FLP 汉英对照经典读本·古典精华③

聊斋志异选

STRANGE TALES FROM MAKE-DO STUDIO

(清)蒲松龄　著

(美)丹尼斯·马尔
维克多·马尔　译

Written by Pu Songling

Translated by Denis C. & Victor H. Mair

外文出版社

FOREIGN LANGUAGES PRESS

图书在版编目(CIP)数据

聊斋志异选:汉英对照/(清)蒲松龄著;(美)马尔等(Mair.)译.—北京:外文出版社,2000.9
(FLP汉英对照经典读本·古典精华:3)
ISBN 7-119-02691-7

Ⅰ.聊… Ⅱ.①蒲…②马… Ⅲ.英语-对照读物:小说-汉、英 Ⅳ.H319.4:I

中国版本图书馆CIP数据核字(2000)第66864号

外文出版社网址:
http://www.flp.com.cn
外文出版社电子信箱:
info@flp.com.cn
sales@flp.com.cn

FLP汉英对照经典读本·古典精华③
聊斋志异选

作　　者　(清)蒲松龄
译　　者　(美)丹尼斯·马尔　维克多·马尔

责任编辑　刘文渊　李晓凤
封面设计　蔡　荣
出版发行　外文出版社
社　　址　北京市百万庄大街24号　邮政编码　100037
电　　话　(010)68320579(总编室)
　　　　　(010)68329514/68327211(推广发行部)
印　　刷　三河市三佳印刷装订有限公司
经　　销　新华书店/外文书店
开　　本　64开(89×127毫米)　字　　数　220千字
印　　数　0001-5000册　印　　张　58(盒)
版　　次　2000年9月第1版第1次印刷
装　　别　盒
书　　号　ISBN 7-119-02691-7/I·668(外)
定　　价　80.00元(盒)

出版前言

本社专事外文图书的编辑出版，几十年来用英文翻译出版了大量的中国文学作品和文化典籍，上自先秦，下迄现当代，力求全面而准确地反映中国文学及中国文化的基本面貌和灿烂成就。这些英译图书均取自相关领域著名的、权威的作品，英译则出自国内外译界名家。每本图书的编选、翻译过程均极其审慎严肃，精雕细琢，中文作品及相应的英译版本均堪称经典。

我们意识到，这些英译精品，不单有对外译介的意义，而且对国内英文学习者、爱好者及英译工作者，也是极有价值的读本。为此，我们对这些英译精品做了认真的遴选，编排成汉英对照的形式，陆续推出，以飨读者。

外文出版社

Publisher's Note

Foreign Languages Press is dedicated to the editing, translating and publishing of books in foreign languages. Over the past several decades it has published, in English, a great number of China's classics and records as well as literary works from the Qin down to modern times, in the aim to fully display the best part of the Chinese culture and its achievements. These books in the original are famous and authoritative in their respective fields, and their English translations are masterworks produced by notable translators both at home and abroad. Each book is carefully compiled and translated with minute precision. Consequently, the English versions as well as their Chinese originals may both be rated as classics.

It is generally considered that these English translations are not only significant for introducing China to the outside world but also useful reading materials for domestic English learners and translators. For this reason, we have carefully selected some of these books, and will publish them successively in Chinese-English bilingual form.

Foreign Languages Press

目 录

CONTENTS

聊斋志异选

STRANGE TALES FROM MAKE-DO STUDIO

考城隍

予姊丈之祖，宋公讳焘，邑廪生。一日，病卧，见吏人持牒，牵白颠马来，云："请赴试。"公言："文宗未临，何遽得考？"吏不言，但敦促之。公力疾乘马从去。路甚生疏。至一城郭，如王者都。移时入府廨，宫室壮丽。上坐十余官，都不知何人，惟关壮缪可识。檐下设几、墩各二，先有一秀才坐其末，公便与连肩。几上各有笔札。俄题纸飞下。视之，八

CANDIDATE FOR THE POST OF CITY GOD

MY brother-in-law's grandfather Master Song Tao, a local recipient of a government stipend for bachelors of letters, was lying sick in bed one day when an officer bearing a summons and leading a white-blazed horse came to him and said, "You are requested to be present at an examination."

"The civil examiner has not yet arrived; how can an examination be held out of the blue?" asked Master Song.

The officer fended the question off by insistently urging him to go. Master Song climbed weakly onto the horse and followed him along an unfamiliar road till they came to a walled city that looked like the seat of a king's authority. Before long they entered a magnificently built official residence. A group of ten or so officials sat at the head of a hall, none of whom he recognized except the God of War, Guan Yu. Two low desks with floor cushions had been set up in front of the hall. A bachelor of letters was already seated at the place farther from the head of the room. Master Song sat down shoulder-to-shoulder with him. On each desk were a pen and a writing pad. Suddenly a slip of paper bearing the composition topic glided down before his eyes. The

字云:“一人二人,有心无心。”二公文成,呈殿上。公文中有云:“有心为善,虽善不赏;无心为恶,虽恶不罚。”诸神传赞不已。召公上,谕曰:“河南缺一城隍,君称其职。”公方悟,顿首泣曰:“辱膺宠命,何敢多辞。但老母七旬,奉养无人,请得终其天年,惟听录用。”上一帝王像者,即命稽母寿籍。有长须吏,捧册翻阅一过,白:“有阳算九年。”共踌躇间,关帝曰:“不妨令张生摄篆九年,瓜代可也。”乃谓公:“应即赴任;今推仁孝之心,给假九年,及期当复相召。”又勉励秀才数语。二公稽首并下。秀才握手,送诸郊野。自言长山张某。以诗赠

eight words on it were "One man, two men: with intent, without intent." The two scholars com-pleted their essays and presented them to the group at the head of the hall. One part of Master Song's essay read: "When a good deed is done with the intent of getting a reward, goodness is not to be rewarded: when an evil deed is done without intent, then evil is not to be punished."

The deities passed the essay around, and there was no end to their praise of it. They called Master Song forward and announced their decision: "There is an opening for a city god in Henan Province that you are qualified to fill." Only then did Master Song realize what was happening. He bumped his head pleadingly on the floor and sobbed: "Since you deign to grant me your most partial appoint-ment, how dare I stubbornly decline? But my old mother is in her seventies and has no one to look after her. Please let me be with her until she lives out her appointed span of years: then I will be at your service."

An emperor-like deity commanded that his mother's longevity entry be checked. A clerk with a long beard brought out a record book and, after leafing quickly through it, reported, "She has nine years left on earth."

Guan Yu resolved the general indecision by saying: "No trouble. Have Scholar Zhang hold the seal of appointment in his stead until the nine years are up. That will be fine." Then he turned to Master Song and said, "Even though you should assume your duties right away, in order to promote benevolence and filial obedience, we will grant you a nine-year extension this time. When that period is over we will summon you again." He then spoke a few words of consolation and encouragement to the unsuccessful candidate. The two scholars kowtowed and left the hall together. The unsuccessful candidate shook Master Song's hand and accompanied him to the environs of the city. He volunteered the information that his name was Zhang, coming from Changshan. His parting gift was a poem which escaped Song's memory

别,都忘其词,中有“有花有酒春常在,无烛无灯夜自明”之句。公既骑,乃别而去。及抵里,豁若梦寤。时卒已三日。母闻棺中呻吟,扶出,半日始能语。问之长山,果有张生,于是日死矣。后九年,母果卒。营葬既毕,浣濯入室而殁。其岳家居城中西门内,忽见公镂膺朱幩,舆马甚众,登其堂,一拜而行。相共惊疑,不知其为神。奔讯乡中,则已殁矣。公有自记小传,惜乱后无存,此其略耳。

except two of the lines: "With flowers and wine, spring is always here; without candle or lamp the night itself is bright." Master Song mounted his horse, said goodbye and left. As he entered his own neighborhood he felt himself waking up as if from a dream.

At that time he had been dead for three days. His mother heard moaning in the coffin and helped him out. Half a day passed before he could speak. Song asked about Changshan and learned that, sure enough, a scholar named Zhang had died there on the same day that he had.

Nine years later his mother died as expected. As soon as Song had finished making her funeral arrangements, he bathed and then entered his bedroom and died. That day his in-laws, who lived just inside the west gate of the city, saw him riding a horse with engraved harness and crimson trappings, followed by a large number of coaches and horses. Song walked into their hall, bowed once and left. In their astonishment they failed to realize that he was a ghost. They ran to his neighborhood to ask about him, only to find that he was already dead. Master Song left a short autobiography but, unfortunately, nothing remained of it after the disorder that swept our land. Here I give only a bare outline.

画　壁

江西孟龙谭，与朱孝廉客都中。偶涉一兰若，殿宇禅舍，俱不甚弘敞，惟一老僧挂搭其中。见客入，肃衣出迓，导与随喜。殿中塑志公像。两壁图绘精妙，人物如生。东壁画散花天女，内一垂髫者，拈花微笑，樱唇欲动，眼波将流。朱注目久，不觉神摇意夺，恍然凝想。身忽飘飘，如驾云雾，已到壁上。见殿阁重重，非复人世。一老僧说法座上，偏袒绕视

THE MURAL

WHILE staying in the capital, Meng Longtan of Jiangxi and Master of letters Zhu once happened upon a monastery. Neither the shrine-hall nor the meditation room was very spacious, and only one old monk was found putting up within. Seeing the guests enter, the monk straightened up his clothes, went to greet them and showed them aound the place. An image of Zen Master Baozhi stood in the shrine-hall. On either side wall were painted fine murals with lifelike human figures. The east wall depicted the Buddhist legend of "Heavenly Maidens Scattering Flowers." Among the figures was a young girl with flowing hair with a flower in her hand and a faint smile on her face. Her cherry-red lips were on the verge of moving, and the liquid pools of her eyes seemed to stir with wave-like glances. After gazing intently for some time, Zhu's self-possession began to waver and his thoughts grew so abstracted that he fell into a trance. His body went adrift as if floating on mist; suddenly he was inside the mural. Peak upon peak of palaces and pavilions made him feel as if he was beyond this earth. An old monk was preaching the *Dharma* on a dais, around which stood a large crowd of viewers in robes with their right shoulders bared out of respect. Zhu mingled in among them.

者甚众。朱亦杂立其中。少间,似有人暗牵其裾。回顾,则垂髫儿,辴然竟去。履即从之。过曲栏,入一小舍,朱次且不敢前。女回首,举手中花,遥遥作招状,乃趋之。舍内寂无人;遽拥之,亦不甚拒,遂与狎好。既而闭户去,嘱勿咳,夜乃复至,如此二日。女伴觉之,共搜得生,戏谓女曰:“腹内小郎已许大,尚发蓬蓬学处子耶?”共捧簪珥,促令上鬟。女含羞不语。一女曰:“妹妹姊姊,吾等勿久住,恐人不欢。”群笑而去。生视女,髻云高簇,鬟凤低垂,比垂髫时尤艳绝也。四顾无人,渐入猥亵,兰麝熏心,乐方未艾。忽闻吉莫靴铿铿甚厉,缧锁锵然。旋有纷嚣腾辨之声。女惊起,与生窃窥,则见一金甲使者,黑面如漆,绾锁挈槌,众女环绕之。使者曰:“全未?”答言:“已全。”使者曰:“如有藏匿下界

Before long, he felt someone tugging furtively at his sleeve. He turned to look, and there was the girl with flowing hair giving him a dazzling smile. She tripped abruptly away, and he lost no time following her along a winding walkway into a small chamber. Once there, he hesitated to approach any farther. When she turned her head and raised the flower with a beckoning motion, he went across to her in the quiet, deserted chamber. Swiftly he embraced her and, as she did not put up much resistance, they grew intimate. When it was over she told him not to make a sound and left, closing the door behind her. That night she came again. After two days of this, the girl's companions realized what was happening and searched together until they found the scholar.

"A little gentleman is already growing in your belly, but still you wear those flowing tresses, pretengding to be a maiden," they said teasingly. Holding out hairpins and earrings, they pressured her to put her hair up in the coiled knot of a married woman, which she did in silent embar-rassment. One of the girls said, "Sisters, let's not outstay our welcome." At this the group left all in a titter.

Looking at the soft, cloudlike chignon piled atop her head and her phoenix ringlets curved low before her ears, the scholar was more struck by her charms than when she had worn her hair long. Seeing that no one was around, he began to make free with her. His heart throbbed at her musky fragrance but, before they had quite finished their pleasure, the heavy tread of leather boots was heard. A clanking of chains and manacles was followed by clamorous, arguing voices. The girl got up in alarm. Peering out, they saw an officer dressed in armor, his face black as lacquer, with chains in one hand and a mace in the other. Standing around him were all the maidens. "Is this all of you?" asked the officer. "We're all here," they answered. "Report if any of you are concealing a man from the lower world. Don't bring trouble on yourselves." "We aren't," said the maidens in unison. The

人,即共出首,勿贻伊戚。"又同声言:"无。"使者反身鹗顾,似将搜匿。女大惧,面如死灰。张皇谓朱曰:"可急匿榻下。"乃启壁上小扉,猝遁去。朱伏,不敢少息。俄闻靴声至房内,复出。未几,烦喧渐远,心稍安;然户外辄有往来语论者。朱跼蹐既久,觉耳际蝉鸣,目中火出,景状殆不可忍,惟静听以待女归,竟不复忆身之何自来也。时孟龙潭在殿中,转瞬不见朱,疑以问僧。僧笑曰:"往听说法去矣。"问:"何处?"曰:"不远。"少时,以指弹壁而呼曰:"朱檀越何久游不归?"旋见壁间画有朱像,倾耳伫立,若有听察。僧又呼曰:"游侣久待矣。"遂飘忽自壁而下,灰心木立,目瞪足软。孟大骇,从容问之。盖方伏榻下,闻叩声

officer turned around and looked malevolently in the direction of the chamber, giving every appearance of an intention to search it. The girl's face turned pale as ashes in fear. "Quick, hide under the bed," she told Zhu in panic. She opened a little door in the wall and was gone in an instant. Zhu lay prostrate, hardly daring to take a little breath. Soon he heard the sound of boots stumping into, then back out of the room. Before long, the din of voices gradually receded. He regained some composure, though the sound of passers-by discussing the matter could be heard frequently outside the door. After cringing there for quite some time, he heard ringing in his ears and felt a burning ache in his eyes. Though the intensity of these sensations threatened to overwhelm him, there was no choice but to listen quietly for the girl's return. He was reduced to the point that he no longer recalled where he had been before coming here.

Just then his friend Meng Longtan, who had been standing in the shrine-hall, found that Zhu had disappeared in the blink of an eye. Perplexed, he asked the monk what had happened. "He has gone to hear a sermon on the *Dharma*, " said the monk laughingly. "Where?" asked Meng. "Not far" was the answer. After a moment, the monk tapped on the wall with his finger and called, "Why do you tarry so long, my good patron?" Presently there appeared on the wall an image of Zhu standing motionless with his head cocked to one side as if listening to something. "You have kept you travelling companion waiting a long time," called the monk again. Thereupon he drifted out of the mural and down to the floor. He stood woodenly, his mind like burned-out ashes, with eyes staring straight ahead and legs wobbling. Meng was terribly frightened, but in time calmed down enough to ask what had happened. It turned out that Zhu had been hiding under the bed when he heard a thunderous knocking, so he came out of the room to listen for the source of the sound.

They looked at the girl holding the flower and saw, instead of

如雷,故出房窥听也。共视拈花人,螺髻翘然,不复垂髫矣。朱惊拜老僧,而问其故。僧笑曰:"幻由人生,贫道何能解。"朱气结而不扬,盂心骇而无主。即起,历阶而出。

异史氏曰:"'幻由人生',此言类有道者。人有淫心,是生亵境;人有亵心,是生怖境。菩萨点化愚蒙,千幻并作,皆人心所自动耳。老婆心切,惜不闻其言下大悟,披发入山也。"

flowing hair, a high coiled chignon on her head. Zhu bowed down to the old monk in amazement and asked the reason for this. "Illusion is born in the mind. How can a poor mendicant like myself explain it?" laughed the monk. Zhu was dispirited and cast down; Meng was shaken and confused. Together they walked down the shrine-hall steps and left.

The Chronicler of the Tales comments: "'Illusion is born in the mind.' These sound like the words of one who has found the truth. A wanton mind gives rise to visions of lustfulness. The mind dominated by lust gives rise to a state of fear. The Bodhisattva made it possible for the ignorant persons to attain realization for themselves. All the myriad transformations of illusion are nothing but the movements of the human mind itself. The old monk spoke in earnest solicitude, but regrettably there is no sign that the youth found enlightenment in his words and entered the mountains with hair unbound to seek the truth."

偷 桃

童时赴郡试，值春节。旧例，先一日，各行商贾，彩楼鼓吹赴藩司，名曰："演春"。余从友人戏瞩。是日游人如堵。堂上四官皆赤衣，东西相向坐。时方稚，亦不解其何官。但闻人语哜嘈，鼓吹聒耳。忽有一人率披发童，荷担而上，似有所白；万声汹动，亦不闻为何语。但视堂上作笑声。即有青衣人大声命作剧。其人应命方兴，问："作何剧？"堂上相顾

THE THEFT OF A PEACH

WHEN young I went to the prefectural seat to take an examination and happened to be there on Spring Festival(Spring Begins). According to custom, on the eve of this day all the shopkeepers decorated their storefronts and organized a musical procession that went through town to the *yamen* of the provincial treasury. This was called the "Spring Performance." Some friends and I went to take it in. The streets were lined with walls of spectators. At the head of the provincial treasury hall sat four officials in red silk robes facing each other, two each on the east and west. I was too young then to know their names and titles. All I could hear was the clamor of voices mingled with the din of the procession outside. In the middle of all this a man with loads on a carrying pole led a long-haired boy to the front of the hall. He seemed to be announcing something, but I could not make out the words in the waves of intermingled sounds. I could see, however, that the people at the head of the hall were laughing. Then a black-robed servant ordered them in a loud voice to perform an cat. As the man got ready to play, he asked, "What act shal I perform?" The officials spoke a few sentences among themselves. A clerk came down and proclaimed their wish to know his best trick.

数语。吏下宣问所长。答言:“能颠倒生物。”吏以白官。少顷复下,命取桃子。术人声诺。解衣覆笥上,故作怨状,曰:“官长殊不了了!坚冰未解,安所得桃?不取,又恐为南面者所怒。奈何!”其子曰:“父已诺之,又焉辞?”术人惆怅良久,乃云:“我筹之烂熟。春初雪积,人间何处可觅?唯王母园中,四时常不凋谢,或有之。必窃之天上,乃可。”子曰:“嘻!天可阶而升乎?”曰:“有术在。”乃启笥,出绳一团,约数十丈,理其端,望空中掷去;绳即悬立空际,若有物以挂之。未几,愈掷愈高,渺入云中;手中绳亦尽。乃呼子曰:“儿来!余老惫,体重拙,不能行,得汝一往。”遂以绳授子,曰:“持此可登。”子受绳有难色,怨曰:“阿翁

"I can transform living creatures," he answered. The clerk relayed this to the officials. After a moment he came down from the hall again and ordered the magician to materialize a peach. The latter agreed to do so, but taking off his coat and laying it over his wicker trunk, he murmured with feigned resetment, "These authorities don't know what they're saying! The ice out there is still inches thick: where am I supposed to get a peach? But if I don't get one, I'm afraid I'll make these lords angry at me. What should I do?"

"You've already agreed to it," said his son. "There is no backing out now."

After grumbling for quite some time, the magician said, "I've mulled it over from every angle. Where on this earth can a peach be found in early spring when snow is still piled on the ground? The only place where one could conceivably be found is in the garden of the Mother Queen of the West, where plants never wither or shed leaves, no matter what the season. But the only way to get a peach would be to steal it from heaven."

"Humph!" exclaimed his son. "Can you scale a ladder up to heaven?"

"I have magic for this," came the answer. Whereupon he opened his trunk and brought out a coil of rope that appeared to be several hundred feet long. He got one end of the rope ready and threw it upwards. The rope stood suspended straight in the air as if it were hanging from something. As he flung more and more rope upwards, the end climbed higher and higher until it was soon lost in the clouds and the coil in his hands was all played out. Then he called to his son: "Come here, son! I'm old and weak. My body is too unwieldy to make the climb. You'll have to be the one to go." He handed the rope to his son saying: "this is the only way up."

His son took the rope reluctantly. "You must be out of your mind, old man!" he said in exasperation. "You want me to grab onto a flimsi-

亦大愦愦！如此一线之绳，欲我附之，以登万仞之高天。倘中道断绝，骸骨何存矣！”父又强呜拍之，曰：“我已失口，悔无及。烦儿一行。儿勿苦，倘窃得来，必有百金赏，当为儿娶一美妇。”子乃持索，盘旋而上，手移足随，如蛛趁丝，渐入云霄，不可复见。久之，坠一桃，如碗大。术人喜，持献公堂。堂上传视良久，亦不知其真伪。忽而绳落地上，术人惊曰：“殆矣！上有人断吾绳，儿将焉托！”移时，一物堕。视之，其子首也。捧而泣曰：“是必偷桃，为监者所觉。吾儿休矣！”又移时，一足落；无何，肢体纷堕，无复存者。术人大悲。一一拾置笥中而阖之，曰：“老夫止此儿，日从我南北游。今承严命，不意罹此奇惨！当负去瘗之。”乃升堂而跪，曰：“为桃故，杀吾子矣！如怜小人而助之葬，当结草以图报耳。”坐官骇诧，各有赐金。术人受而缠诸腰，乃扣笥而呼曰：“八八儿，不出谢赏，将何待？”忽一

ly rope like this and climb into the blue yonder. If it breaks when I'm halfway, there won't even be any bones left of me."

Patting the boy's back, the father urged him to act, "My claim has already been made. I can't take it back now. Would you please go? And don't take it so hard. If you steal one and bring it bak, they'll be sure to give us a wife." The son took hold of the rope and ascended swayingly hand over foot, like a spider on its filament, until he entered the cloud layer and was lost to sight. After some time a bowl-sized peach fell out of the sky. Overjoyed, the magician presented it to those in the hall. The officials took turns examining it for quite some time without being able to tell whether it was real or fake.

Suddenly the rope fell to the earth. "This is awful!" exclaimed the magician. "Someone up above cut my rope. How will my son hold on there?" In a moment an object hurtled to the ground. It turned out to be the boy's head. He held it up and sobbed: "He must have been caught stealing the peach by a guard. It is all over for my boy." Before long a leg fell earthwards, followed by the remaining pieces of a dismembered corpse. The grief-stricken magician gathered up the pieces, placed them in his trunk and snapped it shut, saying "I had only this one son. He was with me in all my wanderings. Now, compelled by his father's command, he has met an unexpected and horrible end. I have no choice but to carry this trunk away and inter his remains." He paused to walk up to the hall, where he knelt and pleaded: "My son lost his life because of that peach. If you take pity on me and help with the burial, I swear that I will repay you even after death." Each of the stunned officials had a sum of gold for him. The magician put it into his waist pouch, then knocked on the trunk and called, "Dear son, won't you come out and thank these men for their presents? What are you waiting for?" Suddenly a tousle-haired boy pushed open the lid with his head, came out and kowtowed toward the north where the officials were seated. And who should it have been but the magician's

蓬头僮首抵笥盖而出，望北稽首，则其子也。以其术奇，故至今犹记之。后闻白莲教，能为此术，意此其苗裔耶？

son!

I remember this even now because it was such an amazing feat of magic. Later I heard that the White Lotus cult was capable of such wizardry. Could these two have perhaps been among its latter-day adherents?

劳山道士

邑有王生，行七，故家子。少慕道，闻劳山多仙人，负笈往游。登一顶，有观宇，甚幽。一道士坐蒲团上，素发垂领，而神观爽迈。叩而与语，理甚玄妙。请师之。道士曰："恐娇惰不能作苦。"答言："能之。"其门人甚众，薄暮毕集。王俱与稽首，遂留观中。凌晨，道士呼王去，授以斧，使随众采樵。王谨受教。过月余，手足重茧，不堪其苦，阴有归志。一夕归，见二人与师共酌，日已暮，尚无灯烛。师乃翦纸如镜，黏壁间。俄顷，月明辉室，光鉴

THE TAOIST OF LAO MOUNTAIN

IN out district lived scholar Wang, the seventh son of an old family. From youth onward he was attracted to Taoist arts. Hearing that immortals abounded on Lao Mountain, he packed his books on his back and set out there on an adventure. Climbing to the top of a peak, Wang came to a Taoist temple set in a wild, secluded spot. A Taoist with white hair hanging past his collar was sitting on a bast mat. He had about him an other-worldly air that was graceful and lofty. Scholar Wang made obeisance to him and struck up a convesation. The Taoist's talk impressed him as quite mysterious and subtle. Wang asked to be accepted as his disciple, to which he replied, "I am afraid you are too soft and lazy to work hard."

"Oh, but I can," answered Wang. The Taoist had a crowd of acolytes, all of whom came together at dusk. Having saluted each of them, Wang settled down in the hermitage.

At the crack of dawn the Taoist woke Wang, gave him an axe and made him go to gather firewood with the others. Wang did exactly as he was told. After more than a month of this, his hands and feet had calluses on top of calluses. Unable to bear the toil, he nursed secret intentions of returning home. One evening on his return he saw two

毫芒。诸门人环听奔走。一客曰:“良宵胜乐,不可不同。”乃于案上取壶酒,分赉诸徒,且嘱尽醉。王自思:七八人,壶酒何能遍给?遂各觅盎盂,竞饮先釂,惟恐樽尽;而往复挹注,竟不少减。心奇之。俄一客曰:“蒙赐月明之照,乃尔寂饮。何不呼嫦娥来?”乃以箸掷月中。见一美人,自光中出。初不盈尺;至地,遂与人等。纤腰秀项,翩翩作“霓裳舞”。已而歌曰:“仙仙乎,而还乎,而幽我于广寒乎!”其声清越,烈如箫管。歌毕,盘旋而起,跃登几上,惊顾之间,已复为箸。三人大笑。

men drinking with his master. The sun had already set but no lamps or candles had yet been lit, so the master cut paper in the shape of a mirror and pasted it on the wall. Suddenly a light as bright as the moon's flooded the room, making even the tiniest hairs visible. The acolytes in attendance ran back and forth at the guests'bidding. One of the guests said, "It's a beautiful night for good times. We ought to share them with everyone here." The Taoist picked up a pitcher of wine from the table and began to pour some for each acolyte, urging them to drink their fill. Wang thought to himself: "How can a pitcher of wine suffice for seven or eight people?" Each of them hunted up a drinking vessel. Thy vied to see who would be first to drain his cup. Their only fear was that the pitcher was empty, but when they went to pour from it again they were astonished to find that the wine had not gone down in the slightest. Soon another guest said, "You have been nice enough to give us moonlight to drink by, but there is still no entertainment. Why don't you call the goddess of the moon to come?" At this the Taoist tossed a chopstick into the moon and a beautiful woman appeared out of the circle of light. At first she was not even a foot tall, but she grew to normal size as she descended to the floor. Her slender waist and graceful neck moved through the fluttering gyrations of the Dance of the Rainbow Skirt and Feathered Blouse. To the tempo of the dance of the Rainbow Skirt and Feathered Blouse. To the tempo of the dance she sang,

Immortal of the mountains
Is it true you're bound for home
Will you leave me all alone
In this icy crystal dome?

Her silvery voice was as piercing as a flute. At the end of the song she arose with a sweeping motion, jumped up on the table and, in the space of an astonished glance, was already a chopstick again. The

又一客曰："今宵最乐，然不胜酒力矣。其饯我于月宫可乎？"三人移席，渐入月中。众视三人，坐月中饮，须眉毕见，如影之在镜中。移时，月渐暗；门人然烛来，则道士独坐而客杳矣。几上肴核尚存。壁上月，纸圆如镜而已。道士问众："饮足乎？"曰："足矣。""足宜早寝，勿误樵苏。"众诺而退。王窃忻慕，归念遂息。又一月，苦不可忍，而道士并不传教一术。心不能待，辞曰："弟子数百里受业仙师，纵不能得长生术，或小有传习，亦可慰求教之心；今阅两三月，不过早樵而暮归。弟子在家，未谙此苦。"道士笑曰："我固谓不能作苦，今果然。明早当遣汝行。"王曰："弟子操作多日，师略授小技，此来为不负也。"道士问："何

three men laughed boisterously.

The other guest spoke up: "This evening has been wonderful, but the wine is getting the better of me. Would it be all right if we had a farewell drink in the palace of the moon?" The three men moved their mats and slowly floated into the moon. The acolytes saw the three seated in the moon drinking, their features distinct as reflections in a mirror. After a time the moon gradually dimmed. When the acolytes brought a lighted candle they found the Taoist sitting alone, his guests nowhere to be seen. The delicacies on the table were just as before, and the moon on the wall was nothing more than a disc of paper.

"Did you have enough to drink?" the Taoist asked the acolytes.

"Enough" they said.

"Then you ought to go right to bed. Don't let this interfere with gathering wood and kindling."

The acolytes said "yes" and retired.

Wang's intention of leaving subsided out of heartfelt admiration. But after another month had passed the grinding toil became too much for him, and the Taoist would not pass on even a single magical technique. Unable to wait any longer, Wang took his leave, saying: "I came a hundred miles to study under such an immortal master as yourself. Even though I cannot learn the art of everlasting life, there may perhaps be some small skill you could impart that would appease my wish for learning. For the past two or three months all I have done is go out to gather wood in the morning and return in the evening. When I was at home, I was not used to this kind of hard work."

The Taoist answered with a laugh: "I said from the start that you would not be able to stand hard work, and you have proven me right. I will send you off tomorrow morning."

"I have labored for many days. If you could just impart some insignificant part of your art, my coming would not be in vain." The Taoist asked what art he hoped to learn.

术之求?"王曰:"每见师行处,墙壁所不能隔,但得此法足矣。"道士笑而允之。乃传以诀,令自咒毕,呼曰:"入之!"王面墙不敢入。又曰:"试入之。"王果从容入,及墙而阻。道士曰:"俯首骤入,勿逡巡!"王果去墙数步,奔而入;及墙,虚若无物;回视,果在墙外矣。大喜,入谢。道士曰:"归宜洁持,否则不验。"遂助资斧遣之归。抵家,自诩遇仙,坚壁所不能阻。妻不信。王效其作为,去墙数尺,奔而入,头触硬壁,蓦然而踣。妻扶视之,额上坟起,如巨卵焉。妻揶揄之。王惭忿,骂老道士之无良而已。

异史氏曰:"闻此事未有不大笑者;而不知世之为王生者,正复不少。今有伧父,喜疢

Wang answered, "I have often noticed that walls are no hindrance to your free motion. I would be satisfied to learn the method of such magic."

The Taoist gave his assent with a laugh. Then he taught Wang the words of a spell and told him to chant it through by himself, at which he cried, "Go through." Wang faced the wall, not daring to walk into it. Again the Taoist cried, "Try to go through it!" Doing as he was told, Wang gingerly approached the wall, but it proved unyielding to his forward movement.

"Lower your head and go through quickly. Don't hold back," instructed the Taoist. So Wang backed several steps away from the wall and ran toward it. When he came to the wall it seemed not to be there at all. Turning around to look, he found that he was already outside the building. Overjoyed, he went back in to thank his master. The Taoist said, "You must live chastely after your return, or the spell will not work." Then he gave Wang money for the trip home and sent him off.

Upon reaching home Wang boasted that he had met with an immortal and that now his power was such that no solid wall could stop him. His wife found this hard to believe. Wang stood several feet from a wall and ran headlong against it as he had done before, but this time his head smacked against the hard wall and he tumbled backward. His wife helped him up and he tumbled backward. His wife helped him up and looked at the goose egg rising mound-like on his forehead. Shamed but incited by her ridicule into a fury, he raved that the old Taoist was nothing but a reprobate.

The Chronicler of the Tales comments: "No one who hears of this incident can keep from laughing out loud, but those who laugh do not realize that the Scholar Wangs of this world are by no means few and far between. Take the case of a worthless official who would 'rather swallow poison than medicines. 'A ' boil-sucking, hemorrhoid-

毒而畏药石，遂有舐痈吮痔者，进宣威逞暴之术，以迎其旨，诒之曰：'执此术也以往，可以横行而无碍。'初试未尝不小效，遂谓天下之大，举可以如是行矣，势不至触硬壁而颠蹶不止也。”

licking'sort of person might cater to his wishes by advocating brutal, self-aggrandizing policies and inveigle him, saying: 'You need only adhere to such and such a policy—nothing will stand in your way. 'The first time he tries, it might yield some small measure of success, thus giving him the idea that such policy can be applied to all cases under heaven. Those who are taken by this will not stop until they run headlong into a solid wall and topple over backward."

妖术

于公者，少任侠，喜拳勇，力能持高壶，作旋风舞。崇祯间，殿试在都，仆疫不起，患之。会市上有善卜者，能决人生死，将代问之。既至，未言。卜者曰："君莫欲问仆病乎？"公骇应之。曰："病者无害，君可危。"公乃自卜。卜者起卦，愕然曰："君三日当死！"公惊诧良久。卜者从容曰："鄙人有小术，报我十金，当代禳之。"公自念，生死已定，术岂能解。不应

BLACK MAGIC

A CERTAIN Master Yu was devoted to chivalry in his youth. He delighted in the might of his fists and was strong enough to do the whirlwind dance with a huge water clock. During the reign of Emperor Chong Zhen (1628-1644), he was in the capital for the palace examination when his servant was laid low by a pestilence. This brought sorrow to his heart.

At that time there was a skilled diviner in the market-place who could foresee life or death. Yu decided to inquire into his servant's fate. Before he had said a word about his reason for coming, the diviner said, "You want to ask about your servant's illness, don't you?" Yu confirmed this in astonishment. "No harm will come to the sick man," said the diviner. "But you, sir, are liable to grave danger." Yu cast the yarrow stalks of divination for himself. The diviner drew up a hexagram, then said in shock: "You will be dead in three days!" The diviner gave this bewildering revelation time to sink in, then went on nonchalantly: "However, I do have mastery of a trifling little spell. If you reward me with ten taels of gold, I will perform invocations for you to exorcise the evil." Yu thought to himself that since his time of death was already fixed, there would be little that magical arts could

而起，欲出。卜者曰："惜此小费，勿悔勿悔！"爱公者皆为公惧，劝罄橐以哀之。公不听。倏忽至三日，公端坐旅舍，静以觇之，终日无恙。至夜，阖户挑灯，倚剑危坐。一漏向尽，更无死法。意欲就枕，忽闻窗隙窣窣有声。急视之，一小人荷戈入；及地，则高如人。公捉剑起，急击之，飘忽未中。遂遽小，复寻窗隙，意欲遁去。公疾斫之，应手而倒。烛之，则纸人，已腰断矣。公不敢卧，又坐待之。逾时，一物穿窗入，怪狞如鬼。才及地，急击之，断而为两，皆蠕动。恐其复起，又连击之，剑剑皆中，其声不软。审视，则土偶，片片已碎。于是移坐窗下，目注隙中。久之，闻窗外如牛

do to forestall it. He got up without answering to walk out of the booth. The diviner called after him: "Don't cling to such a measly sum, or you'll regret it!"

Those who loved Yu were afraid for him and begged him to empty his purse for pity's sake. Yu turned a deaf ear to them. The third day came all too soon. Yu sat in formal posture at his lodgings, watching quietly to see what would happen. The day passed without incident.

At nightfall he locked the door and trimmed the lamp-wick, then sat stiffly, sword at hip. Almost a watch wore on with no sign of anything that would bring his death. He was thinking of going to bed when suddenly a scrab-bling noise came from a crack in the window. He turned his head just in time to see a tiny human figure shouldering a spear coming through the crack. It jumped to the floor and turned imediately into a full-sized man. Yu grabbed his sword, got up, and made a lightning thrust. The sword seemed to go through empty air. The man immediately shrank back to diminutive proportions, then scrambled toward the window. Just as the manikin was about to disappear through the crack, Yu felled it with a swift stroke. The light of a candle revealed nothing but a paper figure cut in two at the waist. Yu dared not lie down, so he sat and waited. A short while later a creature wearing the frightful looks of a ghost came through the window. Yu barely gave it time to hit the floor before he swung his sword and chopped it into two writhing halves. He slashed repeatedly at them, fearing that one would get up and come at him again. Stroke after stroke found its mark, but the sound was nothing like that of a sword sinking into flesh. Looking closely, he saw only an earthen idol that had been hacked to pieces. At this, Yu moved his seat to the window and stared at the crack.

After a while there came a sound like the heavy breathing of a cow from outside the window. A creature pushed against the window frame with such force that the walls of the room shook and threatened to col-

喘,有物推窗棂,房壁震摇,其势欲倾。公惧覆压,计不如出而斗之,遂剨然脱扃,奔而出。见一巨鬼,高与檐齐;昏月中,见其面黑如煤,眼闪烁有黄光;上无衣,下无履,手弓而腰矢。公方骇,鬼则弯矣;公以剑拨矢,矢堕;欲击之,则又弯矣。公急跃避,矢贯于壁,战战有声。鬼怒甚,拔佩刀,挥如风,望公力劈。公猱进,刀中庭石,石立断。公出其股间,削鬼中踝,铿然有声。鬼益怒,吼如雷,转身复剁。公又伏身入;刀落,断公裙。公已及胁下,猛斫之,亦铿然有声,鬼仆而僵。公乱击之,声硬如柝。烛之,则一木偶,高大如人。弓矢尚缠腰际,刻画狰狞;剑击处,皆有血出。公因秉烛待旦。方悟鬼物皆卜人遣之,欲致人于

lapse. Fearing that he would be crushed inside, Yu figured that it would be better to go out and fight. He slid the bolt aside with a clatter and ran out. There stood a huge demon its head even with the eaves. In the dim moonlight he saw its face dark as coal and its eyes glittering with yellow light. It wore no coat or shoes but carried a bow in its hand and a quiver of arrows fastened at its waist. As Yu stood stunned by fright the demon drew its bow. Yu deflected the arrow with his sword, making it glance onto the ground. He raised his sword to attack, but the demon drew its bow again. He leapt aside just in time: the arrow buried its head in the wall with a quivering hum. The enraged demon drew its sword, whirled it like the wind and brought it down on Yu with a forceful blow. However, Yu advanced with a nimble monkey leap to get inside the sword's path. The sword hit a decorative rock and cleaved it through. Yu ran past the demon's legs and slashed an ankle so hard that his sword clanged. Roraring like thunder with insane rage, the demon turned and chopped downward as before. Again Yu ducked inside the blow, which came so close that it cut through his blow, which came so close that it cut through his robe, Yu was directly below the demon's underarm. He hacked fiercely. Again his sword clanged. The demon toppled over and lay stiff on the ground. Yu hacked at the body wildly, producing a sound like a watchman's clapper. By the light of a candle he discovered that he had been chopping at the body of a life-sized wooden puppet. Quiver and bow holder were still fastened at its waist. It had been carved and painted to look fierce and repulsive. Blood was flowing from the sword cuts.

Yu stayed up, candle in hand, until morning, when it finally dawned on him that the monsters had been sent after him by the diviner, who an attempt on his life to verify his prognostications. The next day Yu told this to all his friends and acquaintances, who gathered together and went with him to the diviner's booth. The diviner saw

死,以神其术也。次日,遍告交知,与共诣卜所。卜人遥见公,瞥不可见。或曰:“此翳形术也,犬血可破。”公如言,戒备而往。卜人又匿如前。急以犬血沃立处,但见卜人头面,皆为犬血模糊,目灼灼如鬼立。乃执付有司而杀之。

异史氏曰:“尝谓买卜为一痴。世之讲此道而不爽于生死者几人?卜之而爽,犹不卜也。且即明明告我以死期之至,将复如何?况有借人命以神其术者,其可畏不尤甚耶!”

them coming. Yu, too, spotted him for an instant, but then he was nowhere to be seen. "He's using an invisibility spell. The blood of a dog will break it," someone said. Following this advice, Yu went to make the necessary preparations and then went back to the booth. The diviner vanished as before, but Yu quickly drenched the spot where he had been standing with dog's blood. There the diviner stood, his head all splattered with dog's blood and, floating ghostlike in midair with eyes ablaze. They caught hold of him and turned him over to the authorities for execution.

The Chronicler of the Tales comments: "I have observed that paying for the services of a diviner is one type of folly. How many people pursue this trade without making false predictions of life and death? A false divination is the same as no divination at all. Even if someone tells me plainly when death is to come, what of it? And how much more horrible it is when a man uses another's death to impress people with the accuracy of his predictions!"

青凤

太原耿氏,故大家,第宅弘阔。后凌夷,楼舍连亘,半旷废之。因生怪异,堂门辄自开掩,家人恒中夜骇哗。耿患之,移居别墅,留老翁门焉。由此荒落益甚。或闻笑语歌吹声。耿有从子去病,狂放不羁。嘱翁有所闻见,奔告之。至夜,见楼上灯光明灭,走报生。生欲入觇其异。止之,不听。门户素所习识,竟拨蒿蓬,曲折而入。登楼,殊无少异。穿楼

FOX-GIRL QINGFENG

THE Gengs of Taiyuan were an aristocratic family of long standing who lived in an enomous manor. Eventually their fortunes declined and half of the rambling complex of storied buildings and living quarters was left desolate. This gave rise to hauntings: the door to the main hall often opened and closed by itself, and the household members repeatedly broke the night stillness with terrified cries. Geng found this so disturbing that he moved to a country residence, leaving an old caretaker to watch the gate. From then on the place became even more negelected and overgrown. Laughter and music could sometimes be heard within. Geng had a nephew named Sickness-Free, who was a wild, uninhibited youth. The nephew instructed the caretaker to report anything he saw or heard without delay. One night lamplight was seen flickering in one of the storied buildings.. When the caretaker rushed to inform him of this, the scholar wanted to enter the building and observe the disturbances. Attempts to dissuade him were in vain.

He had long been familiar with the layout of the buildings, but this time he had to push a circuitous way through thick mugworts and brambles. He climbed to the upper story of one building without seeing anything suspicious. Passing through the building, his ears caught the

而过,闻人语切切。潜窥之,见巨烛双烧,其明如昼。一叟儒冠南面坐,一媪相对,俱年四十余。东向一少年,可二十许;右一女郎,裁及笄耳。酒胾满案,团坐笑语。生突入,笑呼曰:"有不速之客一人来!"群惊奔匿。独叟出叱问:"谁何入人闺闼?"生曰:"此我家闺闼,君占之。旨酒自饮,不一邀主人,毋乃太吝?"叟审睇曰:"非主人也。"生曰:"我狂生耿去病,主人之从子耳。"叟致敬曰:"久仰山斗!"乃揖生入,便呼家人易馔。生止之。叟乃酌客。生曰:"吾辈通家,座客无庸见避,还祈招饮。"叟呼:"孝儿!"俄少年自外入。叟曰:"此豚儿也。"揖而坐,略审门阀。叟自言:"义君姓胡。"生素豪,谈议风生,孝儿亦倜傥;倾吐

sibilance of human speech. Peeking into a room lighted in daylike brilliance by a pair of large candles, he saw a man in a scholar's cap seated facing a woman at the south of the room. Both were in their forties. On the east side was a young man, probably in his twenties, and on his right was a young woman who had just reached the hairpin age of fifteen. They sat talking jovially around a table laden with meat and wine. The scholar barged in and cried out laughingly: "An uninvited guest had arrived." The frightened group ran to hide. The old man alone came out and asked in rebuking tones: "Who are you that you dare to enter other people's private chambers?"

"These are my family's chambers," said the scholar. "You have taken them over. You drink exquisite wine by yourselves, without so much as asking the master of the house to join you. Aren't you pushing your stinginess too far?"

"You are not the master of the house," said the old man, inspecting him with a sidelong glance.

"I am the wayward scholar Geng Sickness-Free, nephew of the master of this house."

The old man uttered a respectful greeting: "I've long looked up to your luminosity!"

After bowing the scholar into the room, he called on his servants to replace the food on the table. The scholar stopped him, so the old man poured wine for his guest. The scholar said, "There is friendship between our families, so the guests who were just at table need not remain separate. I earnestly hope you will call them back to have a drink."

"Xiao er!" called the man. A young man came quickly from outside. The older man said, "This is my humble child." The youth bowed and sat down. The conversation opened with inquiries into each other's family back-grounds. The older man volunteered: "My foster-father is surnamed Fox."

间,雅相爱悦。生二十一,长孝儿二岁,因弟之。叟曰:“闻君祖纂涂山外传,知之乎?”答:“知之。”叟曰:“我涂山氏之苗裔也。唐以后,谱系犹能忆之;五代而上无传焉。幸公子一垂教也。”生略述涂山女佐禹之功,粉饰多词,妙绪泉涌。叟大喜,谓子曰:“今幸得闻所未闻。公子亦非他人,可请阿母及青凤来共听之,亦令知我祖德也。”孝儿入帏中。少时,媪偕女郎出。审顾之,弱态生娇,秋波流慧,人间无其丽也。叟指妇云:“此为老荆。”又指女郎:“此青凤,鄙人之犹女也。颇惠,所闻见,辄记不忘,故唤令听之。”生谈竟而饮,瞻顾女郎,停睇不转。女觉之,辄俯其首。生隐蹑莲

The scholar had always been outgoing, and his conver-sation sparkled with wit. Xiao-er, too, had an easy, charming manner. In the course of a forthright conversation, each felt attached to the other. The scholar, being twenty-one years old, was two years older than his friend, so he addressed Xiao-er as a younger brother.

The old man spoke up: "I've heard that your grandfather compiled *The legends of Tushan*. Do you know about it?"

"Yes I do."

"I am descended from the Tushan line," said the old man. "I can remember my family tree to as far back as the Tang Dynasty (618-906), but there are no records of our lineage from the Five Dynasties period and before. I would feel fortunate if you could impart some of what you know."

The scholar gave a brief account of the assistance which the maid of Tushan had rendered to Emperor Yu. He embellished the new story with many fine phrases, and his flow of captivating thoughts gushed forth like a spring. The old man said to his son in great delight: "This is a chance to hear what we've never heard before. The young gentleman is not an outsider: go ahead and ask your mother and Qingfeng to listen with us, so they too will know of my ancestor's glory." Xiao-er went behind a curtain. In a moment the woman appeared with the girl. Geng took a good long look at her. Her dainty poise breathed loveliness, and her eyes rippled with brilliance like autumn pools. Nowhere in the world of men was such beauty to be seen.

The old man pointed first to his wife and then to the girl: "This is my old wife, and this is my niece, Qingfeng. She has quite a head on her shoulders. She always remembers everything she hears and sees, so I called her here to listen."

After the scholar finished telling his tale the drinking began. He turned his eyes to the young woman and let his gaze rest upon her. Sensing his glance she did nothing but lower her head. The scholar

钩，女急敛足，亦无愠怒。生神志飞扬，不能自主，拍案曰："得妇如此，南面王不易也！"媪见生渐醉，益狂，与女俱起，遽搴帏去。生失望，乃辞叟出。而心萦萦，不能忘情于青凤也。至夜，复往，则兰麝犹芳，而凝待终宵，寂无声欬。归与妻谋，欲携家而居之，冀得一遇。妻不从，生乃自往，读于楼下。夜方凭几，一鬼披发入，面黑如漆，张目视生。生笑，染指研墨自涂，灼灼然相与对视。鬼惭而去。次夜，更既深，灭烛欲寝，闻楼后发扃，辟之阍然。生急起窥觇，则扉半启。俄闻履声细碎，有烛光自房中出。视之，则青凤也。骤见生，骇而却退，遽阖双扉。生长跽而致词曰："小生不避险恶，实以卿故。幸无他人，得一握手

furtively placed his foot on her lotus-like slipper. She drew her foot quickly away, but gave no sign of displeasure. The scholar's roving thoughts robbed him of self-command. With a slap on the table he blurted: "If I had a wife like this, I would not trade places with a king facing south on his throne!"

Seeing the scholar become even more boisterous as he succumbed to the wine, the woman and the girl rose, hurriedly parted the curtain and left the room. The disappointed scholar took leave of the old man and departed, but the threads of affection tugged at his heart, and he could not rid his thought of Qingfeng.

At nightfall the next day he went back to the manor. Her orchid-musk remained in the air. He passed the night absorbed in waiting, but not so much as a cough of hers was heard. Returning home, he broached to his wife his plan to take the family there and stay, in hopes of having an encounter. Since his wife did not assent, he went alone. That night, as he sat reading at a desk in the lower story of the mansion, a wild-haired ghost with a lacquer-black face entered and stared wide-eyed at him. He laughingly dipped his fingers in freshly-rubbed ink, smeared it on his face and looked back at the ghost with a burning gaze. The ghost left in shame.

Late the following night he had blown out his candle and was about to retire when he heard a bolt sliding open in the rear of the mansion, followed by the thud of an opening door. He rushed to take a look. A doorleaf was standing ajar. There was a sudden pattering of slippers, and the light of a candle shone from inside. He saw that it was Qingfeng. Frightened at the unexpected sight of the scholar, she backed away and slammed the double-leaved door. The scholar knelt upright before her door and delivered his plea: "It was for your sake that I did not shrink from danger. By good fortune no one else is here. If you were to grant me just once the joy of a touch of your hand, I would face death itself without regret."

为笑,死不憾耳。”女遥语曰:“惓惓深情,妾岂不知,但叔闺训严,不敢奉命。”生固哀之云:“亦不敢望肌肤之亲,但一见颜色足矣。”女似肯可,启关出,捉之臂而曳之。生狂喜,相将入楼下,拥而加诸膝。女曰:“幸有夙分;过此一夕,即相思无用矣。”问:“何故?”曰:“阿叔畏君狂,故化厉鬼以相吓,而君不动也。今已卜居他所,一家皆移什物赴新居,而妾留守,明日即发。”言已,欲去,云:“恐叔归。”生强止之,欲与为欢。方持论间,叟掩入。女羞惧无以自容,俯首倚床,拈带不语。叟怒曰:“贱婢辱吾门户!不速去,鞭挞且从其后!”女低头急去,叟亦出。尾而听之,诃诟万端。闻青凤嘤嘤啜泣。生心意如割,大声曰:“罪在小生,

The girl spoke through the intervening door: "Do not suppose that I know nothing of the heart-gripping longing you fell, but my uncle raised me by a stern code of womanly conduct: I dare not obey your wish."

The scholar kept pleading, nevertheless: "I do not presume to hope for bodily intimacy: it would be enough just to see your face." The girl seemed amenable to this. She opened the door and came out. In a paroxysm of delight the scholar took her arm and drew her into the mansion, where he sat her on his lap and embraced her.

"Tt is fortunate that fate has brought us together," said the girl. "But no matter how much we yearn for each other, it will do us no good after tonight."

"Why is that?" asked the scholar.

"Your wildness frightened my uncle, so he disguised himself as a fierce ghost to frighten you, but you were not fazed. Now he has already found another place to live. The whole family has taken our belongings and moved to our new home. They left me here to watch the place, but I have to leave tomorrow." Then she rose to leave, saying: "T'm afraid my uncle will come back." The scholar, who wanted to enjoy himself with her, did his utmost to detain her. The matter was still under discussion when her uncle entered stealthily. The shamed, frightened girl would have crawled into a hole had there been one handy. She bowed her head and leaned against the bed, wordlessly fingering her sash.

"You are a disgrace to my family, you cheap chamber-maid!" roared the uncle. "If you don't get out of here now, I'll speed you on your way with a whip" The girl rushed from the room, her head lowered abjectly, and her uncle followed. As the scholar trailed behind them listening, the old man's raving curses and Qingfeng's muffled sobs pierced him to the heart.

"I am the guilty one," he shouted after them. "This is not

于青凤何与？倘宥凤也，刀锯铁钺，小生愿身受之！”良久寂然，生乃归寝。自此第内绝不复声息矣。生叔闻而奇之，愿售以居，不较直。生喜，携家口而迁焉。居逾年，甚适，而未尝须臾忘凤也。会清明上墓归，见小狐二，为犬逼逐。其一投荒窜去，一则皇急道上。望见生，依依哀啼，阘耳辑首，似乞其援。生怜之，启裳衿，提抱以归。闭门，置床上，则青凤也。大喜，慰问。女曰：“适与婢子戏，遘此大厄。脱非郎君，必葬犬腹。望无以非类见憎。”生曰：“日切怀思，系于魂梦。见卿如获异宝，何憎之云！”女曰：“此天数也，不因颠覆，何得相从？然幸矣，婢子必以妾为已死，可与君坚永约耳。”生喜，另舍舍之。积二年

Qingfeng's fault. If you'll be lenient with her, I'll gladly bear any punishment, be it by sword, saw, hatcher or axe." All sounds died down into prolonged silence. The scholar went back to bed. From this time on not a breath of noise was heard in the manor. The scholar's uncle, amazed by the news of these events, agreed to sell the manor to his nephew without haggling over the price. The scholar was delighted: he moved into the manor with his family. They lived there quite comfortably for more than a year, but the scholar never forgot Qingfeng.

Then, while returning from the family graves on Tomb Sweeping Day, he happened to see two small foxes closely pursued by hounds. One of them ducked into the brush, but the other was so frightened it kept running on the road. Seeing the scholar, it clung to his side whining pathetically, ears folded back and head hanging, as if to beg for help. The scholar's pity was aroused. He loosened his robe, picked up the fox and carried it home in his arms: When he closed the door to his room and put it onto the bed, it turned into Qingfeng. What joy he felt! He consoled her and asked how she had come to this pass.

"Just now I was out frolicking with a maid servant, when this terrible calamity threatened us. If it had not been for you, I would be buried now in a dog's stomach. I hope you don't hate me for not being one of your kind."

The scholar replied, "My constant yearning for you intrudes into the dreams of my soul. Seeing you is like discovering a precious treasure. How can you say 'hate'?"

"This meeting was fixed by the workings of fate. If it had not been for that near calamity, how could I be able to serve you? Fortunately for us, the maidservant will surely think I am dead. Now we can hold fast to our eternal vow."

With joy in his heart the scholar set the girl up in rooms separate from his family. Two years passed. One night the scholar was in the middle of his reading when Xiao-er came into his room. The startled

余，生方夜读，孝儿忽入。生辍读，讶诘所来。孝儿伏地，怆然曰："家君有横难，非君莫拯。将自诣恳，恐不见纳，故以某来。"问："何事？"曰："公子识莫三郎否？"曰："此吾年家子也。"孝儿曰："明日将过。倘携有猎狐，望君之留之也。"生曰："楼下之羞，耿耿在念，他事不敢预闻。必欲仆效绵薄，非青凤来不可！"孝儿零涕曰："凤妹已野死三年矣！"生拂衣曰："既尔，则恨滋深耳！"执卷高吟，殊不顾瞻。孝儿起，哭失声，掩面而去。生如青凤所，告以故。女失色曰："果救之否？"曰："救则救之；适不之诺者，亦聊以报前横耳。"女乃喜曰："妾少孤，依叔成立。昔虽获罪，乃家范应尔。"生曰："诚然，但使人不能无介介耳。卿果死，定

scholar put down his book and asked the reason for his coming.

Xiao-er prostrated himself and said woefully: "My father is facing an unexpected disaster. Only you can save him. He would have come to plead with you himself, but he feared you would not grant his request, so he sent me."

"Well, what is it?" asked the scholar.

"Do you know Mo the Third Son?"

"He is the son of a man who took examinations the year I did," said the scholar.

Xiao-er said, "He will pass by here tomorrow. If he is carrying a fox taken in the hunt, please ask him to leave it here."

"The shame your father subjected me to in the mansion still burns in my heart. Let me hear no more of what does not concern me. If you insist on my doing what little I can, I will do only if Qingfeng comes to me first!"

"Cousin Qingfeng died in the fields three years ago!" Xiao-er sniffled as he spoke.

The scholar retorted with a sweep of his sleeve, "If so, my resentment is so much the greater!" He picked up his book and loudly intoned a poem, without lifting his gaze in the slightest. Xiao-er rose and cried himself hoarse, then walked out, hiding his face in his hands. The scholar went to Qingfeng's room to let her know.

"Will you save him or not?" she asked, her face gone pale.

"I'll save him all right. My refusal just now was my way of repaying his past spitefulness."

At this the girl brightened: "I was orphaned at an early age, but my uncle took me in and raised me. Though he once offended you, that was only because of the family discipline he had demanded of me."

"True," said the scholar. "But one can't help holding it against him. If you were really dead, I wouldn't lift a finger for him."

"You really are hard-hearted!" she said with a laugh.

不相援。"女笑曰:"忍哉!"次日,莫三郎果至,镂膺虎韔,仆从甚赫。生门逆之。见获禽甚多,中一黑狐,血殷毛革;抚之,皮肉犹温。便托裘敝,乞得缀补。莫慨然解赠。生即付青凤,乃与客饮。客既去,女抱狐于怀,三日而苏,展转复化为叟。举目见凤,疑非人间。女历言其情。叟乃下拜,惭谢前愆。喜顾女曰:"我固谓汝不死,今果然矣。"女谓生曰:"君如念妾,还乞以楼宅相假,使妾得以申返哺之私。"生诺之。叟赧然谢别而去。入夜,果举家来。由此如家人父子,无复猜忌矣。生斋居,孝儿时共谈宴。生嫡出子渐长,遂使傅之;盖循循善教,有师范焉。

Sure enough, Mo the Third Son showed up the next day sporting engraved harness ornaments, a bowcase of tiger skin and an impressive entourage. Meeting him at the gate, the scholar saw that he had bagged a fair amount of game. Among it was a black fox, still warm to the touch, its fur matted with dark red blood. The scholar asked to have it, claiming that he needed the pelt to patch his worn fur coat Mo parted with it magnanimously. The scholar turned it over to Qingfeng and drank wine with his guest. When the guest had gone, the girl held the fox in her arms. After three days it came back to life. Then, through several stages, it changed back into her uncle. Qingfeng was the first to meet his eyes when he looked up, which led him to suspect that he was no longer in the world of men. When the girl had gone through the true story, he bowed down and stammered an apology for his past offence. That done, he turned beamingly to the girl and said, "I kept saying that you weren't dead: now it turns out that I was right!"

The girl said to the scholar: "I also beg you, if you care for me, to give us the use of a building, so that I can care for the one who has cared for me." The scholar assented. The old man then excused himself blushingly and left. That night he returned with his whole family. From then on they lived like one big family, all ill feelings left in the past. The scholar lived a secluded life in his studio, but Xiao-er frequently joined him for wine and conversation. As the son born to the scholar's wife grew older, Xiao-er was asked to act as tutor, because he taught with skill and patience and conducted himself as a teacher should.

画　皮

太原王生,早行,遇一女郎,抱袱独奔,甚艰于步。急走趁之,乃二八姝丽。心相爱乐。问:“何夙夜踽踽独行?”女曰:“行道之人,不能解愁忧,何劳相问。”生曰:“卿何愁忧?或可效力,不辞也。”女黯然曰:“父母贪赂,鬻妾朱门。嫡妒甚,朝詈而夕楚辱之,所弗堪也,将远遁耳。”问:“何之?”曰:“在亡之人,乌有定所。”生言:“敝庐不远,即烦枉顾。”女喜,从

PAINTED SKIN

SCHOLAR Wang of Taiyuan went out for a morning walk and came upon a lone young woman with a bundle in her arms, hurrying along and faltering at every step. Running up behind, he found her to be in the bloom of youthful beauty, and his heart loved and delighted in her.

"Why are you walking all by yourself before the break of day?" he asked.

The girl answered, "Why should a passerby who can do nothing for my misery bother to ask?"

"What is your misery?" asked the scholar. "If there is anything I can do to help, I won't refuse."

The girl answered moodily: "My parents sold me to a rich family as a concubine, thinking of nothing but the marriage gift they would receive. The wife was terribly jealous: mornings she reviled me and evenings she insulted me with beatings. It was too much for me to bear. I must escape to someplace far away."

"Where will you go?" he asked.

"A fugitive does not choose a destination."

"My house is not far. Can I trouble you to pay me a visit?"

之。生代携袱物，导与同归。女顾室无人，问："君何无家口？"答云："斋耳。"女曰："此所良佳。如怜妾而活之，须秘密，勿泄。"生诺之。乃与寝合。使匿密室，过数日而人不知也。生微告妻。妻陈，疑为大家媵妾，劝遣之。生不听。偶适市，遇一道士，顾生而愕。问："何所遇？"答言："无之。"道士曰："君身邪气萦绕，何言无？"生又力白。道士乃去，曰："惑哉！世固有死将临而不悟者！"生以其言异，颇疑女。转思明明丽人，何至为妖，意道士借魇禳以猎食者。无何，至斋门，门内杜，不得入。心疑所作，乃逾垝垣。则室门亦闭。蹑迹而窗窥之，见一狞鬼，面翠色，齿巉巉如

The girl followed him, delighted. The scholar picked up her bundle of possessions and showed her the way home. Seeing that the house was empty, she asked, "Why ins't anyone in your family here?"

"It's only my studio," was the answer.

"This is a wonderful place. If you pity me and wish to save me, my presence here must be a well-guarded secret." Having agreed to this, the scholar took her to bed with him.

He concealed her in a secret room, and several days passed without anyone being the wiser. The scholar revealed something of this to his wife Chen, who suspected that she was a dowry-maid or or concubine from some important family and urged him to send her away. The scholar did not listen.

One day he went to the market, where he came upon a Taoist who turned and looked at him in astonishment, asking: "What have you come up against?"

"Nothing," he answered.

"An aura of evil surrounds you," said the Taoist. "Why do you say *nothing*?" The scholar denied this vigorously, whereupon the Taoist walked away muttering: "Such delusion! It only goes to show there are people in this world who don't even wake death is around the corner." The strangeness of these words stirred suspicion of the girl in the scholar's mind. But then he wondered how such an obviously beautiful girl could be a monster. He concluded that the Taoist probably made use of exorcism to made use of exorcism to make a living.

Soon he came to his studio gate, but it was blocked from inside and he could not enter. Suspicious that something had gone wrong, he leapt over a place where the wall had crumbled. The studio door would not open either. He tiptoed to a window and peeped in to see a frightful demon with green face and jagged, sawlike teeth. It spread a human skin on the bed, and painted the skin with color-dipped

锯。铺人皮于榻上,执采笔而绘之;已而掷笔,举皮,如振衣状,披于身,遂化为女子。睹此状,大惧,兽伏而出。急追道士,不知所往。遍迹之,遇于野,长跪乞救。道士曰:“请遣除之。此物亦良苦,甫能觅代者,予亦不忍伤其生。”乃以蝇拂授生,令挂寝门。临别,约会于青帝庙。生归,不敢入斋,乃寝内室,悬拂焉。一更许,闻门外戢戢有声。自不敢窥也,使妻窥之。但见女子来,望拂子不敢进;立而切齿,良久乃去。少时,复来,骂曰:“道士吓我。终不然,宁入口而吐之耶?”取拂碎之,坏寝门而入。径登生床,裂生腹,掬生心而去。妻号。婢入烛之,生已死,腔血狼藉。陈骇涕不敢声。明日,使弟二郎奔告道士。道士怒曰:“我固怜之,鬼子乃敢尔!”即从生弟来。女子

brushes. That done, the demon threw the brushes aside, lifted the skin and shook the wrinkles out as if it were a piece of clothing. The demon pulled the skin over its body and changed instantly into a young woman.

The scholar slunk away from the studio on all fours, greatly frightened at what he had seen. He ran to see the Taoist, who was nowhere to be found. He went searching everywhere and finally came upon him in a field. There he knelt upright and begged to be saved.

The Taoist said: "With your leave I will drive the monster away. But it has to suffer greatly before it can find someone to take its place. I really can't bear to kill it." With this he handed the scholar a fly-whisk, instructing him to hang it above the door to his bedroom. Before parting, they arranged to meet at the Blue Emperor Temple.

When he returned, the scholar did not dare to enter the studio, so he slept in an inner chamber and hung the whisk over the door. A short time into the second watch of the night, muted sounds could be heard outside. Not daring to look himself, the scholar had his wife Chen peek out. She saw the girl come toward the door and then stop short at the sight of the whisk. She stood there grinding her teeth for quite some time and then left. In a short while she returned and stormed: "That Taoist is trying to scare me off. But don't tell me I should spit out what has come into my mouth!"

She pulled down the whisk and tore it to pieces, battered down the door and came into the room. Jumping right onto the scholar's bed, she tore a gash into his chest, ripped out his heart and ran wawy with it. Chen wailed. A maid came in and held up a candle: the scholar was already dead. Blood from his chest cavity was splattered everywhere. Chen sniveled in terror, not daring to sob out loud. The next day she had the scholar's second brother run to tell the Taoist.

The Taoist exploded: "I took pity on that ghost, but still it had the gall to do such a thing!" He followed the scholar's brother home,

已失所在。既而仰首四望，曰："幸遁未远。"问："南院谁家？"二郎曰："小生所舍也。"道士曰："现在君所。"二郎愕然，以为未有。道士问曰："曾否有不识者一人来？"答曰："仆早赴青帝庙，良不知。当归问之。"去，少顷而返，曰："果有之。晨间一妪来，欲佣为仆家操作，室人止之，尚在也。"道士曰："即是物矣。"遂与俱往。仗木剑，立庭心，呼曰："孽魅！偿我拂子来！"妪在室，惶遽无色，出门欲遁。道士逐击之。妪仆，人皮划然而脱；化为厉鬼，卧嗥如猪。道士以木剑枭其首；身变作浓烟，匝地作堆。道士出一葫芦，拔其塞，置烟中，飗飗然如口吸气，瞬息烟尽。道士塞口入囊。共视人皮，眉目手足，无不备具。道士卷之，如卷画轴声，亦囊之，乃别欲去。陈氏拜迎于

but the girl had disappeared. The Taoist lifted his head and looked upwards in all directions. "Luckily she isn't hiding far from here," he exclaimed, and then asked, "Whose house is that in the south courtyard?"

"I live there," said the second brother.

"She 's in your place now," said the Taoist.

This startled the second brother, but he was not con-vinced.

The Taoist asked, "Has anyone you don't know been here?"

"I went to the Blue Emperor Temple this morning, so I have no idea. I'll go back and ask." The young man left and returned in a short while to say: "There was someone. An old woman came this morning asking for work as a household servant. My wife discouraged her, but she is still there."

"It's her all right," said the Taoist. He and the second brother went to the latter's house. He stood in the middle of the courtyard holding a wooden sword and cried, "Pay me back for my whisk, you hideous fiend!" The old woman's face blanched with panic when she heard his voice. She ran through the gate, trying to escape. The Taoist caught up with her and struck. The old woman fell flat, her human skin peeled away, and she changed into a fearsome demon that lay there bellowing like a pig. The Taosit dealt a death blow, skewered its head with his wooden sword and held it up in the air. The body changed into dense vapor that whirled into a single mass on the ground. The Taoist brought out his bottle gourd, uncorked it, and placed it in the smoke. There was the sound of a mouth sucking in breath, and in the wink of an eye the smoke was gone. The Taoist corked the gourd and put it in his pouch. Everyone stared at the human skin, which was complete with arms, legs and finely detailed eyes. The Taoist rolled it up with a sound like rolling up a scroll painting, then put it too into his pouch, after which he said good-bye and started to leave. The scholar's wife Chen bowed before him at the

门,哭求回生之法。道士谢不能。陈益悲,伏地不起。道士沉思曰:"我术浅,诚不能起死。我指一人,或能之,往求必合有效。"问:"何人?"曰:"市上有疯者,时卧粪土中。试叩而哀之。倘狂辱夫人,夫人勿怒也。"二郎亦习知之。乃别道士,与嫂俱往。见乞人颠歌道上,鼻涕三尺,秽不可近。陈膝行而前。乞人笑曰:"佳人爱我乎?"陈告之故。又大笑曰:"人尽夫也,活之何为?"陈固哀之。乃曰:"异哉!人死而乞活于我。我阎摩耶?"怒以杖击陈。陈忍痛受之。市人渐集如堵。乞人咯痰唾盈把,举向陈吻曰:"食之!"陈红涨于面,有难色;既思道士之嘱,遂强啖焉。觉入喉中,硬如团絮,格格而下,停结胸间。乞人大笑曰:"佳人爱我哉!"遂起行,已,不顾。尾之,入于庙中。追而求之,不知所在;前后冥搜,

gate, begging in tears for a spell that would bring her husband to life. The Taoist apologized that it was beyond him. She was even more stricken and laid on the ground, refusing to get up. The Taoist pondered this and said, "My powers are insufficient to raise the dead. But I will recommend a man who may be able to. Go and ask him, and maybe things will work out."

"Who is he?"

"There is a madman in the market who often lies on piles of refuse. Try asking his advice and imploring his help. Do not be angry if he insults you in his madness." The second-brother, too, had heard of the mad-man. Thereupon he took leave of the Taoist and went to the market with his sister-in-law. They found the beggar singing loonily in the street. Snot dangled in a long string from his nose, and he was unapproachably filthy. Chen approached him on her knees.

The beggar laughed: "So the beauty loves me, does she?" Chen told him what had happened. He howled again with laughter, saying: "Any man could be your husband. Why bring him to life?" Chen would not give up her entreaties. "How strange! Her man dies, and she begs me to give back his life. Am I Yama, king of the underworld?" In a fit of anger he struck Chen with his staff. Chen steeled herself against the pain and took the beating. The crowd in the street gathered round so closely that the two were walled in. The beggar hacked up phlegm until it filled his cupped hand, then held it up to Chen's face, saying: "Eat it."

Chen's face flushed and grimaced with reluctance, but thinking of the Taoist's instructions, she forced it down. As it entered her throat, it felt hard like compacted fuzz. It slid slowly down into her chest and clotted firm.

The beggar howled with laughter: "Oh, the beauty loves me!" He rose and walked away without looking back. She trailed him till he went into a temple and went right in after him, but could not see

殊无端兆,惭恨而归。既悼夫亡之惨,又悔食唾之羞,俯仰哀啼,但愿即死。方欲展血敛尸,家人伫望,无敢近者。陈抱尸收肠,且理且哭。哭极声嘶,顿欲呕。觉鬲中结物,突奔而出,不及回首,已落腔中。惊而视之,乃人心也。在腔中突突犹跃,熱气腾蒸如烟然。大异之,急以两手合腔,极力抱挤,少懈,则气氤氲自缝中出。乃裂缯帛急束之。以手抚尸,渐温。覆以衾裯。中夜启视,有鼻息矣。天明,竟活。为言:"恍惚若梦,但觉腹隐痛耳。"视破处,痂结如钱,寻愈。

异史氏曰:"愚哉世人!明明妖也,而以为美。迷哉愚人!明明忠也,而以为妄。然爱人之色而渔之,妻亦将食人之唾而甘之矣。

where he had gone. Though she searched everywhere in the gloom, there was no sign of him. There was nothing to do but walk through the crowd in embarrassment and return home. Grieving at her husand's horrible death and burning with the humiliation of eating phlegm, she was racked by such sobs of misery she wanted to die then and there.

The time came to drain the blood and put the corpse in its coffin. The servants looked on stock still, not daring to approach. Chen embraced the corpse and put its vitals back into the abdomen, wailing as she got them tidy. When her wails reached their highest pitch her voice gave way: suddenly she felt like vomiting. The clotted thing that had settled on her diaphragm churned suddenly upwards and out. Before she could turn her head it had landed in the corpse's chest cavity. There before her amazed eyes was a human heart, jumping with rythmic beats and giving off a warm, steamy vapor. She was awestruck. She quickly closed the cavity with her hands and squeezed the body with all her strength. When she relaxed her embrace slightly, a breath of warmth issued from the opening. At this she tore plain silk into strips and hastily wrapped them around the torso. The corpse gradually became warm to the touch of her caressing hand. She put a cover over it. In the middle of the night she lifted the cover for a look: breath was coming from her husband's nostrils. In the morning he came to life.

"I was senseless, as if in a dream," he told them. "All I could feel was a burning pain in my chest." They looked for the gash but saw only a coin-sized scab. Even this soon healed.

The Chronicler of the Tale comments: "How foolish are the people of this world! That which is clearly bewitching they think beautiful. How deluded are the fools of this world! What is clearly trustworthy they think absurd. And as for those who net the beauties they adore, their wives must bear the shame of eating what others have disgorged.

天道好还，但愚而迷者不寤耳。可哀也夫！”

The way of heaven is reciprocity, but foolish, deluded people do not wake up. Is this not a pity?!"

陆　判

陵阳朱尔旦,字小明。性豪放。然素钝,学虽笃,尚未知名。一日,文社众饮。或戏之云:"君有豪名,能深夜赴十王殿,负得左廊判官来,众当醵作筵。"盖陵阳有十王殿,神鬼皆以木雕,妆饰如生。东庑有立判,绿面赤须,貌尤狞恶。或夜闻两廊拷讯声。入者,毛皆森竖。故众以此难朱。朱笑起,径去。居无何,门外大呼曰:"我请髯宗师至矣!"众皆起。

JUDGE LU

ZHU Erdan, of Lingyang, whose courtesy name was Xiaoming, was bold and outgoing by nature, though tending to be gullible. He studied industriously but had not yet made a name for himself. One day his literary club gathered for a drinking party, and one member taunted him: "We all know how daring you are. If you can go to the Hall of the Ten Kings of Hell in the middle of the night and bring back the judge in the left gallery, all of us will contribute to a feast in your honor." He was referring to Lingyang's Hall of Ten Kings, where there were lifelike images of gods and demons carved in wood. In the east corridor was a standing judge with green face and red beard, quite frightful in appearance. Sounds of torture and interrogation had been heard in the corridors at night, making the hair of those who entered stand chillingly on end. Zhu's compamions were only using this to embarrass him. But Zhu got up laughing and went straight out.

Not much time passed before a loud yell was heard outside the door: "The bearded master is here by my invitation! Everyone stood up. Presently Zhu came in carrying the judge, set him on a table and poured a libation of three cupfuls of wine. Everyone watched apprehensively, fidgeting in their seats. They asked him to carry the image

俄负判入,置几上,奉觞酹之三。众睹之,瑟缩不安于座。仍请负去。朱又把酒灌地,祝曰:"门生狂率不文,大宗师谅不为怪。荒舍匪遥,合乘兴来觅饮,幸勿为畛畦。"乃负之去。次日,众果招饮。抵暮,半醉而归,兴未阑,挑灯独酌。忽有人搴帘入,视之,则判官也。朱起曰:"意吾殆将死矣!前夕冒渎,今来加斧锧耶?"判启浓髯微笑曰:"非也。昨蒙高义相订,夜偶暇,敬践达人之约。"朱大悦,牵衣促坐,自起涤器爇火。判曰:"天道温和,可以冷饮。"朱如命,置瓶案上,奔告家人治肴果。妻闻,大骇,戒勿出。朱不听,立俟治具以出。易盏交酬,始询姓氏。曰:"我陆姓,无名字。"与谈古典,应答如响。问:"知制艺否?"曰:"妍媸亦颇辨之。阴司诵读,与阳世

away as well. Again Zhu poured wine on the floor as he made this prayer: "Your disciple is willful and uncultivated. May your Honor not take offense. My humble quarters are not far. Please feel free to come for a drink with me anytime you choose. Let there be no barriers between us." Whereupon Zhu carried the image away.

Next day the club members kept their word and invited Zhu to a drinking party. At sundown he went home feeling halfway tipsy. Still being in a party mood, he trimmed the lampwick and poured himself a measure. Suddenly someone parted the curtain and entered. He looked up to see the judge before him.

Zhu stood up and said: "I suppose I'm about to die! Last night I committed sacrilege. Have you come to execute me?"

The judge smiled under his thick beard as he said, "You're wrong. Yesterday I was honored by your kind invitation. Since I happen to have leisure tonight, I am glad to accept an invitation from such a liberal-minded man as yourself." Zhu was overjoyed. He urged the judge to take a seat by tugging at his robe, then went to wash wine vessels and light a fire.

"The weather is pleasantly warm: we can drink it cold," said the judge. Zhu did as directed, putting the pitcher of wine on the table. He ran to tell his servants to prepare a light meal and fruit. His wife, greatly distraught at hearing of their guest, warned him not to leave the inner rooms. Zhu did not listen. He stood waiting for the dishes to be prepared so he could serve them. Having done so, he and his guest toasted back and forth. only then did he ask his guest's name.

"Lu is my family name. I have no given name. When Zhu brought up subjects from the classics, the guest's replies came as quickly as echoes."

"Are you conversant with the examination essay style?" asked Zhu.

"I can distinguish the agreeable from the disgusting fairly well.

略同。"陆豪饮,一举十觥。朱因竟日饮,遂不觉玉山倾颓,伏几醺睡。比醒,则残烛昏黄,鬼客已去。自是三两日辄一来,情益洽,时抵足卧。朱献窗稿,陆辄红勒之,都言不佳。一夜,朱醉,先寝。陆犹自酌。忽醉梦中,觉脏腑微痛;醒而视之,则陆危坐床前,破腔出肠胃,条条整理。愕曰:"夙无仇怨,何以见杀?"陆笑云:"勿惧,我为君易慧心耳。"从容纳肠已,复合之,末以裹足布束朱腰。作用毕,视榻上亦无血迹。腹间觉少麻木。见陆置肉块几上,问之。曰:"此君心也。作文不快,知君之毛窍塞耳。适在冥间,于千万心中,拣得佳者一枚,为君易之,留此以补阙数。"乃起,掩扉去。天明解视,则创缝已合,有綖而赤者存焉。自是文思大进,过眼不忘。数日,又出文

What we read in the court of the underworld is pretty much the same as what you have in the sunlit world." Judge Lu drank mightily, downing ten horns in a single bout. Because Zhu had been drinking all day, his condition was like a jade mountain ready to topple heavily. He leaned against the table in wine-soaked slumber. When he awoke he saw by the sickly light of a guttering candle that his ghostly guest was gone. From that night on the judge came once every few days. Their friendship grew even closer. Sometimes they slept together with the soles of their feet touching. When Zhu presented his practice compositions, Lu always covered the papers with red ink and invariably said they would not do. One night Zhu, being drunk, went to bed first, while Lu stayed up pouring wine for himself. Suddenly, in his drunken dream, Zhu was aware of a slight pain in his viscera. He woke up and looked: Lu was sitting upright by the bed drawing entrails out of Zhu's rent abdomen and putting the coils in order.

"There has never been malice between us," said Zhu, shocked. "Why are you killing me?"

"Never fear. I'm only putting in a brilliant heart in place of yours," said Lu laughingly. He calmly stuffed the intestines back in, pushed the incision together and finally wound strips of footbinding cloth around Zhu's loins. When the operation was completed there were no traces of blood to be seen on the bed. Only Zhu's abdomen felt a bit numb. He asked about the lump of flesh which he noticed the judge putting on the table.

"This is your own heart. From your slowness at writing I knew your heart's apertures were blocked. Just now in the nether regions I picked out one excellent heart among tens of thousands. Now I have exchanged it for yours, which I'll keep to make up for the missing one." He rose and left, closing the door softly behind him. At dawn Zhu undid the bandage to have a look: the incision had already closed, leaving only a thin red line. From then on he showed great improve-

示陆。陆曰:“可矣。但君福薄,不能大显贵,乡、科而已。”问:“何时?”曰:“今岁必魁。”未几,科试冠军,秋闱果中经元。同社生素揶揄之;及见闱墨,相视而惊,细询始知其异。共求朱先容,愿纳交陆。陆诺之。众大设以待之。更初,陆至,赤髯生动,目炯炯如电。众茫乎无色,齿欲相击;渐引去。朱乃携陆归饮。既醺,朱曰:“湔肠伐胃,受赐已多。尚有一事欲相烦,不知可否?”陆便请命。朱曰:“心肠可易,面目想亦可更。山荆,予结发人,下体颇亦不恶,但头面不甚佳丽。尚欲烦君刀斧,如何?”陆笑曰:“诺,容徐图之。”过数

ment in his ability to express thought in writing. When he passed his eyes over a page, he never forgot it. After a few days he brought out another composition and showed it to Lu.

"It will do," said Lu. "But your blessings are meager. You cannot win any great honors. The prefectural and provincial examinations are as far as you'll go."

"When will that be?" asked Zhu.

"You will take top honors in this year's provincial exam."

Not long afterwards he came out first in the prefectural examination and went on to win an honorable title in the provincial examinations. His friends in the literary club who had always poked fun at him looked at one another in amazement when they read copies of his examination papers. Finally, after thorough questioning, they learned of the marvel that lay behind this. They all pleaded with Zhu to say a word on their behalf, so that they might strike up an acquaintance with Lu. Lu consented. The group made elaborate preparations to entertain him. Lu arrived at the beginning of the first watch, his red beard wagging and his eyes glinting like lightning. The group members were pale and dazed; their teeth were on the point of chattering. Gradually they all withdrew.

Zhu, for his part, took Lu by the hand and went home to drink wine. When they were soaked, Zhu said, "By opening my stomach and washing my intestines, you have already given me a great deal. There is one more favor I'd like to ask of you, but I don't know if I should." Without hesitation, Lu offered to do his bidding. Zhu said, "If vitals can be exchanged, I suppose that facial features can be replaced too. My wife and I got married when we came of age. The lower part of her body is not bad at all, but her head and face are not very appealing. I would like to trouble you to put your blade to use once again. What do you say?"

Lu answered with a laugh: "As you wish. Give me time to work

日,半夜来叩关。朱急起延入。烛之,见襟裹一物。诘之,曰:"君曩所嘱,向艰物色。适得一美人首,敬报君命。"朱拨视,颈血犹湿。陆立促急入,勿惊禽犬。朱虑门户夜扃。陆至,一手推扉,扉自辟。引至卧室,见夫人侧身眠。陆以头授朱抱之;自于靴中出白刃如匕首,按夫人项,着力如切腐状,迎刃而解,首落枕畔。急于生怀,取美人头合项上,详审端正,而后按捺。已而移枕塞肩际,命朱瘗首静所,乃去。朱妻醒,觉颈间微麻,面颊甲错;搓之,得血片。甚骇,呼婢汲盥。婢见面血狼籍,惊绝。濯之,盆水尽赤。举首则面目全非,又骇极。夫人引镜自照,错愕不能自解。朱入告之。因反复细视,则长眉掩鬓,笑靥承

out the details." After several days he came knocking on the gate in the middle of the night. Zhu got up quickly and invited him in. The light of a candle revealed an object bulging beneath his coat. Zhu demanded to know what it was.

"What you asked for a while ago has been hard to select, but I just obtained the head of a beautiful woman, which I am now bringing you as you requested. Zhu pulled his lapel aside to look: the neck was still wet with blood. Lu immediately urged him to go inside in order not to arouse dogs and fowl. Zhu was concerned because the doors to the inner rooms had been locked for the night, but when Lu walked up and touched the double-leafed door with one hand, the door opened by itself. Zhu led him to the bedroom, where his wife lay sleeping on her side. Lu had Zhu hold the head in his arms, while he pulled a sharpdaggerlike blade from his boot. He pressed it down on the neck of Zhu's wife as delicately as if he were slicing a piece of curd. The flesh parted before the blade, and the head fell beside the pillow. He quickly took the beautiful woman's head from the scholar's cradled arms and fitted it on the neck. After checking carefully to be sure it was correctly aligned, he pressed down. When that was done he slid a pillow under her shoulders. He ordered Zhu to bury the head in a quiet place and then left.

Zhu's wife awoke with a slight tingling in her neck and a crust on her cheeks. Rubbing them she discovered flakes of dried blood. Horrified, she called for a maid to draw a basin of water. The maid was thoroughly shocked when she saw her mistress's blood-spattered visage. Wishing it clean made the whole basinful of water red. Looking up, the maid saw a set of features that in no way resembled those of her mistress. Nothing could have given her a greater shock. The wife reached for a mirror and was thrown into consternation by what she saw. She had no idea what had happened to herself. Zhu came in and told her all about it. Meanwhile he looked from every possible angles

颧,画中人也。解领验之,有红线一周,上下肉色,判然而异。先是吴侍御有女甚美,未嫁而丧二夫,故十九犹未醮也。上元游十王殿。时游人甚杂,内有无赖贼窥而艳之,遂阴访居里,乘夜梯入;穴寝门,杀一婢于床下,逼女与淫。女力拒声喊。贼怒,亦杀之。吴夫人微闻闹声,呼婢往视。见尸骇绝。举家尽起,停尸堂上,置首项侧,一门啼号,纷腾终夜。诘旦启衾,则身在而失其首。遍挞侍女,谓所守不恪,致葬犬腹。侍御告郡。郡严限捕贼,三月而罪人弗得。渐有以朱家换头之异闻吴公者。吴疑之,遣媪探诸其家;入见夫人,骇走以告吴公。公视女尸故存,惊疑无以自决。

at her long eyebrows that lost themselves beneath the hair at her temples and the dimples on her cheeks when she smiled. She was, in short, a beauty right out of a painting. Zhu loosened her collar for a closer look and found a red line encircling her collar for a closer look and found a red line encircling her neck. The skin above and below her neck was of two distinct colors.

Prior to this, a certain Provincial Censor Wu had a very beautiful daughter who was still unwed at nineteen because her two prospective husbands had died before she could marry them. On the day of the Lantern Festival she went for a visit to the Hall of Ten Kings, at a time when all sorts of sightseers were there. Among them was a scoundrel who stared at her, aroused by her beauty. Unbeknownst to her, he found out which neighborhood she lived in. He went there under cover of night, climbed over the wall with a ladder and cut a hole in the bedroom door. He killed a maid beside the bed, then tried to make love to the young woman by force. She screamed and put up vigorous resistance, which so infuriated the rapist he killed her too. Lady Wu, faintly hearing the commotion, told a maid to go look. The maid fainted at the sight of the body. After the whole family had been roused up, they laid the girl's body in the hall, and her head was laid beside the neck. The entire household was in a screeching, wailing uproar all night. In the morning they lifted the quilt only to find the body there but the head gone. They beat all the waiting maids for not being attentive enough while watching over their mistress and so allowing her head to be buried in the stomachs of dogs.

The Censor reported this to the prefectural government. Though the district imposed a strict time limit for capture of the killer, he was still at large after three months. Eventually Master Wu was apprized of the wondrous head substitution in Zhu's house. His suspicions aroused, Wu sent an old woman there to sound out the family on this matter. She went in and saw the lady of the house, then ran back in

猜朱以左道杀女,往诘朱。朱曰:“室人梦易其首,实不解其何故。谓仆杀之,则冤也。”吴不信,讼之。收家人鞫之,一如朱言。郡守不能决。朱归,求计于陆。陆曰:“不难,当使伊女自言之。”吴夜梦女曰:“儿为苏溪杨大年所贼,无与朱孝廉。彼不艳于其妻,陆判官取儿头与之易之,是儿身死而头生也。愿勿相仇。”醒告夫人,所梦同。乃言于官。问之,果有杨大年;执而械之,遂伏其罪。吴乃诣朱,请见夫人,由此为翁婿。乃以朱妻首合女尸而葬焉。朱三入礼闱,皆以场规被放,于是灰心仕进。积三十年,一夕,陆告曰:“君寿不永矣。”问其期,对以五日。“能相救否?”曰:“惟

fear to tell Master Wu. When he learned that his daughter's body was still intact, the master could not get over his astonishment and suspicion. He surmised that Zhu had used black arts to kill his daughter and went to him to demand the truth.

Zhu said, "My wife's head was changed in a dream, but I have no idea how it came about. It would be unjust to say that I killed your daughter."

Wu was not convinced. He brought charges against Zhu, and the members of his household were summoned for questioning. Everything they said corroborated Zhu's story. The prefectural magistrate could not reach a decision. Zhu went to home and asked Lu for a plan.

"This is not difficult," said Lu. "I'll simply have his daughter tell the truth."

That night Wu dreamed of his daughter, who said, "I was murdered by Yang Danian of Su Creek. Bachelor Zhu had nothing to do with it. He found his wife unattractive, so Judge Lu exchanged my head for hers. This way my head lives on, even though my body is dead. I hope you will bear no grudge against him." Wu awoke and told his wife of the dream. It was identical to what she had dreamed. They notified the authorities of this. Inquiries proved that there was indeed a Yang Danian, who later confessed his guilt after being arrested and shackled. Wu paid Zhu a visit and asked to see the lady of the house. From then on Wu and Zhu were as father and son-in-law. Zhu's wife's head was put together with Wu's daughter's corpse and buried.

Zhu entered the capital examination three times, but was thrown out each time for breaking rules of deportment. At this the goal of official advancement soured on him.

Thirty years passed. One evening Lu told him: "You do not have much longer to live. Zhu asked him when his time would come, and Lu answered that he had five days."

"Can you save me?"

天所命，人何能私？且自达人观之，生死一耳，何必生之为乐，死之为悲？”朱以为然。即治衣衾棺椁，既竟，盛服而没。翌日，夫人方扶柩哭，朱忽冉冉自外至。夫人惧。朱曰：“我诚鬼，不异生时。虑尔寡母孤儿，殊恋恋耳。”夫人大恸，涕垂膺。朱依依慰解之。夫人曰：“古有还魂之说，君既有灵，何不再生？”朱曰：“天数不可违也。”问：“在阴司作何务？”曰：“陆判荐我督案务，授有官爵，亦无所苦。”夫人欲再语，朱曰：“陆公与我同来，可设酒馔。”趋而出。夫人依言营备。但闻室中笑饮，亮气高声，宛若生前。半夜窥之，窅然已逝。自是三数日辄一来，时而留宿缱绻，家中事就便经纪。子玮方五岁，来辄捉抱；至七八岁则灯下教读。子亦惠，九岁能文，十五入邑庠，竟不知无父也。从此来渐疏，日月至焉而已。又一夕来，谓夫人曰：“今与卿永诀矣。”

"What good are personal wishes in the face of heaven's decree? And anyway life and death are one in the eyes of a man of broad perspective. Why should you rejoice at life and grieve at death?"

This made sense to Zhu. He readied a suit of burial clothes, a shroud, a coffin, and an outer coffin. That being done, he dressed himself impeccably and died. The next day, just as his wife was leaning against the coffin in tears, Zhu suddenly floated in from outside. His wife was terrified. Zhu spoke to her: "Yes, I am a ghost, but no different from when I lived. I worry about you two, a widowed mother and an orphaned boy; I simply can't bear parting with you." His wife was so overcome with the grief that snivel dripped onto her chest. Zhu consoled her tenderly. His wife said, "In ancient times men told of souls returning to their bodies. Since your spirit is not extinguished, why not live again?"

Zhu replied, "The workings of fate cannot be defied."

"What do you do in the court of the underworld?"

"Judge Lu recommended me for a position overseeing case records. I have an official title, but it is not too demanding." His wife wanted to say more, but Zhu cut her off: "Master Lu came here with me. Would you set out wine and food?" He walded out with rapid steps. His wife made preparations according to his wishes, and the room was soon filled with laughing toasts and loud, convivial talk, just as when her husband had been alive. Then she peeked into the room in the middle of night: both of them had departed without a trace. From then on Zhu came onceevery few days. Now and then he spent an intimate night with her. While there he advised her on the handling of household matters, and he always hugged his son Wei, who was five years old at the time of his death. When the boy was about seven he taught him to read by lamplight. The boy, too, was brilliant. At nine he could write a composition; at fifteen he entered the local academy, never realizing that he was fatherless. Then Zhu's visits tapered off,

问:“何往?”曰:“承帝命为太华卿,行将远赴,事烦途隔,故不能来。”母子持之哭。曰:“勿尔!儿已成立,家计尚可存活,岂有百岁不拆之鸾凤耶!”顾子曰:“好为人,勿堕父业。十年后一相见耳。”径出门去,于是遂绝。后玮二十五,举进士,官行人。奉命祭西岳,道经华阴,忽有舆从羽葆,驰冲卤簿。讶之。审视车中人,其父也。下马哭伏道左。父停舆曰:“官声好,我目瞑矣。”玮伏不起。朱促舆行,火驰不顾。去数步,回望,解佩刀遣人持赠。遥语曰:“佩之当贵。”玮欲追从,见舆马人从,飘忽若风,瞬息不见。痛恨良久。抽刀视之,制极精工,镌字一行,曰:“胆欲大而心欲小,

until he came only once or so a month. One evening he came and said to his wife: "The time has come for me to say goodbye to your forever."

"Where will you go?" she asked.

"Jade Emperor of Heaven has made me Governor of Hua Mountain. I must go a great distance to assume my post. My duties are many and the road is hard, so I cannot return. His wife and son cried and held him fast." Don't take it so hard! Our son's position in life is assured, and the family fortune will be enough for you to live on. When has there ever been a pair of phoenixes that stayed together for a century? "Turning to his son," he said, "Be a man of character, and don't squander what I've left you. We'll get to se each other ten years from now." He walked straight out the door and was gone.

At the age of twenty-five, Wei was awarded a Master of Letters degree and given the position of inspecting com-missioner. He was ordered to perform ceremonies at Hua Mountain, the Western Sacred Peak, and his route took him through Huayin County. To his surprise there suddenly appeared a carriage with attendants bearing plumed canopies, galloping toward the ranks of his escort. On closer inspection, the man in the carriage proved to be his father. He dismounted and threw himself down, sobbing, at the side of the road. His father stopped the carriage and said, "You have a good reputation as an official. Now I can rest easy." Wei did not rise from his prone position. Without turning his head, Zhu ordered his carriage to leave quickly. When he had gone several paces he turned, unfastened a sword from his waist and had an attendant hand it to his son.

"Wear it and you will prosper," he cried from afar. Wei was about to run after him, but, as he watched, the carriage with its horses and attendants floated airily over the ground and disappeared in the blinking of an eye. For a long time he gave himself up to disappointment and regret. Then he drew the sword and saw that it was a piece

智欲圆而行欲方。"玮后官至司马。生五子，曰沉，曰潜，曰沕，曰浑，曰深。一夕，梦父曰："佩刀宜赠浑也。"从之。浑仕为总宪，有政声。

异史氏曰："断鹤续凫，矫作者妄，移花接木，创始者奇；而况加凿削于肝肠，施刀锥于颈项者哉？陆公者，可谓媸皮裹妍骨矣。明季至今，为岁不远，陵阳陆公犹存乎？尚有灵焉否也？为之执鞭，所欣慕焉。"

of extremely fine workmanship. A line of words was engraved upon it: "Be long on courage and short on foolhardiness; be round in wisdom and square in conduct." Wei later attained the rank of sub-prefect. He had five sons: Chen, Qian, Mi, Hun and Shen. One night he dreamed his father said, "The sword should go to Hun." He acted accordingly. Hun later became a commissioner-general with a high reputation.

The Chronicler of the Tales comments: "To chop short the crane's legs and stretch the duck's is the folly of artificiality, but grafting a flower to a tree is a marvel of creativity. How true these two statements are when vitals are to be hacked up and knives are to be wielded against necks! This Master Lu was repulsive on the outside but attractive on the inside. It has not been all that many years from the end of the Ming Dynasty to the present. Is Master Lu of Lingyang still around? Does his supernatural power still work as of old? I would like nothing more than to serve, whip in hand, as his charioteer."

婴宁

王子服，莒之罗店人。早孤。绝惠，十四入泮。母最爱之，寻常不令游郊野。聘萧氏，未嫁而夭，故求凰未就也。会上元，有舅氏子吴生，邀同眺瞩。方至村外，舅家有仆来，招吴去；生见游女如云，乘兴独遨。有女郎携婢，捻梅花一枝，容华绝代，笑容可掬。生注目不移，竟忘顾忌。女过去数武，顾婢曰："个儿郎目灼灼似贼！"遗花地上，笑语自去。生拾花怅然，神魂丧失，怏怏遂返。至家，藏花枕底，垂头而睡，不语亦不食。母忧之。醮禳

YINGNING

WANG Zifu from Luo Bazaar in Ju County lost his father at an early age. An absolutely brilliant student, he received the baccalaureate at thirteen. His mother held him so dear that she seldom permitted him to go on outings in the country. He had been engaged to a girl of the Xiao family, but she passed away before they could be married, so his phoenix-mate was as yet unfound. On the Lantern Festival, the son of his maternal uncle, a scholar named Wu, invited him to do some sightseeing together. When they got outside the village a servant from his uncle's house came and called Wu home. Seeing that young women were out walking in droves, Scholar Wang gave in to the impulse to stroll by himself. There was a young woman walking arm-in-arm with a maid and toying with a twig of plum blossoms. Her flower-features topped the age, and the smiles playing across her face had a beauty that invited touching. The scholar riveted his gaze upon her, heedless of all scruples. The girl walked several dainty steps away, turned to her maid and said, "That fellow has a roguish glint in his eyes!" She dropped the flowers on the ground and moved off, talking gaily as she went. The scholar picked up the flowers wistfully. The spirit had gone out of him, and he walked pensively home.

益剧,肌革锐减。医师诊视,投剂发表。忽忽若迷。母抚问所由,默然不答。适吴生来,嘱密诘之。吴至榻前,生见之泪下。吴就榻慰解,渐致研诘。生具吐其实,且求谋画。吴笑曰:"君意亦复痴!此愿有何难遂?当代访之。徒步于野,必非世家。如其未字,事固谐矣;不然,拚以重赂,计必允遂。但得痊瘳,成事在我。"生闻之,不觉解颐。吴出告母,物色女子居里,而探访既穷,并无踪绪。母大忧,无所为计。然自吴去后,颜顿开,食亦略进。数日,吴复来。生问所谋。吴绐之曰:"已得之矣。我以为谁何人,乃我姑氏女,即君姨妹行,今尚待聘;虽内戚有婚姻之嫌,实告之,无

At home he hid the flowers under his pillow. He spent his time moping and sleeping, refusing to eat or speak. His worried mother set up an alter and said prayers to drive out evil influences, but his condition only worsened. He soon grew emaciated. A doctor examined him and had himtake medicines to draw the disease out, but he remained in a heartsick daze. His mother caressed him and asked the reason for his malady, but he would not break his silence.

Just then Scholar Wu showed up. He was instructed to get to the root of the matter without letting Wang know what he was about. Seeing Wu at his bedside made tears roll down Wang's cheeks. Wu set on his bed and comfored him, then gradually brought the conversation around to pointed questions. Wang spat out the whole truth and asked Wu to recommend a course of action.

"You are being downright silly!" laughed Wu. "Nothing stands in the way of fulfilling your wish! I will make inquiries for you. Since she was out in the wilds on foot, she could not belong to a noble family. If she is not yet engaged, then everything is fine. Otherwise, a substantial gratuity will very likely win acceptance. All you have to do is recover: leave the rest to me."

When he heard this the scholar grinned broadly in spite of himself. Wu came out and told Wang's mother everything. He checked into the girl's place of residence, but exhausted every avenue of inquiry without turning up a single trace or thread. The mother could do nothing but eat her heart out. However, Wang started smiling and began to show some interest in food after Wu's visit.

A few days later Wu came again. The scholar asked how the matter was progressing.

Wu deceived him saying: "I've found her already. I never would have thought that she is the daughter of my paternal aunt, which makes her your cousin on your mother's side. She is not engaged as yet. Though marriage between maternal relatives is frowned upon,

不谐者。”生喜溢眉宇,问:“居何里?”吴诡曰:“西南山中,去此可三十余里。”生又付嘱再四,吴锐身自任而去。生由此饮食渐加,日就平复。探视枕底,花虽枯,未便凋落。凝思把玩,如见其人。怪吴不至,折柬招之。吴支托不肯赴召。生恚怒,悒悒不欢。母虑其复病,急为议姻;略与商榷,辄摇首不愿。惟日盼吴。吴迄无耗,益怨恨之。转思三十里非遥,何必仰息他人?怀梅袖中,负气自往,而家人不知也。伶仃独步,无可问程,但望南山行去。约三十余里,乱山合沓,空翠爽肌,寂无人行,止有鸟道。遥望谷底,丛花乱树中,隐隐有小里落。下山入村,见舍宇无多,皆茅屋,而意甚修雅。北向一家,门前皆丝柳,墙

everything should work out if we tell them the truth."

Joy shone from the scholar's brow as he asked, "Where does she live?"

Wu concocted another reply: "A little more than ten miles away in the mountains southwest of here." The scholar entrusted him repeatedly with the task. Wu insisted he would take it upon himself. From then on the scholar's intake of food and liquids gradually increased, and he made daily progress toward recovery. Checking under his pillow he saw that the flowers, though dry , had not yet withered away. He toyed with them in rapt absorption, as if he were looking at the one who had left them. He wonderd why Wu did not come, so he sent a letter summoning him. Wu procrastinated and would not go to him. The scholar was procrastinated and would not go to him. The scholar was enraged and despondent. Fearing that he would take sick again, his mother hastened to arrange for him to marry another girl, but he shook his head whenever she tried to discuss it.

Day after day he did nothing but await Wu's coming. Much to his vexation, there was no word from Wu after all this time. Then it occurred to him that ten miles was not far. Why should he depend on anyone else? Putting the twig of plum blossoms in his sleeve, he sullenly set out by himself, without so much as a word to his family. With nobody to ask for directions, he turned toward the mountain to the south and went his solitary way on foot. jumbled mountains closed in upon him. The great expanse of verdure sent a tingle through his body. No one was abroad in the stillness. Only steep trails could be seen traversing the mountains.

Looking toward the bottom of a valley in the distance he could make out a small settlement almost hidden among flowering thickets and dense trees. He descended the mountain and entered the village. The few buildings he saw were all thatched huts, but they were

内桃杏尤繁,间以修竹;野鸟格磔其中。意其园亭,不敢遽入。回顾对户,有巨石滑洁,因据坐少憩。俄闻墙内有女子,长呼“小荣”,其声娇细。方伫听间,一女郎由东而西,执杏花一朵,俛首自簪。举头见生,遂不复簪,含笑捻花而入。审视之,即上元途中所遇也。心骤喜。但念无以阶进;欲呼姨氏,顾从无还往,惧有讹误。门内无人可问。坐卧徘徊,自朝至于日昃,盈盈望断,并忘饥渴。时见女子露半面来窥,似讶其不去者。忽一老媪扶杖出,顾生曰:“何处郎君,闻自辰刻便来,以至于今。意将何为?得勿饥耶?”生急起揖之,答云:“将以盼亲。”媪聋聩不闻。又大言之,

elegantly constructed. One house to the north had weeping willows before the gate. Within the walls grew especially luxuriant peach and apricot trees, interspersed with tall bamboos. Wild birds went clucking here and there among them. Surmising that this was someone's garden, he dared not enter abruptly. A look around revealed a clean, smooth boulder in front of the facing house, so he sat there to make himself comfortable for a spell.

Suddenly from inside the wall he heard a girl's delicate voice calling in drawn-out tones: "Gloria." As he stood listening, a young woman walked past from east to west, holding an almond blossom and lowering her head to fasten it in her hair. Raising her head, she saw the scholar and ceased fastening the flower; she toyed smilingly with the flower and walked into the house. To his sudden joy he recognized that she was the very girl he had met along the road during the Lantern Festival, but then he reflected that this gave him no pretext for presenting himself. He wanted to call at the house as if it were his aunt's, but considering that the two families had never kept in touch, he was afraid there might be some mistake. What was more, there was no one within the gate whom he could ask. Oblivious to hunger and thirst, he sat, reclined, then paced back and forth from morning into the afternoon, till his eager eyes ached with watching. Now and then he caught a glimpse of the girl's face peeking around a corner, as if she was surprised that he had not left.

Suddenly an old matron came out leaning on a cane, took a look at the scholar and said, "I was told a young man from who knows where came early this morning and has been here ever since. What are you here for? Aren't you hungry?"

The scholar quickly got up, raised his folded hands in greeting and replied, "I intended to look up my relatives." The old woman, being hard of hearing, did not catch what he had said. He repeated his words loudly.

乃问:“贵戚何姓?”生不能答。媪笑曰:“奇哉!姓名尚自不知,何亲可探?我视郎君,亦书痴耳。不如从我来,啖以粗粝;家有短榻可卧。待明朝归,询知姓氏,再来探访,不晚也。”生方腹馁思啖,又从此渐近丽人,大喜。从媪入,见门内白石砌路,夹道红花,片片堕阶上;曲折而西,又启一关,豆棚花架满庭中。肃客入舍,粉壁光明如镜;窗外海棠枝朵,探入室中;裀籍几榻,罔不洁泽。甫坐,即有人自窗外隐约相窥。媪唤:“小荣!可速作黍。”外有婢子叫声而应。坐次,具展宗阀。媪曰:“郎君外祖,莫姓吴否?”曰:“然。”媪惊曰:“是吾甥也!尊堂,我妹子。年来以家窭贫,又无三尺男,遂至音问梗塞。甥长成如许,尚不相

scholar was unable to answer. The old woman laughed: "How strange! If you don't even know their names, what relatives are there for you to visit? From the look of you, you're nothing but a book-addled scholar. I suppose you'd better come with me. I'll feed you husked millet, and there's settee inside you can lie on. You can go back tomorrow morning. Once you've gotten the name straight, you'll have plenty of chances to pay a visit." His famished stomach had put him in the mood to wolf down a meal, and this was a chance to approach the beautiful girl, so the scholar was overjoyed. Following the old woman through the gate, he saw a path of white flagstones lined with red flowers. The steps were strewn with fallen petals. The winding path took them westward to another gate, which opened into a courtyard covered by a bean arbor supported on trellises. The woman invited the guest into the house. The whitewashed walls were dazzling white. Branches from a flowering crabapple outside the window reached into the room. Cushions, table, and settee—everything glistened with cleanliness.

As they moved to their seats a face could indistinctly be seen peeking through the window. The old woman called, "Gloria, make some millet right away." The maid's answering cry was heard outside. When they were seated, they both made known their family histories. The old woman asked, "Was your maternal grandfather by any chance named Wu?"

"Yes, he was."

"Then you're my nephew!" she said in wonderment. "Your mother is my little sister. For years now we've been destitute, and there's not even a three-foot manchild in the house, so our connection has been broken off. Look how grown up you are, nephew: I didn't even recognize you."

The scholar said, "I came just to see you, Aunt, but things happened so quickly that I forgot your name."

"My married name is Qin," said the old woman. " I have no de-

识。"生曰:"此来即为姨也,匆遽遂忘姓氏。"媪曰:"老身秦姓,并无诞育;弱息仅存,亦为庶产。渠母改醮,遗我鞠养。颇亦不钝,但少教训,嬉不知愁。少顷,使来拜识。"未几,婢子具饭,雏尾盈握。媪劝餐已,婢来敛具。媪曰:"唤宁姑来。"婢应去。良久,闻户外隐有笑声。媪又唤曰:"婴宁,汝姨兄在此。"户外嗤嗤笑不已。婢推之以入,犹掩其口,笑不可遏。媪瞋目曰:"有客在,咤咤叱叱,是何景象?"女忍笑而立,生揖之。媪曰:"此王郎,汝姨子。一家尚不相识,可笑人也。"生问:"妹子年几何矣?"媪未能解。生又言之。女复笑不可仰视。媪谓生曰:"我言少教诲,此可见矣。年已十六,呆痴裁如婴儿。"生曰:"小于甥一岁。"曰:"阿甥已十七矣,得非庚午属马

scendants. I do have atender young thing, but she was born to a concubine. Her mother remarried and left her upbringing to me. She is not dull, by any means, but she has had little guidance. She is fun-loving and free of care. In a little while I'll have her come to meet you."

Soon the maid served a meal. On the table was a dish of young chickens small enough to fit in the palm of one's hand. When the old woman had finished urging him to eat, the maid came to clear off the dishes. "Call Miss Yingning here," said the old woman. The maid nodded and left.

After a long wait, a muted laugh was heard from outside. The old woman called again: "Yingning, your cousin is here." There was a drawn-out, chortling laugh from outside the door. As the maid pushed her in, Yingning was still covering her mouth and laughing uncontrollably.

The old woman glared at her and said, "There is a guest here. What sort of impression will you make with all this snorting and spluttering?" The girl mastered her laughter and stood still. The scholar joined his hands before his chest in greeting.

"This is Mister Wang, your aunt's son," said the old woman. "It is laughable that members of the same family don't know each other."

"How old is my cousin here?" asked the scholar. The old woman did not hear him clearly, so the scholar had to repeat his question, which made the girl double up with laughter.

The old woman said to him: "I said that she has had little guidance, and nowyou see what I mean. She's already sixteen, but still as silly as a child."

"She is a year younger than I," said the scholar.

"So you're already seventeen, nephew. You were born in the year of the horse, weren't you?"

The scholar answered with a nod.

"And who is your wife?"

者耶?"生首应之。又问:"甥妇阿谁?"答云:"无之。"曰:"如甥才貌,何十七岁犹未聘?婴宁亦无姑家,极相匹敌;惜有内亲之嫌。"生无语,目注婴宁,不遑他瞬。婢向女小语云:"目灼灼,贼腔未改!"女又大笑,顾婢曰:"视碧桃开未?"遽起,以袖掩口,细碎连步而出。至门外,笑声始纵。媪亦起,唤婢袱被,为生安置。曰:"阿甥来不易,宜留三五日,迟迟送汝归。如嫌幽闷,舍后有小园,可供消遣;有书可读。"次日,至舍后,果有园半亩,细草铺毡,杨花糁迳;有草舍三楹,花木四合其所。穿花小步,闻树头苏苏有声,仰视,则婴宁在上。见生来,狂笑欲堕。生曰:"勿尔,堕矣!"女且下且笑,不能自止。方将及地,失手而堕,笑乃

"I have none," he replied.

"How could someone with your ability and good looks still be unengaged at seventeen at seventeen? Yingning has no in-laws yet either. You two would make a wonderful match. Unfortunately, there remains the objection that you are close kin."

The scholar gave no answer. He was too busy staring wordlessly at Yingning to glance at anything else. The maid whispered to the girl: "See how his eyes gleam: he's still a rogue inside!"

The girl burst out laughing again. "Let's go see if the peach blossoms are out yet," she said, turning to the maid. She rose abruptly, hid her mouth with a sleeve and walked out with dainty, pattering steps. Once outside the gate she loosed a peal of laughter. The old woman also rose and called the maid to make the scholar's bed.

"Your coming was not easy, nephew. I hope you stay for a few days before we get around to sending you home. If you feel restless, there is a small garden behind the house to amuse yourself in, and there are books to read."

On the next day, he went behind the house where a small plot had been given over to a garden carpeted with fine grass. The walks were strewn with poplar catkins. Flowers and trees surrounded three rows of thatched huts. Threading his way among the flowers, he heard a tittering coming from the top of a tree. Looking up, he saw Yingning above him. The scholar's coming had sent her into gales of laughter that threatened to tumble her from the tree.

"Don't act like that: you're going to fall," said the scholar. As she climbed down the girl kept laughing, unable to contain herself. When she almost reached the ground she lost her grip and fell, whereupon she finally stopped laughing. Helping her, the scholar gave her wrist a slight pinch. Her laugh started up again. She leaned against the tree for a long time, unable to walk, before it stopped. The scholar gave her laughter time to die down, then pulled the flowers from his sleeve

止。生扶之,阴捘其腕。女笑又作,倚树不能行,良久乃罢。生俟其笑歇,乃出袖中花示之。女接之曰:“枯矣。何留之?”曰:“此上元妹子所遗,故存之。”问:“存之何意?”曰:“以示相爱不忘也。自上元相遇,凝思成疾,自分化为异物;不图得见颜色,幸垂怜悯。”女曰:“此大细事。至戚何所靳惜?待郎行时,园中花,当唤老奴来,折一巨捆负送之。”生曰:“妹子痴耶?”“何便是痴?”曰:“我非爱花,爱捻花之人耳。”女曰:“葭莩之情,爱何待言。”生曰:“我所谓爱,非瓜葛之爱,乃夫妻之爱。”女曰:“有以异乎?”曰:“夜共枕席耳。”女俯思良久,曰:“我不惯与生人睡。”语未已,婢潜至,生惶恐遁去。少时, 会母所。母问:“何往?”女答

to show her.

She took them in her hand saying: "They are withered. Why do you keep them?"

"These are the ones you left behind on Lantern Festival day, so I kept them."

"What's the point in keeping them?"

"To show that my love for you is not forgotten. Since I met you on Lantern Festival day, I pined for you till I grew ill: I thought that I would surely end up a dead man. Now unexpectedly I have this chance to gaze at your beautiful face. Please take pity on me."

The girl said, "This is a mere trifle. Close relatives should never be stingy to one another. When you leave I'll tell the old servant to pick a giant bundle of flowers from the garden and send them along with you."

"Are you being silly?" asked the scholar.

"What's so silly about that?"

"I don't love the flowers; I love the one who was holding the flowers in her fingers."

Between relatives love goes without saying.

"What I mean by love is not the love between gourds on the same vine, but the love between husband and wife."

"What makes that different?"

"They share pillow and mat at night."

The girl lowered her head in thought for a long while, then said, "I'm not used to sleeping with people I don't know well." The maid stole up in the middle of the conversation, frightening the scholar away. A little later they met in the mother's room.

"Where did you go?" asked the mother. The girl replied that they had been talking together in the garden. "The meal has been ready for quite some time. What subject kept you gabbing so long?" asked the old woman.

以园中共话。媪曰:“饭熟已久,有何长言,周遮乃尔?”女曰:“大哥欲我共寝。”言未已,生大窘,急目瞪之,女微笑而止。幸媪不闻,犹絮絮究诘,生急以他词掩之。因小语责女。女曰:“适此语不应说耶?”生曰:“此背人语。”女曰:“背他人,岂得背老母。且寝处亦常事,何讳之?”生恨其痴,无术可以悟之。食方竟,家中人捉双卫来寻生。先是,母待生久不归,始疑;村中搜觅几遍,竟无踪兆。因往询吴。吴忆曩言,因教于西南山村行觅。凡历数村,始至于此。生出门,适相值,便入告媪,且请偕女同归。媪喜曰:“我有志,匪伊朝夕。但残躯不能远涉;得甥携妹子去,识认阿姨,大好!”呼婴宁。宁笑至。媪曰:“有何喜,笑辄不辍?若不笑,当为全人。”因怒之以目,乃

"Cousin wants to sleep with me," said the girl. She would have kept talking, but the mortified scholar gave her an anxious look. She smiled and stopped. Luckily the old woman was still prattling along with her longwinded question and did not hear what the girl said. The scholar covered up by speaking of something else. In a low voice he reproved the girl.

"Shouldn't I have what I did just now?" she asked.

"That should only be talked about behind people's backs."

"I might hide things from other people, but I would never do anything behind my mother's back? Besides, sleeping is an everyday matter: why treat it like a taboo?" Irritated as he was with her simple-mindedness, he had no way to make her grasp his meaning.

Some days earlier, the scholar's mother had grown worried when he failed to return after a long wait. She serched nearly everywhere in the village without finding a sign of him, so she went to ask Wu. Recalling what he had said in the past, Wu told her to look for him in a mountain village to the southwest. The servant had passed through several villages before reaching this one.

When the scholar finished his meal he went to the gate, and there he met the servant from home, leading a pair of donkeys in search of him. He returned to tell the old woman and ask if he could take the girl back with him.

The old woman replied happily: "That has been my intention for a long time. But my weak old bones cannot venture far. It's wonderful, nephew, that we have you to take her back and let her get to know her aunt." She called for Yingning, who came laughing. "What makes you so happy that you can't stop laughing?" asked the old woman. "You would be perfect if you didn't laugh." Anger showed in her eyes. "Your cousin wants to take you with him. Go ahead and pack." Then, after she had served food and wine to the servant, she saw the girl out the gate, saying: "Your aunt's family has ample landholdings and can sup-

曰:“大哥欲同汝去,可便装束。”又饷家人酒食,始送之出曰:“姨家田产丰裕,能养冗人。到彼且勿归,小学诗礼,亦好事翁姑。即烦阿姨,为汝择一良匹。”二人遂发。至山坳,回顾,犹依稀见媪倚门北望也。抵家,母睹姝丽,惊问为谁。生以姨女对。母曰:“前吴郎与儿言者,诈也。我未有姊,何以得甥?”问女,女曰:“我非母出。父为秦氏,没时,儿在褓中,不能记忆。”母曰:“我一姊适秦氏,良确;然殂谢已久,那得复存?”因审诘面庞、志赘,一一符合。又疑曰:“是矣。然亡已多年,何得复存?”疑虑间,吴生至,女避入室。吴询得故,惘然久之。忽曰:“此女名婴宁耶?”生然之。吴亟称怪事。问所自知,吴曰:“秦家姑去世后,姑丈鳏居,祟于狐,病瘠死,狐生女

port extra people. Once you're there you don't have to come back. Learn something of poetry and rites, so you'll be able to serve your in-laws well. Trouble your aunt to choose a good mate for you."

The two of them set out. They went down into a glen, from which, looking back, they could make out the shape of the old woman leaning against the gate and looking northward. When they reached home his mother, surprised at the sight of the beautiful young woman, asked who she might be. The scholar answered that this was her niece.

The mother said, "What Master Wu told you before was false. I don't have a sister: how can I have a niece?"

When questioned, the girl replied, "I am not my mother's child by birth. My father's family name was Qin, and he died when I was still in swaddling clothes. I don't remember him."

The mother said, "True, my older sister did marry a Qin, but she passed away long ago. How could she be alive now?" She questioned the girl closely about her mother's facial features and the location of warts and moles. Everything the girl said tallied perfectly. But the mother was still suspicious: "That may well be, but she's been dead for many years. How could she be alive now?"

Scholar Wu came, at which the girl retreated to her room. When he learned her story, he seemed lost in thought for quite some time. Suddenly he asked, "Is the girl's name Yingning?" The scholar nodded. Wu declared that this was indeed a strange matter.

When asked how he knew, Wu said, "After my aunt who married into the Qin family died, uncle remained single. He was beset by a werefox until he wasted away and died. The spirit gave birth to a daughter named Yingning. Everyone in my family used to see her lying in a crib in her baby clothes. The werefox kept coming after uncle died. Then we procured a Heavenly Preceptor charm, which we pasted to the wall, and the werefox spirit fled with the girl. Could this be

名婴宁，绷卧床上，家人皆见之。姑丈殁，狐犹时来；后求天师符黏壁间，狐遂携女去。将勿此耶？”彼此疑参。但闻室中吃吃皆婴宁笑声。母曰：“此女亦太憨生。”吴请面之。母入室，女犹浓笑不顾。母促令出，始极力忍笑，又面壁移时，方出。才一展拜，翻然遽入，放声大笑。满室妇女，为之粲然。吴请往觇其异，就便执柯。寻至村所，庐舍全无，山花零落而已。吴忆姑葬处，仿佛不远；然坟垅湮没，莫可辨识，诧叹而返。母疑其为鬼。入告吴言，女略无骇意；又吊其无家，亦殊无悲意，孜孜憨笑而已。众莫之测。母令与少女同寝止。昧爽即来省问，操女红精巧绝伦。但善笑，禁之亦不可止；然笑处嫣然，狂而不损其

her?" The three discussed each of their suspicions. All this time the snorting sounds of Yingning's laughter could be heard from the inner room.

"That girl is just too mindless," said the mother. Wu asked to see her. The mother went into the inner room, but the girl was laughing so hard she paid no attention. When the mother prevailed on her to go out, she finally did her best to stifle her chuckles by turning her face to the wall for some time before making an appearance. No sooner had she made gestures of greeting than she turned right back into the inner rooms and loosed a loud peal of laughter, much to the amusement of all the women in the room.

Wu offered to go to her village to look into the mystery and, while he was at it, to act as go-between. He found the spot where the village had been, but not a building was there, only a scattering of mountain flowers. Wu remembered that his aunt's burial spot was somewhere nearby, but the grave was overgrown beyond recognition. With a sigh of bewilderment, he headed back.

Thereafter, Wang's mother suspected the girl was a ghost. When she went in to relay the news that Wu had brought, the girl did not betray the slightest astonishment. The mother consoled her for having no family, but she, without showing a sign of grief, only persisted in laughing giddily. No one could fathom her.

The mother made her stay with the other young women. She always presented herself at the break of day to ask after the mother's health. She surpassed all her peers in cleverness at sewing. The only thing wrong was her predisposition to laughter, which she could not stop evenwhen forbidden. But there was a winning beauty in her laugh, an abandon that did not detract from her charm. Everyone found it delightful. The girls and young wives in the neighborhood vied in making overtures to her. The mother, in spite of her persistent fear that the girl was a ghostly being, selected an auspicious day for

媚,人皆乐之。邻女少妇,争承迎之。母择吉将为合卺,而终恐为鬼物。窃于日中窥之,形影殊无少异。至日,使华妆行新妇礼;女笑极不能俯仰,遂罢。生以其憨痴,恐漏泄房中隐事;而女殊密秘,不肯道一语。每值母忧怒,女至,一笑即解。奴婢小过,恐遭鞭楚,辄求诣母共话;罪婢投见,恒得免。而爱花成癖,物色遍戚党;窃典金钗,购佳种,数月,阶砌藩溷,无非花者。庭后有木香一架,故邻西家。女每攀登其上,摘供簪玩。母时遇见,辄诃之。女卒不改。一日,西人子见之,凝注倾倒。女不避而笑。西人子谓女意已属,心益荡。女指墙底笑而下,西人子谓示约处,大

toasting with nuptial winecups. She observed the girl stealthily when the sun was behind her, but there was nothing abnormal about the shadow cast by her body. When the day came they tried to make her perform the bridal ceremony in her wedding finery, but they had to give it up because she laughed so hard she could not go through the motions.

Thinking that she was mindless and silly, the scholar feared she would reveal private, bedroom matters, but she proved to be close-mouthed and would not say a word.

Whenever the mother was depressed or angry the girl would come and lift her spirits with a single laugh. Servants and maids who feared beatings for minor mistakes would beg her to go with them to intercede with the mistress. Guilty maids who threw themselves on her mercy were always excused. She loved flowers to the point of mania and made rounds of every relative and family friend to search for what would catch her eye. She secretly pawned her jewelry to buy fine varieties. In a few months there was not a step, path, fence or outhouse that did not have flowers growing on or around it.

At the rear of the courtyard was an arbor of banksia roses adjoining the yard of the neighbor on the west. The girl often climbed onto it and amused herself by picking flowers to fasten in her hair. The mother reprimanded her every time she found her doing this, but the girl would not give it up. One day the son of the neighbor was staring fixedly at her, infatuated with her beauty. She laughed and made no attempt to get out of sight. The neighbor's son thought that the girl was showing an interest in him, and his heart began to churn. The girl pointed to a spot overjoyed, thinking that she was making an assignation. When dusk came he went to the place, and she was waiting. He went to her and entered her. At that moment something in her private parts pierced him like an awl: the pain of it shot through him to his heart. With a loud wail he stumbled back and fell. He peered at her

悦。及昏而往，女果在焉。就而淫之，则阴如锥刺，痛彻于心，大号而踣。细视，非女，则一枯木卧墙边，所接乃水淋窍也。邻父闻声，急奔研问，呻而不言。妻来，始以实告，爇火烛窍，见中有巨蝎，如小蟹然。翁碎木捉杀之。负子至家，半夜寻卒。邻人讼生，讦发婴宁妖异。邑宰素仰生才，稔知其笃行士，谓邻翁讼诬，将杖责之。生为乞免，遂释而出。母谓女曰："憨狂尔尔，早知过喜而伏忧也。邑令神明，幸不牵累；设鹘突官宰，必逮妇女质公堂，我儿何颜见戚里？"女正色，矢不复笑。母曰："人罔不笑，但须有时。"而女由是竟不复笑，

but saw, instead of the girl, a dead log lying beside the wall. What he had joined with was a water-moistened knothole.

Hearing the scream, the neighbor dashed to the spot and asked what had happened. His son moaned and would not answer. When the neighbor's wife came he finally told them the truth. They lit a torch and held it to the knothole: inside was a huge scorpion, the size of a small crab. The father chopped the log apart, caught the scorpion and killed it. He carried his son home, and the young man died suddenly in the middle of the night.

The neighbor brought charges against Scholar Wang and exposed Yingning as a witch. The district magistrate, having long admired the scholar's genius, knew well that he was a gentleman of irreproachable conduct. Concluding that the neighbor was making false accusations, he would have punished him with a beating had the scholar not begged to have him pardoned. The neighbor was released and driven from the courthouse.

The mother said to the girl: "As mindless and brash as you are, I knew that your silliness would cause a tragedy. Because of the magistrate's wise judgment, you were lucky enough not to be entangled. If he had been a muddle-headed official, you would surely have been arrested and interrogated in court. How could my son have faced our relatives and neighbors after that?" The girl made a sober face, promising not to laugh again.

"There is no one who doesn't laugh, but it has its proper time," said the mother.

The girl never laughed again, even when she was teased on purpose, but not even once did she make a grim face.

Then one night she cried and sniveled before the scholar. This was something strange to him.

"I did not say this earlier, when I had not been with you long, for fear you would be shaken," she sobbed. "Now I see how sincerely you

虽故逗,亦终不笑;然竟日未尝有戚容。一夕,对生零涕。异之。女哽咽曰:“曩以相从日浅,言之恐致骇怪。今日察姑及郎,皆过爱无有异心,直告或无妨乎?妾本狐产。母临去,以妾托鬼母,相依十余年,始有今日。妾又无兄弟,所恃者惟君。老母岑寂山阿,无人怜而合厝之,九泉辄为悼恨。君倘不惜烦费,使地下人消此怨恫,庶养女者不忍溺弃。”生诺之,然虑坟冢迷于荒草。女但言无虑。刻日,夫妻舆榇而往。女于荒烟错楚中,指示墓处,果得媪尸,肤革犹存,女抚哭哀痛。异归,寻秦氏墓合葬焉。是夜,生梦媪来称谢,寤而述之。女曰:“妾夜见之,嘱勿惊郎君耳。”生恨不邀留。女曰:“彼鬼也,生人多,阳气胜,何能久居?”生问小荣,曰:“是亦狐,最黠。狐

and your mother lavish affection on me. There can't be any harm in being honest, can there? I am a werefox's child. Before mother died she entrusted me to my ghost mother, who gave me a home for over ten years. That is why I am here today. What is more, I have no brothers: you are the one I rely on. My mother lies in forlorn stillness on the slope of a mountain, with no one to take pity on her and bury her in a grave beside her husband. This is the constant grief she bears there in the underwould. If you don't grudge the trouble and expense of easing the unjust suffering of the departed, then those who rear daughters will perhaps not be so hard-hearted as to drown or abandon them.

The scholar gave his consent, but worried that the burial mound might be lost under wild grasses. The girl simply told him not to worry. On the arranged day husband and wife loaded a coffin on a cart and set out. The girl pointed out the burial place among the mists of a dense thicket. There they found the old woman's body, flesh still on the bones. The girl bent over it and cried dolefully. After transporting it back, they located the Qin family graves and buried her with her husband. That night the scholar dreamed the old woman came to express thanks. Upon awakening he told the dream.

The girl said, "I saw her during the night, but she told me not to rouse you." The scholar regretted that Yingning had not invited her to stay. The girl said, "She is a ghost. There are many living people about and vital forces are overpowering here. How could she stay long?" The scholar asked about Gloria". She too is a fox, and quite a clever one," was the answer. "My werefox mother left her to watch over me. She often fed me choice morsels with her own hands, so I will always be grateful to her. When I asked about her last night, mother said she has already found her a husband."

From then on, every year when the Cold Food Festival rolled around, husband and wife never failed to vistit the Qins'grave, sweep-

母留以视妾，每摄饵相哺，故德之常不去心。昨问母，云已嫁之。”由是岁值寒食，夫妻登秦墓，拜扫无缺。女逾年，生一子。在怀抱中，不畏生人，见人辄笑，亦大有母风云。

异史氏曰：“观其孜孜憨笑，似全无心肝者；而墙下恶作剧，其黠孰甚焉。至凄恋鬼母，反笑为哭，我婴宁殆隐于笑者矣。窃闻山中有草，名‘笑矣乎’。嗅之，则笑不可止。房中植此一种，则合欢、忘忧，并无颜色矣；若解语花，正嫌其作态耳。”

ing and paying respects to the dead. When a year had passed the girl gave birth to a son. While still in his mother's arms, he was unafraid of strangers. He laughed at anyone he saw, much in the manner of his mother.

The Chronicler of the Tales comments: "Judging from her persistent mindless laughter, she seemed wholly lacking in sensibility, and what could be more deviously cunning than her wicked prank beneath the wall? But her sorrowful yearning for her ghostly mother and her switch from laughter to tears lead one to think that laughter was merely a mask for the real Yingning. I have heard of a mountain herb called Laugharia which, when smelled, makes men laugh without stopping. If some of these were planted in a room, then herbs like Forget-Your-Sorrow and Joy of Union would not make much of an impression, while the flower that understands speech" would seem to be putting on air.

聂小倩

宁采臣，浙人。性慷爽，廉隅自重。每对人言："生平无二色。"适赴金华，至北郭，解装兰若。寺中殿塔壮丽，然蓬蒿没人，似绝行踪。东西僧舍，双扉虚掩；惟南一小舍，扃键如新。又顾殿东隅，修竹拱把；阶下有巨池，野藕已花。意甚乐其幽杳。会学使按临，城舍价昂，思便留止，遂散步以待僧归。日暮，有士人来，启南扉。宁趋为礼，且告以意。士

NIE XIAOQIAN

NING Caichen, a native of Zhejiang, was bold and forthright by nature. He disciplined himself to uprightness and valued his own integrity. He often told people that there was only one woman in his life.

It happened that he went to Jinhua. Arriving at the north wall, he set down his baggage in a monastery. The shrine-hall and pagoda within were magnificent, but tangled grasses grew head high and no traces of human presence were seen. The double-leaved doors of the monks'quarters to the east and west were closed but a knocker and latch that looked new. At the eastern corner of the shrine-hall were tall bamboos one or two hands in circumference. Below the steps was a large pond blooming with wild lotuses. The hidden, faraway quality of the place pleased Ning greatly. At that time high rents were being charged for rooms in the city, because the Commissioner of Education was there to preside over examinations. These considerations made Ning decide to stay in the monastery, so he strolled about to pass the time until the monks return. At sundown a gentleman came in and opened the south door. Ning went to greet him with rapid steps and told him of his plans.

人曰:“此间无房主,仆亦侨居。能甘荒落,旦晚惠教,幸甚。”宁喜,藉藁代床,支板作几,为久客计。是夜,月明高洁,清光似水,二人促膝殿廊,各展姓字。士人自言:“燕姓,字赤霞。”宁疑为赴试诸生,而听其音声,殊不类浙。诘之,自言:“秦人。”语甚朴诚。既而相对词竭,遂拱别归寝。宁以新居,久不成寐。闻舍北喁喁,如有家口。起伏北壁石窗下,微窥之。见短墙外一小院落,有妇可四十余;又一媪衣黦绯,插蓬沓,鲐背龙钟,偶语月下。妇曰:“小倩何久不来?”媪云:“殆好至矣。”妇曰:“将无向姥姥有怨言否?”曰:“不闻,但意似蹙蹙。”妇曰:“婢子不宜好相识!”言未已,有一十七八女子来,仿佛艳绝。媪笑曰:“背

"There is no landlord here," said the gentleman. "I am a squater too. If you can put up with the desolation and be kind enough to share your knowledge when time permits, I will be fortunate." Ning was delighted. Anticipating a long stay, he bound up sheaves of straw for a mattress and long stay, he bound up sheaves of straw for a mattress and put up boards to do duty for a desk. That night the moon was high and bright, and its clear light was like water. The two men sat face to face on the shrine-hall gallery, telling each other their names and courtesy titles. The gentleman gave the family name Yan and the soubriquet Chixia. Ning thought he might be one of the scholars who had come for the examination, but he certainly did not speak with a Zhejiang accent. Ning asked him. Yan told him in a plain, forthright manner that he hailed from Shaanxi. When they had finished what they had to say to each other, each joined his hands before his chest by way of leavetaking and retired.

Ning did not fall asleep for a long time because of the unfamiliar surroundings. He heard an undertone of voices north of his quarters, as if a family lived there. He got out of bed and, crouching beneath the stone windowsill at the north wall, peeked outside. There in a small courtyard beyond a low wall he saw a woman in her forties talking in the moonlight with an old decrepit stoop-backed lady dressed in faded red silk and a large decorative comb stuck in her hair.

"What's keeping Xiaoqian?" asked the woman.

"She'll be here any minute," said the old lady.

"Don't tell me she has grumbled to you?"

"Not to my face, but she looks down in the mouth."

"We shouldn't show too much of friendship toward that little maid."

A girl of sixteen or seventeen arrived while the woman was talking. From what Ning could see she was utterly ravishing

The old lady said laughingly: "It only goes to show we shouldn't

地不言人,我两个正谈道,小妖婢悄来无迹响。幸不訾着短处。”又曰:“小娘子端好是画中人,遮莫老身是男子,也被摄魂去。”女曰:“姥姥不相誉,更阿谁道好?”妇人女子又不知何言。宁意其邻人眷口,寝不复听。又许时,始寂无声。方将睡去,觉有人至寝所。急起审顾,则北院女子也。惊问之,女笑曰:“月夜不寐,愿修燕好。”宁正容曰:“卿防物议,我畏人言;略一失足,廉耻道丧。”女云:“夜无知者。”宁又咄之。女逡巡若复有词。宁叱:“速去!不然,当呼南舍生知。”女惧,乃退。至户外复返,以黄金一铤置褥上。宁掇掷庭墀,曰:“非义之物,污吾囊橐!”女惭,出,拾金自言曰:“此汉当是铁石。”诘旦,有兰溪生携一仆来候试,寓于东厢,至夜暴亡。足心有小孔,如锥刺者,细细有血出。俱莫知故。经

speak of others behind their backs. You sneaked up on us without a sound, just when we were talking about you, little witchmaid. Fortunately, we weren't backbiting you." She went on, "Young lady, you sure do look like you're right out of a painting. If I were a man you'd even steal my soul away."

The girl said, "If Granny didn't praise me, who else would say a good word for me?"

The women and the girl went to talking about something or other. Ning lay down and stopped listening, assuming they belonged to a family in the neighborhood. After a while the voices died away. As he was about to fall asleep, he became aware that someone was in his room. He jumped up and took a close look: it was the girl from the north courtyard. Startled, he asked what brought her there.

The girl said with a laugh: "The moonlight tonight is keeping me awake: I'd like to enter into an intimate friendship."

"You should guard against scandal," said Ning, giving her a stern look. "I fear what others will say. If you take one false step, you will stray from the path of virtue and modesty."

"It is night: no one will be the wiser," said the girl.

Again Ning rebuked her. The girl shilly-shallied as if she had more to say. "Leave quickly," snapped Ning. "Or I'll shout loud enough for the scholar in the south apartment to know." At this the frightened girl withdrew. She got outside the door, but came back in and placed a gold ingot on his cover. Ning grabbed the ingot and hurled it onto the courtyard steps, saying: "This ill-gotten stuff would soil my pouch!"

The girl picked up the gold in shame and went out, saying to herself: "This man must be made of iron or stone."

In the morning a student from Lanxi came in the company of a servant and put up in the east chamber to await the examination. That night he died suddenly. Blood trickled from small punctures in the soles of his feet that seemed to have been made by an awl. Nobody

宿，仆一死，症亦如之。向晚，燕生归，宁质之，燕以为魅。宁素抗直，颇不在意。宵分，女子复至，谓宁曰："妾阅人多矣，未有刚肠如君者。君诚圣贤，妾不敢欺。小倩，姓聂氏，十八夭殂，葬寺侧，辄被妖物威胁，历役贱务；觍颜向人，实非所乐。今寺中无可杀者，恐当以夜叉来。"宁骇求计。女曰："与燕生同室可免。"问："何不惑燕王？"曰："彼奇人也，不敢近。"问："迷人若何？"曰："狎昵我者，隐以锥刺其足，彼即茫若迷，因摄血以供妖饮；又或以金，非金也，乃罗刹鬼骨，留之能截取人心肝：二者，凡以投时好耳。"宁感谢。问戒备之期，答以明宵。临别泣曰："妾堕玄海，求岸不得。郎君义气干云，必能拔生救苦。倘肯囊妾朽骨，归葬安宅，不啻再造。"宁毅然诺之。

knew what had happened. The next night the servant also died in a similar condition. Toward evening Scholar Yan returned. In answer to Ning's queries, he gave the opinion that it was a banshee. Ning, bold in his uprightness, did not let the matter weigh on his mind.

At nighttime the girl came again and said to him: "I've had experience with many men, but never was there anyone with your moral integrity. You are truly a saint: I dare not deceive you. My name is Xiaoqian, my family name Nie. I died prematurely at eighteen and was buried beside the monastery. Since then I have been forced by a demon to do one low-down deed after another. I have to force myself on people immodestly. I certainly did it against my will. Now there is nobody in the monastery to kill: I fear he will take the form of a *yaksa* demon and come here." In dismay, Ning begged her to recommend a course of action. The girl said, "You can escape harm if you are in the same room with Scholar Yan."

"Why haven't you tried to tempt Scholar Yan?" he asked.

"He is an extraordinary man: I dare not go near him."

"What happens to the deluded ones?" he asked.

"When someone has relations with me I catch them unawares and puncture their feet with an awl. Then they go into a delirium, and I draw their blood for the demon to drink. Or I tempt them with gold which really isn't gold-it is the demon bone of a *yaksa*. He who keeps it will have his heart and liver cut out. Of the two methods, I use whichever happens to have the greater appeal at the time."

Ning thanked her and asked when he should prepare himself She answered that tomorrow night was the time. While taking her leave she sobbed, "I have fallen into a dark sea. Though I cast about for the shore, I fail to reach it. Your sense of honor, sir, towers to the very clouds: you can surely rescue me from my misery. If you would wrap up my remains, take them back with you and give them a resting place, this would be a clemency greater than resurrection."

因问葬处,曰:“但记取白杨之上,有乌巢者是也。”言已出门,纷然而灭。明日,恐燕他出,早诣邀致。辰后具酒馔,留意察燕。既约同宿,辞以性癖耽寂。宁不听,强携卧具来。燕不得已,移榻从之。嘱曰:“仆知足下丈夫,倾风良切。要有微衷,难以遽白。幸勿翻窥箧袱,违之,两俱不利。”宁谨受教。既而各寝。燕以箱箧置窗上,就枕移时,齁如雷吼。宁不能寐。近一更许,窗外隐隐有人影。俄而近窗来窥,目光睒闪。宁惧,方欲呼燕,忽有物裂箧而出,耀若匹练,触折窗上石棂,欻然一射,即遽敛入,宛如电灭。燕觉而起,宁伪睡以觇之。燕捧箧检征,取一物,对月嗅视,白光晶莹,长可二寸,径韭叶许。已而数重包固,仍置破箧中。自语曰:“何物老魅,直尔大

Ning gave his forthright consent and asked where she was buried.

"Just remember that it is under a white poplar—the one with a birds'nest." With these words she went out the gate and vanished in a whirl. The next day, fearing that Yan would go elsewhere, Ning paid an early visit to invite him over. At midmorning he set out wine and victuals while observing Yan attentively. When he got around to inviting Yan to stay overnight, Yan declined, claiming to be eccentric and found of solitude. Ning refused to listen and insisted on bringing Yan's bedding. Yan had no choice but to follow, bearing his cot.

"I know you are an upstanding man," Yan cautioned his host. "And I have the highest admiration for you. But there is a trifling personal matter which cannot be revealed just now. Please do not open or peek into my chest and bundle. If you go against this, the consequences will be unfaorable for both of us."

Ning solemnly acquiesced to these instructions, where-upon they went to bed. Yan placed the chest above the window. Not long after laying head to pillow, he commenced snoring thunderously. Ning could not sleep.

Shortly after the first watch a dim human shape appeared outside the window. Suddenly it came close to the window and peered inside with glittering eyes. In his fright, Ning was about to call out to Yan when an object suddenly split the side of the chest and flew out, flashing like a jet of water in instantaneous arc; it broke through the stone cornice above the window, then flicked abruptly back into the chest like a vanishing bolt of lightning. Yan awoke and got out of bed as Ning watched, pretending to be asleep. Yan picked up the chest and examined it, then pulled out a gleaming crystalline object, about two inches long and hardly broader than the stalk of a scallion, which he sniffed and stared at in the moonlight. After wrapping it tightly in several layers of cloth he placed it back in the broken chest and muttered, "The nerve of that banshee! My wooden chest is ruined on account of him."

胆,致坏箧子。”遂复卧。宁大奇之,因起问之,且以所见告。燕曰:“既相知爱,何敢深隐。我,剑客也。若非石棂,妖当立毙;虽然,亦伤。”问:“所缄何物?”曰:“剑也。适嗅之,有妖气。”宁欲观之。慨出相示,荧荧然一小剑也。于是益厚重燕。明日,视窗外,有血迹。遂出寺北,见荒坟累累,果有白杨,乌巢其颠。迨营谋既就,趣装欲归。燕生设祖帐,情义殷渥。以破革囊赠宁,曰:“此剑袋也,宝藏可远魑魅。”宁欲从授其术。曰:“如君信义刚直,可以为此;然君犹富贵中人,非此道中人也。”宁乃托有妹葬此,发掘女骨,敛以衣衾,赁舟而归。宁斋临野,因营坟葬诸斋外。祭而祝曰:“怜卿孤魂,葬近蜗居,歌哭相闻,庶不见陵于雄鬼。一瓯浆水饮,殊不清旨,幸

He laid back down again. Ning was greatly amazed, so he rose and asked about it, telling Yan what he had seen.

Yan said, "Since you have shown your understanding and affection, why should I hide the fact that I am a swordsman. If it had not been for that stone cornice, the demon would have died instantly. He was wounded as it was."

"What was that you wrapped up?"

"A sword. I smelled a demon aura about it just now." Ning wanted to have a look. Yan generously showed it to him. It was a gleaming, miniature sword. Ning found himself admiring Yan all the more. The next day Ning looked outside the window and saw traces of blood. He went to the north of the monastery, where untended graves were crowded one against the other. Sure enough there was a poplar with birds nesting at its tip.

When Ning had discharged his business, he hurriedly packed his bags for the return trip. Scholar Yan gave him a send-off dinner and showered him with friendliness. He presented Ning with a torn leather pouch, saying: "The sword was kept in this bag. If you guard it like a treasure, it will keep banshees and goblins away."

Ning wished to learn swordsmanship from him, but Yan demurred: "A person of your firm integrity would be capable of it, but you are ultimately a man of worldly prospects, not a man of the Way."

On the pretext that this was his sister's burial place, Ning dug up the girl's remains, laid them out in new burial gown and shroud, and then rented a boat for the trip home. Ning's studio looked out over the wilds, so he had a grave dug and buried her outside his studio. He made a burial offering and said an invocation: "Out of pity for your solitary soul I have buried you near my humble dwelling, within hearing of your songs and wails, in hopes that you will not be tortured by vicious demons I offer you a jarful of wine to drink. The flavor is certainly not pure and sweet: I hope you will not frown on it." The invoca-tion

不为嫌。"祝毕而返。后有人呼曰:"缓待同行!"回顾,则小倩也。欢喜谢曰:"君信义,十死不足以报。请从归,拜识姑嫜,媵御无悔。"审谛之,肌映流霞,足翘细笋,白昼端相,娇艳尤绝。遂与俱至斋中,嘱坐少待,先入白母。母愕然。时宁妻久病,母戒勿言,恐所骇惊。言次,女已翩然入,拜伏地下。宁曰:"此小倩也。"母惊顾不遑。女谓母曰:"儿飘然一身,远父母兄弟。蒙公子露覆,泽被发肤,愿执箕帚,以报高义。"母见其绰约可爱,始敢与言,曰:"小娘子惠顾吾儿,老身喜不可已。但生平止此儿,用承祧绪,不敢令有鬼偶。"女曰:"儿实无二心。泉下人,既不见信于老母,请

over, he was heading homeward when someone called him from behind: "Slow down and wait for me to walk along?" He turned to look: it was Xiaoqian.

She thanked him joyfully: "Ten deaths would not be enough to repay your integrity. I wish to go back with you and make the acquaintance of my in-laws. I will have no regrets, even if I am treated like a concubine or dowry maid." Ning scrutinized her carefully. Her face shone as with the hues of a dawn sky; her feet in their upturned slippers were like tapering shoots of bamboo. Now that he could look at her closely in the daylight, she was even more matchless in grace and allure. So they went together into his studio, where he had her sit and wait while he went in to let his mother know. His mother was dumbfounded. She warned him not to say anything to his wife, who had long been sick, for fear of giving her a fright. As they were talking, the girl whisked in and prostrated herself on the floor. Ning said, "This is Xiaoqian." The mother was too surprised to do anything but stare.

The girl said to the mother: "I was adrift all alone, far from my parents and brothers, but now that I have bathed in the dew of this young man's kindness, I am willing to serve him as a slave to repay his chivalry."

Seeing how etherial and lovely she was, the mother found the courage to speak to her: "I am delighted by the gracious favor you have shown my son, young lady, but I have only this one son to carry on the offering of ancestral sacrifices, and I dare not let him have a ghost mate."

"Rest assured there is no other aim in my heart. Since you, venerable mother, cannot give your trust to a person from the nether world, I beg leave to treat him as an elder brother. I will place myself in your hands and serve you day and night. May I?"

The mother, moved to pity by her earnestness, gave approval.

以兄事,依高堂,奉晨昏,如何?”母怜其诚,允之。即欲拜嫂。母辞以疾,乃止。女即入厨下,代母尸饔,入房穿榻,似熟居者。日暮,母畏惧之,辞使归寝,不为设床褥。女窥知母意,即竟去。过斋欲入,却退,徘徊户外,似有所惧。生呼之。女曰:“室有剑气畏人。向道途之不奉见者,良以此故。”宁悟为革囊,取悬他室。女乃入,就烛下坐。移时,殊不一语。久之,问:“夜读否?妾少诵楞严经,今强半遗忘。浼求一卷,夜暇,就兄正之。”宁诺。又坐,默然,二更向尽,不言去。宁促之。愀然曰:“异域孤魂,殊怯荒墓。”宁曰:“斋中别无床寝,且兄妹亦宜远嫌。”女起,容颦蹙而欲啼,足劻儴而懒步,从容出门,涉阶而没。宁窃怜之。欲留宿别榻,又惧母嗔。女朝旦朝母,捧匜沃盥。下堂操作,无不曲承母志。黄

The girl wished to make a call on her sister-in-law, Ning's wife, but when the mother declined by reason of the woman's illness, she gave up the idea. Then the girl entered the kitchen and presided over preparation of meals in the mother's stead. She threaded her way in and out of rooms and around the furniture like a longtime resident. At sundown the mother, frightened by her presence, bid her goodnight without setting out a bed and covers. Seeing what the mother had in mind, the girl finally left the house. When she passed the studio, she was about to enter but backed away. She walked back and forth before the door, as if something were frightening her.

The scholar called to her. She said, "There is a fearsome sword-aura in this room: that is why I did not come to see you on the way home." Ning realized she was speaking of the leather pouch, so he got it down and hung it up in another room. At this the girl entered and sat down by the candle. For a while she did not utter a word. At last she asked, "Do you read at night? In my childhood I could recite the Sūrangama Sūtras. I've forgotten most of it now. If you could get hold of a copy, I could have you are free at night." Ning said he would. Again they sat in silence, until the second watch was almost at an end, and still she said nothing of leaving. Ning urged her to go.

"A barren grave in a strange place is mighty frightening to a solitary soul," she said glumly.

"I have no other bed in my studio," said Ning. "And even brother and sister should keep themselves above suspicion." The girl rose, knitting her brows as if she were on the verge of weeping. Her feet shuffled lingeringly, carrying her slowly through the gate. She walked onto the steps and descended out of sight. Deep in his heart Ning pitied her. He wanted to let her stay the night on another bed, but he feared his mother's anger. The girl went to serve the mother every morning, bringing a basin and helping her wash. When she left the main hall to do chores, she always accommodated herself to the

昏告退,辄过斋头,就烛诵经。觉宁将寝,始惨然去。先是,宁妻病废,母劬不可堪;自得女,逸甚。心德之。日渐稔,亲爱如己出,竟忘其为鬼;不忍晚令去,留与同卧起。女初来未尝食饮,半年渐啜稀饱。母子皆溺爱之,讳言其鬼,人亦不之辨也。无何,宁妻亡。母阴有纳女意,然恐于子不利。女微窥之,乘间告母曰:"居年余,当知儿肝鬲。为不欲祸行人,故从郎君来。区区无他意,止以公子光明磊落,为天人所钦瞩,实欲依赞三数年,借博封诰,以光泉壤。"母亦知无恶,但惧不能延宗嗣。女曰:"子女惟天所授。郎君注福籍,有亢宗子三,不以鬼妻而遂夺也。"母信之,与子议。宁喜,因列筵告戚党。或请觌新妇,女慨

mother's wishes. At dusk she would leave off her work, pass by the studio and read aloud from sutras by candlelight. Only when she noticed that Ning was ready for bed did she go out dejectedly.

Prior to this, when Ning's wife had fallen ill, the mother had been unbearably overworked. Since the girl's coming she had been quite at ease. In her heart she appreciated the girl and, as she came to know her better every day, loved her like a daughter and even forgot she was a ghost. She could not bear to send the girl out late at night, so she let her stay and sleep in her room. The girl never ate or drank when she first came, but after half a year she began to sip thin rice gruel. Mother and son showered her with affection. They avoided mentioning that she was a ghost, nor could other people tell by looking at her. Before long Ning's wife died. His mother was secretly inclined to bring the girl into the family, but she feared harm would come to her son. The girl, divining this, took advantage of an available moment to tell her: "After living with me for a year, you should know my innermost feelings. I did not wish to keep harming travellers and that's why I followed your son here. The young master is a man of shining openheartedness. He looked on admiringly both in Heaven and among men. And so I have no other intention but to stay close to him and do my part for a few years; this way I can gain a title of nobility that will bring glory on me in the nether world."

The mother knew she harbored no evil intent. Nev-ertheless, she feared that the girl would be unable to continue the clan's line of descent. The girl said, "Children are given according to the will of heaven. The entry under your son's name in the *Register of Fated Blessings* lists three sons who will be a credit to their clan. This cannot be taken from him on account of a ghost wife." Believing what she said, the mother discussed it with her son. Delighted, Ning laid out a banquet and broke the news to his relatives. Someone asked to have a look at the bride. The girl agreed cheerfully and came out in formal dress.

然华妆出，一堂尽眙，反不疑其鬼，疑为仙。由是五党诸内眷，咸执贽以贺，争拜识之。女善画兰梅，辄以尺幅酬答，得者藏什袭以为荣。一日，俯颈窗前，怊怅若失。忽问："革囊何在？"曰："以卿畏之，故缄置他所。"曰："妾受生气已久，当不复畏，宜取挂床头。"宁诘其意，曰："三日来，心怔忡无停息，意金华妖物，恨妾远遁，恐旦晚寻及也。"宁果携革囊来。女反复审视，曰："此剑仙将盛人头者也。敝败至此，不知杀人几何许！妾今日视之，肌犹粟慄。"乃悬之。次日，又命移悬户上。夜对烛坐，约宁勿寝。欻有一物，如飞鸟堕。女惊匿夹幙间。宁视之，物如夜叉状，电目血舌，睒闪攫拿而前。至门却步；逡巡久之，渐近革囊，以爪摘取，似将抓裂。囊忽格然一响，大

The whole hall stared in amazement, not because they suspected she was a ghost, but because they thought she was a fairy. After this, all the female relatives came with get-acquainted gifts to congratulate her, vying with one another to become her friend. The girl painted excellent orchids and plum blossoms, so she repaid them with picture scrolls. Those who got them treasured them proudly.

One day Ning found her before the window, hanging her head and lost in moody thought. Suddenly she asked: "Where is the leather pouch?"

"I wrapped it up and put it somewhere else, because you're afraid of it," said Ning.

"I've been sbsorbing the breath of life for some time now, so I shouldn't be afraid any more. You had better bring it and hang it above the bed." Ning asked what she had in mind. "For three days my heart has not stopped fluttering," she said. "I think the demon from Jinhua hates me for escaping. I fear he'll find this place any time now." Ning brought the leather pouch. The girl turned it over in her hands as she examined it and said, "This is what the sword-immortal put men's heads in. See how worn it is. Who knows the number of men he has killed! Even now when I look at it my flesh crawls." At this they hung it over the bed. The next day she told him to hang it above the door instead. That night they sat beside the lamp, the girl having arranged with Ning not to sleep. In an instant something swooped out of the sky like a bird. The startled girl having arranged with Ning not to sleep. In an instant something swooped out of the sky like a bird. The startled girl hid among the curtains. Ning watched as a *yaksa*-like figure with sparking eyes and blood-red tongue came toward him, its arms flailing out and its eyes glittering. At the gate it stepped back, hesitated for a time, then sidled up to the leather pouch. It snatched at the pouch went "pfft" and grew to the size of a hod basket. In a barely visible flash, a creature stuck its body halfway out and pulled

可合箦;恍惚有鬼物,突出半身,揪夜叉人,声遂寂然,囊亦顿缩如故。宁骇诧。女亦出,大喜曰:“无恙矣!”共视囊中,清水数斗而已。后数年,宁果登进士。女举一男。纳妾后,又各生一男,皆仕进有声。

the *Yaksa* inside. Then there was silence, and the pouch shrank back to its original size. Ning was stunned. The girl came out from her hiding place and joyfully exclaimed, "No need to worry any more!" Together they looked into the pouch, which contained nothing but a few dipperfuls of clear water.

Several years later Ning did indeed receive a Doctorate of Letters. The girl gave birth to a son. A concubine was brought into the family, and she and the girl each bore a son. All three became well-known in their official careers.

地震

康熙七年六月十七日戌刻，地大震。余适客稷下，方与表兄李笃之对烛饮。忽闻有声如雷，自东南来，向西北去。众骇异，不解其故。俄而几案摆簸，酒杯倾覆；屋梁椽柱，错折有声。相顾失色。久之，方知地震，各疾趋出。见楼阁房舍，仆而复起；墙倾屋塌之声，与儿啼女号，喧如鼎沸。人眩晕不能立，坐地上，随地转侧。河水倾泼丈余，鸡鸣犬吠

EARTHQUAKE

QN the seventeenth day of the sixth lunar month in the seventh year of the Kangxi reign period(1668)between seven and nine in the evening, there was a great earth-quake. I was staying at Jixia and drinking by candlelight with my cousin Li Duzhi, when suddenly we heard a sound like thunder coming from the southeast and going north-west. Everyone was shocked and amazed, puzzling about the sound. Soon the table started heaving and winecups fell over. The rafters, beams, and pillars of the room twisted and creaked. We looked at each other, each face turning pale. It took us awhile to realize it was an earthquake. Each of us hastened outside. Storied buildings and houses were tottering and righting themselves again. The sound of falling walls and collapsing houses, with the cries of children and the wails of women, bleaded into a seething uproar. People were too dazed and dizzy to stand, so they sat on the ground and were tossed about with the bucklings of the earth. The water in the river was flung over ten feet high in the air. The crowing of cocks and barking of dogs resounded through the streets. Something like two hours passed before the tremors quieted down slightly. We looked at the street, where unclad men and women were gathered talking frantically to one another, for-

满城中。逾一时许，始稍定。视街上，则男女裸聚，竞相告语，并忘其未衣也。后闻某处井倾仄，不可汲；某家楼台南北易向；栖霞山裂；沂水陷穴，广数亩。此真非常之奇变也。

有邑人妇，夜起溲溺，回则狼衔其子。妇急与狼争。狼一缓颊，妇夺儿出，携抱中。狼蹲不去。妇大号。邻人奔集，狼乃去。妇惊定作喜，指天画地，述狼衔儿状，己夺儿状。良久，忽悟一身未着寸缕，乃奔。此与地震时男妇两忘者，同一情状也。人之惶急无谋，一何可笑！

getting that they had not gotten dressed. Later I heard that the well at such-and-such a place had caved in and water could not be drawn; the north end of a certain family's pavilion was now pointing south; Qixia Mountain had split open; and the Yi river had disappeared into a crater an acre across. This was a truly incredible anomaly in the order of nature.

The wife of a man in my district arose one night to urinate. She returned to the house: there was a wolf holding her son in its jaws. The woman immediately fought with the wolf for the child. When the wolf relaxed its jaws for an instant, the woman pulled the child away and held it in her arms. The wolf squatted down and would not leave. The woman let out a great screech, which brought the neighbors running, whereupon the wolf went away. The woman was happy when she got over the shock. She pointed and gesticulated as she described how the wolf had held her child in its jaws and how she pulled it away. This continued for quite a while before she suddenly realized she was not wearing a thread on her body. Off she ran. This situation was the same as after the earthquake, when men and women forgot themselves. How laughable is the heedlessness of panic-stricken people.

侠女

顾生，金陵人。博于材艺，而家綦贫。又以母老，不忍离膝下，惟日为人书画，受贽以自给。行年二十有五，伉俪犹虚。对户旧有空第，一老妪及少女，税居其中。以其家无男子，故未问其谁何。一日，偶自外入，见女郎自母房中出，年约十八九，秀曼都雅，世罕其匹，见生不甚避，而意凛如也。生入问母。母曰："是对户女郎，就吾乞刀尺。适言其家亦止一母。此女不似贫家产。问其何为不字，则以母老为辞。明日当往拜其母，便风以意；倘所望不奢，儿可代养其母。"明日造其室，其

A CHIVALROUS WOMAN

SCHOLAR Gu of Jinling was a man of diverse accom-plishments. His mother's age, combined with their straitened circumstances, made him reluctant to leave her side. Instead he spent his days painting and doing calligraphy on request, supporting the family with the gifts he received. In his twenty-fifth year, his marital plans were still undecided. Then the vacant house across the lane was rented by an old lady and a young woman. Since there were no men in the house, he did not ask who they were. One day he happened to be returning home when he saw the young woman come out of his mother's room. She was eighteen or nineteen years of age, with graceful charm and elegance that are seldom rivalled in this world. Seeing the scholar, she made no move to turn away, but there was an icy aloofness about her.

The scholar went in to ask his mother, who said, "That was the young woman from across the lane. She was here to borrow scissors and a ruler from me. Just now she said that she has only a mother in her family too. She doesn't strike me as the product of a poor family. When I asked why she isn't engaged, she gave her mother's age as the reason. I will go visit her mother tomorrow and drop a hint about what I'm thinking. If her sights aren't set too high, you can support her

母一聋媪耳。视其室,并无隔宿粮。问所业,则仰女十指。徐以同食之谋试之,媪意似纳,而转商其女;女默然,意殊不乐。母乃归。详其状而疑之曰:"女子得非嫌吾贫乎?为人不言亦不笑,艳如桃李,而冷如霜雪,奇人也!"母子猜叹而罢。一日,生坐斋头,有少年来求画。姿容甚美,意颇儇佻。诘所自,以"邻村"对。嗣后三两日辄一至。稍稍稔熟,渐以嘲谑;生狎抱之,亦不甚拒,遂私焉。由此往来昵甚。会女郎过,少年目送之,问为谁。对以"邻女"。少年曰:"艳丽如此,神情一何可畏!"少间,生入内。母曰:"适女子来乞米,云不举火者经日矣。此女至孝,贫极可悯,宜少

mother for her."

In the morning she paid a call at their house. The mother turned out to be hard of hearing. A look around the house showed that there were no provisions for the next day. Asked how they made a living, the old woman replied that they relied on her daughter's skilled fingers. Gu's mother gradually sounded out her feelings toward a joint dining arrangement. The old woman seemed willing, but when she turned to discuss it with her daughter, the girl kept silent and looked displeased. At this Gu's mother went home.

Gu asked his mother for all the details, then said in bewilderment: "Don't tell me she objects to my poverty. She is quiet and never laughs, as beautiful as peaches and plums but cold as frost and snow. What a strange person!" Mother and son sighed as they tried to figure her out, then let the matter drop.

One day as the scholar sat in his studio a young man came and asked for a painting. He had striking good looks and gave the impression of being rather frivolous. Asked where he was from, he replied "a neighboring village." Afterwards he came once every two or three days. As they got to know each other a bit, they began to banter back and froth. When the scholar embraced him familiarly, he did little to resist, and the two of them became intimate. From then on their relationship was quite close. Once the young woman walked past them. The young man followed her with his eyes and asked who she was. Gu replied that she was a "neighbor girl."

The young man said, "Such a stunning girl, but how forbidding her manner is!"

In a litter while the scholar went inside. His mother said, "Just now the girl came to borrow rice. She said they haven't lit a fire for days. She treats her mother remarkably well. It's pity they are in such desperate straits. We should give them a little relief." In accordance with his mother's words, the scholar carried a peck of rice to

周恤之。”生从母言，负斗米款门达母意。女受之，亦不申谢。日尝至生家，见母作衣履，便代缝纫；出入堂中，操作如妇。生益德之。每获馈饵，必分给其母，女亦略不置齿颊。母适疽生隐处，宵旦号咷。女时就榻省视，为之洗创敷药，日三四作。母意甚不自安，而女不厌其秽。母曰：“唉！安得新妇如儿，而奉老身以死也！”言讫悲哽。女慰之曰：“郎子大孝，胜我寡母孤女什百矣。”母曰：“床头蹀躞之役，岂孝子所能为者？且身已向暮，旦夕犯雾露，深以祧续为忧耳。”言间，生入。母泣曰：“亏娘子良多！汝无忘报德。”生伏拜之。女曰：“君敬我母，我勿谢也；君何谢焉？”于是益敬爱之。然其举止生硬，毫不可干。一日，女出门，生目注之。女忽回首，嫣然而笑。生

their door and communicated her feelings. The girl took the rice without giving thanks. Every day thereafter she went to the scholar's house, and when she saw his mother making clothes or shoes, she did the sewing for her. She bustled in and out of the hall, doing housework like a wife. The scholar appreciated her even more. Whenever he was given a gift of choice food, he would share it with her mother, but she never bothered to say a word of acknowledgement for this either.

Then the scholar's mother developed boils on her private parts, which had her sobbing and wailing night and day. The girl frequently went to her bed to look after her by washing the affected place and applying salve three or four times a day. This made the mother quite ill at ease, but the girl was not revolted by her foulness.

"Ai!" sighed the mother. "Where can I find a daughter-in-law like you to care for my old body until the end!" This was said with such sorrow that the last words stuck in her throat.

The girl comforted her: "You have a highly filial son. That is a hundred times better than being a widowed mother with an orphan."

"A filial son could not have nursed me as tirelessly as you have," said the mother. "Anyway, I am in the sunset of my life: any time now my body will be left out in the mist and dew. I am deeply worried that there will be no one to continue to making offerings to our family's ancestors." The scholar came in as she was talking.

"You owe the little Miss an awful lot," sobbed his mother. "Don't you forget to repay for kindness!" The scholar went down on his knees before the girl.

"You showed respect for my mother, but I would not thank you," she protested. "Why should you be grateful to me?" The scholar revered and loved her all the more for this, but her bearing was hard and distant. She was completely unapproachable.

One day the scholar was gazing at the girl as she went out the

喜出意外，趋而从诸其家。挑之，亦不拒，欣然交欢。已，戒生曰："事可一而不可再！"生不应而归。明日，又约之。女厉色不顾而去。日频来，时相遇，并不假以词色。少游戏之，则冷语冰人。忽于空处问生："日来少年谁也？"生告之。女曰："彼举止态状，无礼于妾频矣。以君之狎昵，故置之。请更寄语：再复尔，是不欲生也已！"生至夕，以告少年，且曰："子必慎之，是不可犯！"少年曰："既不可犯，君何犯之？"生白其无。曰："如其无，则猥亵之语，何以达君听哉？"生不能答。少年曰："亦烦寄告：假惺惺勿作态；不然，我将遍播扬。"生甚怒之，情见于色，少年乃去。一夕方独坐，女忽至，笑曰："我与君情缘未断，宁非天数！"生狂喜而抱于怀。欻闻履声籍籍，两

door, when suddenly she turned her head and smiled alluringly. The scholar had never thought such happiness would be his. He hurried after her to her house. He made advances and she put up no resistance. They merged joyfully.

When it was over she warned him: "It happened once, but it won't happen again."

The scholar went home without answering. The next day he tried to set up a rendezvous. A furious look came over her face, and she walked away without looking back. They encountered each other frequently during her daily visits, but she would not spare him a word or a warm look. When he tried a little good-humored teasing, she froze him with icy replies.

Once in an unoccupied moment she suddenly asked him: "who is the young man who comes every day?" The scholar told her.

"He has affronted me many times, both in behavior and attitude. I have let it pass because of your intimacy with him. But tell him for me that if he behaves that way again, he will not live long."

That night the scholar gave the message to the young man and said, "You'd better watch out. She is not to be toyed with!"

The young man said, "If she is not to be toyed with, why did you toy with her?" The scholar protested that he had not.

"If you haven't, then how did you hear those malicious remarks about me?" The scholar was unable to answer.

"Well, let me trouble you to give her this message," said the young man. "Don't give yourself aris, or I'll let everyone know about you!" The scholar made no attempt to hide his fury, whereupon the young man left.

One night the girl came suddenly while the scholar was sitting alone and said with a laugh: "The affinity between us is not yet broken. It must be the workings of fate!" He embraced her in wild joy. Just then they heard footsteps clattering. They stood up in surprise: it

人惊起,则少年推扉入矣。生惊问:“子胡为者?”笑曰:“我来观贞洁人耳。”顾女曰:“今日不怪人耶?”女眉竖颊红,默不一语。急翻上衣,露一革囊,应手而出,则尺许晶莹匕首也。少年见之,骇而却走。追出户外,四顾渺然。女以匕首望空抛掷,戛然有声,灿若长虹;俄一物堕地作响。生急烛之,则一白狐,身首异处矣。大骇。女曰:“此君之娈童也。我固恕之,奈渠定不欲生何!”收刃入囊。生曳令入。曰:“适妖物败意,请来宵。”出门迳去。次夕,女果至,遂共绸缪。诘其术,女曰:“此非君所知。宜须慎秘,泄恐不为君福。”又订以嫁娶,曰:“枕席焉,提汲焉,非妇伊何也?业夫妇矣,何必复言嫁娶乎?”生曰:“将勿憎吾贫耶?”曰:“君固贫,妾富耶?今宵之聚,正以怜君贫耳。”临别嘱曰:“苟且之行,不可以屡。

was the young man who pushed open the door and entered.

"What are you doing here?" asked the startled scholar.

"I came to have a look at a chaste woman." laughed the young man. He looked at the girl and said, "Doesn't this make a person wonder?" The girl's brows arched and her cheeks reddened, but she was silent. She turned up her blouse with a quick movement, revealing a leather bag, and deftly drew out a long glitening dagger. At the sight of this the young man backed up in fright. They chased him out the door: he was nowhere to be seen. The girl hurled the dagger upward. It screamed through the air, tracing a brilliant arc. Suddenly an object plopped down on the ground. The scholar hurried over with a candle: it was a white fox, its head severed from its body. What a shock!

"This is your pleasure-boy," said the girl. "I did my best to forgive him, but what could I do when he insisted on parting with his life?" She put the knife back in its bag. The scholar pulled her toward the house, but she said, "That creature put me out of the mood. Could we make it tomorrow night?" She went straight out the gate.

The girl did indeed come the next night and intertwine her body with his. Afterwards he asked about her knife-craft, but she said, "That is not for you to know. It is a secret that must be carefully guarded. It would not, I fear, be in your best interests for me to divulge it." He made a proposal of marriage, to which she replied. "I've slept with you and carried water for you. If that isn't being a wife, then what is? We are already husband and wife: why must we talk of marriage?"

"Is it because you hate my lack of wealth?"

"You are poor, all right, but am I wealthy? I have joined with you tonight precisely because I was moved to pity by your poverty. Before they parted she warned him: "Indulgent acts should not be repeated. It it is necessary for me to come, I will come on my own. If it is not, trying to force it will do no good."

当来,我自来;不当来,相强无益。”后相值,每欲引与私语,女辄走避;然衣绽炊薪,悉为纪理,不啻妇也。积数月,其母死,生竭力葬之。女由是独居。生意孤寝可乱,逾垣入,隔窗频呼,迄不应。视其门,则空室扃焉。窃疑女有他约。夜复往,亦如之。遂留佩玉于窗间而去之。越日,相遇于母所。既出,而女尾其后曰:“君疑妾耶?人各有心,不可以告人。今欲使君无疑,乌得可?然一事烦急为谋。”问之,曰:“妾体孕已八月矣,恐旦晚临盆。‘妾身未分明’,能为君生之,不能为君育之。可密告母,觅乳媪,伪为讨螟蛉者,勿言妾也。”生诺,以告母。母笑曰:“异哉此女!聘之不可,而顾私于我儿。”喜从其谋以待之。又月余,女数日不至。母疑之,往探其门,萧萧闭

Later when they met he often tried to tempt her into a private conversation, but she always avoided him. Nevertheless, she was as good as a wife in the way she tended to clothes mending, cooking, and all the other household chores. After several months her mother died. The scholar buried her as well as his means permitted. From then on the girl lived alone. The scholar, thinking that it would be possible to have his way with her now that she slept alone, climbed over the wall. He called several times through the window without getting an answer. He found that the gate was bolted on an empty house. He suspected the girl of having made a rendezvous with someone else. He went again during the night and found things the same way, so he left his jade waist-pendant on the windowsill and left.

A day later he met the girl in his mother's room. When he went out the girl trailed behind and said, "Do you doubt me?" Everyone has something that can't be told to others. Now, even though I try to lay your suspicions to rest, it is no use. But there is one thing I would like you to arrange for me, quickly. He asked what it was.

"I am already eight months pregnant. I am likely to give birth any time now. Since 'my identity as wife is not clear, 'I can bear you a child but cannot raise it. Please tell your mother to find a wet nurse secretly. Make it seem that you are adopting an orphan, and don't say anything about me. The scholar consented, then told this to his mother.

"What a strange girl!" said his mother with a laugh. "She refuses an offer of marriage, and yet goes ahead and has relations with my son." She was glad to prepare for the event in accordance with the girl's plan.

Over a month went by. When the girl did not show up for several days the mother, thinking that something was amiss, went to her house to check. She found the closed-up house deserted and still. She knocked for quite some time before the girl came out, her hair hanging

寂。叩良久，女始蓬头垢面自内出。启而入之，则复阖之。入其室，则呱呱者在床上矣。母惊问："诞儿时矣？"答云："三日。"捉绷席而视之，则男也，且丰颐而广额。喜曰："儿已为老身育孙子，伶仃一身，将焉所托？"女曰："区区隐衷，不敢掬示老母。俟夜无人，可即抱儿去。"母归与子言，窃共异之。夜往抱子归。更数夕，夜将半，女忽款门入，手提革囊，笑曰："我大事已了，请从此别。"急询其故，曰："养母之德，刻刻不去诸怀。向云'可一而不可再'者，以相报不在床笫也。为君贫不能婚，将为君延一线之续。本期一索而得，不意信水复来，遂至破戒而再。今君德既酬，妾志亦遂，无憾矣。"问："囊中何物？"曰："仇人头耳。"检而窥之，须发交而血模糊。骇绝，复致

untidily and her face smudged. The girl opened the door to admit her, then closed it again. They went to her bedroom, where a bawling infant was lying on the bed.

"When was it born?" asked the surprised mother.

"Three days ago," was the reply.

Gu's mother lifted the wrapping-cloth for a look: it was a boy with full cheeks and broad forehead. She exclaimed happily: "Now you have given me a grandson. You are unattached and alone: who will you look to for support?"

The girl said, "I dare not expose my paltry inner motive to you, mother. Wait till night when no one is around; then you can carry the child away."

The mother returned and told this to her son, and neither of them knew what to make of it. That night they went and carried the child home.

Several evenings later the girl rapped on the door in the middle of the night and entered, carrying a leather bag in her hand. "I have accomplished an enormous task. Now I beg leave to part forever." He immediately asked the reason.

"Your kindness to my mother has never been out of my mind for a moment. Earlier I told you that it could happen once, but it would not happen again, because going to bed together was not my way of repaying you. Since you are poor and unable to marry, I thought to give you a thread to carry on your family line. At first I planned to get it at one attempt, but my period came again, which is why I broke my vow and let it happen a second time. Now your kindness has been repaid and my goal has been realized: I have no more regrets."

"What is that in the bag?" he asked.

"Only the head of my mortal enemy."

He hefted the bag and peeked inside: the head's hair and beard were matted and the face was smeared with blood. Thoroughly

研诘。曰:“向不与君言者,以机事不密,惧有宣泄。今事已成,不妨相告:妾浙人。父官司马,陷于仇,彼籍吾家。妾负老母出,隐姓名,埋头项,已三年矣。所以不即报者,徒以有母在;母去,又一块肉累腹中:因而迟之又久。曩夜出非他,道路门户未稔,恐有讹误耳。”言已,出门。又嘱曰:“所生儿,善视之。君福薄无寿,此儿可光门闾。夜深不得惊老母,我去矣!”方凄然欲询所之,女一闪如电,瞥尔间遂不复见。生叹惋木立,若丧魂魄。明以告母,相为叹异而已。后三年,生果卒。子十八举进士,犹奉祖母以终老云。

异史氏曰:“人必室有侠女,而后可以畜娈童也。不然,尔爱其艾豭,彼爱尔娄猪矣!”

shocked, he questioned her further.

"I did not tell you before for fear that you would fail to preserve secrecy, and word of my undertaking would get out. Now the task is accomplished, so it will not hurt to tell you. I am from Zhejiang. My father held the position of Department Magistrate, but he was implicated in crimes by an enemy, who confiscated our family property. I carried my old mother away. I have been laying low and living under an assumed name for three years. First I did not take immediate revenge because my mother was alive. My mother left this world, but then I still had an encumberence of flesh in my belly, so again there was a long delay. I used to leave home at night, not for any other reason, but because I was not yet sure of the roads and the appearance of his house. I might have made a dreadful mistake." With that she went through the gate, then stopped to give him parting instructions: "Take good care of the son I bore. Your blessings are scanty and your lifewill not be long, but the child will win glory for your family. We must not rouse mother at this late hour. I'm off!"

Before the sorrowful scholar could ask where to, the girl was off in a lightning-like flas. In the space of a glance she was gone. The scholar sighed at his loss and stood woodenly, like one bereft of spirit. In the morning he told his mother. They sighed and marveled without end. After three years the scholar died, just as expected. At eighteen his son attained the Doctorate of Letters, and he continued to care for his grandmother to the end of her years, or so the story goes.

The Chronicler of the Tales comments: "In order to keep a pleasure-boy, it is necessary that one's wife be a chivalrous woman. Otherwise, while you are loving your fine young boar, he will be loving your brood-sow!"

阿　宝

粤西孙子楚，名士也。生有枝指。性迂讷，人诳之，辄信为真。或值座有歌妓，则必遥望却走。或知其然，诱之来，使妓狎逼之，则赪颜彻颈，汗珠珠下滴。因共为笑。遂貌其呆状，相邮传作丑语，而名之“孙痴”。邑大贾某翁，与王侯埒富。姻戚皆贵胄。有女阿宝；绝色也。日择良匹，大家儿争委禽妆，皆不当翁意。生时失俪，有戏之者，劝其通媒。生殊不自揣，果从其教。翁素耳其名，而贫

PRECIOUS

SUN Zichu, a celebrated man of letters of Guangxi, had a sixth finger growing on one of his hands. He was unrealistic by nature, halting in speech and inclined to accept the deceitful words of others at face value. If singing girls or courtesans happened to be present at a gathering, he would invariably run off as soon as he caught sight of them. When those who knew of his peculiarity tricked him into coming and had prostitutes press themselves upon him, he would redden to the base of his neck, and sweat would trickle down his face. He was made the butt of everyone's laughter. People wrote descriptions of his witless antics, circulated them as items of abusive gossip and nicknamed him Sun the Fool.

Old Man Jia, a big merchant in the district, had wealth enough to rival a prince, and his relations were all of noble blood. His daughter Precious was incomparably beautiful. When the time came to choose her a suitable mate, sons of major families rushed to offer marriage presents, but none measured up to the old man's wishes. The scholar had been bereaved of his wife sometime before, and some-one tricked him into sending a go-between. The scholar, singularly unmindful of his own limitations, went ahead and followed this suggestion. The old

之。媒媪将出,适遇宝,问之,以告。女戏曰:“渠去其枝指,余当归之。”媪告生。生曰:“不难。”媒去,生以斧自断其指,大痛彻心,血益倾注,滨死。过数日,始能起,往见媒而示之。媪惊,奔告女。女亦奇之。戏请再去其痴。生闻而哗辨,自谓不痴;然无由见而自剖。转念阿宝未必美如天人,何遂高自位置如此?由是曩念顿冷。会值清明,俗于是日,妇女出游,轻薄少年,亦结队随行,恣其月旦。有同社数人,强邀生去。或嘲之曰:“莫欲一观可人否?”生亦知其戏己;然以受女揶揄故,亦思一见其人,忻然随众物色之。遥见有女子憩树下,恶少年环如墙堵。众曰:“此必阿宝也。”趋之,果宝。审谛之,娟丽无双。少顷,人益稠。女起,遽去。众情颠倒,品头题足,

man had long heard of the scholar's reputation but considered him too poor. As the go-between left the house she came upon Precious, who asked the purpose of her coming. When the go-between told her, the girl said jokingly: "If he gets rid of that extra finger, I'll be his."

The go-between reported this to the scholar, who said, "That won't be difficult." After the go-between left the scholar chopped off his finger with a hatchet. Excruciating pain pierced him to the heart, and blood spurted out till he was on the brink of death. Several days passed before he could rise from his bed. He went to see the go-between and showed her the finger. The startled woman ran to tell the girl. She too was taken aback. She jokingly required that he also get rid of his folly. When the scholar heard this he protested loudly that he was not a fool, but he had no way to see her and bare his heart to her. Then it occurred to him that Precious might not have the beauty of an angel after all. What gave her the right to rate herself so highly? His earlier ardor cooled abruptly.

Then came Tomb-Sweeping Day. According to custom this was the day when girls and women went outdoors to stroll, and frivolus young men followed after them in groups, brazenly discussing their merits. Several members of his club strongly urged the scholar to go along with them. One said mockingly: "Don't you want to have a look at your Precious?" The scholar knew they were making fun of him, but the ridicule he had suffered at the girl's hands made him want to see her in person. He gladly followed the group to get a look at her. From a distance they saw a young woman resting beneath a tree, surrounded by a wall of obnoxious young men. The members of the group exclaimed, "That must be Precious." They hurried over, and sure enough it was she. Close scrutiny proved her to be matchlessly beautiful. Soon the crowd became thicker. The girl rose and walked abruptly away. Everyone was bowled over. They set up a wild hubbub of appraisals of her face and comments on her legs. Only the scholar kept

纷纷若狂;生独默然。及众他适,回视,生犹痴立故所,呼之不应。群曳之曰:"魂随阿宝去耶?"亦不答。众以其素讷,故不为怪,或推之,或挽之,以归。至家,直上床卧,终日不起,冥如醉,唤之不醒。家人疑其失魂,招于旷野,莫能效。强拍问之,则朦胧应云:"我在阿宝家。"及细诘之,又默不语。家人惶惑莫解。初,生见女去,意不忍舍,觉身已从之行,渐傍其衿带间,人无呵者。遂从女归,坐卧依之,夜辄与狎,甚相得;然觉腹中奇馁,思欲一返家门,而迷不知路。女每梦与人交。问其名,曰:"我孙子楚也。"心异之,而不可以告人。生卧三日,气休休若将澌灭。家人大恐,托人婉告翁,欲一招魂其家。翁笑曰:"平昔不相往还,何由遗魂吾家?"家人固哀之,翁始允。巫执故服、草荐以往。女诘得其故,骇极,不听他往,直导入室,任招呼而去。巫归

silent. When the group went elsewhere, they looked back and saw the scholar, still standing numbly in the same spot. They called to him, but there was no response. They pulled at his arm, saying: "Has your soul left you to follow after Precious?" Still he did not answer. No one thought this strange, because they knew him to be slow of speech. Some pushed and some pulled until they got him back. Once home he climbed straight into bed and lay there all day without fising. He was in stupor, as if drunk, and could not be roused. His family suspected that his soul had left his body. They went to deserted fields and prayed for his soul's return without success. When they slapped him and forced him to respond to their questions, he answered indistinctly: "I am at Precious'house." They asked specificquestions, but he would say no more. His family was dismayed and baffled.

Earlier, when watching the girl walk away, the scholar could not bear to see her go, and felt his body walking behind her. He gradually moved toward her and leaned against her sash, without anyone reprimanding him. He followed her home and stayed beside her every moment. At night he made love to her, to the great delight of both. Then he felt a tremendous hollowness in his stomach. He wanted to make the trip back to his home gate, but he did not know the way. The girl herself dreamed repeatedly of copulating with a man. When she asked his name he said "I am Sun Zichu." She was unable to confide her amazement to anyone.

The scholar lay at home for three days, drawing each halting breath as if it might be his last. Deeply frightened, his family sent someone to communicate the matter to the old man in a roudabout way and ask if they could say soul-summoning prayers in his house, at which he laughed and said "Our two families have never visited back and forth: how could he have left his soul in my house?" Sun's family would not give up their pleading, so the old man finally assented. The shaman went to his house, carrying Sun's sleeping mat and a suit of

至门,生榻上已呻。既醒,女室之香奁什具,何色何名,历言不爽。女闻之,益骇,阴感其情之深。生既离床寝,坐立凝思,忽忽若忘。每伺察阿宝,希幸一再遘之。浴佛节,闻将降香水月寺,遂早旦往候道左,目眩睛劳。日涉午,女始至。自车中窥见生,以掺手搴帘,凝睇不转。生益动,尾从之。女忽命青衣来诘姓字。生殷勤自展,魂益摇。车去,始归。归复病,冥然绝食,梦中辄呼宝名。每自恨魂不复灵。家旧养一鹦鹉,忽毙,小儿持弄于床。生自念倘得身为鹦鹉,振翼可达女室。心方注想,身已翩然鹦鹉,遽飞而去,直达宝所。

his clothes. The girl was greatly shocked to learn his reason for coming. She led him straight to her chamber, not letting him go anywhere else, and instructed him to leave after summoning Sun's soul. By the time the shaman returned to the Sun family gate, the scholar was moaning on his bed. Upon waking, he unerringly named and described all the toiletries and possessions in the girl's chamber. Hearing of this, the girl was amazed and secretly moved by the depth of his affection.

Upon leaving the bed the scholar spent his waking hours absorbed in thought and lost in forgetfulness. He constantly watched for Precious, in hopes that fortune would favor him with another encounter. He learned that she would offer incense at the Moon-in-the-Water Monastery on Buddha-Bathing Festival, so he went early in the morning and stationed himself beside the road to wait. He watched the crowd until his eyes blurred and ached in their sockets. The sun had passed its zenith before the girl arrived. Glimpsing the scholar from within her carriage, she pulled aside the curtain with slender fingers and redoubled his excitement by fixing her gaze upon him. He fell in line behind her. Unexpectedly, she sent a servant to ask his name and courtesy title. He eagerly identified himself, losing what little composure he still had left. He did not return until the carriage left. At home he fell ill again. He lapsed into a fog and stopped eating. He kept calling out Precious'name in his dreams, and cursed his soul for failing to do what it could before.

A parrot which the family had kept for a long time suddenly died. As his young son sat on the bed, holding and stroking it, the scholar thought to himself that if only he were a parrot he could arrive at the girl's room with a few flaps of his wings. As his mind immersed itself in these thoughts, his body turned into a parrot with fluttering suddenness. In an instant he was off and flying straight to Precious' place.

女喜而扑之,锁其肘,饲以麻子。大呼曰:“姐姐勿锁!我孙子楚也!”女大骇,解其缚,亦不去。女祝曰:“深情已篆中心。今已人禽异类,姻好何可复圆?”鸟云:“得近芳泽,于愿已足。”他人饲之不食,女自饲之则食。女坐,则集其膝;卧,则依其床。如是三日。女甚怜之。阴使人瞷生,生则僵卧气绝,已三日,但心头未冰耳。女又祝曰:“君能复为人,当誓死相从。”鸟云:“诳我。”女乃自矢。鸟侧目若有所思。少间,女束双弯,解履床下,鹦鹉骤下,衔履飞去。女急呼之,飞已远矣。女使妪往探,则生已寤。家人见鹦鹉衔绣履来,堕地死,方共异之。生既苏,即索履。众莫知故。适妪至,入视生,问履所在。生曰:“是阿宝信誓物。借口相覆:小生不忘金诺也。”妪反命。女益奇之,故使婢泄其情于母。母审之确,乃

The delighted girl embraced the parrot, chained its leg to a perch and fed it with hempseeds. She was taken aback when it cried, "Don't chain me, sister. I am Sun Zichu!" She untied its bond, but it did not fly away. The girl offered a prayer, saying "Your deep affection is engraved upon my heart, but now we are different in kind—a human being and a bird. How can we ever join in marriage?"

"All I wish for is to be near your fragrance," said the bird. He would not eat when others fed him, but only when the girl fed him herself. When she sat he roosted on her knees; when she lay down he moved next to her bed. This went on for three days. The girl pitied him sorely and secretly sent someone to have a look at the scholar. He had lain stiff and unbreathing for three days, but the area around his heart was not yet cold. Once more the girl prayed to the parrot: "If you can turn back into a man, I vow to remain with you until death."

"You are fooling me," said the bird, but the girl swore she was not. The bird cocked its head thougtfully. Soon the girl removed the slippers from her bound feet and put them under her bed. The parrot leapt down all of a sudden, sized a shoe in its beak, and flew away. The girl anxiously called after it, but it had already flown far. An old servant-woman she sent to probe for news of the scholar found on her arrival that he had already awakened.

Moments before, his family had been thrown into consternation by a parrot which had flown in holding an embroidered shoe in its beak and dropped dead on the floor. Immediately afterwards the scholar awoke and im-mediately asked for the shoe. No one knew what lay behind his strange request. The servant-woman who had just arrived went in to see the scholar, and asked where the shoe was.

"I am keeping it as a token of Precious promise," said the scholar. "Give her this reply: 'I will not forget your golden vow.'"

When the servant woman reported back, the girl was doubly impressed and so had a maid reveal these events to her mother. After

曰:“此子才名亦不恶,但有相如之贫。择数年得婿若此,恐将为显者笑。”女以履故,矢不他。翁媪从之。驰报生。生喜,疾顿瘳。翁议赘诸家。女曰:“婿不可久处岳家;况郎又贫,久益为人贱。儿既诺之,处蓬茆而甘藜藿,不怨也。”生乃亲迎成礼,相逢如隔世欢。自是家得奁妆,小阜,颇增物产。而生痴于书,不知理家人生业,女善居积,亦不以他事累生。居三年,家益富。生忽病消渴,卒。女哭之痛,泪眼不晴,至绝眠食。劝之不纳,乘夜自经。婢觉之,急救而醒,终亦不食。三日,集亲党,将以殓生。闻棺中呻以息,启之,已复活。自言:“见冥王,以生平朴诚,命作部

confirming the truth of this, the mother said, "This young man has quite a reputation for literary talent, but he is as poor as Xiangru. If we don't do any better than this after all those years of trying to choose you a husband, I fear that people of good families will langh at us." But because of the shoe, the girl vowed she would have no one else. Her parents gave in and sent a messenger running to notify the scholar, whose malady was instantly cured by joy. When the old man suggested that he be brought into the family as a live-in son-in-law, the girl said, "It is not good for a man to remain long in the home of his in-laws. What is more, he is poor and such a step would eventually cause people to look down on him all the more. Now that I have given him my hand, I will gladly live under a thatched roof and eat wild greens without complaint."

The scholar then went to escort her home, and the wedding ceremony was completed. They came together like lovers from a past lifetime. With the help of the girl's dowry his family became moderately prosperous and acquired sizeable new assets. The scholar, however, was book-addled and did not know enough to handle the family enterprises. The girl was skilled in management and did not embroil the scholar in extraneous matters. Within three years the family was wealthy.

Then the scholar fell abruptly ill and succumbed to diabetes. The girl mourned him so grievously that she ceased eating and sleeping. She refused to be consoled, and under cover of night she hung herself. Amaid discovered her and rushed to her rescue. She came to her senses, but refused to eat. Three days later when the scholar's relatives gathered for the funeral, they heard moaning and gasping in the coffin. Lifting the lid, they found that he had come back to life.

"I was called before the king of the underworld," he told them. "Because of my lifelong honesty, I was appointed to serve on an official board. Suddenly a man came and informed the king: 'The wife of

曹。忽有人白：'孙部曹之妻将至。'王稽鬼录，言：'此未应便死。"又白：'不食三日矣。'王顾谓：'感汝妻节义，姑赐再生。'因使驭卒控马送余还。"由此体渐平。值岁大比，入闱之前，诸少年玩弄之，共拟隐僻之题七，引生僻处与语，言："此某家关节，敬秘相授。"生信之，昼夜揣摩，制成七艺。众隐笑之。时典试者虑熟题有蹈袭弊，力反常经，题纸下，七艺皆符。生以是抡魁。明年，举进士，授词林。上闻异，召问之。生具启奏。上大嘉悦。后召见阿宝，赏赉有加焉。

异史氏曰："性痴则其志凝：故书痴者文

Board Official Sun is about to arrive. 'The king checked the ghost register and said, 'It is not yet her time to die.'"

"'She didn't eat for three days, 'the man explained."

"Turning to look at me, the king said, 'In consideration of your wife's sense of honor. I will allow you to live again for the time being. 'Then he ordered a driver to hitch up horses and escort me back here."

After this, his health gradually returned to normal. Then came the annual provincial examinations. As the time for entering the examination cells drew near, some young men played a joke on Sun by making up seven obscure composition topics. They dragged the scholar off to an out-of-the-way spot and said, "We got hold of these through certain family connections. To show our respect, we are giving them to you secretly."

The scholar believed them and turned the questions over in his mind night and day until he succeeded in writing seven practice compositions. The group laughed at him behind his back. At that time the officiating examiner, concerned lest the familiar topics encourage plagiarism, made efforts to go against the convention. When the list of topics was handed out, all seven tallied with the ones Sun had prepared, and so the scholar took top honors. The year after that he was awarded the Doctorate of Letters and given a position in the Imperial Academy. The emperor, hearing of his wondrous story, summoned him and asked if it were true. The scholar informed the throne of every-thing, winning considerable favor from the emperor. Later he summoned Precious to an audience and bestowed presents of even greater munificence.

The Chronicler of the Tales comments: "'Foolishness'or fixation in a man's character makes for dedication. Thus one who is fixated on books will surely write proficiently and one who is fixated on a craft will have consummate skill. The down-and-out losers of this world are

必工，艺痴者技必良；世之落拓而无成者，皆自谓不痴者也。且如粉花荡产，卢雉倾家，顾痴人事哉！以是知慧黠而过，乃是真痴；彼孙子何痴乎！”

all people who claim to be free of fixation. Look at those who throw money away on powdered ladies and ruin their families for gambling! Are they not playing the fool's part? From this we can see that the worst foolishness is cleverness and cunning carried to extremes. What was so foolish about Master Sun?"

口 技

村中来一女子，年二十有四五。携一药囊，售其医。有问病者，女不能自为方，俟暮夜问诸神。晚洁斗室，闭置其中。众绕门窗，倾耳寂听；但窃窃语，莫敢欬。内外动息俱冥。至夜许，忽闻帘声。女在内曰："九姑来耶？"一女子答云："来矣。"又曰："腊梅从九姑来耶？"似一婢答云："来矣。"三人絮语间杂，刺刺不休。俄闻帘钩复动，女曰："六姑至矣。"乱言曰："春梅亦抱小郎子来耶？"一女曰："拗哥子！呜呜不睡，定要从娘子来。身

VENTRILOQUISM

A WOMAN in her mid-twenties came to our village, carrying a medicine bag on her arm and offering medical treatment. Someone went to her to have an illness treated. The woman could not make up a prescription herself: she had to wait till nightfall and take counsel with spirits. In the evening she swept her cubbyhole of a room clean and closed herself inside. A hushed crowd gathered around the window and the door, straining to eavesdrop. They exchanged whispers, but no one dared cough. Sound and movement were stilled both inside and out. When night came they suddenly heard the sound of a curtain being drawn. Inside the room the woman said "Is that you, Ninth Mistress?"

"It is me," answered another woman's voice.

"Did Winter-Plum come with you?"

A voice that seemed to belong to a maid answered: "Here I am."

The three women chattered ceaselessly about odds and ends. Before long the crowd heard curtain hooks sliding again. The woman's voice said "Sixth Mistress has come."

Stray voices said, "Has Spring-Plum come with the young master in her arms?"

"You naughty little boy," came a woman's voice. "Bawl-ing and

如百钧重,负累煞人!"旋闻女子殷勤声,九姑问讯声,六姑寒暄声,二婢慰劳声,小儿喜笑声,一齐嘈杂。即闻女子笑曰:"小郎君亦大好耍,远迢迢抱猫儿来。"既而声渐疏,帘又响,满室俱哗,曰:"四姑来何迟也?"有一小女子细声答曰:"路有千里且溢,与阿姑走尔许时始至。阿姑行且缓。"遂各各道温凉声,并移坐声,唤添坐声,参差并作,喧繁满室,食顷始定。即闻女子问病。九姑以为宜得参,六姑以为宜得芪,四姑以为宜得术。参酌移时,即闻九姑唤笔砚。无何,折纸戢戢然,拔笔掷帽丁丁然,磨墨隆隆然;既而投笔触几,震震作响,便闻撮药包裹苏苏然。顷之,女子推帘,呼病者授药并方,反身入室,即闻三姑作

refusing to sleep. You had to come with your mother. It feels like you weigh three thousand catties. Carrying you is enough to tire a person to death!"

They soon heard the woman's words of greeting, Ninth Mistress' questions about health, Sixth Mistress' formalities, the maids' sympathetic remarks, the happy laughter of the child—all blended into a cacophony of voices.

Then they heard the woman laugh: "The little master certainly is a funloving kid: he came all this way holding a kitty-cat."

Gradually the voices came few and far between. Again there was the sound of the curtain being drawn, and the whole room rang with voices saying: "Why have you come so late, Fourth Mistress?"

A dainty voice answered: "The way here was more than three hundred miles long. Mother-in-law and I have been hurrying along all this time and we've only gotten here now. She's such a slow walker." Then each of them made some perfunctory remarks about the weather by way of salutation. The room rang with mingled sounds of scraping chairs and cries for more chairs. This went on for the duration of a meal. Then the crowd heard the woman ask about her patient's illness. Ninth Mistress said ginseng was indicated; Sixth-Mistress, yellow vetch; and Fourth Mistress, atractylis. This was discussed for a while. Then Ninth Mistress was heard calling for brush and inkstone. Soon came the crinkling of paper, the tinkling of the inkbrush cap being pulled off and thrown on the table, and the grating of an ink-stik being rubbed on a slab. Then there was the click of the inkbrush being dropped on the desk, and the tiny sounds of herbs being measured out and wrapped.

Soon the woman pushed aside the curtain at the entrance of the room and told her patient to come and get the medicine and prescription. She turned back into the room. The farewells of the three mistresses and the three maids, the burbling of the child, and the mewing

别，三婢作别，小儿哑哑，猫儿唔唔，又一时并起。九姑之声清以越，六姑之声缓以苍，四姑之声娇以婉，以及三婢之声，各有态响，听之了了可辨。群讶以为真神。而试其方，亦不甚效。此即所谓口技，特借之以售其术耳。然亦奇矣！

昔王心逸尝言：在都偶过市廛，闻弦歌声，观者如堵。近窥之，则见一少年曼声度曲。并无乐器，惟以一指捺颊际，且捺且讴；听之铿铿，与弦索无异。亦口技之苗裔也。

of the cat all rang out at once. Ninth Mistress'voice was clear and piercing; Sixth Mistress'halting and flat; and Fourth Mistress'coy and appealing. These, along with the voices of the three maids, each had its own clearly distinguishable intonation. The amazed crowd thought these were truly spirit visitors. But the prescription was tried without much effect. This was what is known as ventriloquism, employed to sell medical art, but amazing nonetheless!

Wang Xinyi once said he was passing through a mar-ketplace in the capital when he heard a song accompanied by a string instrument. Onlookers were packed together as densely as a wall. He moved closer for a look and saw a young man performing an aria in rich voice. He had no instrument. Instead, he pressed a finger against his cheek as he sang, producing a twanging sound just like one made by a string instrument. He too was an adept in the skill of ventriloquism that has been handed down from long ago.

连　城

乔生，晋宁人。少负才名。年二十余，犹偃蹇。为人有肝胆。与顾生善；顾卒，时恤其妻子。邑宰以文相契重；宰终于任，家口淹滞不能归，生破产扶柩，往返二千余里。以故士林益重之，而家由此益替。史孝廉有女，字连城，工刺绣，知书。父娇爱之。出所刺"倦绣图"，征少年题咏，意在择婿。生献诗云："慵鬟高髻绿婆娑，早向兰窗绣碧荷；刺到鸳鸯魂

LIANCHENG

SCHOLAR Qiao of Jinning was hailed as a genius at an early age, but was still frustrated and unrecognized in his twenties. He was a man of chivalrous qualities. He was close to a scholar named Gu, and when Gu died he gave frequent aid to his wife and children. When the district magistrate, who had prized his talent, died in office, leaving the members of his household stranded far from home, the scholar liquidated his holdings to escort the coffin of the deceased to his hometown, which entailed a round trip of nearly a thousand miles. This gave the scholarly community an even higher opinion of him, but it also furthered the decline of his family's fortunes.

Master of Letters Shi had a daughter with the soubriquet Liancheng who was skilled at embroidery and well-read in books. Her father pampered her with affection. He brought forth a tapestry done by her needle entitled "Weary With Embroidery" and invited young men to write poems about it, intended as a means to select a son-in-law. Scholar Qiao presented a poem which read:

The languid coils of her chignon
Are tumbled waves of darkest shade
By morning's orchid window light

欲断，暗停针线蹙双蛾。”又赞挑绣之工云：“绣线挑来似写生，幅中花鸟自天成；当年织锦非长技，幸把回文感圣明。”女得诗喜，对父称赏。父贫之。女逢人辄称道；又遣媪矫父命，赠金以助灯火。生叹曰：“连城我知己也！”倾怀结想，如饥思啖。无何，女许字于鹾贾之子王化成，生始绝望；然梦魂中犹佩戴之。未几，女病瘵，沈痼不起。有西域头陀自谓能疗；但须男子膺肉一钱，捣合药屑。史使人诣王家告婿。婿笑曰：“痴老翁，欲我剜心头肉也！”使返，史乃言于人曰：“有能割肉者

Lily pads of green thread are made
But a linking lovebird pattern
Disturbs the calm that time allows
Her needle pausing furtively
She pouts and knits her mothwing brows
With nimble stitch of colored thread,
She turns to life for her designs;
The scene is filled with birds and blooms
And all are formed to nature's lines.
No special skill was used to make
The brocade legends tell us of
T'was the palindromic poem thereon
That won the monarch's love.

The girl was delighted with the poems and praised them to her father, but he objected to the scholar's poverty. The girl spoke highly of the scholar to everyone she met and even sent an old woman with money to help him buy lamp oil for reading, ostensibly upon instructions from her father. The scholar sighed, "Liancheng is the one person who truly knows me!" His heart inclined toward her, and his thoughts were tied to her as those of a starving man are to food.

But soon the girl was betrothed to Wang Huacheng, the son of a salt merchant. The scholar finally lost hope, but his dreaming soul still attached to her. Before long the girl was stricken so badly with consumption that she could not rise. An ascetic from the Western Regions claimed that he could heal her, if only he had a tenth of a tael of flesh from a man's chest to grind up and mix with other medicinal powders. Master Shi sent a man to the Wang house to notify his son-in-law, who laughed and said, "Foolish old man! He wants me to slice away the flesh that covers my heart."

After the messenger returned, Shi announced: "I will give my

妻之。"生闻而往，自出白刃，刲膺授僧。血濡袍裤，僧敷药始止。合药三丸。三日服尽，疾若失。史将践其言，先告王。王怒，欲讼官。史乃设筵招生，以千金列几上，曰："重负大德，请以相报。"因具白背盟之由。生怫然曰："仆所以不爱膺肉者，聊以报知己耳，岂货肉哉！"拂袖而归。女闻之，意良不忍，托媪慰谕之。且云："以彼才华，当不久落。天下何患无佳人？我梦不祥，三年必死，不必与人争此泉下物也。"生告媪曰："'士为知己者死'，不以色也。诚恐连城未必真知我，但得真知我，不谐何害？"媪代女郎矢诚自剖。生曰："果尔，相逢时，当为我一笑，死无憾！"媪既去，逾

daughter's hand in marriage to the man who can part with this bit of flesh." Hearing of this, the scholar went to Shi's house. He drew out a keen blade, sliced his chest and handed the flesh to the monk. Blood soaked his robe and trousers, but finally stopped when the monk applied a compress. The monk compounded three pills. After three days, when she had taken all the pills, the girl's disease was healed in an instant.

Shi let Wang know that he intended to keep his promise. Wang was infuriated and threatened to take his case to the authorities, so Shi invited the scholar to a feast and, spreading one thousand taels of gold out on the table, said, "Please accept this as payment for the great debt of gratitude I owe you." Then he explained his reason for going back on his word.

The scholar replied indignantly: "I did not grudge the flesh from my chest, because I wanted to show appreciation for one who truly knows me. Do you think I want to sell my flesh?" He walked out with a disdainful flourish of his sleeves.

Hearing of this, the girl felt unbearably sorry for him, so she entrusted the old woman to go comfort him and let him know feelings.

"With his genius he will not be frustrated for long." the girl added. "Why should he worry that there is no beautiful woman for him in this wide world? My ill-omened dreams foretell that I will die within three years. He need not fight for someone who already has one foot in the grave."

The scholar told the old woman. "'A man of hnor gives his life for the one who knows him, not because of sexual attraction. My real fear is that Liancheng may not recognize my worth. If only she does, our union could fail to work out and I sitll would not care."

The old woman conveyed the girl's soul-baring vows of faithfulness.

"If she truly feels that way," said the scholar, "She should smile

数日,生偶出,遇女自叔氏归,睨之。女秋波转顾,启齿嫣然。生大喜曰:"连城真知我者!"会王氏来议吉期,女前症又作,数月寻死。生往临吊,一痛而绝。史舁送其家。生自知已死,亦无所戚。出村去,犹冀一见连城。遥望南北一道,行人连绪如蚁,因亦混身杂迹其中。俄顷,入一廨署,值顾生,惊问:"君何得来?"即把手将送令归。生太息,言:"心事殊未了。"顾曰:"仆在此典牍,颇得委任。倘可效力,不惜也。"生问连城。顾即导生旋转多所,见连城与一白衣女郎,泪睫惨黛,藉坐廊隅。见生至,骤起似喜,略问所来。生曰:"卿死,仆何敢生!"连城泣曰:"如此负

at me next time we meet. Then I could die without regrets!"

The old woman left. Several days later the scholar happened to go out and meet the girl as she returned from her uncle's house. He looked at her intently. Her limpid eyes turned in his direction, and her mouthparted winningly. The scholar exclaimed joyfully: "Liancheng is the one who truly knows me!"

Just when the Wang family came to discuss an auspicious day for the wedding, the girl had a relapse. Within a few months she was dead. The scholar went to mourn her and collapsed in anguish. As Shi was having him carried home, the scholar was well aware of his own death but did not feel upset. He walked out of the village, but still hoped to see Liancheng again. In the distance he saw an antilike line of people walking on a north-south road, so he mingled in among them. Soon he came to an office building, where he encountered Scholar Gu, who asked in surprise: "What brought you here?" He grabbed Scholar Qiao's arm and stared to escort him back.

With a heavy sigh Qiao said, "What has been weighing on my mind is far from resolved."

"Quite a lot of responsibility has been delegated to me since I began handling documents here," said Gu, "I will not hesitate to do anything within my power for you."

When Qiao asked about Liancheng, Scholar Gu led him around from place to place until they saw Liancheng and a white-robed young woman sitting in the corner of a veranda, their eyes forlorn and wet with tears. Seeing Scholar Qiao arrive, Liancheng leapt up with apparent pleasure and inquired into the manner of his coming.

"Now that you have died, how can I go on living?" answered the scholar.

The tears rolled down as she said, "I behaved like such an ingrate and still you did not spurn me. Why should you sacrifice your life for me? It is impossible to give myself to you in this life: I want nothing

义人，尚不吐弃之，身殉何为？然已不能许君今生，愿矢来世耳。”生告顾曰：“有事君自去，仆乐死不愿生矣。但烦稽连城托生何里，行与俱去耳。”顾诺而去。白衣女郎问生何人，连城为缅述之。女郎闻之，若不胜悲。连城告生曰：“此妾同姓，小字宾娘，长沙史太守女。一路同来，遂相怜爱。”生视之，意态怜人。方欲研问，而顾已返，向生贺曰：“我为君平章已确，即教小娘子从君返魂，好否？”两人各喜。方将拜别，宾娘大哭曰：“姊去，我安归？乞垂怜救，妾为姊捧帨耳。”连城凄然，无所为计，转谋生。生又哀顾。顾难之，峻辞以为不可。生固强之。乃曰：“试妄为之。”去食顷而返，摇手曰：“何如！诚万分不能为力矣！”宾娘闻之，宛转娇啼，惟依连城肘下，恐其即去。惨怛无术，相对默默；而睹其愁颜戚

more than to promise my next life to you."

The scholar told Gu: "You can go on about your business. I am glad for death and have no wish to live. But I would like to bother you to look up the locality of Liancheng's next incarnation, so I can go there with her." Gu left after promising to do so. The white-robed woman asked who the scholar was, so Liancheng told her the whole story. The sadness of it seemed to overwhelm her as she listened.

"She and I share the same family name," Liancheng told the scholar. "Her youth-name is Binniang. She is the daughter of the prefect Shi of Changsha. We became close as we walked together on the road here."

The scholar took a good look and found her to have a charming manner. He was about to ask more about her when Gu returned and congratulated the scholar, saying: "I already have everything worked out for you. I'm going to have the young lady follow your soul back to the world of the living. How would you like that?"

The two were overjoyed. They were about to take their leave when Binniang broke into loud sobs and said, "When you go, sister, where am I to turn to? If you are generous enough to come to my rescue, I will wait on you hand and foot." Liancheng was distressed and at a loss so she turned to ask for the scholar's advice. The scholar begged Gu to give them further help, but Gu considered this too difficult and protested strongly that it could not be done. At last, worn down by the scholar's pleading, he said, "I'll give it my best, for what that's worth." He went out for the time it takes to eat a meal and returned, waving his hands and saying: "I told you so! I simply cannot do anything for you."

Hearing this made Binniang break into plaintive, drawn-out sobs. She held fast to Liancheng's arm, fearful of being left behind that very moment. They could do nothing but look at one another in silent despair. To see her wretched, forlorn countenance was enough to make

容,使人肺腑酸柔。顾生愤然曰:“请携宾娘去。脱有愆尤,小生拚身受之!”宾娘乃喜,从生出。生忧其道远无侣。宾娘曰:“妾从君去,不愿归也。”生曰:“卿大痴矣。不归,何以得活也?他日至湖南,勿复走避,为幸多矣。”适有两媪摄牒赴长沙,生属宾娘,泣别而去。途中,连城行蹇缓,里余辄一息;凡十余息,始见里门。连城曰:“重生后,惧有反覆。请索妾骸骨来,妾以君家生,当无悔也。”生然之。偕归生家。女惕惕若不能步,生伫待之。女曰:“妾至此,四肢摇摇,似无所主。志恐不遂,尚宜审谋,不然,生后何能自由?”相将入侧厢中。嘿定少时,连城笑曰:“君憎妾耶?”生惊问其故。赧然曰:“恐事不谐,重负君矣。请先以鬼报也。”生喜,极尽欢恋。因徘徊不

a person's heart ache. "Take Binniang away with you," Scholar Gu said hotly. "Should any blame be incurred, I will accept it, even if it costs me my life!" Binniang happily followed Scholar Qiao out. The scholar worried about her going on such a long journey home without any companion. Binniang said, "I'll go with you. I don't want to go back to Hunan."

"You are carrying your foolishness too far," said the scholar: "If you don't go back, how can you be reincarnated? I'll be going to Hunan someday, and will be pleased if you don't run away from me then." At that moment two old women walked by, carrying travelling papers for Changsha. The schloar commended Binniang to their care. They parted tearfully and left. Liancheng was hampered by lameness on the trip and had to take a rest after walking a little more than a third of a mile. They made more than ten stops before they saw the gate to their residential quarter.

Liancheng said, "I'm afraid complications may crop up after we come back to life. Please ask for my remains and bring them here. If I come to life in your house, nothing will happen that we might regret later." This made sense to the scholar. Both of them headed toward his house. The girl shrank back timidly with fear and seemed unable to go forward, so the scholar stood waiting for her. "I've come a long way, and my arms and legs are shaking," said the girl. "They won't do what I tell them to. I'm afraid our intentions may not be realized. We should talk it over further. Otherwise, after we have regained our lives, how can we carry out our wishes?" She tugged him into a side chamber. There were a few moments of quiet and then Liancheng said laughingly: "Do you hate me?" The bewildered scholar asked the reason for this question. Blushingly, she replied: "I'm afraid our plans won't work out and I'll end up betraying you again. First let me repay your love with my ghostly body." The scholar was overjoyed. They abandoned themselves to tender ecstasy. Since they were afraid to

敢遽生，寄厢中者三日。连城曰：“谚有之：‘丑妇终须见姑嫜。’戚戚于此，终非久计。”乃促生入。才至灵寝，豁然顿苏。家人惊异，进以汤水。生乃使人要史来，请得连城之尸，自言能活之。史喜，从其言。方舁入室，视之已醒。告父曰：“儿已委身乔郎矣，更无归理。如有变动，但仍一死！”史归，遣婢往役给奉。王闻，具词申理。官受赂，判归王。生愤懑欲死，亦无奈之。连城至王家，忿不饮食，惟乞速死。室无人，则带悬梁上。越日，益惫，殆将奄逝。王惧，送归史。史复舁归生。王知之，亦无如何，遂安焉。连城起，每念宾娘，欲遣信探之，以道远而艰于往。一日，家人进

come to life right away, they dallied in the chamber for three days.

Then Liancheng said, "As the saying goes—'Even an ugly bride must eventually meet her in-laws.' Staying here on pins and needles is not a long-term plan." With this she urged the scholar to go in. The moment he reached the bier he revived suddenly. The stunned members of his family poured warm water down his throat. The scholar then sent for Shi. He asked to have Liancheng's remains, claiming that he could bring them to life. Shi was glad to do as he asked. As soon as the girl's body was carried into the room, she was seen to waken.

"I've already given myself to Master Qiao," the girl told her father. "There is no reason for me to go home again. If anything happens to thwart me in this, my only alternative will be to die again!" Shi returned home and sent a maid to wait upon her.

When Wang heard of this, he drew up a statement presenting his position and bribed the magistrate, who then determined that Wang was the rightful husband. The scholar was close to expiring from indignation, but there was no help for it. When she arrived at the Wang house, Liancheng's resentment was such that she would not eat or drink, but only begged that they allow her to die quickly. When she was left alone in her room, she tried to hang herself from a rafter with her sash. In a few days she had wasted away to the point of imminent death. Wang was frightened and sent her back to her father, who then had her carried back to the scholar's house. Wang knew of this, but there was nothing he could do, so he let the matter rest.

After her recovery Liancheng often thought of Binniang and, owing to the difficulty of making such a long trip, she hesitated to send a messenger to inquire after her. One day a servant ran in to say: "There is a horse and carriage at the gate." Husband and wife went out to look and found that Binniang was already there in their courtyard. It was a tearful, happy reunion. The scholar invited the pre-

曰:“门有车马。”夫妇出视,则宾娘已至庭中矣。相见悲喜。太守亲诣送女,生延入。太守曰:“小女子赖君复生,誓不他适,今从其志。”生叩谢如礼。孝廉亦至,叙宗好焉。生名年,字大年。

异史氏曰:“一笑之知,许之以身,世人或议其痴;彼田横五百人,岂尽愚哉。此知希之贵,贤豪所以感结而不能自已也。顾茫茫海内,遂使锦绣才人,仅倾心于蛾眉之一笑也。悲夫!”

fect, who had escorted his daughter there personally, to come in.

"My daughter owes her renewed life to you, sir," said the prefect. "She swears that she will marry no one else, so I have decided to go along with her wishes." The scholar touched his head to the floor in gratitude as etiquette demanded. Shi, the Master of Letters, came too, and the two gentlemen confirmed their clan ties.

By the way, Scholar Qiao's name was Nian and his soubriquet, Danian.

The Chronicler of the Tales comments: "Some may call it foolish for a man to commit himself to a woman when no more recognition than a smile has passed between them. But could the five hundred followers of Tian Heng have all been fools? From them we learn how highly men value those who recognize their worth, and what makes able, outstanding men rally around a leader without thinking of themselves. And yet, it would surely be tragic if a young man in all the splendor of his gifts could find nothing more in this vast world on which to pin hopes for recognition than the smiles of a young beauty!"

罗刹海市

马骥，字龙媒，贾人子。美丰姿。少倜傥，喜歌舞。辄从梨园子弟，以锦帕缠头，美如好女，因复有“俊人”之号。十四岁，入郡庠，即知名。父衰老，罢贾而居。谓生曰：“数卷书，饥不可煮，寒不可衣。吾儿可仍继父贾。”马由是稍稍权子母。从人浮海，为飓风引去，数昼夜，至一都会。其人皆奇丑；见马

THE RAKSASAS AND THE OCEAN BAZAAR

MA Jun, also known as Dragon Messenger, was a merchant's son. He had striking good looks and in his untrammeled youth gave himself up to the pleasures of singing and dancing. He frequented the Pear Garden, where he amused himself in the company of the actors. Wrapping his head in a brocade turban he had all the charm of an attractive woman, and hence was given the nickname "Stunner." He also made a name for himself by being admitted to the prefectural academy at fourteen.

When age and decliing health made the young scholar's father give up business and go into retirement, he said these words to his son: "Those books you have read cannot feed you when you are hungry and cannot keep you warm when you are cold. You should take over my business, son." From then on Ma devoted part of his attention to matters of investment and profit.

Ma embarked on an ocean voyage with a party of other passengers, but it happened that they were blown off course by a typhoon. After several days the ship came to a city in which all the inhabitants were freakishly ugly. They ran off in an uproar as Ma approached,

至,以为妖,群哗而走。马初见其状,大惧;迨知国人之骇己也,遂反以此欺国人。遇饮食者,则奔而往;人惊遁,则啜其余。久之,入山村。其间形貌亦有似人者,然褴褛如丐。马息树下,村人不敢前,但遥望之。久之,觉马非噬人者,始稍稍近就之。马笑与语。其言虽异,亦半可解。马遂自陈所自。村人喜,遍告邻里,客非能搏噬者。然奇丑者望望即去,终不敢前。其来者,口鼻位置,尚皆与中国同。共罗浆酒奉马。马问其相骇之故。答曰:“尝闻祖父言:西去二万六千里,有中国,其人民形象率诡异。但耳食之,今始信。”问其何贫。曰:“我国所重,不在文章,而在形貌。其美之极者,为上卿;次任民社;下焉者,亦邀贵人宠,故得鼎烹以养妻子。若我辈初生时,父母皆以为不祥,往往置弃之;其不忍

taking him for a monster. When Ma first saw this he was greatly frightened, but once he realized they were afraid of him, he used their fear to gain the upper hand. Finding a group of them sitting at table, he rushed toward them and, after they dashed away in fright, gulped down the food they left. After a time he went into a mountain village, where some of the inhabitants looked almost human, though they wore the tattered fags of beggars. Ma sat down to rest beneath a tree. The villagers watched him from a distance, not daring to approach. After a while, when they realized that Ma was not a man-eating monster, they finally edged toward him. Ma smiled and talked with them. Although their speech was strange, it was halfway comprehensible. Without being asked, Ma told where he had come from. The delighted villagers told everyone in the neighborhood that the stranger was not violent. Still the freakishly ugly ones stole furtive looks at him and ran off, never daring to come near. Those who did come close had mouths and noses in just about the same places as we do here in China. Together they hunted up wine and served it to Ma.

Ma asked why they had been afraid of him. "I once heard my grandfather say," one of them replied, "that 8,500 miles to the west lies a land called the Middle Kingdom, and the people there are all grotesque in appearance. I knew it only by hearsay, but now I believe it."

Ma asked why they were so poor. Someone answered, "In our country what is valued is appearance rather than literary ability. The most handsome among us become high ministers at court; the fairly handsome are given posts in local administrative offices; and the somewhat handsome can support their wives and children in style by winning the favor of some nobleman. As for people like us, we are thought to be bearers of evil fortune, and our parents often abandon us at birth. All the people who cannot bear to abandon their offspring straightaway are thinking about the continuity of their family line.

遽弃者，皆为宗嗣耳。”问：“此名何国？”曰：“大罗刹国。都城在北去三十里。”马请导往一观。于是鸡鸣而兴，引与俱去。天明，始达都。都以黑石为墙，色如墨。楼阁近百尺。然少瓦，覆以红石；拾其残块磨甲上，无异丹砂。时值朝退，朝中有冠盖出，村人指曰：“此相国也。”视之，双耳皆背生，鼻三孔，睫毛覆目如帘。又数骑出，曰：“此大夫也。”以次各指其官职，率狰狞怪异；然位渐卑，丑亦渐杀。无何，马归，街衢人望见之，噪奔跌蹶，如逢怪物。村人百口解说，市人始敢遥立。既归，国中无大小，咸知村有异人，于是搢绅大夫，争欲一广见闻，遂令村人要马。然每至一家，阍人辄阖户，丈夫女子窃窃自门隙中窥语；终一日，无敢延见者。村人曰：“此间一执戟郎，曾

"What is the name of this kingdom?" asked Ma.

"The Great Kingdom of the Raksasas," was the answer. "The capital is ten miles north of here." Ma asked them to lead him there for a look. And so they arose at cock's crow the next day and took him there. They reached the capital after daybreak. The walls of the city were built of stone as black as ink, and the storied buildings were nearly a hundred feet high. There were few rooftiles to be seen. Instead, the buildings were covered with shingles of red stone. Ma picked up a loose piece and rubbed it against his armor; it was exactly like cinnabar.

Just then came the time for dismissal of the morning court session at the palace. The villagers pointed to one of the dignitaries who were coming out of the palace gate: "That is the prime minister." Ma saw that his ears were attached to the back of his head, his nose had three nostrils and his eyelashes covered his eyes like curtains. Then several men came out on horseback. "Those are privy counselors," said the villagers. As the officials came out in succession, the villagers pointed out their ranks. All of them had grotesque, monstrous faces, but as the lower ranks came out the degree of ugliness gradually abated. Before long Ma started back toward the village. People in the streets who saw him screamed and fell over one another trying to run away, as if they had met with a monster. Only when the villagers had gone to great lengths to reassure them did the city dwellers dare to stand and watch from a distance.

After they returned to the village, everyone in the kingdom, regardless of rank, knew there was an unusual person there. Members of the gentry and court officials, eager to broaden their horizons, told the villagers to invite Ma to visit them, but whenever he showed up at someone's house, the gatekeeper would close the door, and the men and women alike would only venture to peer at him and speak with him through cracks in the door. This would go on all day without anyone

为先王出使异国,所阅人多,或不以子为惧。”造郎门。郎果喜,揖为上宾。视其貌,如八九十岁人。目睛突出,须卷如猬。曰:“仆少奉王命,出使最多;独未尝至中华。今一百二十余岁,又得睹上国人物,此不可不上闻于天子。然臣卧林下,十余年不践朝阶,早旦,为君一行。”乃具饮馔,修主客礼。酒数行,出女乐十余队,更番歌舞。貌类如夜叉,皆以白锦缠头,拖朱衣及地。扮唱不知何词,腔拍恢诡。主人顾而乐之。问:“中国亦有此乐乎?”曰:“有。”主人请拟其声,遂击桌为度一曲。主人喜曰:“异哉!声如凤鸣龙啸,得未曾

asking him in for a visit.

One villager said, "There is an officer of the guard living in this district who was sent abroad as emissary by our former king. He has had experience with many sorts of people, so he may not be frightened of you."

They went to the officer's house and, as the villager had foreseen, he was delighted at their visit and received Ma as an honored guest. Apparently between eighty and ninety years of age, he had goggle eyes and hair that stood out like a hedgehog's.

"In my youth I went on more diplomatic missions for the king than anyone else, but the Middle Kingdom of China is the one place I have never been. Now I am over a hundred and twenty years old, and at last I have the chance to see someone from your esteemed country. The king simply must be informed of this. Though I have been leading a life of retirement and have not set foot upon the palace steps these past ten years or more. I will make the trip for your sake in the morning."

Observing all the formalities of a host to his guest, he then had wine and victuals set out. After they had drunk several rounds, he brought out ten or so female entertainers with faces like *yaksa* monsters, who took turns singing and dancing. All of them wore white brocade turbans on their heads and flowing red robes that dragged on the ground. Ma could not make out the lyrics, but he found the tune and rhythm oddly fascinating. The host watched them with immense enjoyment.

"Do you have entertainment like this in the Middle Kingdom?" he asked.

"Oh yes," answered Ma.

The host asked him to imitate the music for them, so Ma drummed on the table and performed a song.

"Well if that isn't most extraordinary!" exclaimed the delighted

闻。”翼日，趋朝，荐诸国王。王忻然下诏。有二三大臣，言其怪状，恐惊圣体。王乃止。即出告马，深为扼腕。居久之，与主人饮而醉，把剑起舞，以煤涂面作张飞。主人以为美，曰：“请客以张飞见宰相，宰相必乐用之，厚禄不难致。”马曰：“嘻！游戏犹可，何能易面目图荣显？”主人固强之，马乃诺。主人设筵，邀当路者饮，令马绘面以待。未几，客至，呼马出见客。客讶曰：“异哉！何前媸而今妍也！”遂与共饮，甚欢。马婆娑歌“弋阳曲”，一座无不倾倒。明日，交章荐马。王喜，召以旌节。既见，问中国治安之道，马委曲上陈，大蒙嘉叹，赐宴离宫。酒酣，王曰：“闻卿善雅乐，可

host. "The melody makes me think of phoenixes calling and dragons roaring. It is unlike anything I have ever heard." The next day he went to court and recommended Ma to the king. The king gladly commanded that Ma be brought before him, but when a few high counselors claimed that Ma's monstrous appearance might result in a shock injurious to His Majesty's health, the order was rescinded. The old officer of the guard came out and gave Ma the news of this crushing disappointment.

Ma stayed with the officer for a long while. One day, when he and his host were in their cups, he smeared his face with soot to look like Zhang Fei and began to dance with sword in hand. The host thought he was attractive and said, "Why don't you make yourself up as Zhang Fei and go to see the prime minister. I am sure he will be delighted to find a place for you. An ample salary is within your grasp."

"Hah! It is one thing to paly games, but why should I put on a new face to chase after honor and fame?" But when the host insisted, Ma gave in. The host invited the ranking officials to a feast and long the guests arrived, and Ma was called out to meet them.

"Isn't that strange!" said the guests in surprise. "How could someone who was once so ugly turn into such a good looking fellow? Whereupon they all drank together with exceeding joy. Ma swayed with the rhythm as he sang the Yiyang Melody, and every person at the table was positively bowled over. The next day a number of petitions recommending Ma were sent to the throne. The king was so delighted he summoned Ma with a big fanfare. During their first audience the king asked how law and order were maintained in the Middle Kingdom. Ma gave a detailed explanation which met with sighs of admiring approval. The king granted him the favor of dining with him in the royal hostel. When both were mellow with wine, the king said," I have heard that you are skilled in fine music. Might I be so fortunate as to hear you perform? "So Ma got up to dance. He sang softly and

使寡人得而闻之乎?”马即起舞,亦效白锦缠头,作靡靡之音。王大悦,即日拜下大夫。时与私宴,恩宠殊异。久而官僚百执事,颇觉其面目之假;所至,辄见人耳语,不甚与款洽。马至是孤立,惆然不自安。遂上疏乞休致,不许;又告休沐,乃给三月假。于是乘传载金宝,复归山村。村人膝行以迎。马以金赀分给旧所与交好者,欢声雷动。村人曰:“吾侪小人受大夫赐,明日赴海市,当求珍玩,用报大夫。”问:“海市何地?”曰:“海中市,四海鲛人,集货珠宝;四方十二国,均来贸易。中多神人游戏。云霞障天,波涛间作。贵人自重,不敢犯险阻,皆以金帛付我辈,代购异珍。今其期不远矣。”问所自知,曰:“每见海上朱鸟来往,七日即市。”马问行期,欲同游瞩。村人

languidly, in the style of the white-turbaned entertainers. The king was overjoyed. On that very day he gave Ma the title of deputy minister. He often dined privately with Ma and showered him with exceptional generosity and favor. After a time the other officials and administrators were fairly certain of the falseness of Ma's countenance. Wherever he went, he would see people whispering to one another instead of greeting him cordially. Being thus ostracized made Ma ill at ease, so he submitted a request for retirement, but this was not granted. Again he requested official leave, and was given a vacation of three months.

Ma lost no time loading his gold and jewels onto a stage coach and returning to the mountain village. The villagers came out to greet him on their knees. Joyful cries rang through the air when Ma divided gold coins among his old friends.

The villagers said, "Since we lowly folk have been honored by your gifts, we will set out for the ocean bazaar tomorrow and seek precious gems to repay you."

"Where is the ocean bazaar?" asked Ma.

"Mermen from the four seas gather at the ocean bazaar to trade in pearls and jewels. People from four directions and twelve kingdoms all come to trade with them. Many deities are engaged in pleasurable pastimes there. The sky is filled with clouds, and great waves roll ashore from time to time. People of rank are too concerned for their personal stafety to expose themselves to these dangers, so they entrust us with their gold and silk in order to purchase rare treasures for them. Now the date of the bazaar is not disant.

Ma asked how they knew it.

"When red birds are seen flying back and forth over the sea, the opening of the bazaar is seven days away."

Ma asked their time of departure and expressed a desire to make the trip with them and do some sightseeing. The villagers begged him

劝使自贵。马曰:“我顾沧海客,何畏风涛?”未几,果有踵门寄货者,遂与装货入船。船容数十人,平底高栏。十人摇橹,激水如箭。凡三日,遥见水云幌漾之中,楼阁层叠;贸迁之舟,纷集如蚁。少时,抵城下。视墙上砖,皆长与人等。敌楼高接云汉。维舟而入,见市上所陈,奇珍异宝,光明射眼,多人世所无。一少年乘骏马来,市人尽奔避,云是“东洋三世子”。世子过,目生曰:“此非异域人。”即有前马者来诘乡籍。生揖道左,具展邦族。世子喜曰:“既蒙辱临,缘分不浅!”于是授生骑,请与连辔。乃出西城。方至岛岸,所骑嘶跃入水。生大骇失声。则见海水中分,屹如壁立。俄睹宫殿,玳瑁为梁,鲂鳞作瓦;四壁晶明,鉴影炫目。下马揖入。仰见龙君在上,世

to consider his personal safety.

"But I am a seafarer. Do you suppose I fear rough weather? Before long there were people at the gate bringing valuables to invest in the voyage. Ma helped the crew stow the valuables on board the ship. It was a flat-bottomed craft with high gunwales and room for several dozen men. With ten men at the oars it churned up a seething wake and skimmed along like an arrow. After three days they glimpsed buildings and towers one behind the other through the shifting clouds that hung over the water. Trading ships converged on the place like ants. In no time they drew up beneath the city wall, which was made of bricks as long as a man's body. The battlements towered into the clouds above. Having moored their ship and entered the city, they saw displayed in the bazaar strange treasures and rare gems of dazzling brilliance, many never seen in the world of men."

Just then a young man mounted on a splendid stallion rode up to them. The shopkeepers and buyers scattered before him, saying that he was the "third crown prince of the Eastern Ocean." As the crown prince rode by he eyed the scholar and said, "Isn't this man from a faraway country?" Arunner came over to Ma and wanted to know his native land. Ma greeted him from the side of the road and people of his birth.

"Since you've honored us by coming here, it is plain that there is a deep bond of fate between us!" exclaimed the prince happily. He gave the scholar a mount and invited him to ride alongside. Riding beyond the western wall, they came to the shore of the island, where their mounts neighed and plunged into the water. The scholar was struck dumb with terror, but he soon saw that they were in an open space, with walls of seawater arching above them. Suddenly a palace appeared ahead, its beams made of tortoise shell and its roof tiled with scales of bream. The crystalline walls mirrored the shapes around them with blinding brilliance. Dismounting, the prince motioned Ma

子启奏："臣游市廛，得中华贤士，引见大王。"生前拜舞。龙君乃言："先生文学士，必能衙官屈、宋。欲烦椽笔赋'海市'，幸无吝珠玉。"生稽首受命。授以水精之砚，龙鬣之毫，纸光似雪，墨气如兰。生立成千余言，献殿上。龙君击节曰："先生雄才，有光水国多矣！"遂集诸龙族，燕集采霞宫。酒炙数行，龙君执爵而向客曰："寡人所怜女，未有良匹，愿累先生。先生倘有意乎？"生离席愧荷，唯唯而已。龙君顾左右语。无何，宫人数辈，扶女郎出。珮环声动，鼓吹暴作，拜竟睨之，实仙人也。女

inside. At the head of the hall before them was the Dragon Lord. The crown prince informed the throne: "While riding through the bazaar I found this worthy scholar from the Middle Kingdom whom I have brought for an audience with Your Highness." The scholar stepped forward and made an elaborate bow.

"I see sir, that you are a man of literary accomplishment," said the Dragon Lord. "I am sure you are good enough to lord it over famous poets of antiquity like Qu Yuan and Song Yu. Might I trouble you to brandish your rafter-sized inkbrush to write a rhapsody on the ocean bazaar? Please do not grudge us your precious words."

The scholar touched his forehead to the floor in ac-knowledgement. He was given a crystal inkstone, a gragon-bristle inkbrush, paper with the bright smoothness of snow and an inkstick exuding the fragrance of orchids. Without stopping to think, he completed a piece of over a thousand words and offered it to the throne. The dragon lord beat time while reciting the rhymed prose.

"Sir, your great talent has brought much glory to my acquatic kingdom!" he said.

So it was that the hosts of dragondom were assembled for a feast in Glowing-Cloud Palace. After several rounds of wine and several courses of roast meat, the dragon lord raised his cup and said to his guest: "I have not yet found a good match for my beloved daughter. Sir, I would like to inflict her upon you. Would this be in accordance with your wishes?"

The scholar rose to his knees from the mat, so overcome with gratitude that he could only stammer, "Yes, yes." The Dragon Lord turned and spoke to his attendants. Before long a group of court maids led forth a young woman, Jade rings thinkling at her waist as she moved. A sudden fanfare rang out. When he had finished bowing the scholar gave her an appraising glance: She was a veritable fairy maiden. She bowed and withdrew.

拜已而去。少时，酒罢，双鬟挑画灯，导生入副宫。女浓妆坐伺。珊瑚之床，饰以八宝；帐外流苏，缀明珠如斗大；衾褥皆香软。天方曙，则雏女妖鬟，奔入满侧。生起，趋出朝谢。拜为驸马都尉。以其赋驰传诸海。诸海龙君，皆专员来贺；争折简招驸马饮。生衣绣裳，驾青虬，呵殿而出。武士数十骑，皆雕弧，荷白棓，晃耀填拥。马上弹筝，车中奏玉。三日间，遍历诸海。由是“龙媒”之名，噪于四海。宫中有玉树一株，围可合抱；本莹澈，如白琉璃；中有心，淡黄色；稍细于臂；叶类碧玉，厚一钱许，细碎有浓阴。常与女啸咏其下。花开满树，状类薝蔔。每一瓣落，锵然作响。拾视之，如赤瑙雕镂，光明可爱。时有异

Soon the drinking ceased. Maids with hair done up in double buns bearing painted candles led the scholar into a side palace. The girl sat there waiting in her finest adornments. The coral bed was studded with a galaxy of gems, and shining pearls the size of spoons were knotted into the tassels that hung outside the canopy. The quilts were fragrant and yielding.

At the crack of dawn, budding young girls and bewiching maids ran in and stood in a row around the bed. The scholar rose, hurried to court and thanked the king. He was given the title of royal son-in-law. Because his rhapsody was rapidly disseminated throughout the four seas, the dragon lords from all quarters sent special envoys to congratulate him and deliver invitations to banquets. The scholar dressed in brocades and rode about on a green, horned dragon. He set forth from the palace with warning shouts to clear his way. An entourage of several dozen mounted knights bearing carved bows and white staffs clustered about him, their armor flashing. There were mounted musicians strumming zithers and others in a carriage playing jade flutes. Within three days the scholar had journeyed to all the oceans. From then on the name Dragon Messenger resounded throughout the four seas.

A jade tree as big in girth as a man's embrace grew in the palace. The trunk was shimmeringly transparent, like clear glass, with a pale yellow center slightly thinner than an arm. The leaves resembled green jade and were a bit thicker than copper coins. This profuse foliage cast dense shade, in which the scholar and his bride often sang and chanted poetry The whole tree was blooming with flowers that looked like gardenias. Each time a petal fell a distinct tinkle could be heard. Upon closer inspection each gleaming, delicate petal seemed to be sculpted of red agate.

Rare birds with feathers of iridescent blue and tails longer than their bodies often alighted on the tree and sang strains every bit as heart-rending as notes from a plaintive jade flute. Everytime the

鸟来鸣,——毛金碧色,尾长于身,——声等哀玉,恻人肺腑。生每闻辄念乡土。因谓女曰:“亡出三年,恩慈间阻,每一念及,涕膺汗背。卿能从我归乎?”女曰:“仙尘路隔,不能相依。妾亦不忍以鱼水之爱,夺膝下之欢。容徐谋之。”生闻之,泣不自禁。女亦叹曰:“此势之不能两全者也!”明日,生自外归。龙君曰:“闻都尉有故土之思,诘旦趣装,可乎?”生谢曰:“逆旅孤臣,过蒙优宠,衔报之诚,结于肺肝。容暂归省,当图复聚耳。”入暮,女置酒话别。生订后会。女曰:“情缘尽矣。”生大悲。女曰:“归养双亲,见君之孝。人生聚散,百年犹旦暮耳,何用作儿女哀泣?此后妾为君贞,君为妾义,两地同心,即伉俪也,何必旦

scholar heard them, he thought of his homeland. One day he spoke of this to his wife: "Three years have passed since I lost touch with my family. Everytime I think of separation from my parents, snivel drips onto my chest and sweat drenches my back. Would you go back with me?"

"Faerie and earth have separate roads," she said. "They cannot remain together. I cannot bear, for the sake of our marital love, to deny you the happiness of being at your parents'side. Give me time to think of a way." The scholar could not help but cry to hear her. His wife, too, heaved a sigh and said, "You cannot have it both ways!"

The next day when the scholar came back to the palace the dragon lord said to him: "I am told that you are homesick. How will it be if we have your baggage ready the first thing tomorrow morning?"

The scholar thanked him: "I was a solitary wanderer far from home until you made me your subject and lavished your favor and concern upon me. From the depths of my heart I feel a sincere wish to repay you. Let me go home to visit for a time; I will try to meet with you again."

When evening came, the girl had set out wine for a farewell. The scholar wanted to set a time to meet again, but she said, "The affinity that bound us together has run out." The scholar was deeply grieved.

"Go back and care for your parents," she said. "Show them what a filial son you are. The hundred years of a human life, with its meetings and partings, is like a single day. What is the good of whining like a child? From this day on I shall remain chaste for your sake, and you will be true to me in your thoughts. Though we will be in different places, our hearts will be as one, so we will still be husband and wife. We can grow old together without having to remain side by side day and night. If either of us transgresses this vow, heaven will not bless our marriage. If you worry that there is no one to do the housekeeping, you can take a maid. I have one more thing to tell you. After

夕相守，乃谓之偕老乎？若渝此盟，婚姻不吉。倘虑中馈乏人，纳婢可耳。更有一事相嘱：自奉裳衣，似有佳朕，烦君命名。”生曰：“其女耶，可名龙宫，男耶，可名福海。”女乞一物为信。生在罗刹国所得赤玉莲花一对，出以授女。女曰：“三年后四月八日，君当泛舟南岛，还君体胤。”女以鱼革为囊，实以珠宝，授生曰：“珍藏之，数世吃着不尽也。”天微明，王设祖帐，馈遗甚丰。生拜别出宫。女乘白羊车，送诸海涘。生上岸下马，女致声珍重，回车便去，少顷便远。海水复合，不可复见。生乃归。自浮海去，咸谓其已死；及至家，家人无不诧异。幸翁媪无恙，独妻已他适。乃悟龙女“守义”之言，盖已先知也。父欲为生再婚，生不可，纳婢焉。谨志三年之期，泛舟岛中。见两儿坐浮水面，拍流嬉笑，不动亦不沉。近引之。儿哑然捉生臂，跃入怀中。其

serving you all this time, I have noticed singns of a joyous event to come. Would you please give this child a name?"

"If the baby is a girl, name her Dragon-Palace; if it is a boy, name him Blessing-Sea," said the scholar.

His wife begged for a token of their vow. The scholar brought out a pair of red jade lotuses he had gotten in the Kingdom of Raksasas and gave them to her.

"Three year from now on the eighth day of the fourth month make sure to sail around South Island," she said. "I will return your flesh and blood to you." She filled a will return your flesh and blood to you." She filled a fish-skin pouch with pearls and gems, gave it to him and said," Keep this well. Your family can live off it for generations."

At the first faint light of dawn the king had a farewell party set up for the departure, and there bounteous gifts were heaped before the scholar. With a parting bow the scholar left the palace. The girl, riding in a cart drawn by white rams, saw him to the shore. He rode onto the beach and dismounted. She bid him farewell, then turned the cart around and left. In a few short moments, she was far away. The waters of the sea closed back together, hiding her from view.

Then the scholar started homeward. His voyage had lasted so long that everyone assumed him dead, but now, to his family's amazement, he turned up at home. Fortunately his parents were in good health, but his wife had married again. The meaning of the dragon girl's words "be true to me" finally became clear to him. She must have known of this already. The father wanted to arrange another marriage, but the scholar would not allow it and took a maid instead.

With the appointed time engraved in his mind, the scholar sailed to the island three years later. There he saw two children sitting afloat on the surface of the water. They were amusing themselves by splashing with their hands, yet this neither caused them to move nor to sink. He drew up to them and held out his hands. One child grabbed

一大啼,似嗔生之不援己者。亦引上之。细审之,一男一女,貌皆婉秀。额上花冠缀玉,则赤莲在焉。背有锦囊,拆视,得书云:"翁姑计各无恙。忽忽三年,红尘永隔;盈盈一水,青鸟难通。结想为梦,引领成劳,茫茫蓝蔚,有恨如何也!顾念奔月姮娥,且虚桂府;投梭织女,犹怅银河。我何人斯,而能永好,兴思及此,辄复破涕为笑。别后两月,竟得孪生。今已啁啾怀抱,颇解笑言;觅枣抓梨,不母可活。敬以还君。所贻赤玉莲花,饰冠作信。膝头抱儿时,犹妾在左右也。闻君克践旧盟,意愿斯慰。妾此生不二,之死靡他。奁中珍物,不蓄兰膏;镜里新妆,久辞粉黛。君似征

his wrist and jumped giggling into his arms. The other wailed as if vexed at the scholar for not lending a helping hand. This one too was lifted aboard. A closer look showed that one was a girl and the other a boy. Both had fair, appealing features. On their heads were coronets studded with jade; in the middle of each was one of the red lotuses. One of them bore a brocade pouch. The scholar opened it and found a letter which read:

"I trust that father and mother are in good health. Three years have gone by in a flash: the world of red dust is forever out of reach. The messenger is hard put to cross this great expanse water. Longing has taken shape as dreams: my neck is weary with gazing into the boundless blue. What good are my regrets? My thoughts now turn to Chang'e, who ran away to the moon only to spend a lone life of loneness in Cassia Mansion, and Weaving Maid, who once threw down her shuttle but to this day ruefully watches her lover from across the Milky Way. Who am I, that I should have everlasting love? Once this thought arises, tears give way to laughter. Two months after we parted, I was blessed, to my amazement, with twins. Now they are babbling in arms, and understand something of speech and laughter. They grab whatever fruits they see and can live without their mother's milk. Now I worshipfully return them to you. I have decorated their coronets with the red jade lotus flowers you gave me, as a token of the fulfillment of my vow. When you lift the children to your knees and embrace them, it will be like having me at your side. I felt comforted to hear that you are conscien-tiously observing your vow of yesteryear. I will be faithful to you all my life; unto death there will be no change. I no longer keep perfumed unguents within my trousseau, and the reflection in my mirror has long ago said farewell to powder and mascara. You are like a wayfarer, and I am the wayfarer's wife. But yet, though the lute and harp are left long unplayed, no one can say they do not harmonize. Now, I trust, my in-laws can be with their grandchil-

人,妾作荡妇,即置而不御,亦何得谓非琴瑟哉?独计翁姑亦既抱孙,曾未一觌新妇,揆之情理,亦属缺然。岁后阿姑窀穸,当往临穴,一尽妇职。过此以往,则'龙宫'无恙,不少把握之期;'福海'长生,或有往还之路。伏惟珍重,不尽欲言。"生反复省书揽涕。两儿抱颈曰:"归休乎!"生益恸,抚之曰:"儿知家在何许?"儿亟啼,呕哑言归。生望海水茫茫,极天无际,雾鬟人渺,烟波路穷。抱儿返棹,怅然遂归。生知母寿不永,周身物悉为预具,墓中植松槚百余。逾岁,媪果亡。灵舆至殡宫,有女子缞绖临穴。众方惊顾,忽而风激雷轰,继以急雨,转瞬间已失所在。松柏新植多枯,至是皆活。福海稍长,辄思其母,忽自投入海,

dren, though they have never met their daughter-in-law. Thinking of my duty to them, I cannot help feeling much regret. When the time comes for mother's interment, I will perform my duty by going to mourn at her tomb. Here's hoping that Dragon-Palace will henceforth remain in good health, and that I will not miss the chance to hold her in my arms. May Blessing-Sea live long and travel back and forth between us. Not having finished all that I wished to say, I entreat you to take good care of yourself." The scholar pored repeatedly over the letter, wiping tears from his eyes. His two children threw their arms around his neck, saying: "Oh please, let's go back!"

This only added to the scholar's misery. He caressed them and asked, "Do you children know how to find your home?" Their only answer was to burst into sobs and wail that they wanted to go home.

The scholar looked out over the boundless sea; as far as the eye could see stretched a ravelling mist devoid of human presence, a road leading nowhere through the foggy waves. He held his children close as he made for the ship, and returned in discouragement.

The scholar, knowing that his mother's days were num-bered, made ready her burial accoutrements beforehand and planted over a hundred pine and catalpa trees in the enclosure around her tomb. Sure enough, after a year passed, the old woman died. When the hearse reached the final resting place, a woman in hempen mourning clothes stood before the tomb. Suddenly, as the mourners stared in surprise, a fierce wind began to blow and thunder rumbled. This was followed by heavy rain. In the blink of an eye she was gone. Many of the pines and catalpas had died from being transplanted, but after this they all came to life.

As Blessing-Sea grew a little older he thought often of his mother. One day he was seen to throw himself into the sea, and he did not return till several days later. Dragon-Palace, being a girl, could not go, and so she cried in her room day after day. One day the light of

数日始还。龙宫以女子不得往,时掩户泣。一日,昼暝,龙女忽入,止之曰:“儿自成家,哭泣何为?”乃赐八尺珊瑚一树、龙脑香一帖、明珠百颗、八宝嵌金合一双,为作嫁资。生闻之,突入,执手啜泣。俄顷,疾雷破屋,女已无矣。

异史氏曰:“花面逢迎,世情如鬼。嗜痂之癖,举世一辙。‘小惭小好,大惭大好’;若公然带须眉以游都市,其不骇而走者,盖几希矣。彼陵阳痴子,将抱连城玉向何处哭也?呜呼!显荣富贵,当于蜃楼海市中求之耳!”

the sun dimmed; in an instant the dragon lord's daughter appeared and calmed her: "Someday you will have a family of your own. What good will crying do?" She gave her daughter a dowry consisting of an eight-foot tree of coral, a packet of borneol camphor, one hundred gleaming pearls and a pair of small gold boxes set with eight sorts of gems. Hearing her voice, the scholar burst into the room and took her by the hand, sobbing. In a moment a sharp clap of thunder shook the room, and she was gone.

The Chronicler of the Tales comments: "The ways of the world are no different from the ways of goblins: both would have us paint our faces to curry favor. When it comes to proclivities for eating scabs and such, the whole world is in the same rut. Moderately embarrassing actions receive moderate praise; greatly embarrassing actions receive great praise. If a person were to amble through a city with his true face exposed for all to see, few must be the ones who would not take to their heels in fright. Whose shoulder can the Fool of Lingyang cry on with his fabled jade worth fifteen cities? Alas! Glory and wealth can only be found in castles in the air and ocean bazaars."

促　织

宣德间，宫中尚促织之戏，岁征民间。此物故非西产；有华阴令欲媚上官，以一头进，试使斗而才，因责常供。令以责之里正。市中游侠儿，得佳者笼养之，昂其直，居为奇货。里胥猾黠，假此科敛丁口，每责一头，辄倾数家之产。邑有成名者，操童子业，久不售。为人迂讷，遂为猾胥报充里正役，百计营谋不能脱。不终岁，薄产累尽。会征促织，成不敢敛

THE CRICKET

DURING the Xuande reign period (1426-1435) of the Ming Dynasty cricket keeping was a popular amusement in the palace. The insects were levied annually from the populace. Live crickets were not originally a Shaanxi product until a magistrate in Huayin County who was anxious to win favor with his superiors presented one, which was tried in the ring and found to be an outstanding fighter. From then on Huayin county was charged with providing crickets to the court regularly. The magistrate delegated the responsibility to the headman in each ward. Young idlers in the marketplace kept the best of them in cages, forcing prices up by cornering the market. Cunning ward administrators used this as an excuse to impose a head tax on the peasants. For every cricket that was requisitioned, several families were driven into bankruptcy.

In the district there was a man named Cheng Ming, a long unsuccessful candidate for the Bachelor of Letters degree. The crafty ward administrator, seeing that Cheng was impractical and slow of speech, recommended him for the position of headman. Cheng made numerous frtile attempts to free himself from the obligations of this office. Before a year had passed his meager resources were used up. Then came

户口，而又无所赔偿，忧闷欲死。妻曰："死何裨益？不如自行搜觅，冀有万一之得。"成然之。早出暮归，提竹筒铜丝笼，于败堵丛草处，探石发穴，靡计不施，迄无济；即捕得三两头，又劣弱不中于款。宰严限追比；旬余，杖至百，两股间脓血流离，并虫亦不能行捉矣。转侧床头，惟思自尽。时村中来一驼背巫，能以神卜。成妻具资诣问。见红女白婆，填塞门户。入其舍，则密室垂帘，帘外设香几。问者爇香于鼎，再拜。巫从傍望空代祝，唇吻翕辟，不知何词。各各竦立以听。少间，帘内掷一纸出，即道人意中事，无毫发爽。成妻纳钱案上，焚拜如前人。食顷，帘动，片纸抛落。拾视之，非字而画。中绘殿阁，类兰若；后小

the cricket levy. Cheng did not dare collect money from the households, nor could he fulfil the duty out of his own funds. He was so despondent he wanted to kill himself.

"What good would killing yourself do?" said his wife. "It would be better to look for a cricket yourself. There is a slight chance you might find one."

This made sense to Cheng. He went out in the mornings and returned at nightfall, bamboo pail and wire cage in hand, poking under stones and opening burrows amid crumbling walls and thick growths of grass. There was nothing he did not try, but it was no use. The few that he did manage to catch were too puny to fit the regulations. The magistrate's deadline was rigorously enforced, and he was given a total of a hundred strokes with a cane over a period of ten days. Blood and puss oozed from his buttocks and, what was worse, he was unable to go looking for the insects at all. He tossed and turned on his bed, his mind filled with thoughts of suicide.

It was then that a hunchbacked shamaness who perfromed divinations with the help of a spirit-familiar came to the village. Cheng's wife scraped up a sum of money and went to call on her. Smartly dressed young women and white-haired old ladies were milling around the door. Inside the house was a curtained-off sanctum, with an altar standing outside the curtain. Petitioners lit incense in the censer and kowtowed twice, while the shamaness stood to one side looking off into space and pronouncing an invocation for them, her lips contorted with unintelligible mutterings. Everyone stood stiffly listening until shortly a piece of paper, bearing a message that dealt with the petitioner's troubles, was thrown out from within the curtain. The messages were never off by a hair.

Cheng's wife placed her money on the table, lit incense, and kowtowed like those before. After the time it takes to eat a meal passed by, the curtain moved and a slip of paper was tossed out onto

山下，怪石乱卧，针针丛棘，青麻头伏焉；旁一蟆，若将跳舞。展玩不可晓。然睹促织，隐中胸怀。折藏之，归以示成。成反复自念，得无教我猎虫所耶？细瞻景状，与村东大佛阁真逼似。乃强起扶杖，执图诣寺后。有古陵蔚起；循陵而走，见蹲石鳞鳞，俨然类画。遂于蒿莱中，侧听徐行，似寻针芥；而心目耳力俱穷，绝无踪响。冥搜未已，一癞头蟆猝然跃去。成益愕，急逐趁之。蟆入草间。蹑迹披求，见有虫伏棘根；遽扑之，入石穴中。掭以尖草，不出；以筒水灌之，始出。状极俊健。逐而得之。审视，巨身修尾，青项金翅。大

the ground. Picking it up, she saw not words but a drawing depicting a group of buildings, apparently those of a monastery. Behind it at the foot of a hill was a jumble of odd-looking boulders. There, at the edge of a dense bramble thicket, crouched a shiny black cricket. Beside it was a toad that seemed to be on the point of leaping. She spread the drawing out and pored over it, unable to make out its meaning. Still the cricket was just what she had been looking for. She folded the paper up, tucked it away and took it back to show Cheng who, after much reflection, wondered if the picture were not telling him where to hunt for a cricket. Careful scrutiny of the scene in the drawing revealed a close resemblance to the Great Buddha Abbey east of the village.

Cheng dragged himself out of bed, propped himself up with a cane and proceeded, drawing in hand, to the rear of the monastery. The overgrown ruins of an ancient tomb stood before him. Following the edge of the tomb, he saw boulders squatting one on top of the other like fish scales, precisely as in the drawing. He walked slowly through a jungle of weeds, cocking his head to catch the slightest sound and looking for all the world as if he were searching for a needle or a mustard seed. He could no longer maintain the intentness of eyes, ears and mind, but he had not yet seen or heard a cricket. He was still groping about, when suddenly to his great amazement a wart-headed toad leapt from underfoot. He stayed close behind it as it ducked into a dense growth of grass. He stepped gingerly into the grass, spreading the blades apart with his hands to get a better look. There, crouching at the base of a bramble-bush was an insect. He hurriedly grabbed for it, but it ducked into a hole in the stones. He poked at it with a sharp blade of grass, but it would not come out. Finally, by pouring water from his bucket into the hole, he was able to flush the robust-looking cricket out. He gave chase and caught it. A closer look showed it to have a thick torso, a long tail, a blue-green neck and metallic wings.

喜，笼归。举家庆贺，虽连城拱璧不啻也。上于盆而养之，蟹白栗黄，备极护爱，留待限期，以塞官责。成有子九岁，窥父不在，窃发盆。虫跃掷径出，迅不可捉。及扑入手，已股落腹裂，斯须就毙。儿惧，啼告母。母闻之，面色灰死，大骂曰："业根！死期至矣！而翁归，自与汝覆算耳！"儿涕而出。未几成归，闻妻言，如被冰雪。怒索儿，儿渺然不知所往；既得其尸于井。因而化怒为悲，抢呼欲绝。夫妻向隅，茅舍无烟，相对默然，不复聊赖。日将暮，取儿藁葬。近抚之，气息惙然。喜寘榻上，半夜复苏。夫妻心稍慰。但蟋蟀笼虚，顾之则气断声吞，亦不敢复究儿，自昏达曙，目不交

Great was Cheng's joy as he put it in the cage and returned home.

The whole family rejoiced as if he had found a treasure more precious than the legendary piece of jade to the worth of fifteen cities. They put it in a basin and nourished it on crab meat and chestnuts, going to every extreme to give it the best of care. They planned to keep it until the deadline, when Cheng would use it to discharge his official duty.

But one day Cheng's nine-year-old son, seeing that his father was out, furtively lifted the lid off the basin. The cricket hopped straight out, so quickly that the boy could not grab it. He jumped and caught it in his hand, breaking off a leg and cracking its abdomen. In a few short moments it was dead. The terrified boy ran crying to tell his mother. Her face paled to the hue of ashes at what she heard.

"A bad seed, that's what you are!" she cursed him loudly, "Your day of doom will not be long now! When your father comes home he'll settle accounts with you." The boy ran out sniveling. Cheng soon returned. When his wife told him what had happened, it was as if a heap of freezing snow had been dumped on his head. He called angrily for his son but the boy was nowhere to be seen. Soon afterwards, they found his body in a well. Cheng's rage turned to sorrow. Stricken half-dead with grief, he struck his head on the ground and cried out to heaven. Husband and wife went inside and each turned their sobbing faces toward separate corners. No cooking fire was lit in their thatched hut that night. They had come to their wit's end and could only stare only stare dumbly at one another. As the day drew to an end, they prepared to wrap their son in a grass mat for burial. Touching him, they found that he was now breathing haltingly. Joyfully they placed him on the bed. In the middle of the night he regained consciousness, which relieved his parents somewhat, but his breath came in gasps and he had the vacant look of a sleepwalker. Looking at the empty cricket cage was enough to rob them of breath and make their

睫。东曦既驾，僵卧长愁。忽闻门外虫鸣，惊起觇视，虫宛然尚在。喜而捕之。一鸣辄跃去，行且速。覆之以掌，虚若无物；手裁举，则又超忽而跃。急趁之。折过墙隅，迷其所往。徘徊四顾，见虫伏壁上。审谛之，短小，黑赤色，顿非前物。成以其小，劣之。惟彷徨瞻顾，寻所逐者。壁上小虫，忽跃落衿袖间。视之，形若土狗，梅花翅，方首长胫，意似良。喜而收之。将献公堂，惴惴恐不当意，思试之斗以觇之。村中少年好事者，驯养一虫，自名"蟹壳青"，日与子弟角，无不胜。欲居之以为利；而高其直，亦无售者。径造庐访成。视成所蓄，掩口胡卢而笑。因出己虫，纳比笼中。

voices die in their throats, but they dared not question their son again. Their eyes did not close for the whole night. When the sun in the esat began its course through the heavens they lay down stiffly, brooding sleep-lessly.

Suddenly there was a chirping outside their door. They got up in amazement to observe: there was the cricket looking as sound as ever. Jumping for joy, they ran to catch it, but it gave a chirp and hopped rapidly away. Cheng covered it with a cupped hand, but he seemed to have grasped nothing but thin air. As soon as he lifted his hand the cricket leapt swiftly out from under it. He followed it closely, but lost it when it rounded the corner of a wall. As he walked about distractedly, looking all around him, he saw a cricket crouching on the wall. A careful look showed that it was short, small and reddish-black in color -certainly not the one he had been chasing. It was worthless to him because of its small size. He went on walking aimlessly and staring in all directions for the one he had been chasing. All of a sudden the little cricket jumped off the wall and landed on the side of his robe. It was built like a mole cricket, with finely veined wings, a square head and long neck. It impressed him as a good specimen, so he was glad to keep it. His plan was to present it at the yamen, but the thought that it might not meet the magistrate's expectations made him shudder, so he decided to observe how it would perform in a fight.

A young man known as a busybody in the village was keeping a cricket which he had named Crabshell Blue. He matched it daily with the crickets of other young men, and it was always emerged victorious. He was holding onto it until he could turn a nice profit, but nobody would pay the high price he asked. One day this young man went to Cheng's house for a visit. Seeing the cricket Cheng was keeping, he had to stifle a laugh with his hand. He took out his cricket and put it into the cage. Cheng was discomfited at the sight of its huge build. He dared not pick up the gauntlet, but the young man insisted. It oc-

成视之,庞然修伟,自增惭怍,不敢与较。少年固强之。顾念蓄劣物终无所用,不如拚博一笑。因合纳斗盆。小虫伏不动,蠢若木鸡。少年又大笑。试以猪鬣毛,撩拨虫须,仍不动。少年又笑。屡撩之,虫暴怒,直奔,遂相腾击,振奋作声。俄见小虫跃起,张尾伸须,直龁敌领。少年大骇,解令休止。虫翘然矜鸣,似报主知。成大喜。方共瞻玩,一鸡瞥来,径进以啄。成骇立愕呼。幸啄不中,虫跃去尺有咫;鸡健进,逐逼之,虫已在爪下矣。成仓猝莫知所救,顿足失色。旋见鸡伸颈摆扑;临视,则虫集冠上,力叮不释。成益惊喜,掇置笼中。翼日进宰。宰见其小,怒诃成。成述其异。宰不信。试与他虫斗,虫尽靡;又试之鸡,果如成言。乃赏成,献诸抚军。抚军大悦,以金笼进上,细疏其能。既入宫中举天下所贡蝴蝶、螳螂、油利挞、青丝额,……一切异状,遍试之,无出其右者,每闻琴瑟之声,则

curred to Cheng that keeping an inferior specimen would be useless anyway, and that he might as well set his cricket against the other for a laugh. Both insects were placed in a fighting basin. The small one crouched motionless, looking as foolish as a wooden chicken. The young man guffawed once more as he used a boar bristle to poke at the cricket's antennae. Still it did not move, provoking the young man into another burst of laughter. He prodded it repeatedly. The insect exploded with rage and ran at its opponent. They attacked one another with flying leaps, rousing themselves to battle with defiant chirps. In an instant the small cricket jumped up, its antennae and tail stiffly erect, and bit down on its opponent's neck. The frightened young man pulled them apart and put an end to the fight. The small cricket drew itself up and chirped proudly, as if it were reporting victory to its master.

Cheng was overjoyed. As he and his guests were admiring the winner, a chicken caught sight of it, ran over and delivered a peck at the small cricket. Cheng stood there numb with dread and cried out in alarm. Luckily the chicken's beak had missed its mark; the cricket leaped a foot and some inches away. The chicken lunged forward and bore down upon it. Before Cheng could come to its rescue, the insect was under the chicken's claws; he turned pale and stamped his feet helplessly. But in the next moment he saw the chicken stretching its neck and flut-tering about. Much to his amazed delight upon closer inspection, he found the criket hanging tenaciously onto the fowl's comb. He picked it up, put it in its cage and presented it to the magistrate the next day.

The magistrate berated Cheng angrily for bringing such a puny cricket, nor was he convinced by Cheng's account of the cricket's extraordinary prowess. The cricket was tried in the ring against others of its kind: all were vanquished. When it was tried against a chicken the outcome confirmed Cheng's story. The magistrate thereupon re-

应节而舞。益奇之。上大嘉悦，诏赐抚臣名马衣缎。抚军不忘所自，无何，宰以“卓异”闻。宰悦，免成役。又嘱学使，俾入邑庠。后岁余，成子精神复旧。自言身化促织，轻捷善斗，今始苏耳。抚军亦厚赉成。不数岁，田百顷，楼阁万椽，牛羊蹄躈各千计。一出门，裘马过世家焉。

异史氏曰：“天子偶用一物，未必不过此已忘；而奉行者即为定例。加以官贪吏虐，民日贴妇卖儿，更无休止。故天子一跬步，皆关

warded him and presented the cricket to the provincial governor. The governor, greatly delighted, presented it to the emperor in a golden cage along with a memorial detailing its abilities.

After the champion was taken into the palace, all sorts of unusual crickets, such as "butterflies," "mantises," "oily beaters" and "silky green foreheads" were tried against it, but none could get the better of it. When it heard the music of lutes and zithers it hopped to the beat, which made people marvel at it all the more. The emperor was so pleased that he called for the provincial governor and gave him thoroughbred horses and satins for clothing. The governor did not forget the source of his good fortune: before long word was going around that the magistrate was an "outstanding" official. The delighted magistrate released Cheng from his duties as headman and instructed the civil examiner to grant him admission to the district academy.

A little more than a year later Cheng's son regained his faculties, claiming that he had been transformed into an agile, combative cricket and that today his soul had finally re-entered his body. The provincial governor rewarded Cheng generously. Within a few years Cheng possessed 1, 500 acres of fields; pavilions and storied buidings in such number that thousands of rafters had been used to roof them over; and sheep and horses numbering in the hundreds. The furs he wore and the horses he rode when he went out could not have been equalled by an aristocratic family.

The Chronicler of the Tales comments: "The emperor may use something once on a whim and give it no more thought, but for the people who carry out his wishes it becomes a fixed article of tribute. With the greed of officials and the cruelty of administrators on top of this, there is no end to hardships which make peasants give up their wives and sell their children. Thus every time the emperor takes a step the lives of the people are affected. There is no room for carelessness. Cheng's case was unique: after being reduced to poverty by

民命,不可忽也。独是成氏子以蠹贫,以促织富,裘马扬扬。当其为里正、受扑责时,岂意其至此哉!天将以酬长厚者,遂使抚臣、令尹,并受促织恩荫。闻之:一人飞升,仙及鸡犬。信夫!"

the depradations of corrupt officials, a criket brought him wealth enough to go about flaunting furs and fine horses. Back in the days when he was beaten for failing to fulfill his duties as headman, how could he have foreseen that such a fortune was in store for him? Heaven made the provincial governor and magistrate enjoy the benefits of the cricket's favor as a means of rewarding one man's honesty. When the Taoist master in the old story perfected the elixir and rose to heaven, immortality redounded even to his dogs and chickens. There is much truth in this!"

姊妹易嫁

掖县相国毛公，家素微。其父常为人牧牛。时邑世族张姓者，有新阡在东山之阳。或经其侧，闻墓中叱咤声曰："若等速避去，勿久溷贵人宅！"张闻，亦未深信。既又频得梦警曰："汝家墓地，本是毛公佳城，何得久假此？"由是家数不利。客劝徙葬吉，张听之，徙焉。一日，相国父牧，出张家故墓，猝遇雨，匿身废圹中。已而雨益倾盆，潦水奔穴，崩洵灌注，遂溺以死。相国时尚孩童。母自诣张，愿

SISTERS SWITCH PLACES

MASTER Mao, the prime minister from Ye county, was born of a humble family. His father often tended cows for other people. At one time the Zhangs, a noble family of the district, had a new family gravesite south of East Mountain. Someone passing by the grounds heard a scolding voice from inside the grave say, "Clear out now, all of you. Don't keep defiling a nobleman's house!" Zhang learned of this and did not give it much credence, but then he had recurring dreams of a voice that warned, "Your family cemetery was intended to be Master Mao's grave-yard. Why do you keep using it?" After this the Zhang family's fortunes declined. A retainer urged them to move the body to a more auspicious site. Zhang complied with his suggestion and had the body reburied.

One day the father of the future prime minister was tending cows beside the Zhangs' vacant gravesite when he was caught in a sudden rain and took shelter in the empty vault. Soon the rain became a steady downpour. The crashing torrent of a flash flood poured into the vault and drowned the unfortunate man. The prime minister was still a child at the time. His mother called on Zhang and begged for a few feet of ground in which to bury the boy's father. Zhang was greatly amazed

丐咫尺地，掩儿父。张徵知其姓氏，大异之。行视溺死所，俨然当置棺处，又益骇。乃使就故圹窆焉。且令携若儿来。葬已，母偕儿诣张谢。张一见，辄喜，即留其家，教之读，以齿子弟行。又请以长女妻儿。母骇不敢应。张妻云："既已有言，奈何中改?"卒许之。然此女甚薄毛家，怨惭之意，形于言色。有人或道及，辄掩其耳。每向人曰："我死不从牧牛儿!"及亲迎，新郎入宴，彩舆在门；而女掩袂向隅而哭。催之妆，不妆；劝之亦不解。俄而新郎告行，鼓乐大作，女犹眼零雨而首飞蓬也。父止婿，自入劝女。女涕若罔闻。怒而逼之，益哭失声。父无奈之。又有家人传白："新郎欲行。"父急出，言："衣妆未竟，乞郎少停待。"即又奔入视女，往来者无停履。迁延

to learn that their family name was Mao. He was even more shocked when he went to examine the spot of the drowning and found it was precisely where one of his family coffins had previously been situated. He gave permission for the man to be buried in the old vault and told the woman to bring her son to his house.

After the burial mother and son called on Zhang to thank him. Zhang took an immediate liking to the boy and invited him to stay at his house. The boy was taught to read and treated as one of the family. Later Zhang offered to give the young man his elder daughter's hand in marriage, but the mother was too intimidated to accept.

"Now that we have made the offer, why should we go back on it?" said Zhang's wife.

The betrothal was thus settled. The bride-to-be, however, despised Mao's family. Chagrin and disdain were evident in her every word and expression. When anyone spoke to her of the marriage, she would cover her ears with her hands. She invariably told people: "I would rather die than be the wife of a cowherd's son."

The day came for the groom to receive the bride. The groom went in to the Zhangs' banquet, leaving the bridal carriage at the gate, but the girl hid her face in her sleeves and turned weeping toward a corner. Her relatives pressed her to dress, but she would not. None of their appeals could move her. Soon the groom announced that it was time to go. A loud fanfare was sounded. The girl's face was wet with tears and her hair as disorderly as a tumbleweed. The father kept his son-in-law from leaving and went in to urge his daughter. She went on crying as if his words did not register. In his anger he tried to force her, but she cried until her voice grew hoarse. There was nothing father could do about it. Just then a servant came in and informed them: "The groom is about to leave."

The father rushed out and said, "She hasn't finished dressing: I beg you to stay and wait a bit longer," then ran back in to look after

少时,事愈急,女终无回意。父无计,周张欲自死。其次女在侧,颇非其姊,苦逼劝之。姊怒曰:“小妮子,亦学人喋聒!尔何不从他去?”妹曰:“阿爷原不曾以妹子属毛郎;若以妹子属毛郎,更何须姊姊劝驾也。”父以其言慷爽,因与伊母窃议,以次易长。母即向女曰:“忤逆婢不遵父母命,欲以儿代若姊,儿肯之否?”女慨然曰:“父母教儿往也,即乞丐不敢辞;且何以见毛家郎便终饿莩死乎?”父母闻其言,大喜,即以姊妆妆女,仓猝登车而去。入门,夫妇雅敦逑好。然女素病赤鬝,稍稍介公意。久之,浸知易嫁之说,由是益以知己德女。居无何,公补博士弟子,应秋闱试。道经王舍人店,店主人先一夕梦神曰:“旦日当有

his daughter. By scurrying ceaselessly back and forth he managed to stall for a while. The matter was drawing to a head, but the girl would not reconsider. The father had reached his wit's end: he looked wildly about him, wishing he were dead. His younger daughter, who stood beside him, spoke critically to her sister and did her best to pressure and persuade her.

"So now you are mouthing other people's drivel, you little flunky!" the elder sister spat out angrily. "Why don't you go off with him?"

"Father did not give me to Master Mao," said her sister. "If he had, I wouldn't need any urging from you."

Hearing her unabashed words, the father quietly proposed to his wife that the two sisters switch places. The mother turned to her younger daughter and said, "This insolent chambermaid will not obey her parents. We would like you to take her place. Would you be willing?"

The girl accepted readily: "Now that you have told me to go, I would not refuse even if he were a beggar. Anyway, what reason is there to suppose that the young master of the Mao family is doomed to starve to death?"

The father and mother were overjoyed to hear their daughter's words. After they dressed her in her elder sister's finery, she hurriedly climbed into the carriage and left. Once home, husband and wife gracefully consummated their union. However, the girl suffered from chronic *favus* of the scalp, a disfigurement that preyed ever so slightly on Master Mao's mind. As time went by, he came to learn that his present wife had taken the place of his intended bride which made him appreciate her all the more for recognizing his true worth.

Before long Mao was entered on the roll of Attending Scholars which qualified him to take part in the autumn provincial examinations. His road there took him past the Master Wang Inn, where the

毛解元来，后且脱汝于厄。”以故晨起，专伺察东来客。及得公，甚喜。供具殊丰善，不索直；特以梦兆厚自托。公亦颇自负。私以细君发鬑鬑，虑为显者笑，富贵后，念当易之。已而晓榜既揭，竟落孙山，咨嗟蹇步，懊惋丧志。心赧旧主人，不敢复由王舍，以他道归。后三年，再赴试，店主人延候如初。公曰：“尔言初不验，殊惭祗奉。”主人曰：“秀才以阴欲易妻，故被冥司黜落，岂妖梦不足以践？”公愕而问故，盖别后复梦而云。公闻之，惕然悔惧，木立若偶。主人谓：“秀才宜自爱，终当作解首。”未几，果举贤书第一人。夫人发亦寻

innkeeper had dreamt the night before of a spirit that said to him, "Tomorrow a Head Master of Letters Mao will come: someday he will deliver you from calamity." And so the host rose with the sun and watched for a traveller from the east. Great was his delight when he saw Master Mao at last. He received his guest with generous fare and services without asking for payment. Instead, he threw himself upon Master Mao's willingness to do as the dream had foretold. The latter, for his part, began to have a rather high opinion of himself.

Concerned that his wife, with her straggly hair, might be laughed at by people of high society, he decided to abandon her for another woman when his fortune was made. Later, the examination results were posted, but his name was nowhere on the list. He stumbled away moaning and cursing in frustration, his strength of will obliterated by remorse. The mere thought of his onetime host made his face turn crimson, so he went home by a different route, not daring to pass by the Master Wang Inn.

Three years later when he went to take part in the examinations a second time, the innkeeper extended the same hospitality as before.

"Your hospitality is especially embarrassing because the truth of your words has not yet been borne out," said Master Mao.

"You had a secret wish to change your wife for another." replied the innkeeper. "That is why the officials of the unseen worldstruck your name from the rolls. Do not think for a minute that my prophetic dream was false. The amazed Mao asked for an explanation and learned that after their last parting the innkeeper had had another dream in which this revelation was made. Upon hearing this Mao was shot through with dread and grief: he stood in numb immobility, like a puppet.

"It behooves you, Bachelor of Letters, to maintain your self-respect: then you will eventually take top honors."

Before long Mao did indeed win first place among the successful

长，云鬟委绿，转更增媚。姊适里中富室儿，意气颇自高。夫荡惰，家渐陵夷，空舍无烟火。闻妹为孝廉妇，弥增惭怍。姊妹辄避路而行。又无何，良人卒，家落。顷之，公又擢进士。女闻，刻骨自恨，遂忿然废身为尼。及公以宰相归，强遣女行者诣府谒问，冀有所贻。比至，夫人馈以绮縠罗绢若干匹，以金纳其中，而行者不知也。携归见师。师失所望，恚曰："与我金钱，尚可作薪米费，此等仪物，我何须尔！"遂令将回。公及夫人疑之。及启视而金具在，方悟见却之意。发金笑曰："汝师百余金尚不能任，焉有福泽从我老尚书也。"遂以五十金付尼去，曰："将去作尔师用

provincial candidates. His wife's hair, too grew out rapidly. Her cloudlike tresses, coiled and gleaming, added much to her charms.

Her elder sister married the son of a wealthy family in the neighborhood—a match over which she became puffed up with self-importance. But her husband was a wastrel and a no-account who brought his family by degrees to ruin. They soon found themselves living in an empty house with no fire in the hearth. News that her younger sister was now the wife of a Master of Letters only intensified her humiliation. She took pains to avoid meeting her younger sister on the street. Not long afterwards her husband died, leaving his family destitute. After a time, when she learned that Master Mao had taken the Doctorate of Letter, she was shot through to the very bones with such self-loathing that she bitterly parted with secular life and became a nun.

Master Mao returned home holding the rank of prime minister, whereupon the elder sister ordered one of her disciples to pay a call at his mansion, hoping for a present. When she got there, the lady of the house presented as gifts a few bolts each of twilled silk, crepe, gauze and raw silk. Unbeknownst to the messenger she slipped gold in among them. The messenger carried them back to her mistress, whose high hopes were dashed.

"If they had given me money, I could have spent it on wood and rice," she said in disappointment. "What good are presents like these?" She had them taken back. The prime minister and his wife wondered why their gifts had been turned down until they unrolled the cloth and found the gold still there.

Mao uncovered the gold and said laughingly: "Even a hundred or so taels of gold was too much for your mistress: no wonder she did not have the good fortune to pair up with an old minister like myself!" Then he sent off the messenger with fifty taels of gold, saying: "Taken this back to use for your mistress'living expenses. I am afraid that more gold would be too much of a burden for a person of her scant

度;多,恐福薄人难承荷也。"行者归,具以告。师默然自叹,念平生所为,辄自颠倒,美恶避就,繄岂由人耶?后店主人以人命事逮系囹圄,公为力解释罪。

异史氏曰:"张公故墓,毛氏佳城,斯已奇矣。余闻时人有'大姨夫作小姨夫,前解元为后解元'之戏,此岂慧黠者所能较计邪?呜呼!彼苍者天久不可问,何至毛公,其应如响?"

blessings."

After the messenger returned, she told all of this to her mistress, who gave a quiet sign and reflected that throughout her life the results of her actions had been the opposite of her intentions. Alas-people may attempt to seek the blessings and avoid evils, can they be sure it is up to them?

Later the innkeeper was arrested in connection with a murder case and thrown in jail. Master Mao used his influence to gain his release and have the charges against him dropped.

The Chronicler of the Tales comments: "The old burial grounds of Master Zhang became a final resting place for the Mao family: this in itself is already strange. As the current saying has it: "The elder sister's bridegroom marries the younger sister: This year's top examinee has to wait another three years. Such twists of fortune cannot be traced even by the clever-witted, can they? Ah well! The blue heaven above has long held itself aloof from men's pleas. Why, when Master Mao came along, did it respond with as unfailingly as an echo?"

续黄粱

福建曾孝廉，高捷南宫时，与二三新贵，遨游郊郭。偶闻毗卢禅院，寓一星者，因并骑往诣问卜。入揖而坐。星者见其意气，稍佞谀之。曾摇箑微笑，便问："有蟒玉分否？"星者正容许二十年太平宰相。曾大悦，气益高。值小雨，乃与游侣避雨僧舍。舍中一老僧，深目高鼻，坐蒲团上，偃蹇不为礼。众一举手登

SEQUEL TO THE "YELLOW MILLET DREAM"

When Master of Letters Zeng of Fujian placed highly in the doctoral examination held at South Palace, he and a few other newly successful examinees went on an excursion to the outskirts of the city. Rumor had it that an astrologer was staying at the Contemplative Priory of Vairocana, so they rode there together to ask their fortunes. They bowed with folded hands on entering and then took their seats. The astrologer took note of their smugness and proceeded to flatter them with what they wished to hear. Zeng waved his fan and grinned as he listened and hear. Zeng waved his fan and grinned as he listened and then asked, "Does my future hold a python robe and jade sash pendants?" The diviner assured him with a straight face that he would hold the prime ministership for twenty peaceful years. Zeng was overjoyed and ever more pleased with himself.

Just then a small rainstorm came along, so Zeng and his companions took shelter in the monk's quarters. There on a rush mat sat an old monk with deepset eyes and aquiline nose, indifferent to their presence. The group raised their hands in greeting, then sat on the couches and began to converse among themselves. They all congratu-

榻自话，群以宰相相贺。曾心气殊高，指同游曰："某为宰相时，推张年丈作南抚，家中表为参、游，我家老苍头亦得小千把，于愿足矣。"一坐大笑。俄闻门外雨益倾注，曾倦伏榻间，忽见有二中使，赍天子手诏，召曾太师决国计。曾得意疾趋入朝。天子前席，温语良久。命三品以下，听其黜陟；即赐蟒玉名马。曾被服稽拜以出。入家，则非旧所居第，绘栋雕榱，穷极壮丽。自亦不解，何以遽至于此。然捻髯微呼，则应诺雷动。俄而公卿赠海物，伛偻足恭者，叠出其门。六卿来，倒屣而迎；侍郎辈，揖与语；下此者，颔之而已。晋抚馈女乐十人，皆是好女子。其尤者为袅袅，为仙

lated Zeng on his imminent prime-ministership, causing him to be carried away with himself. Turning to the companions, he said, "When I am prime minister I will recommend my classmate Zhang, here to be Governor of the Southern Provinces; my cousins will be staff officers; and even the grey-haired servants in my house will be adjutants—then I will be satisfied." All present burst into loud guffaws.

Just then they heard the rain begin to pour down harder outside. Already tired, Zeng lay down on the couch. Suddenly two palace messengers appeared before him bearing an edict handwritten by the emperor himself summoning Grand Tutor Zeng to give counsel on state affairs. Zeng rushed to court in great high spirits. The emperor sat eagerly on the edge of his throne during their long, intimate conversation. He decreed that all officials of the third grade and below were subject to dismissal or promo-tion as Zeng saw fit. He then presented Zeng with a python robe, a jade sash-pendant and a thoroughbred horse. Zeng donned the robe, pressed his forehead reverently to the floor and made his exit.

He went to his house and found it was not the one he had left that morning. Now he was surrounded by painted beams and carved refters in a mansion of extreme magnificence. He did not understand how all of this had come about so quickly. When he so much as stroked his whiskers or make a sound, the chorus of responses from his followers was like thunder. Soon there was a steady stream of noblemen and high ministers at his door bearing gifts of seafood and hunching their backs in deference. If one of the six high ministers came, Zeng would rise so hastily to greet them that he could barely put his slippers on straight; to vice ministers he bowed with folded hands and made conversation; but to anyone lower than that he gave nothing more than a nod. The governor of Shanxi presented him with ten female entertainers, all fine women. The best among them were Willowette and Flutter, both of whom he favored with special regard. On days when he

仙,二人尤蒙宠顾。科头休沐,日事声歌。一日,念微时尝得邑绅王子良周济我,今置身青云,渠尚蹉跎仕路,何不一引手?早旦一疏,荐为谏议,即奉俞旨,立行擢用。又念郭太仆曾睚眦我,即传吕给谏及侍御陈昌等,授以意旨;越日,弹章交至,奉旨削职以去。恩怨了了,颇快心意。偶出郊衢,醉人适触卤簿,即遣人缚付京尹,立毙杖下。接第连阡者,皆畏势献沃产。自此富可埒国。无何而袅袅、仙仙,以次殂谢,朝夕遐想。忽忆曩年见东家女绝美,每思购充媵御,辄以绵薄违宿愿,今日

lounged bareheaded at home, bathing or relaxing, the two of them stayed at his side singing songs.

One day Zeng recalled how he had been helped through a difficult period by Wang Ziliang, one of the gentry in his district. "Now I am up here in the clouds," thought Zeng, "while he is still mired down along the road to advancement. Why don't I give him a hand?" The first thing next morning Zeng handed up a memorial recommending next morning Zeng handed up a memorial recommending Wang as a counselor. An edict was then issued for Wang's immediate promotion.

Again Zeng recalled that Master-Steward Guo had once given him a dirty look. He lost no time in calling Imperial Advisor Lu, Censor Chen Chang and a few others before him and communicating his wish to them. The next day letters of accusation flooded in from all quarters. An edict was issued by the emperor ordering that the culprit be stripped of official rank and sent out of the capital.

Zeng found it quite pleasurable to pay off his old grudges and debts of gratitude. Once, as he made his way along a thoroughfare on the outskirts of the city, a drunk was found in the way of his retinue procession. Zeng ordered his underlings to bind the man and hand him over to the metropolitan prefect, where summary execution was carried out by beating the man to death. People who owned land adjacent to Zeng's houses and fields offered him fertile acreage and property out of fear of his power. Henceforth he had wealth enough to rival the resources of a kingdom.

Later Willowette and Flutter passed away, one after another, and Zeng's mind was filled morning and night with straying thoughts. Suddenly he remembered the time, years ago, when he had seen the daughter of his neighbors to the east and found her beautiful beyond compare. He had often thought of buying her as a concubine, but his wish had been denied because of his meagre wealth. Now that he was fortunate enough to have the wherewithal for realizing his aim, he

幸可适志。乃使干仆数辈，强纳资于其家。俄顷，滕舆舁至，则较昔之望见时，尤艳绝也。自顾生平，于愿斯足。又逾年，朝士窃窃，似有腹非之者。然各为立仗马；曾亦高情盛气，不以置怀。有龙图学士包上疏，其略曰："窃以曾某，原一饮赌无赖，市井小人。一言之合，荣膺圣眷，父紫儿朱，恩宠为极。不思捐躯摩顶，以报万一；反恣胸臆，擅作威福。可死之罪，擢发难数！朝廷名器，居为奇货，量缺肥瘠，为价重轻。因而公卿将士，尽奔走于门下，估计夤缘，俨如负贩，仰息望尘，不可算数。或有杰士贤臣，不肯阿附，轻则置之闲

sent several capable servants to force a marriage payment on the family. Before long they re-turned bearing a wicker sedan chair. The girl was even more stunning than when he had caught sight of her in the past. Looking back over his life thus far, he was sure that the girl marked the complete fulfillment of his wishes.

As the year passed, courtiers began to whisper among themselves: some seemed in wardly opposed to Zeng, but all were like palace horses trained to stand stock-still on guard. Zeng was too wrapped up in his arrogance and sense of power to let it bother him.

Then a scholar from the Hall of Dragon Symbols sent up a memorial that went something like this:

It is this writer's humble opinion that Zeng was originally no more than a gambler and a drunk—a rascal straight out of the marketplace. Owing to a single agreeable conversation, he was honored with Your Majesty's sagely regard. His father was clothed in ministerial purple and his son in official crimson: such were the extremes of generosity and favor Your Majesty showered on him. But he gives no thought to sacrificing himself in weary toil to repay even one ten-thousandth of Your Majesty's kindness. On the contrary he indulges his whims and tyranically a buses the powers he has arrogated to himself. All the hairs on a person's head are hardly enough to count his capital offenses! He monopolizes the offices of the Imperial Court as if they were commodities for speculation, assessing vacancies according to their potential for gain and fixing their prices accordingly. That is why dukes, ministers, generals, and scholars flock to his door and scheme to establish connections with him in such blatantly mercenary fashion. Innumerable are the people who wait in suspense for his every breath and gaze after the dust trail he leaves behind. Some outstanding scholars and worthy counselors will not today to him: in mild cases they are relegated to positions of obscurity, and in serious cases they are

散，重则褫以编氓。甚且一臂不袒，辄迕鹿马之奸；片语方干，远窜豺狼之地。朝士为之寒心，朝廷因而孤立。又且平民膏腴，任肆蚕食；良家女子，强委禽妆。沴气冤氛，暗无天日！奴仆一到，则守、令承颜；书函一投，则司、院枉法。或有厮养之儿，瓜葛之亲，出则乘传，风行雷动。地方之供给稍迟，马上之鞭挞立至。荼毒人民，奴隶官府，扈从所临，野无青草。而某方炎炎赫赫，怙宠无悔。召对方承于阙下，萋菲辄进于君前；委蛇才退于自公，声歌已起于后苑。声色狗马，昼夜荒淫；国计民生，罔存念虑。世上宁有此宰相乎！内外骇讹，人情汹汹。若不急加斧锧之诛，势

stripped of their titles and reduced to commoners. Failure to stand on his side of the fence may provoke him so far as to condemn his victims for alleged treachery; even one word that displeases him is cause for banishment to a region of bobcats and wolves. Hence courtiers have no stomach for involvement, and the court has become isolated.

To make matters worse, he indiscriminately gobbles up the fertile lands of the common people and forces marriage payments upon girls of decent families. Amiasma of injustice has shrouded the sun and sky in darkness. His slaves and servants are greeted wherever they go by the ingratiating smiles of prefacts and magistrates A letter from him is sufficient to make judges and procurators bend the law. His domestic familiars and distant relatives raise thunderous and stormy commotions where they go about in official carriages. When locals are late forwarding supplies, they immediately receive a thorough whipping from his mounted henchmen. Common people are savagely tormented and officials treated like slaves. Wherever his entourage passes the fields are left desolate.

Despite all this, the flames of the accused's ascend-ancy continue to blaze hotly: he relies on Your Majesty's favor and acts without scruple. Whenever Zeng is summoned to the palace explaining himself, then he presents Your Majesty with an elaborately overdrawn account of the peccadillos of his rivals. Moments after he smugly withdraws from court to his own house, music and singing can be heard from his rear garden. His days and nights are dissipated in sensual indulgence, horsemanship, and dog racing. The people's livelihood and affairs of the empire mean nothing to him. What sort of prime minister is this? There are alarms and vague rumors within and outside of the capital: public sentiment has become threateningly restless. Unless this man is immediately turned over to the excutioner, a usurpation of imperial authority on the scale of that committed by the traitors Cao Cao(155-220) and Wang Mang (45 B. C. -A. D. 23) will surely develop. It is

必酿成操、莽之祸。臣夙夜祗惧，不敢宁处，冒死列款，仰达宸听。伏祈断奸佞之头，籍贪冒之产，上回天怒，下快舆情。如果臣言虚谬，刀锯鼎镬，即加臣身”云云。疏上，曾闻之，气魄悚骇，如饮冰水。幸而皇上优容，留中不发。又继而科、道、九卿，交章劾奏；即昔之拜门墙、称假父者，亦反颜相向。奉旨籍家，充云南军。子任平阳太守，已差员前往提问。曾方闻旨惊怛，旋有武士数十人，带剑操戈，直抵内寝，褫其衣冠，与妻并系。俄见数夫运资于庭，金银钱钞以数百万，珠翠瑙玉数百斛，幄幕帘榻之属，又数千事，以至儿襁女舄，遗堕庭阶。曾一一视之，酸心刺目。又俄而一人掠美妾出，披发娇啼，玉容无主。悲火

impossible for me to sit calmly by while such fears preoccupy me day and night, and offer them for Your Majesty's perusal. I humbly beseech Your Majasty to have this wicked traitor beheaded and his ill-gotten property confiscated, to appease the anger of Heaven above and gratify public opinion here below. If my words prove to be false or misleading, may my body be consigned to the axe or the oil cauldron. (And so forth.)

The news of this memorial had as chilling an effect on Zeng's spirits as a drink of icewater has on a man's internal warmth. Luckily for him the emperor was lenient, leniency and the document was shelved. But then section heads, government inspectors and the nine high ministers sent up one accusation after another. Even those who had bowed at Zeng's gate and called him godfather now faced him defiantly. An imperial command was issued to confiscate his home and exile him to Yunnan. A special commissioner had already been assigned to try his son, who was the prefect of Pingyang in Shanxi. Zeng was in a state of shock and dread, having just heard the command, when several dozen soldiers, bearing swords and spears, precipitately barged into his inner chamber, stripped him of his robe and official headpiece and bound both him and his wife. Soon he saw several porters carrying his valuables into the courtyard. There were gold, silver, coins and notes worth milions of taels; hundreds of bushels of pearls, jadeite, agate and nephrite; and netting, canopies, curtains and beds to the sum of several thousand articles. Nothing was left unturned; even baby clothes and women's shoes were scattered here and there on the courtyard steps. Zeng looked at the remnants one by one with aching heart and stinging eyes. Suddenly he heard a plaintive cry: someone was dragging out his beautiful concubine, her hair now dishevelled and her jade countenance forlorn. Flames of anguish seared his heart, but he dared not give vent to his outrage.

烧心,含愤不敢言。俄楼阁仓库,并已封志。立叱曾出。监者牵罗曳而出。夫妻吞声就道,求一下驷劣车,少作代步,亦不得。十里外,妻足弱,欲倾跌,曾时以一手相攀引。又十余里,己亦困惫。欻见高山,直插霄汉,自忧不能登越,时挽妻相对泣。而监者狞目来窥,不容稍停驻。又顾斜日已坠,无可投止,不得已,参差蹩躠而行。比至山腰,妻力已尽,泣坐路隅。曾亦憩止,任监者叱骂。忽闻百声齐噪,有群盗各操利刃,跳梁而前。监者大骇,逸去。曾长跪,言:"孤身远谪,橐中无长物。"哀求宥免。群盗裂眦宣言:"我辈皆被害冤民,只乞得佞贼头,他无索取。"曾叱怒曰:"我虽待罪,乃朝廷命官,贼子何敢尔!"贼

No sooner had the doors to his mansion and storehouse been sealed with notices of confiscation than Zeng was gruffly told to leave the premises. Guards tied a rope to him and dragged him away. Husband and wife swallowed their resentment and set out on foot. Now they could not even get a team of nags or a broken-down cart as a conveyance to spare them a few steps. When they had gone four miles his wife's legs were ready to give out. Zeng braced her from time to time and helped her along with his arm, but after another four miles he too was exhausted. Soon they saw a huge mountain towering into the clouds ahead. Fearing what would happen if they could not make the climb, the couple joined hands repeatedly and looked at each other with tear-filled eyes, but each time the guards approached them and leered threateningly, not allowing them to stop for a moment. They looked up and saw the slanting rays of the setting sun, but there was no place to take shelter for the night. They had no choice but to hobble onward falteringly. Halfway up the mountain his wife's strength gave out, and she sat down sobbing at the side of the road. Zeng too ignored the curses and shouts of the guards and stopped for a rest. Suddenly they heard a hundred voices whooping and shouting all at once. A party of bandits brandishing sharp swords approached, sending the guards fleeing in terror.

Zeng knelt before the bandits saying: "I am being exiled to a faraway place. There is nothing of value in my bag." He begged them to let him free.

The bandits glowered at him and announced, "All of us here have suffered from injustice. Your head is the only thing we want, you bootlicker. We don't We don't care about any-thing else!"

"Even though charges have been pressed against me, I am an appointed court official," Zeng bellowed angrily. "How dare you petty thieves treat me this way?" The bandits, too, lost their tempers. One of them swung a huge axe at Zeng's neck. He felt his head hitting the

亦怒，以巨斧挥曾项。觉头堕地作声，魂方骇疑，即有二鬼来，反接其手，驱之行。行逾数刻，入一都会。顷之，睹宫殿；殿上一丑形王者，凭几决罪福。曾前，匐伏请命。王者阅卷，才数行，即震怒曰："此欺君误国之罪，宜置油鼎！"万鬼群和，声如雷霆。即有巨鬼捽至墀下。见鼎高七尺已来，四围炽炭，鼎足尽赤。曾觳觫哀啼，窜迹无路。鬼以左手抓发，右手握踝，抛置鼎中。觉块然一身，随油波而上下；皮肉焦灼，痛彻于心；沸油入口，煎烹肺腑。念欲速死，而万计不能得死。约食时，鬼方以巨叉取曾出，复伏堂下。王又检册籍，怒曰："倚势凌人，合受刀山狱！"鬼复捽去。见一山，不甚广阔，而峻削壁立，利刃纵横，乱如

ground with a thud, to the terror and bewilderment of his soul.

Then two ghosts came to him at once, tied his hands behind his back and prodded him forward. He walked for several notches until he entered a metropolis. Moments later he found himself in a palace hall, at the head of which a hideous looking king leaned against a desk passing judgement. Zeng went forward and prostrated himself to beg for his life.

The king read only a few lines from Zeng's file and exploded with anger: "For deceiving your lord betraying your country, you must be thrown into the oil cauldron!" Ten thousand ghosts applauded the decision with a thunderous roar. A giant demon dragged him to the foot of the stairs. There stood a cauldron at least seven feet high, with blazing charcoal around its base, its three legs glowing red. Zeng shuddered and wailed, but there was no escape. A ghost grabbed Zeng's hair with its left hand and his ankles in its right, then hurled him into the cauldron. Zeng felt his body dragged under the surface and then lifted by the currents of boiling oil. The pain from his scorching flesh pierced through him. The seething oil flowed into his mouth and fried his vital organs. He wished himself dead at that every moment, but he could think of nothing to make death come. This went on for the time it takes to eat a meal before a ghost lifted him out with a huge pitchfork and deposited him prone at the foot of the hall.

The king examined the file again and raged, "For using your power to mistreat others, you must be tortured on the mountain of knoves!" The demon dragged him out again to a mountain. It was not very broad, but its sides were sheer, wall-like cliffs. Keen blades were everywhere on its surface like a dense growth of bamboo shoots. Several people were already on its slopes, their abdomens pierced and their intestines hanging on the blades. The ghastliness of their wails and screams was heart rending. The demon drove Zeng forward and, when he sobbed loudly and cringed, it raised a poison-tipped awl and

密筭。先有数人胃肠刺腹于其上，呼号之声，惨绝心目。鬼促曾上，曾大哭退缩。鬼以毒锥刺脑，曾负痛乞怜。鬼怒，捉曾起，望空力掷。觉身在云霄之上，晕然一落，刃交于胸，痛苦不可言状。又移时，身躯重赘，刀孔渐阔；忽焉脱落，四支蠖屈。鬼又逐以见王。王命会计生平卖爵鬻名，枉法霸产，所得金钱几何。即有髯须人持筹握算，曰："三百二十一万。"王曰："彼既积来，还令饮去！"少间，取金钱堆阶上，如丘陵。渐入铁釜，熔以烈火。鬼使数辈，更以杓灌其口，流颐则皮肤臭裂，入喉则脏腑腾沸。生时患此物之少，是时患此物之多也！半日方尽。王者令押去甘州为女。行数步，见架上铁梁，围可数尺，绾一火轮，其大不知几百由旬，焰生五采，光耿云霄。鬼挞使登轮。方合眼跃登，则轮随足转，似觉倾坠，遍体生凉。开眸自顾，身已婴儿，而又

punctured his skull. Over-come by pain, Zeng begged for mercy. The infuriated demon lifted him and hurled him in the air. He felt himself flying up through the clouds, and then came a dizzying fall onto knives that pierced his ribcage from all sides, causing an agony beyond the power of words to describe. After a time the wounds in his sagging body gaped larger and larger until he slid off the blades, his limbs clenched as thought he were an inchworm. Again the ghosts drove him before the king, who ordered his officials to calculate the amount of money he had made while alive by selling official posts and titles, twisting the law, and seizing property. A man with a tangled beard manipulated his tally chips and reported: "3, 210, 000 taels'worth."

The king roared, "As much as he has hoarded, let him devour!"

Within moments, gold coins had been laid out in piles on the steps. They were moved load by load into iron pots and melted over blazing fires. Several ghosts poured ladlefuls of the molten metal down Zeng's mouth. Some ran down his chin, sending up an odor of charred flesh. The rest went down his throat and made his guts seethe. While alive he had worried that he would never get enough of the stuff, but now he worried that there was too much. Half a day passed before it was gone.

The king ordered that Zeng be taken to Ganzhou for rebirth as a woman. A few steps brought him to a frame supporting an iron beam several feet in cirumference, around which turned a wheel of fire uncountable li in diameter. Five colors glowed in its flames and its light flickered against the clouds. The ghosts beat him, forcing him to climb onto the wheel. No sooner had he closed his eyes and jumped on than the wheel turned beneath his feet. He seemed to be hurtling downward, and a cool feeling spread through his body. He opened his eyes to find himself in an infant's body, and a female one at that. The girl's parents were dressed in as tattered as a quail tail; a beggar's staff and gourd leaned against the wall of the earthen room. He knew that '

女也。视其父母,则悬鹑败焉。土室之中,瓢杖犹存。心知为乞人子。日随乞儿托钵,腹辘辘然常不得一饱。着败衣,风常刺骨。十四岁,鬻与顾秀才备媵妾,衣食粗足自给。而冢室悍甚,日以鞭箠从事,辄以赤铁烙胸乳。幸而良人颇怜爱,稍自宽慰。东邻恶少年,忽逾垣来逼与私。乃自念前身恶孽,已被鬼责,今那得复尔。于是大声疾呼,良人与嫡妇尽起,恶少年始窜去。居无何,秀才宿诸其室,枕上喋喋,方自诉冤苦。忽震厉一声,室门大辟,有两贼持刀入,竟决秀才首,囊括衣物。团伏被底,不敢复作声。既而贼去,乃喊奔嫡室。嫡大惊,相与泣验。遂疑妾以奸夫杀良人,因以状白刺史;刺史严鞫,竟以酷刑定罪案,依律凌迟处死,縶赴刑所。胸中冤气扼塞,距踊声屈,觉九幽十八狱,无此黑黯也。

had been reborn as a beggar's daughter.

Every day she went along with the other beggars, holding out an almsbowl. Her rumbling stomach was hardly ever filled. The wind pierced her to the bone through her tattered clothes. At fourteen she was sold to Bachelor of Letters Gu as a concubine. Her food and clothing were barely sufficient, and the mistress of the house was a terrible shrew. She served the girl every day with whip or bamboo rod and branded her breast with a red hot iron. Luckily the girl could take comfort in the loving regard shown by her husband. One day a no-good youth who lived east of them climbed the wall and forced himself upon her. She thought of how the ghosts had punished her for the sins of her past life: No, it must not happen again! She screamed and hollered until her husband and the mistress were aroused and the no-good youth slunk away. Soon afterward her husband was spending the night in her room. She was rattling along with her head next to his on the pillow, complaining of her troubles and the wrongs done to her, when two knife-wielding robbers burst through the door with a fierce shout. They cut off the scholar's head, and bagged all clothes and other articles. The girl huddled under the covers, not daring to make a sound. When the robbers had gone, she ran screaming to them broke out in sobs when they found him truly dead. The mistress, suspecting that the concubine had conspired with a lover to kill her husband, accused the girl before the district magistrate. The magistrate subjected her to severe interrogation and finally used torture to establish her guilt. The sentence prescribed by law was death by dismemberment. She was bound and taken to the execution ground . Outrage at this injustice swelled within her chest till she could no longer contain it. She stamped frenziedly and screamed that she had been wronged. There could be no darkness worse than this, she thought, not even in the nine dungeons and eighteen levels of hell. In the midst of her wailing the voices of Zeng's fellow sightseers were heard calling: "Are you

正悲号间，闻游者呼曰："兄梦魇耶?"豁然而寤，见老僧犹跏趺座上。同侣竞相谓曰："日暮腹枵，何久酣睡?"曾乃惨淡而起。僧微笑曰："宰相之占验否?"曾益惊异，拜而请教。僧曰："修德行仁，火坑中有青莲也。山僧何知焉。"曾胜气而来，不觉丧气而返。台阁之想，由此淡焉。入山不知所终。

异史氏曰："福善祸淫，天之常道。闻作宰相而忻然于中者，必非喜其鞠躬尽瘁可知矣。是时方寸中，宫室妻妾，无所不有。然而梦固为妄，想亦非真。彼以虚作，神以幻报。黄粱将熟，此梦在所必有，当以附之邯郸之后。"

having a nightmare, brother?"

Zeng came back to himself with a start: he saw the old monk still sitting in lotus posture on the mat. Zeng's companions all spoke at the same tie: "The sun is going down and we haven't had a thing to eat. What made you sleep so deeply all this time?" Zeng gave them a grim look and rose.

"Did the prediction that you would be prime minister turn out to be true?" asked the monk with a smile. This amazed Zeng all the more. He bowed to the monk and asked to be instructed.

"If you cultivate virtue and act with benevolence, you can make a blue lotus grow out of a pit of fire," said the monk. But you can't expect a mountain monk like me to know about it?"

Zeng's spirits had been high when he set out that morning, but on his return they were unexpectedly low. Henceforth, his ardor for the prime ministership waned. He went into the mountains, and no one knows what became of him.

The Chronicler of the Tales comments: "Blessings are given to the good and calamity is visited upon the decadent: this has always been the way of Heaven. A man who takes secret delight at predictions that he will be prime minister is obviously not glad for the chance to work himself to the bone for his country. Palaces, houses, wives, and concubines all appeared within the small space of Zeng's imagination—nothing was lacking. But dreams are reducible to delusion, and wishes are unreal. When a man acts with hypocrisy, the spirits counter with illusion. When yellow millet is on the fire and nearly finished cooking, the time for this dream is bound to come. It deserves to be appended as a sequel to what another young man dreamt along the road to Handan."

莲花公主

胶州窦旭，字晓晖。方昼寝，见一褐衣人立榻前，逡巡惶顾，似欲有言。生问之。答云："相公奉屈。""相公何人？"曰："近在邻境。"从之而出。转过墙屋，导至一处，叠阁重楼，万椽相接，曲折而行。觉万户千门，迥非人世。又见宫人女官，往来甚夥，都向褐衣人问曰："窦郎来乎？"褐衣人诺。俄，一贵官出，迎见甚恭。既登堂，生启问曰："素既不叙，遂

PRINCESS LOTUS

DOU XU of Jiaozhu, also known as Xiaohui, was lying in bed one day when he noticed a man in a robe of coarse cloth standing hesitantly at the foot of his bed and looking about nervously as if he had something to say. Scholar Dou asked his business, and he answered, "The prime minister awaits your pleasure."

"What prime minister?"

"He is here in the vicinity," said the man. Dou followed him out and around the corner of his house. The man led the way to a place with row upon row of pavilions and mansions supported by thousands of parallel beams. The scholar found himself in a maze of gates opening onto doors and doors opening onto gates-a scene totally unlike anything in this world. Numerous palace attendants and ladies-in-waitling back and forth all asked the cloth-robed man: "Is this Master Dou?" Each time the man answered yes.

Soon a distinguished looking official came out and welcomed the scholar with great civility. When they had climbed a staircase into a hall, Dou opened with a question: "Not having enjoyed your acquaintance, I have never gotten around to paying you a visit. I cannot help but entertain some misgivings at the undue regard you have shown by

疏参谒。过蒙爱接,颇注疑念。”贵官曰:“寡君以先生清族世德,倾风结慕,深愿思晤焉。”生益骇,问:“王何人?”答云:“少间自悉。”无何,二女官至,以双旌导生行。入重门,见殿上一王者,见生入,降阶而迎,执宾主礼。礼已,践席,列筵丰盛。仰视殿上一匾曰“桂府”。生踢蹙不能致辞。王曰:“忝近芳邻,缘即至深。便当畅怀,勿致疑畏。”生唯唯。酒数行,笙歌作于下,钲鼓不鸣,音声幽细。稍间,王忽左右顾曰:“朕一言,烦卿等属对:‘才人登桂府。’”四座方思,生即应云:“君子爱莲花。”王大悦曰:“奇哉!莲花乃公主小字,何

having me brought here."

The high official answered, "The long-standing virtue and honesty of your family have earned His Majesty's admiration; it is his heartfelt wish to meet you."

Dou was all the more disconcerted. "What king are you talking about?" he demanded.

"In a little while you will see for yourself," was the reply. Soon two ladies-in-waiting came and led the way with a pair of banners. They passed through one gate after another and approached a hall, at the head of which waited a king. As Dou entered, the king descended the steps and greeted him with polite formality. That done, they stepped over to take their seats at a table on which was spread a lavish feast. The scholar glanced upward and saw a plaque at the head of the hall which read "Cassia Manor." He was too ill at ease to begin the conversation.

"My proximity to such an honorable neighbor as yourself proves that the bond of fate between us is quite deep," said the king. "So it is fitting for us to open our hearts and not to show mistrust."

The scholar murmured in agreement. After several rounds of wine, reed organs and singing were heard at the foot of the hall. There was no percussion, so the music had an airy, serene quality. Soon the king turned to his courtiers on both sides and said, "I have a line of verse here and I'd like to ask for another line to make a couplet: 'A talented scholar ascends to Cassia Manor!'"

While those around the king were still pondering, the scholar came up with a ready answer: "The gentleman loves lotus flowers."

"Marvelous!" said the king delightedly. "Lotus is the princess' nickname. How did you hit on it like that? Could there be a tie between you and her from former life? Send word to the princess that she absolutely must come out and make the acquaintance of this young gentleman."

适合如此？宁非夙分？传语公主，不可不出一晤君子。”移时，珮环声近，兰麝香浓，则公主至矣。年十六七，妙好无双。王命向生展拜，曰：“此即莲花小女也。”拜已而去。生睹之，神情摇动，木坐凝思。王举觞劝饮，目竟罔睹。王似微察其意，乃曰：“息女宜相匹敌，但自惭不类，如何？”生怅然若痴，即又不闻。近坐者蹑之曰：“王揖君未见，王言君未闻耶？”生茫乎若失，忪愣自惭，离席曰：“臣蒙优渥，不觉过醉，仪节失次，幸能垂宥。然日旰君勤，即告出也。”王起曰：“既见君子，实惬心好，何仓卒而便言离也？卿既不住，亦无敢于强。若烦萦念，更当再邀。”遂命内官导之出。途中内官语生曰：“适王谓可匹敌，似欲附为婚姻，何默不一言？”生顿足而悔，步步追恨，

After a time the tinkle of sash pendants was heard approaching, fragrance of orchid and musk filled the air, and the princess appeared. She was sixteen or seventeen years of age and graced with matchless beauty. The king ordered her to bow to the scholar and introduced her: "This is my daughter Princess Lotus." Having made an obeisance, she withdrew.

The scholar's self-possession was much shaken at the sight of her: he sat there woodenly, immersed in thought and oblivious even to the toast offered by the king. The king seemed to perceive what preoccupied him, for he said, "My daughter would be a good match for you, but I am ashamed that we are not of your kind. What do you say?"

Again the scholar, in heartsick befuddlement, was oblivious to his words. The man sitting beside him nudged his foot and said, "The king greeted you politely, but you didn't respond. Don't tell me you didn't hear what the king just said to you!"

The scholar was lost in a daze and greatly ashamed of himself. He rose from his seat and said, "Your Majesty has entertained me with such hospitality that, without my knowing it, the wine has gone to my head and I have behaved improperly, for which I beg your forgiveness. But now the day is late and you are busy, so I must ask leave to depart."

"Meeting with you is truly the fulfillment of my heart's wishes. Why must you speak so abruptly of leaving? But since you are not inclined to stay, I dare not force you. If you would be so kind as to remember us, I should like to invite you again." With this the king ordered a lady-in-waiting to lead him out.

On the way she said to the scholar, "Just now the king said that his daughter would be a good match for you. He seems willing to connect himself to you through marriage. Why didn't you speak up?"

The scholar stamped his feet in remorse. He agonized over his

遂已至家。忽然醒寤,则返照已残。冥坐观想,历历在目。晚斋灭烛,冀旧梦可以复寻,而邯郸路渺,悔叹而已。一夕,与友人共榻,忽见前内官来,传王命相召。生喜,从去。见王伏谒。王曳起,延止隅坐,曰:“别后知劳思眷。谬以小女子奉裳衣,想不过嫌也。”生即拜谢。王命学士大臣,陪侍宴饮。酒阑,宫人前白:“公主妆竟。”俄见数十宫女,拥公主出。以红锦覆首,凌波微步,挽上氍毹,与生交拜成礼。已而送归馆舍。洞房温清,穷极芳腻。生曰:“有卿在目,真使人乐而忘死。但恐今日之遭,乃是梦耳。”公主掩口曰:“明明妾与君,那得是梦?”诘旦方起,戏为公主匀铅黄;已而以带围腰,布指度足。公主笑问:“君颠

mistake with each step he took until he arrived at home. Suddenly he was awake, his eyes open to the last rays of the setting sun. He sat quietly letting the images from his dream pass one by one before his mind's eye. Later that night he blew out the candles in his studio, hoping to find his way back to the same dream, but the road was lost in haze. All he could do was heave a sigh of regret.

One night as he lay in bed with a friend, the same lady-in-waiting suddenly came to him to relay a summons from the king. The scholar gladly followed. When he came before the king he knelt down and announced himself. The king pulled him to his feet, showed him to a seat in a private corner, and said, "I know that since our parting you have devoted a great deal of thought to us. Would it be brash to suppose that you will not mind to having my daughter wait on you?"

The scholar bowed in gratitude. The king ordered his councillors and ministers to be present at the weding banquet. When the wine had gone the rounds a palace attendant came forward to say: "The princess has finished dressing."

Soon several dozen palace maids emerged, clutered about the princess, who wore on her head a bridal veil of red brocade. She walked forward with steps delicate enough to skim over waves and was led onto a felt rug. There she performed, with the scholar, the mutual kowtow by which the wedding ceremony was completed. Then they were escorted to their residence. In the comfortable warmth of the nuptial chamber, he was treated to all the rich fragrance that human senses can absorb.

"Having you before my eyes is such a joy that I can forget death," he said to his bride. "But I fear that what happened today is only a dream."

"Here we are, you and I, clear as day. How could it be a dream?" asked the princess, covering her mouth to hold back a laugh.

As soon as he rose early the next morning he playfully applied

耶?"曰:"臣屡为梦误,故细志之。倘是梦时,亦足动悬想耳。"调笑未已,一宫女驰入曰:"妖入宫门,王避偏殿,凶祸不远矣!"生大惊,趋见王。王执手泣曰:"君子不弃,方图永好。讵期孽降自天,国祚将覆,且复奈何!"生惊问何说。王以案上一章,授生启读。章云:"含香殿大学士臣黑翼,为非常妖异,祈早迁都,以存国脉事:据黄门报称:自五月初六日,来一千丈巨蟒,盘踞宫外,吞食内外臣民一万三千八百余口;所过宫殿尽成丘墟,等因。臣奋勇前窥,确见妖蟒:头如山岳,目等江海;昂首则殿阁齐吞,伸腰则楼垣尽覆。真千古未见之凶,万代不遭之祸!社稷宗庙,危在旦夕!

cream to the princess'face and kohl to her eye-brows. When that was done, he encircled her waist with a sash and measured her feet with his fingers.

"Are you losing your mind?" she asked.

"I have been misled by dreams many times before, so now I am making a detailed record. Even if it turns out to be a dream, this will be enough to refresh my memory."

They were still poking fun at each other when a palace maid ran in and said, "A monster has entered the palace gate, and the king has fled to a side hall. An evil calamity is upon us!"

Greaty shocked, the scholar hurried to see the king, who took the scholar's hand in his own and said in a voice broken by sobs: "Since you did not spurn us, I was looking forward to a long friendship. Who could have foreseen that Heaven would send this great evil down upon us? My kingdom is on the brink of collapse: what can I do?"

In reply to the bewildered scholar's questions, the king took a memorial from the desk and gave it to him to read. The memorial was as follows:

"Your subject Black-Wing, Grand Councillor of Incense-Redolent Hall, prays that you will quickly move the capital, so that the heart of our kingdom may continue beating. According to a report by the privy council, a giant python ten thousand feet in length appeared on the sixth day of the fifth month, coiled feet in length appeared on the sixth day of the fifth month, coiled itself outside the palace, then proceeded to devour 13, 800 of your subjects and courtiers. All the palace halls and mansions the snake crawled over were reduced to rubble. I mustered up the courage to observe the disaster, and did indeed see a monstrous python—its head as massive as a mountain and its eyes like bodies of water—gulp down halls and pavilions with a toss of its head and flatten towers and walls by flexing its waist. It is truly a disaster unparalleled throughout history and a calamity of a scope never met

乞皇上早率宫眷，速迁乐土”云云。生览毕，面如灰土。即有宫人奔奏：“妖物至矣！”阖殿哀呼，惨无天日。王仓遽不知所为，但泣顾曰：“小女已累先生。”生坌息而返。公主方与左右抱首哀鸣，见生入，牵衿曰：“郎焉置妾？”生怆恻欲绝，乃捉腕思曰：“小生贫贱，惭无金屋。有茅庐三数间，姑同窜匿可乎？”公主含涕曰：“急何能择？乞携速往！”生乃挽扶而出。未几，至家。公主曰：“此大安宅，胜故国多矣。然妾从君来，父母何依？请别筑一舍，当举国相从。”生难之。公主号咷曰：“不能急人之急，安用郎也！”生略慰解，即已入室。公主伏床悲啼，不可劝止。焦思无术，顿然而

with in past ages! The danger to our state and ancestral temple is imminent. I beg Your Majesty to lead the royal family to a safe place immediately. Would that I could say more." By the time the scholar had finished reading his face was like the shade of ashes.

At that point a palace servant ran in and reported, "The monster has come!" All through the palace people set up such a wretched howling that the sky and sun seemed blotted out by their misery. The king, immobilized by panic, simply stared at the scholar and sobbed as he said, "I must entrust my daughter to you."

The scholar gasped at the news and went back to where the princess was huddled wailing with her servants. She grasped the front of his robe when she saw him enter and said, "What will you do with me, husband?"

The scholar was nearly overcome with grief, but he grasped her wrist as he thought aloud, "I am only a poor student. It shames me that I have no room of gold to accommodate you. What I do have is a thatched hut with several rooms. We can hide away there for a time, can't we?"

"What choice do we have?" sniffed the princess. "Please give me your arm and take me there right away!" So the scholar wrapped his arm around her and led her out. Soon they reached his house.

"This is a great, invulnerable house—much better than our palace. But who will my parents rely on now that I have come here with you? Please construct another house; then I can have the whole kingdom move in." The scholar expressed qualms at this.

"People are in danger, but you have no sympathy for them," wailed the princess. "What good are you?"

The scholar made an effort to comfort her, but she ignored him and ran to his room, where she threw herself on the bed and sobbed uncontrollably. Just as he was racking his brains for a way to calm her, he suddenly awoke and realized he had been dreaming. But still

醒,始知梦也。而耳畔啼声,嘤嘤未绝。审听之,殊非人声,乃蜂子二三头,飞鸣枕上。大叫怪事。友人诘之,乃以梦告。友人亦诧为异。共起视蜂,依依裳袂间,拂之不去。友人劝为营巢。生如所请,督工构造。方竖两堵,而群蜂自墙外来,络绎如绳。顶尖未合,飞集盈斗。迹所由来,则邻翁之旧圃也。圃中蜂一房,三十余年矣,生息颇繁。或以生事告翁。翁觇之,蜂户寂然。发其壁,则蛇据其中,长丈许。捉而杀之。乃知巨蟒即此物也。蜂入生家,滋息更盛,亦无他异。

the sound of her sobbing hummed in his ear. Turning to look, he found that it was not a human voice at all but the buzzing of a few bees that flew around his pillow. The strangeness of this brought a loud exclamation to his lips. When his friend questioned him, he told him the dream. His amazed friend, too, knew that this was no ordinary dream. They got up and looked at the bees, which were hovering close to the scholar's sleeve and would not let themselves be brushed away. The friend urged him to build a hive. The scholar accepted his suggestion and directed a workman to construct it. No sooner were two of the walls been in place than a swarm of bees from over the wall flew into it in a steady stream. Before the roof was on a peck basketful of them had come. Tracing the direction of their flight, he found that they came from an old garden kept by an elderly man next door. For the past thirty years there had been a highly prolific hive of bees in the garden. After hearing of the scholar's dream, the old man examined the hive and found no sign of activity. Removing a wall, he found the hive occupied by a snake over ten feet long, which he pulled out and killed. Now it was plain that this snake was the giant python in the dream. After the bees swarmed into the hive built against the scholar's house, they were more productive than ever, and there were no more strange occurrences.

云 翠 仙

梁有才，故晋人，流寓于济，作小负贩。无妻子田产。从村人登岱。岱，四月交，香侣杂沓。又有优婆夷、塞，率众男子以百十，杂跪神座下，视香炷为度，名曰“跪香”。才视众中有女郎，年十七八而美，悦之。诈为香客，近女郎跪；又伪为膝困无力状，故以手据女郎足。女回首似嗔，膝行而远之。才又膝行近之；少间，又据之。女郎觉，遽起，不跪，出门去。才亦起，出履其迹，不知其往。心无望，怏怏而行。途中见女郎从媪，似为女也母者。

YUN CUIXIAN

LIANG Youcai was originally from Shanxi; but his wanderings took him to the area around Jinan in Shandong, where he worked as a peddler. He had neither wife, children, nor land. On the first day of summer he climbed Mt. Tai along with some villagers. On that day Mt. Tai is crowded with pilgrims, as lay Buddhists, both male and female, lead groups of men numbering about a hundred before the image of a deity, where both sexes kneel together for the length of time a stick of incense burns. This is called "kneeling to incense." Youcai spotted a beautiful young woman, seventeen or eighteen years old, in the crowd and felt a liking for her. He knelt beside her, pretending to be a pilgrim. Then, acting as if his knees had given out, he put his hand on her leg. She turned her head to give him an exasperated look, then moved away from him on her knees. Youcai moved over to her also on his knees, and after a moment, touched her again. Realizing what he was up to, the young woman rose abruptly, gave up trying to kneel and went out the gate.

Youcai stood up and followed on her trail, but he did not know which way she had gone. Giving up hope, he walked along dejectedly. Then, seeing the young woman walking with an old woman, apparent-

才趋之。媪女行且语。媪云:“汝能参礼娘娘,大好事!汝又无弟妹,但获娘娘冥加护,护汝得快婿,但能相孝顺,都不必贵公子、富王孙也。”才窃喜,渐渍诘媪。媪自言为云氏,女名翠仙,其出也。家西山四十里。才曰:“山路濇,母如此蹜蹜,妹如此纤纤,何能便至?”曰:“日已晚,将寄舅家宿耳。”才曰:“适言相婿,不以贫嫌,不以贱鄙,我又未婚,颇当母意否?”媪以问女,女不应。媪数问,女曰:“渠寡福,又荡无行,轻薄之心,还易翻覆。儿不能为遢伎儿作妇!”才闻,朴诚自表,切矢皦日。媪喜,竟诺之。女不乐,勃然而已。母又强拍咻之。才殷勤,手于橐,觅山兜二,舁媪

ly her mother, on the road ahead, he hurried toward them and heard them talking as they walked.

"I'm so glad you went to worship the goddess! You don't have any brothers or sisters, but the Goddess will be your Guardian Angel and secretly arrange for you to find a fine husband. As long as he can treat me with respect and deference, he need not be a noble young gentleman or the son of a rich family."

Youcai was relieved to hear these words. He started a conversation and bit by bit began to ply the old woman with questions. The old woman said that her surname was Yun, that the girl, named Cuixian, was her daughter and that their house was in the mountains forty li to the west.

"This is a steep mountain road," said Youcai. "With your feet dragging the way they are, and Sister being as delicate as she is, do you really think you can make it?"

"It's getting late," said Cuixian. "We're going to stay the night at my uncle's house."

Youcai said, "Just now you were saying that when you look for a son-in-law you won't turn a person away because of his poverty or low station. I am still single. Do you think I might meet your wishes, Mother?"

The old woman asked her daughter but received no answer. Ater she asked several times the girl said, "He is a man of scant blessings: besides, he is loose and immoral. He has a wanton heart and is liable to grow restless. I will not be the wife of a wild, dissipated man."

Upon hearing this, Youcai insisted that he was perfectly sincere and swore by the sun above. The old woman, who found this to her liking, finally gave her approval. The girl could only show her disapproval with a scowl. The mother patted her and spoke reassuringly to make her give in. Youcai graciously reached into his pouch and hired two mountain sedan chairs to carry the woman and the girl. He himself

及女。已步从，若为仆。过隘，辄诃兜夫不得颠摇动，良殷。俄抵村舍，便邀才同入舅家。舅出翁，妗出媪也。云兄之嫂之。谓："才吾婿。日适良，不须别择，便取今夕。"舅亦喜，出酒肴饵才。既，严妆翠仙出，拂榻促眠。女曰："我固知郎不义，迫母命，漫相随。郎若人也，当不须忧偕活。"才唯唯听受。明日早起，母谓才："宜先去，我以女继至。"才归，扫户闼。媪果送女至。入视室中，虚无有。便云："似此何能自给？老身速归，当小助汝辛苦。"遂去。次日，有男女数辈，各携服食器具，布一室满之。不饭俱去，但留一婢。才由此坐温饱，惟日引里无赖，朋饮竞赌，渐盗女郎簪珥佐博。女劝之，不听；颇不耐之，惟严守箱奁，如防寇。一日，博党款门访才，窥见女，适

followed on foot like their servant. As they passed through rugged stretches he obligingly scolded the porters for giving the ladies a bumpy ride. Soon they approached a village, and the woman invited him to go along to the house of Cuixian's uncle. The uncle, a bearded old man, and the aunt, an old woman, came to the door. They were Madame Yun's elder brother and sister-in-law. "This is Youcai, my son-in-law," she told them. "Today happens to be auspicious; there is no need to choose a later date. Let's make it tonight." The girl's uncle happily brought out wine and viands to feed Youcai. Afterwards Cuixian was brought out in fromal dress, and the two were hustled off to a freshly swept bedroom.

"I knew from the start that you were no good, but I had to go along with my mother's wishes. If you can behave as a human being, you need not worry about our life together." Youcai heard her out and agreed with everything she said. They rose early the next morning.

"It's best for you to go on ahead," the mother told Youcai. "I will be there later with my daughter." Youcai returned home to clean up his house. The old woman showed up later with her daughter as promised. After looking around the empty, unfurnished house she said, "How can we live in a place like this? I'll be back at once with some things that will make life easier for you." Whereupon she left.

The next day several men and women came carrying food, clothing and utensils enough to fill the whole house. They all went away without eating, leaving only a maid.

From this time on Youcai could sit back and enjoy comfort and plenty, but every day he got together with the neighborhood idlers to drink and gamble. Grandually he began to steal his wife's hairpins and earrings to provide himself with gambling funds. She tried to reason with him, but he would not listen. She was exasperated by his behavior and took precautions to guard her hope chest closely, as if she were warding off a bandit. One day when one of Youcai's cronies knocked at

适惊。戏谓才曰："子大富贵，何忧贫耶？"才问故。答曰："曩见夫人，实仙人也。适与子家道不相称。货为媵，金可得百；为妓，可得千。——千金在室，而听饮博无资耶？"才不言，而心然之。归辄向女欷歔，时时言贫不可度。女不顾，才频频击桌，抛匕箸，骂婢，作诸态。一夕，女沽酒与饮。忽曰："郎以贫故，日焦心。我又不能御穷，分郎忧，中岂不愧怍？但无长物，止有此婢，鬻之，可稍稍佐经营。"才摇首曰："其直几许！"又饮少时，女曰："妾于郎，有何不相承？但力竭耳。念一贫如此，便死相从，不过均此百年苦，有何发迹？不如以妾鬻贵家，两所便益，得直或较婢多。"才故愕言："何得至此！"女固言之，色作庄。才喜

his gate for a visit he caught a glimpse of the girl and was stunned by her beauty.

"You are a rich man," he told Youcai jokingly. "You will never have to worry about being poor."

When Youcai asked what he meant he answered, "I just saw your wife. No doubt about it, she is a fairy maiden. You and she were simply not made for each other. If you sell her as a concubine, you can get a hundred taels of gold; as a courtesan she would go for one thousand taels. With a thousand taels of gold to your name, you would ever have to cramp your style for lack of money?"

Youcai said nothing, but in his heart he agreed. Back home he sighed heavily in front of his wife and said over and over that they were too poor to get by. When she ignored him he slammed the table repeatedly with his fist, threw down his soup spoon and chopsticks, raged at the maid and did everything else he could to be obnoxious.

One night his wife bought wine to drink with him and, without leading up to the subject, said, "You fret day in and day out over being poor. I feel guilty for not being able to end our poverty or share the burden of worry. But I own nothing worthy of mention except this maid. Selling her will help our finances a bit."

Youcai shook his head and said, "We couldn't get much for her!"

After they had been drinking a while longer she said, "There is nothing I would not do to help you. but I am powerless. I was willing to spend my life with you, even in poverty like this, but if staying with you means nothing more than sharing a lifetime of despair, what is the good of it? You might as well sell me to a rich family. It would be a good deal for both sides, and you would probably get more for me than for the maid."

Youcai looked shocked and said, "How can I let that happen?" The girl repeated what she said, this time insistently and seriously.

"Let me think it over," said Youcai delightedly. So he offered to

曰:“容再计之。”遂缘中贵人,货隶乐籍。中贵人亲诣才,见女大悦,恐不能即得,立券八百缗,事滨就矣。女曰:“母日以婿家贫,常常萦念,今意断矣,我将暂归省;且郎与妾绝,何得不告母?”才虑母阻。女曰:“我顾自乐之,保无差贷。”才从之。夜将半,始抵母家。挝阖入,见楼舍华好,婢仆辈往来憧憧。才日与女居,每请诣母,女辄止之,故为甥馆年余,曾未一临岳家。至此大骇,以其家巨,恐媵妓所不甘也。女引才登楼上。媪惊问夫妻何来。女怨曰:“我固道渠不义,今果然!”乃于衣底出黄金二铤置几上,曰:“幸不为小人赚脱,今仍以还母。”母骇问故。女曰:“渠将鬻我,故藏金无用处。”乃指才骂曰:“豺鼠子!曩日负肩担,面沾尘如鬼。初近我,熏熏作汗腥,肤

sell her, through the good offices of a eunuch at court, to the Registry of Entertainers. The eunuch visited Youcai and was overjoyed when he saw her. Fearing that he might not get her after all, he made a down payment of 800 strings of a thousand cash each, and the deal was virtually closed.

"Our poverty has been a matter of constant concern for my mother," said the girl. "Now that it is over between us, I will go home and visit my mother for a while. It would hardly be right not to tell her we are parting."

When Youcai voiced his fear that her mother would interfere, she said, "I am going through with this because it pleases me. I guarantee you nothing will go wrong."

Youcai went along with her. They did not reach her mother's house until almost midnight. They knocked on the gate and were admitted to a magnificent manor house with servants running about ceaselessly. During their days together Youcai had often asked if they could visit her mother's, but she had always refused. So he had been a son-in-law for over a year without ever visiting his in-laws' house. What he now saw filled him with dread: he feared that a family of such a magnitude would not tolerate one of its daughters being sold as a concubine or courtesan.

Cuixian led Youcai to the upper floor of a storied building. The old woman was startled to see them and asked why they had come. "I told you he was no good, and that's just how he turned out," said the girl reproachfully. She pulled two ingots from underneath her clothes and placed them on the table, saying: "Fortunately the low-down snake did not trick these away from me. Now I am returning them to you." Her shocked mother asked for an explanation.

"He is going to sell me, so there is no use keeping this gold in reserve." She pointed to Youcai and reviled him: "You son of a rat and a lynx! Awhile ago you were carrying a shoulder pole, and your face was

颜 氏

顺天某生，家贫，值岁饥，从父之洛。性钝，年十七，裁能成幅。而丰仪秀美，能雅谑，善尺牍。见者不知其中之无有也。无何，父母继殁，孑然一身，授童蒙于洛汭。时村中颜氏有孤女，名士裔也。少惠。父在时，尝教之读，一过辄记不忘。十数岁，学父吟咏。父曰："吾家有女学士，惜不弁耳。"钟爱之，期择贵婿。父卒，母执此志，三年不遂，而母又卒。

MISS YAN

A STUDENT from a poor family of Shuntian prefecture moved to Luoyang in Henan province with his father during a year of famine. He was slow to develop and could not write a complete composition until the age of seventeen. On the other hand, he had fine, handsome features; he was a witty conversationalist and an excellent letter writer. These gifts drew people's attention away from his deficiencies. Before long his father and mother died in quick succession. Alone in the world, he began tutoring at a village school near where the Luo River flows into the Yellow River. At that time there lived in the village an orphaned girl from the Yan family, who was the daughter of a renowned scholar. She had shown considerable intellectual powers in childhood. When her father was alive he taught her to read, and she could retain in her memory anything that passed before her eyes. In her early teens she learned poetry from her father, who once remarked, "We have a female scholar in my family: if only she wore scholar's hat!"

Owing to his deep fondness for her, he hoped to find her a husband from a noble family. After his death the girl's mother held to this aim without success for three years, until she also died. Some people

或劝适佳士,女然之而未就也。适邻妇逾垣来,就与攀谈。以字纸裹绣线,女启视,则某手翰,寄邻生者。反复之而好焉。邻妇窥其意,私语曰:“此翩翩一美少年,孤与卿等,年相若也。倘能垂意,妾嘱渠侬胹合之。”女脉脉不语。妇归,以意授夫。邻生故与生善,告之,大悦。有母遗金鸦镮,托委致焉。刻日成礼,鱼水甚欢。及睹生文,笑曰:“文与卿似是两人,如此,何日可成?”朝夕劝生研读,严如师友。敛昏,先挑烛据案自哦,为丈夫率,听漏三下,乃已。如是年余,生制艺颇通;而再试再黜,身名蹇落,饔飧不给,抚情寂漠,嗷嗷悲泣。女呵之曰:“君非丈夫,负此弁耳!使

advised the girl to marry a promising student. The girl concurred, but the right man had not yet come along.

Then one day the woman who lived next door climbed over the wall to talk with her. She showed the girl a paper parcel enclosing silk threads for embroidery. The girl opened it and found the paper to be a letter in the youngstudent's hand to the scholar who lived next door. Reading it over and over, she began to feel attracted to the youth who had written it. The woman saw what was on her mind and said in a low voice: "This was written by a lively, handsome young man who is an orphan like yourself and close to you in age. If you are favorably disposed, I will have my husband bring the two of you together."

The girl responded with a meaningful silence. The woman went home and communicated her plan to her husband, who was on good terms with the young man. The young man was overjoyed to hear the news brought by his friend. He had a gold sun-ring left him by his mother, which he asked his friend to give to Miss Yan. A date was set and the wedding was held, whereupon the two of them were as happy as fish finding their way to water. But the girl laughed when she read the young man's compositions and said, "I can't help thinking that you and the writer of these had to be two different people. With writing like this, how are you ever going to make it?"

Morning and evening, with the strictness of a teacher or well-meaning friend, she urged him to pore over his books. When daylight was fading she would bring out a candle and sit at the desk reciting passages until the third watch—an example for her husband to follow. After a year of this the young man had a fair mastery of examination writing, but then he failed two examinations in a row. His fortunes and reputation were mired in decline, and he could not provide two proper meals a day. Brooding over his miserable situation, he filled the room with the noise of sobbing.

"You are no man," the girl chided. "You don't live up to that hat

我易髻而冠，青紫直芥视之!”生方懊丧，闻妻言，睊睊而怒曰：“闺中人，身不到场屋，便以功名富贵似汝厨下汲水炊白粥；若冠加于顶，恐亦犹人耳!”女笑曰：“君勿怒。俟试期，妾请易装相代。倘落拓如君，当不敢复藐天下士矣。”生亦笑曰：“卿自不知蘖苦，真宜使请尝试之。但恐绽露，为乡邻笑耳。”女曰：“妾非戏语。君尝言燕有故庐，请男装从君归，伪为弟。君以襁褓出，谁得辨其非?”生从之。女入房，巾服而出，曰：“视妾可作男儿否?”生视之，俨然一顾影少年也。生喜，遍辞里社。交好者薄有馈遗，买一羸蹇，御妻而归。生叔兄尚在，见两弟如冠玉，甚喜，晨夕恤顾之。又见宵旰攻苦，倍益爱敬。雇一剪发雏奴，为

you wear. If I could exchange my topknot for a top hat, winning the purple robe of an official would be like stooping over to pluck a blade of grass."

The student was already feeling dejected when his wife spoke these words. He glared at her and replied angrily: "You've been in an isolation booth at the examination hall—but you suppose that winning fame and fortune is like fetching water for the kitchen and boiling gruel. If a scholar's hat were placed on your head, I'm afraid you wouldn't do any better than a man."

The girl laughed and said, "Don't be angry with me. When examination time comes, let me disguise myself and take your place. If I fail as badly as you have, I will never dare to look on a scholar again."

The student also laughed and said, "Since you have not yet sampled oak gall for yourself, I really should let you have a taste, but I am afraid that if this slips out our neighbors will laugh at us."

"I am not joking," said the girl. You once said your family home is in Hebei. Why don't you go back, and I'll go with you dressed as a man, pretending to be your younger brother. You left home when you were practically still in swaddling clothes, so who will know the difference? "The student agreed, so she went into the bedroom, came out in a scholar's kerchief and robe, and asked, "Do I pass inspection as a young man?"

The student found her to be the very picture of a young dandy. He delightedly went around taking leave of all his neighbors. Using the meager gifts of his young friends, he bought a bony ass, mounted his wife on it and returned to his family home. His elder cousin on his father's side, who had remained there, was delighted to see two cousins as fine as jade hatpins, and he looked after them day and night. His esteem for them doubled when he saw them slaving over their books from early in the morning until late at night. He engaged a short-haired young slave to provide for their needs, but when night

供给使。暮后，辄遣去之。乡中吊庆，兄自出周旋；弟惟下帷读。居半年，罕有睹其面者。客或请见，兄辄代辞。读其文，瞲然骇异。或排闼而迫之，一揖便亡去。客睹丰采，又共倾慕。由此名大噪，世家争愿赘焉。叔兄商之，惟辗然笑。再强之，则言："矢志青云，不及第，不婚也。"会学使案临，两人并出。兄又落。弟以冠军应试，中顺天第四；明年成进士；授桐城令，有吏治；寻迁河南道掌印御史，富埒王侯。因托疾乞骸骨，赐归田里。宾客填门，迄谢不纳。又自诸生以及显贵，并不言娶，人无不怪之者。归后，渐置婢。或疑其私；嫂察之，殊无苟且。无何，明鼎革，天下大乱。乃谓嫂曰："实相告：我小郎妇也。以男

came they sent him away. Whenever there was a funeral or happy occasion in the area, the elder brother went out to socialize, but the younger drew his curtains and went on studying. Half a year passed, but seldom had anyone seen his face. If guests asked to see him, the elder brother would make excuses for him. When people read his essays, their eyes bulged with amazement. A few tried to force their acquaintance on him by breaking into his room, but he simply greeted them with a bow and turned away. Everyone who glimpsed his fine features became an admirer. So it was that his reputation was spread over a wide area, and noblemen vied to have him marry into their families. When his cousin brought up the subject, he responded with a bemused smile. When urged further he replied, "I have vowed to attain to the height of honors. Until my name is posted on the notice board, there will be no marriage for me."

At that time the civil examiner came to preside over an examination, and the two went up for it. The elder brother failed again, but the younger took top honors in the qualifying examination and placed fourth in Shuntian prefecture. The year after he took the Doctorate and was given the magistracy of Tongcheng in Anhui province, where he had a good record as an administrator. He was soon promoted to censor with imperial credentials of the Henan circuit. He possessed the wealth of a prince or marquis.

On the pretext of ill health, he asked to be allowed to resign and was given permission to return to his family lands. Guests milled about his door, but all were turned away. Everyone thought it strange that from his student days right up to this time of prosperity and renown, he had never spoken of marriage. Upon his return he gradually staffed his household with maids. Some surmised that he was having relations with them, but investigations by his cousin's wife proved that there were no licentious goings-on.

Before long came the widespread disorder following the fall of the

子阘茸，不能自立，负气自为之。深恐播扬，致天子召问，贻笑海内耳。”嫂不信。脱靴而示之足，始愕；视靴中，则败絮满焉。于是使生承其衔，仍闭门而雌伏矣。而生平不孕，遂出资购妾。谓生曰：“凡人置身通显，则买姬媵以自奉；我宦迹十年，犹一身耳。君何福泽，坐享佳丽？”生曰：“面首三十人，请卿自置耳。”相传为笑。是时生父母，屡受覃恩矣。搢绅拜往，尊生以侍御礼。生羞袭闺衔，惟以诸生自安，终身未尝舆盖云。

异史氏曰：“翁姑受封于新妇，可谓奇矣。然侍御而夫人也者，何时无之？但夫人而侍御者少耳。天下冠儒冠、称丈夫者，皆愧死矣！”

Ming Dynasty. The younger brother finally confessed to his cousin's wife: "To tell the truth, I am the young gentleman's wife, not his brother. He is a nobody who cannot stand on his own feet, so I insisted on doing it myself. I fear that if this gets out I'll be summoned for questioning by the emperor, and my husband and I will be the laughing stocks of the empire." The cousin's wife could not believe this. He removed 'his' boots to expose 'his' feet: much to her amazement, the boots were stuffed with old cotton.

From then on the woman had her husband assume her title, while she withdrew behind closed doors as most females do. She had never gotten pregnant, so she put up the money to buy a concubine and said to the student: "Any man who makes a success of himself buys a concubine to serve him. After ten years as an official I still have only one partner. What makes you so fortunate, that you can sit back and have a pretty woman come to you."

"Go ahead and provide yourself with a stable of thirty male concubines," said the student. People often retell this witty exchange for amusement.

During this period the student's deceased parents were frequently honored on occasions of imperial bounty granting. The gentry came to pay their respects to the student and honored him as though he were censor. The student was ashamed to accpet the title his wife had earned. He felt comfortable only when treated as a scholar and lived out his days without riding in a carriage under an official canopy.

The Chronicler of the Tales comments: "For parents to receive posthumous titles because of a daughter-in-law is remarkable, but when have we ever been without people who become censors and proceed to act like women? The rare thing is a woman who becomes a censor. That would be enough to make everyone in this world who wears a scholar's hat and calls himself a man die of shame!"

小　谢

渭南姜部郎第，多鬼魅，常惑人。因徙去。留苍头门之而死，数易皆死；遂废之。里有陶生望三者，夙倜傥，好狎妓，酒阑辄去之。友人故使妓奔就之，亦笑内不拒；而实终夜无所沾染。尝宿部郎家，有婢夜奔，生坚拒不乱，部郎以是契重之。家綦贫，又有"鼓盆之戚"，茆屋数椽，溽暑不堪其热；因请部郎，假废第。部郎以其凶故，却之。生因作《续无鬼论》献部郎，且曰："鬼何能为！"部郎以其请之坚，诺之。生往除厅事。薄暮，置书其中；返

GHOST-GIRL XIAOXIE

THE mansion of Ministry Secretary Jiang in Weinan was haunted by a large number of supernatural beings that misled people. Because of this the Jiang family moved away, leaving an old man to watch the gate, This man died, as did several others that were sent to take his place, so the house was deserted. In the same neighborhood lived a scholar named Tao Wangsan, a carefree, self-assured sort, who enjoyed the companionship of courtesans but always left them when the drinking was over. Some friends had a courtesan follow him to his place. He let her in with a smile but did not lay a hand on her all night. Once while staying overnight at the secretary's mansion, he earned a high place in his host's estimation by firmly refusing the advances of a maid who went to him at night.

Tao lived in dire poverty. Moreover, he had just been bereaved of his wife, and his tiny thatched hut was unbearably hot in sweltering summer. For these reasons he asked the secretary if he might make use of the vacant mansion. The secretary refused because of the hauntings. This inspired the scholar to write an essay entitled "Further Arguments on the Non-Existence of Ghosts" and present it to the secretary with the comment: "What can a ghost do to me?"

取他物，则书已亡。怪之，仰卧榻上，静息以伺其变。食顷，闻步履声，睨之，见二女自房中出，所亡书，送还案上。一约二十，一可十七八，并皆姝丽。逡巡立榻下，相视而笑。生寂不动。长者翘一足踹生腹，少者掩口匿笑。生觉心摇摇若不自持，即急肃然端念，卒不顾。女近以左手捋髭，右手轻批颐颊，作小响。少者益笑。生骤起，叱曰："鬼物敢尔！"二女骇奔而散。生恐夜为所苦，欲移归，又耻其言不掩；乃挑灯读。暗中鬼影憧憧，略不顾瞻。夜将半，烛而寝。始交睫，觉人以细物穿鼻，奇痒，大嚏；但闻暗处隐隐作笑声。生不语，假寐以俟之。俄见少女以纸条捻细股，鹤行鹭伏而至；生暴起呵之，飘窜而去。既寝，

At last the secretary gave in to his determined requests, and the scholar went there to clean up and move into one of the rooms. At dusk he set down a book and went out to bring in some other things. When he came back the book was gone. Baffled by this turn of events, he lay quietly on his bed looking at the ceiling and waiting for what would happen next. After the duration of a meal he heard footsteps. Looking out of the corner of his eyes, he saw two young women coming from an inner chamber and replacing the missing book on the desk. One was about twenty and the other seventeen or eighteen. Both of them were beautiful. They walked hesitantly to the side of his bed and exchanged grins. The scholar kept quiet and did not stir. The older girl raised her foot and planted it on the scholar's belly: the younger one covered her mouth with her hand to stifle a giggle. The scholar felt himself wavering: he made a sober effort to straighten his thoughts and succeeded in turning his eyes away. The girl came closer and stroked his whiskers with her left hand as she patted his cheek with her right, which caused the younger to laugh all the more. The scholar leapt up and shouted, "How dare you ghosts behave this way?"

The two girls ran off in fright. The scholar feared they would bother him at night and wanted to move back home, but he felt ashamed not to back up his words with deeds, so he lit a lamp and stayed up reading. Spectral froms flitted about in the dark, but he did not ever glance at them. When it was almost the middle of the night, he went to bed with a candle burning. The minute his eyelids shut he felt someone poking a fine object into his nose. The exceedingly itching sensation was too much for him: he let loose with a mighty sneeze, which was answered by muffled laughter from laughter a dark corner. Saying nothing, he pretended to be asleep and waited for them to try again. Soon he saw the younger girl roll a slip of paper into the shape of a toothpick and then come toward him, placing each foot carefully like crane and crouching like an egret. He leapt up and railed at her.

又穿其耳。终夜不堪其扰。鸡既鸣，乃寂无声，生始酣眠，终日无所睹闻。日既下，恍惚出现。生遂夜炊，将以达旦。长者渐曲肱几上，观生读。既而掩生卷。生怒捉之，即已飘散；少间，又抚之。生以手按卷读。少者潜于脑后，交两手掩生目，瞥然去，远立以哂。生指骂曰："小鬼头！捉得便都杀却！"女子即又不惧。因戏之曰："房中纵送，我都不解，缠我无益。"二女微笑，转身向灶，析薪溲米，为生执爨。生顾而奖曰："两卿此为，不胜憨跳耶？"俄顷，粥熟，争以匕、箸、陶碗置几上。生曰："感卿服役，何以报德？"女笑云："饭中溲合砒、鸩矣。"生曰："与卿夙无嫌怨，何至以此相加。"啜已，复盛，争为奔走。生乐之，习以

She floated into hiding. Again he lay down, and this time she stuck something in his ear. He had to put up with these torments the whole night.

At cockcrow the sounds finally died down, and the scholar slept soundly. He saw and heard nothing of the girls all day, but at sundown they were there before he knew it. That night he started a cooking fire, intending to stay up until morning. The older girl gradually approached, leaned her forearm against the table and watched him read. Without warning she reached over and closed his book. He grabbed angrily at her, but she had already floated out of reach. A little while passed, and again she flipped it shut, so he pressed down on the book with his hands as he read. Before long the younger girl stole up behind him, put her hands over his eyes, darted away and stood at a distance giggling.

The scholar shook his finger at her and scolded, "You little imp! It will be all over for you when I catch you."

This did nothing to deter them, so he said playfully: "I don't know the first thing about riding young fillies in bed, so what's the use of pestering me?" The two girls grinned and turned toward the stove, where they set to work splitting firewood, rinsing rice and doing the cooking for him. He looked up and praised them: "Now isn't this better than the idiotic way you were acting?"

Soon the rice gruel was done, and they raced to set chopsticks, a spoon and earthenware bowl on the desk. "How can I show my gratitude for your helpfulness?"

"No need. We mixed arsenic and esssnce of falcon feathers with your rice."

"There has never been any ill-will between us," he said. "I don't think you would do that to me?" When his bowl was empty, they filled it again: they ran back and forth trying to outdo one another in helpfulness. He enjoyed their attentions and grew accustomed to them. As

为常。日渐稔,接坐倾语,审其姓名。长者云:"妾秋容,乔氏;彼阮家小谢也。"又研问所由来。小谢笑曰:"痴郎!尚不敢一呈身,谁要汝问门第,作嫁娶耶?"生正容曰:"相对丽质,宁独无情;但阴冥之气,中人必死。不乐与居者,行可耳;乐与居者,安可耳。如不见爱,何必玷两佳人?如果见爱,何必死一狂生?"二女相顾动容,自此不甚虐弄之;然时而探手于怀,捋裤于地,亦置不为怪。一日,录书未卒业而出,返则小谢伏案头,操管代录。见生,掷笔睨笑。近视之,虽劣不成书,而行列疏整。生赞曰:"卿雅人也!苟乐此,仆教卿为之。"乃拥诸怀,把腕而教之画。秋容自外入,色乍变,意似妒。小谢笑曰:"童时尝从父学书,久不作,遂如梦寐。"秋容不语。生喻

time passed they became more familiar, until one day he invited them to sit down for a talk and asked their names.

"My name is Qiurong and my surname is Qiao: she is Xiaoxie of the Ruan family," said the older.

When he inquired into their backgrounds, Xiaoxie said laughingly: "Silly man. Why should you ask about our families when you haven't shown your true feelings toward us. Are you thinking about marriage?"

"Do you think I am so unfeeling as to be unmoved by your beauty?" he asked earnestly. "But any man who is touched by dark, supernatural forces must die. If you don't like living with me, you can leave. If you like living with me, it's all right to stay. If you don't care for me, why should two nice girls like you lower yourselves? If you do have love in your heart, why would you wish to cause the death of a book-crazed scholar?"

Visibly moved, the two girls exchanged glances. From then on they were less froward in their playfulness. Still they sometimes slipped their hands under his shirt or pulled down his pants, but he did not let it bother him. One day he got up from a book he was in the middle of copying and went out. On his return he found Xiaoxie hunch over the desk, writing brush in hand, copying for him. Seeing him, she threw down the brush and laughed, looking at him with sidelong glances. He took a close look: her characters were too ill-formed to be called calligraphy, but the lines were evenly spaced.

"You are a woman of refinement," he praised her. "If you enjoy this, I'll teach you." He took her on his lap and guided her hand to show her how to make the strokes. When Qiurong came into the room her face fell abruptly, obviously out of jealousy.

Xiaoxie laughed and said, "I learned calligraphy from my father when I was little, but I haven't practiced for ages, so it feels like it's coming back to me in a dream." Qiurong said nothing. The scholar

其意,伪为不觉者,遂抱而授以笔,曰:“我视卿能此否?”作数字而起,曰:“秋娘大好笔力!”秋容乃喜。生于是折两纸为范,俾共临摹;生另一灯读。窃喜其各有所事,不相侵扰。仿毕,祗立几前,听生月旦。秋容素不解读,涂鸦不可辨认,花判已,自顾不如小谢;有惭色。生奖慰之,颜始霁。二女由此师事生,坐为抓背,卧为按股,不惟不敢侮,争媚之。逾月,小谢书居然端好,生偶赞之。秋容大惭,粉黛淫淫,泪痕如线;生百端慰解之,乃已。因教之读,颖悟非常,指示一过,无再问者。与生竞读,常至终夜。小谢又引其弟三郎来,拜生门下。年十五六,姿容秀美。以金如意一钩为贽。生令与秋容执一经,满堂咿唔,生于此设鬼帐焉。部郎闻之喜,以时给其

sensed what she felt but, pretending not to notice, he set her on his lap, handed her a brush and said, "Let me see if you can do it."

She wrote several characters and got up. "Miss Qiurong wields a mighty pen!" was his comment, which brightened Qiurong's face.

The scholar thereupon folded a piece of paper, tore it into halves and wrote model characters on each one for them to copy while he went to read under another lamp, secretly relieved that they would stop bothering him now they had something to keep them busy. When they were done copying, they stood respectfully before the desk waiting for his comments. Qiurong had never learned to recognize characters, and her scribbling was undecipherable. When he finished making a few offhand corrections, a humiliated look came over her face as she realized she was not Xiaoxie's rival, but the scholar's praise and reassurance finally cleared the clouds on her brow.

Frow then on the two girls treated the scholar as their teacher. When he sat they scratched his back; when he lay down they massaged his thighs. Far from affronting him, they vied to please. After a month Xiaoxie was writing in an unexpectedly neat and elegant hand, for which he occasionly praised her. Qiurong was sorely abashed: her rouge and mascara were streaked with trickling tears that would not stop until the scholar went to great lengths to reassure her. To make her feel better, he taught her to read and found her to possess remarkable powers of comprehennsion. Once he had pointed something out, she never-needed to ask a second time. Often she stayed up all night trying to outread the scholar.

Xiaoxie also brought her third brother to bow before the scholar and become his student. He was fifteen or sixteen years old and well-favored in face and bearing. His gift to his teacher was an as-you-will sceptre of gold. The scholar assigned him the same classic that Qiurong was studying. Soon the hall was filled with reciting voices: the scholar had founded a private school for ghosts. The ministry secre-

薪水。积数月,秋容与三郎皆能诗,时相酬唱。小谢阴嘱勿教秋容,生诺之;秋容阴嘱勿教小谢,生亦诺之。一日,生将赴试,二女涕泪持别。三郎曰:“此行可以托疾免;不然,恐履不吉。”生以告疾为辱,遂行。先是,生好以诗词讥切时事,获罪于邑贵介,日思中伤之。阴赂学使,诬以行简,淹禁狱中。资斧绝,乞食于囚人,自分已无生理。忽一人飘忽而入,则秋容也。以馔具馈生。相向悲咽,曰:“三郎虑君不吉,今果不谬。三郎与妾同来,赴院申理矣。”数语而出,人不之睹。越日,部院出,三郎遮道声屈,收之。秋容入狱报生,返身往侦之,三日不返。生愁饿无聊,度一日如

tary was delighted by the news of this and began to pay him a regular salary. After several months Qiurong and third brother were accomplished in poetry and frequently presented poems to each other. Xiaoxie secretly told the scholar not to teach Qiurong: he agreed not to. When Qiurong told him to stop teaching Xiaoxie, he assented to her too.

The day came when the scholar left to take part in an examination. The girls sniffed and tears ran down their cheeks as they said their farewells.

"Maybe you should ask to be excused from this exami-nation on grounds of illness," said third brother. "Other-wise, I'm afraid you will land in an unfortunate predicament."

The scholar considered it degrading to ask for leave on account of illness, so he went anyway. Prior to this the scholar, who was fond of writing topical poems in a satirical vein, had offended a nobleman in the district, who brooded daily over how he could retaliate. He secretly bribed the civil examiner to have Tao thrown in prison on a trumped-up charge of misconduct. The scholar ran out of pocket money and was forced to beg for food from other prisoners. He had already resigned himself to death when suddenly a person appeared out of nowhere in his cell. It was Qiurong. She set dishes of food before him, gave him a long sorrowful look and quavered: "Third brother's fear that you would come to harm was well-founded. He and I came together: now he is going to the governor's yamen to lodge an appeal." She slipped out unnoticed after speaking only these few words.

The next day when the governor went out, third brother stopped him in the street crying "Injustice!" The governor agreed to read his appeal.

After appearing in the prison to let the scholar know of third brother's plan, Qiurong had gone back to watch the outcome. Three days went by without her showing up again. For the scholar, helpless-

年岁。忽小谢至，怆惋欲绝，言："秋容归，经由城隍祠，被西廊黑判强摄去，逼充御媵。秋容不屈，今亦幽囚。妾驰百里，奔波颇殆；至北郭，被老棘刺吾足心，痛彻骨髓，恐不能再至矣。"因示之足，血殷凌波焉。出金三两，跛踦而没。部院勘三郎，素非瓜葛，无端代控，将杖之，扑地遂灭。异之。览其状，情词悲恻。提生面鞫，问："三郎何人？"生伪为不知。部院悟其冤，释之。既归，竟夕无一人。更阑，小谢始至。惨然曰："三郎在部院，被廨神押赴冥司；冥王以三郎义，令托生富贵家。秋容久锢，妾以状投城隍，又被按阁，不得入，且复奈何？"生忿曰："黑老魅何敢如此！明日仆

ness and the misery of hunger made each day pass like a year. Suddenly Xiaoxie appeared in his cell in great anguish and said, "On her way back Qiurong passed through shrine to the City-God. The Black Judge of the Western Corridor abducted her and tried to force her to be his chambermaid, but she would not give in, so now she too is in captivity. I ran the hundred li here so fast I nearly dropped. When I reached the northern wall the sole of my foot was punctured by a nasty thorn. The pain went right through to the marrow of my boness. I'm afraid I won't be able to come again." She showed him her foot covered with crimson blood, then pulled out three taels of gold, hobbled away, and disappeared.

Meanwhile the governor, having ascertained that third brother lacked even a tenuous relationship with the accused and was making an appeal for no good reason, ordered his men to beat him with staffs only to see him dive to the ground and disappear. The amazed governor read the written appeal which the strange visitant had just given him and was touched by the content and the manner of writing. He had the scholar brought out for questioning and asked "Who is this third brother?" The scholar pretended not to know. The governor realized the injustice of the sentence and released him.

The whole evening of the scholar's return passed without anyone coming. It was late in the night before Xiaoxie finally came and reported gloomily: "Third brother was seized by a corridor spirit in the governor's *yamen* and taken to the underworld court. The king of the underworld sent him to be reborn into a rich family in consideration of his commendable deeds. I submitted a statement to the city god speaking out against Qiurong's undue detainment, but the case was pigeonholed and I was not given an audience. Now what can I do. ?"

The scholar flew into a rage and spluttered, "Who does that black fiend think he is, taking liberties like this? Tomorrow I'm going to knock his image over and grind it to mud under my feet. While I'm at

其像,践踏为泥,数城隍而责之;案下吏暴横如此,渠在醉梦中耶!"悲愤相对,不觉四漏将残。秋容飘然忽至。两人惊喜,急问。秋容泣下曰:"今为郎万苦矣!判日以刀杖相逼,今夕忽放妾归,曰:'我无他,原以爱故;既不愿,固亦不曾污玷。烦告陶秋曹,勿见谴责。'"生闻少欢,欲与同寝,曰:"今日愿为卿死。"二女戚然曰:"向受开导,颇知义理,何忍以爱君者杀君乎?"执不可;然俯颈倾头,情均伉俪。二女以遭难故,妒念全消。会一道士途遇生,顾谓"身有鬼气。"生以其言异,具告之。道士曰:"此鬼大好,不拟负他。"因书二符付生,曰:"归授两鬼,任其福命:如闻门外有哭女者,吞符急出,先到者可活。"生拜受,

it I'll give that city god a piece of my mind for letting his underlings get out of hand like this. Is he off in some drunken dream or what?"

The two of them sat there sharing their indignation and sorrow. Before they knew it the fourth watch was nearly at an end. Suddenly Qiurong appeared out of thin air. When they had gotten over their joyful surprise, they pressed her to tell all that had happened.

Tears ran down Qiurong's face as she said, "I suffered terribly because of you! The judge threatened me with knives and clubs every day, but today he suddenly let me go. He said, 'I only behaved as I did out of my tender feelings for you. But you were unwilling, and anyway I did not molest you. Please convey that fact to Tao, who is foreordained to be minister of punishments, and ask him not to reproach me.'"

The scholar was elated by this and found himself wishing he could sleep with her. "Today I want to die in your arms," he said.

The two women answered glumly: "Now that you have opened our eyes for us, we known a little something about right and wrong. We could not bear it if what we did to show our love caused you to die."

They persisted in refusing, but they submissively bowed their heads with wifelike tenderness. The difficulties they had gone through had completely done away with their feelings of jealousy.

One day as the scholar walked along the road he met a Taoist priest who turned to him and said, "You are giving off a ghost aura."

Because the Taoist's manner of speaking was so extraor-dinary, the scholar told him everything. The Taoist said, "These ghosts are too good to let down."

With this he wrose out two paper charms and gave them to the scholar, saying: "When you get home give one to each ghost, and let fate decide who will be the lucky one. The moment you hear a funeral procession for a young woman outside your gate, have the ghosts swallow the charms and run out. The one who gets there first will come to

归嘱二女。后月余,果闻有哭女者。二女争奔而去。小谢忙急,忘吞其符。见有丧舆过,秋容直出,入棺而没;小谢不得入,痛哭而返。生出视,则富室郝氏殡其女。共见一女子入棺而去,方共惊疑;俄闻棺中有声,息肩发验,女已顿苏。因暂寄生斋外,罗守之。忽开目问陶生。郝氏研诘之。答云:“我非汝女也。”遂以情告。郝未深信,欲舁归;女不从,径入生斋,偃卧不起。郝乃识婿而去。生就视之,面庞虽异,而光艳不减秋容,喜惬过望,殷叙平生。忽闻呜呜鬼泣,则小谢哭于暗陬。心甚怜之,即移灯往,宽譬哀情,而衿袖淋浪,痛不可解。近晓始去。天明,郝以婢媪赍送香奁,居然翁婿矣。暮入帷房,则小谢又哭。如

life."

The scholar took the charms with a bow, returned home and relayed the instructions to the girls. Sure enough, a little more than a month later they heard the sound of people mourning the death of a young woman in their family. The two girls raced to the spot. Xiaoxie was so flustered that she forgot to swallow her charm. As the hearse passed by, Qiurong ran straight to it, jumped into the coffin and disappeared. Xiaoxie, who was unable to find away in, sobbed miserably and turned back. The scholar went out for a look and found that it was a funeral procession for a daughter of the wealthy Hao family. Everyone present had seen a girl jump through the top of the coffin and disappear. Now while they gaped in bewilderment, a voice was heard from within the coffin. The bearers took the coffin off their shoulders and opened it for a look. The girl had come back to life. They put her down outside the scholar's studio and formed a circle around her. The girl opened her eyes with a start and asked for the scholar. In response to Mr. Hao's questions she answered, "I am not your daughter."

Then she told him the truth, but this was not enough to convince Hao, who wanted to have her carried back to his house. The girl refused to go: instead, she darted into the scholar's studio, lay down, and would not rise. Where-upon Hao acknowledged the scholar as his son-in-law and left. The scholar went to her and took a good look: her features were different, but this face was a no less radiantly beautiful than Qiurong's own. This was a joyful blessing beyond his expectations. He was making an earnest declaration of his everlasting affection when they were interrupted by a muffled ghostly sobbing—it was Xiaoxie crying in a dark concr. Pitying her from the depths of his heart he picked up the lamp, walked over to her and spoke eloquent words of consolation. Still the sleeves and front of her blouse were soaked with tears, and nothing he said could relieve her misery. She

此六七夜,夫妇俱为惨动,不能成合卺之礼。生忧思无策。秋容曰:“道士,仙人也。再往求,倘得怜救。”生然之。迹道士所在,叩伏自陈。道士力言“无术”。生哀不已。道士笑曰:“痴生好缠人!合与有缘,请竭吾术。”乃从生来,索静室,掩扉坐,戒勿相问。凡十余日,不饮不食。潜窥之,瞑若睡。一日晨兴,有少女搴帘入,明眸皓齿,光艳照人。微笑曰:“跋履终夜,惫极矣!被汝纠缠不了,奔驰百里外,始得一好庐舍,道人载与俱来矣。待见其人,便相交付耳。”敛昏,小谢至,女遽起迎抱之,翕然合为一体,仆地而僵。道士自室中出,拱手径去。拜而送之。及返,则女已

did not leave until near dawn. At daybreak Hao, every bit the new father-in-law, sent maids and serving women with dowry chests. That night when the scholar walked through the bedroom curtain, Xiaoxie started crying again. This went on every night for a week. Husband and wife were so affected by her dismal presence that they could not consummate their marriage. The scholar worried over the matter, but he could not come up with a solution.

"That Taoist priest is surely an immortal," said Qiurong. "If you go and plead with him, he might take pity on her and save her."

This seemed sensible to the scholar. He trailed the Taoist to where he was staying, kowtowed to him and stated his reason for coming. The Taoist protested that he had "no magical abilities," but the scholar would not give up his distraught pleading.

"This foolheaded scholar won't give a person a moment's peace. I suppose there is a bond of fate between us. All right, I'll do whatever lies within my power."

He went home with the scholar, asked for a quiet room and warned that he was not to be disturbed. Then he closed the door behind him and assumed a sitting position. For over ten days he did not eat or drink. Peeking in on him, they saw that he was deep in a trance. One morning as they were getting up a young woman parted the curtains and entered. The radiance of her bright eyes and gleaming teeth shone into their eyes.

"I've been trudging the whole night through," she said with a little laugh, "and now I am utterly worn out! You would not leave me alone, so I had to run myself ragged; I was a hundred li from here before I found a nice bodily dwelling. She is coming with the Taoist. When she shows up, he will turn her over to you."

As dusk closed in that evening, Xiaoxie appeared. The strange girl jumped up and ran to embrace her. Their outlines overlapped and then merged into a single body which fell stiffly on the floor. The

苏。扶置床上，气体渐舒，但把足呻言趾股痠痛，数日始能起。后生应试得通籍。有蔡子经者，与同谱，以事过生，留数日。小谢自邻舍归，蔡望见之，疾趋相蹑；小谢侧身敛避，心窃怒其轻薄。蔡告生曰："一事深骇物听，可相告否？"诘之，答曰："三年前，少妹夭殒，经两夜而失其尸，至今疑念。适见夫人，何相似之深也？"生笑曰："山荆陋劣，何足以方君妹？然既系同谱，义即至切，何妨一献妻孥。"乃入内，使小谢衣殉装出。蔡大惊曰："真吾妹也！"因而泣下。生乃具述本末。蔡喜曰："妹子未死，吾将速归，用慰严慈。"遂去。过数

Taoist came out of his room, joined his hands before his chest, and turned to leave. The scholar bowed to him and saw him off. When he came back in, the girl had regained consciousness. He hepled her onto the bed. As she rested the circulation of vital energy through her body was gradually restored, but she cluched at legs and moaned of sharp muscular pain in her feet and thighs. Several days passed before she was on her feet.

Later the scholar went up for examinations and won a place on the roster of prospective officials. A fellow examinee named Cai Zijing visited him on some matter or other and stayed several days. When Cai caught sight of Xiaoxie returning from next door, he ran over to her and practically trod on her heels. Xiaoxie turned away and ran from the room, seething inwardly at his rashness. Cai turned and unburdened himself to the scholar: There is something on my mind which could be a shock to people who bear of it. Can I confide in you?"

The scholar questioned him until he let it out: "Three years ago my little sister died young. Two nights later her body disappeared. To this day this remains a mystery to me. I saw your wife just now, and I wonder how she came to bear such a startling resemblance to my sister?"

The scholar answered jokingly, "My wife is homely, how can she compare with your sister? But since you are my fellow candidate and my close friend, there could not be any harm in introducing my wife to you."

With this he entered the inner chamber and had Xiaoxie dress in her burial clothes to greet the guest.

"She really is my sister," Cai exclaimed in great aston-ishment. Tears began to run down his face. The scholar then told him the whole story. Cai howled gleefully: "My sister is still alive! I must hurry home and give my parents the comfort of knowing she is alive." And so he left. After a few days the whole family came, and afterward they

日。举家皆至,后往来如郝焉。

异史氏曰:“绝世佳人,求一而难之,何遽得两哉!事千古而一见,惟不私奔女者能遘之也。道士其仙耶?何术之神也!苟有其术,丑鬼可交耳。”

exchanged visits with the scholar just as the Hao family did.

The Chronicler of the Tales comments: "To find one matchless beauty is no easy matter, not to speak of two at once! This is something that only to a man who can keep himself from running off with whatever woman is available. Was the Taoist priest an immortal? What made his magic so powerful? With the right magic, hideous ghouls can be worth befriending."

考　弊　司

闻人生，河南人。抱病经日，见一秀才入，伏谒床下，谦抑尽礼。已而请生少步，把臂长语，刺刺且行，数里外犹不言别。生伫足，拱手致辞。秀才云："更烦移趾，仆有一事相求。"生问之。答云："吾辈悉属考弊司辖。司主名虚肚鬼王。初见之，例应割髀肉，浼君一缓颊耳。"生惊问："何罪而至于此？"曰："不必有罪，此是旧例。若丰于贿者，可赎也。然

THE INSPECTORATE OF MISDEEDS

WEN Rensheng of Henan had been laid up with an illness for days when a bachelor of letters appeared and kowtowed a deferential greeting at the foot of his bed. That done, he invited the scholar to go on a stroll. He took the scholar by the arm and chattered ceaselessly as they walked, but made no mention of leaving him even after they had gone a couple of li. The scholar stopped, joined his hands before his chest and said farewell.

"I must trouble you to keep walking," said the bachelor of letters. "I would like you to do a favor for me." The scholar asked what it was, and he answered, "People of my rank are all under the authority of the Inspectorate of Misdeeds. Its chief is called the Empty-Bellied Ghoul-King. When new subordinates have a first audience with him, the rules require that we offer him pieces of flesh cut form our thighs. May I impose on you to put in a good word for me."

"What crime have you committed that you must suffer this?" asked the scholar.

"One need not be guilty of a crime. This is an established precedent. Anyone who gives a generous bribe can buy his way out of it,

而我贫。”生曰:“我素不稔鬼王,何能效力?”曰:“君前世是伊大父行,宜可听从。”言次,已入城郭。至一府署,廨宇不甚弘敞,惟一堂高广,堂下两碣东西立,绿书大于栲栳,一云“孝弟忠信”,一云“礼义廉耻”。躇阶而进,见堂上一匾,大书“考弊司”。楹间,板雕翠字一联云:“曰校、曰序、曰庠,两字德行阴教化;上士、中士、下士,一堂礼乐鬼门生。”游览未已,官已出,鬈发鲐背,若数百年人;而鼻孔撩天,唇外倾,不承其齿。从一主簿吏,虎首人身。又十余人列侍,半狞恶若山精。秀才曰:“此鬼王也。”生骇极,欲却退。鬼王已睹,降阶揖生上,便问兴居。生但诺。又问:“何事见临?”生以秀才意具白之。鬼王色变曰:“此有

but I am penniless."

"But I have never been connected in any way with the Ghoul-King. How can I help you?"

"In a former life you were of the same generation as his grandfather. He is likely to listen to you on that account."

What with all their talking, they were inside the walls of a city before they knew it. They came to a *yamen* housed in a none-too-spacious building, only the central hall of which was highroofed and roomy. At the foot of the raised hall, to the east and the west stood two stone tablets bearing green characters, each a square foot in size. One tablet read: "Filiality, fraternity, loyalty, faithfulnes" and the other"Propriety, justice, honesty, honor." Walking up the entrance steps, they saw a plaque with the words "Inspectorate of Misdeeds" at the head of the hall. A couplet in malachite-tinted characters was carved on two opposing pillars: "Be they institutes, academies or schools, the essence of subterranean teaching is 'virtuous behavior': Be they superior, mediocre or inferior, the hall of music and etiquette educates ghostly disciples." Before they had finished looking the place over, an official whose frizzy hair and hunched back made him look hundreds of years old came toward them. His nostrils were turned up to the sky and his lips protruded, unable to contain his teeth. Behind him trailed a clerk in charge of files, who had a tiger's head and human body. Last of all came ten or so men who lined up in attendence, half of whom had the fierce ugliness of trolls.

"That is the Ghoul-King," said the bachelor of letters. The scholar recoiled in terror, but before he could get away the Ghoul-King caught sight of him, descended the steps, invited him into the hall with hands clasped obsequiously and inquired after his health. The scholar merely grunted in acknowledgement, whereupon the king asked, "To what do I owe the honor of this visit?"

The scholar answered by telling him exactly what the bachelor of

成例,即父命所不敢承!”气象森凛,似不可入一词。生不敢言,骤起告别;鬼王侧行送之,至门外始返。生不归,潜入以观其变。至堂下,则秀才已与同辈数人,交臂历指,俨然在徽缠中。一狞人持刀来,裸其股,割片肉,可骈三指许。秀才大嗥欲嗄。生少年负义,愤不自持,大呼曰:“惨惨如此,成何世界!”鬼王惊起,暂命止割,跷履逆生。生忿然已出,遍告市人,将控上帝。或笑曰:“迂哉!蓝蔚苍苍,何处觅上帝而诉之冤也?此辈惟与阎罗近,呼之或可应耳。”乃示之途。趋而往,果见殿陛威赫,阎罗方坐;伏阶号屈。王召讯已,立命诸鬼绾绁提锤而去。少顷,鬼王及秀才

letters had asked him to say. A displeased look came over the Ghoul-King's face as he said, "In a case like this, when there is a fixed rule to go by, I could not change things if my father ordered me to." He delivered these words with an icy finality that made prusuing the matter seem futile. Not daring to say another word, the scholar rose abruptly and asked to be excused. The Ghoul-King saw him all the way to the door, walking sideways.

Instead of going home, the scholar slipped back in to watch what happened. From the foot of the hall he saw the bachelor of letters and his fellows with their arms tied behind backs and their fingers held tightly between torture clamps: obviously they had already been bound and trussed. A hideous man came out carrying a knife and proceeded to strip their thighs bare and slice off chunks of flesh three fingers in breadth. The bachelor of letter's shrieks trailed off into hoarse gurgling.

The scholar, being a young man with a sense of justice, could not help but shout in indignation: "What sort of world are you trying to create with such brutality?"

The Ghoul-King got up with a start, ordered a short halt to the slicing and strode menacingly in the scholar's direction. But the scholar stormed out, telling every towns-man he met that he would bring an accusation before the Lord on High.

People jeered at him: "What a deluded fool! Where in the deep blue sky can you find a Lord on High to complain of injustice to? Officials like these are subject to no spirit but Yama. If you call upon him you may get a response."

With this they pointed out the road. The scholar hurried along it until he came to the steps of an imposing hall. He crouched on the steps before Yama's throne and cried out that a great wrong had been committed. Yama called the scholar forward and, after questioning him, immediately dispatched a number of ghosts carring ropes and

并至。审其情确，大怒曰："怜尔夙世攻苦，暂委此任，候生贵家；今乃敢尔！其去若善筋，增若恶骨，罚令生生世世不得发迹也！"鬼乃箠之，仆地，颠落一齿；以刀割指端，抽筋出，亮白如丝。鬼王呼痛，声类斩豕。手足并抽讫，有二鬼押去。生稽首而出。秀才从其后，感荷殷殷。挽送过市，见一户，垂朱帘，帘内一女子，露半面，容妆绝美。生问："谁家？"秀才曰："此曲巷也。"既过，生低徊不能舍，遂坚止秀才。秀才曰："君为仆来，而令踽踽以去，心何忍。"生固辞，乃去。生望秀才去远，急趋入帘内。女接见，喜形于色。入室促坐，相道

iron-tipped clubs. Before long the Ghoul-King and the bachelor of letters appeared. When Yama ascertained the truth of the case, he roared at the Ghoul-King: "out of consideration of your studiousness in your former life, I temporarily assigned you this post while you were on call for rebirth into a wealthy family. How dare you behave so shamelessly! It is my judgement that your sinews of goodness be removed and your bones of wickedness be increased. You are condemned to being a nonentity for endless lives to come!"

The ghosts caned the Ghoul-King until he toppled to the ground, knocking out a tooth. They cut off the tips of his fingers and pulled out white sinews that gleamed like silk. The Ghoul-King howled like a pig being butchered. When the strands had been drawn from his hands and feet, two ghosts led him away.

The scholar touched his forehead to the ground and went out, followed by the bachelor of letters, who was eager for a chance to show his gratitude. The latter took the scholar's arm and led him through a busy district, where they glimpsed a face of matchless beauty peeking from behind the crimson curtains of one of the buildings.

"Whose home is this?" asked the scholar.

"This is one of those 'back alley houses,'" said the bachelor of letters.

As they walked past the scholar, unable to tear himself away, insisted that the bachelor of letters leave him to himself.

"You came here for my sake," said the bachelor of letters. "I cannot bear to make you go back all by yourself." He finally left when the scholar firmly refused his offer to accompany him farther. The scholar watched till he was out of sight, then lost no time going through the door curtain. The girl received him with obvious pleasure on her face. They entered a parlour and she sat down next to him, after which they introduced themselves.

"My surname is Liu, and I go by the name Qiuhua," offered the

姓名。女自言:“柳氏,小字秋华。”一妪出,为具肴酒。酒阑,入帷,欢爱殊浓,切切订婚嫁。既曙,妪入曰:“薪水告竭,要耗郎君金资,奈何!”生顿念腰橐空虚,惶愧无声。久之,曰:“我实不曾携得一文,宜署券保,归即奉酬。”妪变色曰:“曾闻夜度娘索逋欠耶?”秋华颦蹙,不作一语。生暂解衣为质。妪持笑曰:“此尚不能偿酒直耳!”呶呶不满志,与女俱入。生惭。移时,犹冀女出展别,再订前约;久久无音,潜入窥之,见妪与秋华,自肩以上化为牛鬼,目睒睒相对立。大惧,趋出;欲归,则百道歧出,莫知所从。问之市人,并无知其

girl.

An old woman came to set out viands and wine. When they had drunk their fill they went behind bed curtains. Their lovemaking was of rare intensity, and they fervently vowed to become man and wife. The next morning the old woman came in and said, "I have nothing left to pay for household expenses. As much as I hate to speak out, I must ask the young gentleman for some money."

The sudden recollection that his pouch was empty plunged the scholar into guilty silence for an awkward interval before he answered, "To tell the truth, I didn't bring a single along. What I can do is write out a note of credit, which I will make good as soon as I get back home."

An ominous look came over the old woman's face as she snarled:" Have you ever heard of an overnight girl going to collect a debt?"

Qiuhua knit her brows in silence. The scholar stripped off his robe to serve for the time being as a guarantee of payment. The old woman held it up and jeered, "Ha! This doesn't even cover the wine!" She continued to gibber disappointedly as she led the girl from the room.

The scholar was mortified. Hours passed but still be waited, hoping that the girl would come back to bid him farewell and reaffirm her vow. More time went by without a sign of her. He stole toward the inner chamber and peered through a doorway: there were the woman and Qiuhua, but from the shoulders up they had transformed into ox-demons. They stood there looking right at him, their eyes flashing fire. He ran outside in terror. He wanted to go home, but a hundred roads branched out in all directions. Which one should he take? He asked the people in the market, but nobody knew the name of his village. He wandered aimlessly among the stalls and shops for two days and two nights, his heart aching with loss and his hungry stomach rumbling complainingly. He could not make up his mind to go one way

村名者。徘徊廛肆之间，历两昏晓，凄意含酸，响肠鸣饿，进退无以自决。忽秀才过，望见之，惊曰："何尚未归，而简亵若此？"生腼颜莫对。秀才曰："有之矣！得勿为花夜叉所迷耶？"遂盛气而往，曰："秋华母子，何遽不少施面目耶！"去少时，即以衣来付生，曰："淫婢无礼，已叱骂之矣。"送生至家，乃别而去。生暴绝，三日而苏，言之历历。

or another. It was then that the bachelor of letters passed by and happened to see him.

"Why haven't you gone home yet, and why are you dressed so scantily?" he asked in amazement. The scholar was too embarrassed to reply.

"I know!" exclaimed the bachelor of letters. "You got trapped by that seductive she-devil, didn't you?" With that he stormed off indignantly, shouting: "Qiuhua and Ma-dame! Why don't you show regard for my friends any more?" He left for a little while, came back with the robe and gave it to the scholar, saying: "That sex-hungry chambermaid won't behave herself. I just gave her a piece of my mind." He accompanied the scholar home, then said good-bye and left, the scholar, who had died suddenly three days before, came back to life and told of these events in detail.

山　市

奂山山市，邑八景之一也。数年恒不一见。孙公子禹年，与同人饮楼上，忽见山头有孤塔耸起，高插青冥。相顾惊疑，念近中无此禅院。无何，见宫殿数十所，碧瓦飞甍，始悟为山市。未几，高垣睥睨，连亘六七里，居然城郭矣。中有楼若者，堂若者，坊若者，历历在目，以亿万计。忽大风起，尘气莽莽然，城

THE CITY ON THE MOUNTAIN

THE "city on the mountain" at Mt. Huan is one of the eight scenic wonders of my district, but it is usually not seen for years at a time. Young master Sun Yunian and his companions were drinking in a pavilion when they suddenly noticed a lone pagoda standing high on the mountain and towering into the deep blue sky. They looked at one another in bewilderment. They knew there was no such monastery anywhere in the area. Before long scores of palace buildings with green-glazed tiles and high roof ridges appeared: at last they realized that it was the "City on the mountain." Soon they saw a high wall with battlements extending for six or seven li—the city wall, obviously. Inside it the shapes of what appeared to be storied buidings, halls, and lanes by the tens of thousands could be discerned. Suddenly a great wind blew up clouds of dust that hid the city in obscurity. After the wind settled down and the sky cleared, all was gone but the single lofty tower that touched the very clouds. Five shuttered windows were wide open on each story, and the light of the sky shining through from the other side made lines of five bright spots. By counting the lines, one could count the stories. The farther up the tower, the less light shone through. By the eighth story they were no bigger than stars: above

市依稀而已。既而风定天清，一切乌有；惟危楼一座，直接霄汉。五架窗扉皆洞开；一行有五点明处，楼外天也。层层指数：楼愈高，则明愈少；数至八层，裁如星点；又其上，则黯然缥缈，不可计其层次矣。而楼上人往来屑屑，或凭或立，不一状。逾时，楼渐低，可见其顶；又渐如常楼；又渐如高舍，倏忽如拳如豆，遂不可见。又闻有早行者，见山上人烟市肆，与世无别，故又名"鬼市"云。

that they were there and yet not there in the twilight, going an uncountable number of stories farther up. People were coming and going busily on the tower, while some leaned or stood, all in different poses. After a while, the tower grew lower and the top became invisible. Gradually it diminished into a regular storied buiding, then to the size of a tall house, and then quickly into something the size of a fist, then a bean, till finally it dwindled to nothing. I have also heard that an early morning wayfarer once saw habitations and market shops on the mountain that were no different from those of this world, for which reason the apparition was also named the "city of ghosts."

青　娥

霍桓,字匡九,晋人也。父官县尉,早卒。遗生最幼,聪惠绝人。十一岁,以神童入泮。而母过于爱惜,禁不令出庭户,年十三,尚不能辨叔伯甥舅焉。同里有武评事者,好道,入山不返。有女青娥,年十四,美异常伦。幼时窃读父书,慕何仙姑之为人。父既隐,立志不嫁。母无奈之。一日,生于门外瞥见之。童子虽无知,祇觉爱之极,而不能言;直告母,使

FAIRY QING-E

HUO Huan, alias Kuangjiu, was a native of Shanxi. His father, a onetime district garrison commander, had died young. Huo Huan, the youngest survivor, possessed intellectual powers that outshone his peers. His precocity gained him admission to the government academy at the age of eleven. However, his mother was excessively protective and would not allow him to leave the house. At thirteen he still could not distinguish between his paternal and maternal uncles and nephews. In the same neighborhood lived Assessor Wu, a man with a penchant for Taoism, who went into the mountains and never came back. His fourteen-year-old daughter Qing-E was beautiful beyond compare. As a child she had secretly read her father's books and come to admire the deeds of Fairy-Mistress He. After her father left to be a hermit, she resolved not to marry. Her mother was forced to respect her wishes.

One day Huo Huan caught sight of her outside her door. Though he was an adolescent with no understanding of these matters, he was sure of thing, and that was the surge of longing he felt for her, which he could not express in words. He went straight to his mother and asked her to send gifts of betrothal to the Wus. His mother, knowing it was hopeless, was reluctant. The student could no longer feel at

委禽焉。母知其不可,故难之。生郁郁不自得。母恐拂儿意,遂托往来者致意武,果不谐。生行思坐筹,无以为计。会有一道士在门,手握小镵,长裁尺许。生借阅一过,问:"将何用?"答云:"此劚药之具;物虽微,坚石可入。"生未深信。道士即以斫墙上石,应手落如腐。生大异之,把玩不释于手。道士笑曰:"公子爱之,即以奉赠。"生大喜,酬之以钱,不受而去。持归,历试砖石,略无隔阂。顿念穴墙则美人可见,而不知其非法也。更定,逾垣而出,直至武第;凡穴两重垣,始达中庭。见小厢中,尚有灯火,伏窥之,则青娥卸晚妆矣。少顷,烛灭,寂无声。穿墉入,女已熟眠。轻解双履,悄然登榻;又恐女郎惊觉,必遭呵逐,遂潜伏绣褶之侧,略闻香息,心愿窃慰。而半夜经营,疲殆颇甚,少一合眸,不

peace within himself and lapsed into frustration His mother, afraid to cross his wishes, asked a frequent visitor at both houses to convey her wish to the Wus. Just as she had feared, the answer was not favorable. The student thought while he walked and schemed as he sat, but he could not come up with a plan.

One day a Taoist priest turned up at the door, holding a tiny spade hardly more than a foot long. The student asked to have a look at it and asked"What is it for?"

"This is a tool for digging up medicinal roots," was the answer. "It may be small, but it can penetrate solid rock."

The student was incredulous, whereupon the Taoist took the spade and hacked at a stone in the wall, causing it to crumble like a piece of curd. The dumbstruck student took the spade and fondled it every which way, unwilling to let it out of his hands.

"Since you've taken a fancy to it, young master, I'll make you a present of it."

The student was overjoyed and tried to give him money for it but he refused and went on his way. The student carried the spade back toward the house, testing it on bricks and rocks without meeting the slightest resistance. The thought struck him that he could get a look at the beautiful girl boring a hole in her wall: it did not occur to him that this was against the law. In the quiet hours of the night he slipped over the wall and proceeded to the Wu manor. He had to dig through two walls before he came to the courtyard. In a small side chamber a lamp was still burning. He peered from the shadows: it was Qing-E getting ready for bed In a moment the lamp was blown out and all was still. He dug his way in through the thick wall and found the girl fast asleep. He gingerly took off his shoes and eased himself onto the bed. Fearing the inhospitable reception the young woman would surely give him if she were roused, he slid over only as far as the edge of her embroidered coverlet. Faint inhalations of her aroma were enough to

觉睡去。女醒,闻鼻气休休;开目,见穴隙亮入。大骇,急起,暗中拔关轻出,敲窗唤家人妇,共爇火操杖以往。见一总角书生,酣眠绣榻;细审,识为霍生。推之始觉,遽起,目灼灼如流星,似亦不大畏惧,但靦然不作一语。众指为贼,恐呵之。始出涕曰:"我非贼,实以爱娘子故,愿以近芳泽耳。"众又疑穴数重垣,非童子所能者。生出镵以言其异。共试之,骇绝,讶为神授。将共告诸夫人。女俯首沉思,意似不以为可。众窥知女意,因曰:"此子声名门第,殊不辱玷。不如纵之使去,俾复求媒焉。诘旦,假盗以告夫人,如何也?"女不答。众乃促生行。生索镵。共笑曰:"骇儿童!犹不忘凶器耶?"生觑枕边,有凤钗一股,阴纳袖

what he was doing. She told the girl, who said nothing, and showed no anger. One serving old woman patted him on the neck and said, "Don't let that silly look on his face fool you: he knows well enough what he's up to."

They led him away, and he went out through the holes in the walls where he had come from. Back home, he dared not tell his mother everything, so he merely asked her to send another go-between. His mother, who could not bear to refuse him bluntly, merely asked all the local go-betweens to find some other likely prospect quickly.

Learning of this made Qing-E chafe with anxiety. She sent her confidante to drop a hint to Huo's mother. The old woman, glad for the new development, sent a go-between to the Wus. But right about that time a serving maid let out word of the previous incident. Madame Wu was enraged at the news of this dishonor. The coming of a go-between at such a time goaded her into even greater fits of anger. Strikin her staff on the ground, she reviled the student and even threw in a few curses at his mother. The rightened go-between slunk back to the Huos and told of the reception she had met. The student's mother, too, flew into a passion: "I don't have the slightest idea what that idiotic son of mine has done. But why does she have to add insult to injury? Why didn't she have my debauched son and that little tart of hers killed together while thay were in the act?"

From then on she told her relatives the whole story every chance she got. The girl felt like dying for shame when she heard of this. Madame Wu terribly regretted causing this to happen, but she could not stop Mrs. Huo from talking. The girl secretly sent someone to convey her wish to the student's mother, along with her own vow never to love another. It was a soul-stirring message, and the mother was touched by it. She left off spreading vicious stories, but by this time neither side wanted to pursue plans for the marriage.

At that time a certain Master Ou of Shaanxi, who was serving as

切。母感之,乃不复言;而论亲之谋,亦遂辍矣。会秦中欧公宰是邑,见生文,深器之,时召入内署,极意优宠。一日,问生:"婚乎?"答言:"未。"细诘之,对曰:"夙与故武评事女小有盟约;后以微嫌,遂致中寝。"问:"犹愿之否?"生觋然不言。公笑曰:"我当为子成之。"即委县尉、教谕,纳币于武。夫人喜。婚乃定。逾岁,娶归。女入门,乃以镵掷地曰:"此寇盗物,可将去!"生笑曰:"勿忘媒妁。"珍佩之恒不去身。女为人温良寡默,一日三朝其母,余惟闭门寂坐,不甚留心家务。母或以吊庆他往,则事事经纪,罔不井井。年余,生一子孟仙。一切委之乳保,似亦不甚顾惜。又四五年,忽谓生曰:"欢爱之缘,于兹八载。今

district magistrate, read the student's essays. He had a high opinion of the boy's potential, often invited him to his private chambers, and did all he could to see the boy got the best of everything. One day he asked the student: "Are you married?"

"Not yet."

To more specific questions the boy replied, "At one time I had an understanding with the daughter of Assessor Wu, but owing to a slight discord it was left up in the air."

"Do you still want her?" asked the magistrate. The student was too embarrassed to reply.

"I'll fix everything for you," said the magistrate with a laugh. Then he told the district garrison commander and the superintendant of education to send silk and jade to the Wus as gifts of betrothel. This made Madame Wu happy, and soon the engagement was finalized.

A year later the girl was brought to her husband's home. As soon as she came in, she threw down the spade and said "Get this burglar's tool out of my sight!"

"Don't act so ungratefully toward our go-between," laughed the student. He wore it everyday dangling from his sash like a precious pendant.

The girl was good-hearted but quiet. Aside from paying her respects to her mother-in-law three times a day, she spent her time sitting in silence behind closed doors and did not give much attention to household affairs. Once in a while the mother would go away to a funeral, wedding or birthday, in which case the girl would take charge and set everything in order. After little more than a year she gave birth to a son named Mengxian, whom she entrusted completely to the care of a nursemaid. She gave few signs of fondness for the child.

After four or five more years she said to the student one day out of the blue: "The bond of love has kept us together for eight years. Now I foresee a lifelong parting and only a short time of togetherness

离长会短，可将奈何！”生惊问之，即已默默，盛妆拜母，返身入室。追而诘之，则仰眠榻上而气绝矣。母子痛悼，购良材而葬之。母已衰迈，每每抱子思母，如摧肺肝，由是遘病，遂惫不起。逆害饮食，但思鱼羹，而近地则无，百里外始可购致。时厮骑皆被差遣；生性纯孝，急不可待，怀资独往，昼夜无停趾。返至山中，日已沉冥，两足跛踦，步不能咫。后一叟至，问曰：“足得毋泡乎？”生唯唯。叟便曳坐路隅，敲石取火，以纸裹药末，熏生两足讫。试使行，不惟痛止，兼益矫健。感极申谢。叟问：“何事汲汲？”答以母病，因历道所由。叟

remaining. Ah well, there is nothing we can do!"

The student plied her with bewildered questions, but she lapsed into silence. She put on her finest clothes, went to kowtow to his mother, then turned and went back to her room. He chased after her, demanding to know what she meant, only to find her lying face up in bed, her breathing already stopped. Mother and son mourned her bitterly. A coffin of fine wood was bought for the burial.

As she held the boby and thought of its mother, the old woman, already burdened by advanced age, felt pain tearing through her vitals. She contracted an illness and became too feeble to rise. Food and drink tasted revolting to her, but she thought continually of fish broth. No fish were available in the vicinity: the closest place they were to be had was over a hundred li away, and all the servants who could ride happened to be off on errands. But the student's devotion to his mother made him too anxious to wait. Taking some money with him, he set out alone, making the whole trip without stopping day or night. On the way back he found himself in the middle of the mountains as the sun sank and twilight came. His legs ached too much to go another step. Then an old mountain man appeared and asked, "Do you have blisters on your feet?"

The student said yes. The old man took his arm and had him sit by the side of road. Then he struck two stones together to make a fire and fumigated the student's feet by heating a paper package of powder over the fire. He had the student try walking: not only was the pain gone, there was even an added springiness to his steps. He told the old man he was deeply grateful.

"And what makes you run about so frantically?" asked the old man. The student answered first by telling him of his mother's illness, and then with an account of everything that had led up to it.

"Why don't you marry again?" asked the old man.

"I haven't found the right woman," was the answer.

问:"何不另娶?"答云:"未得佳者。"叟遥指山村曰:"此处有一佳人,倘能从我去,仆当为君作伐。"生辞以母病待鱼,姑不遑暇。叟乃拱手,约以异日入村,但问老王,乃别而去。生归,烹鱼献母。母略进,数日寻瘳。乃命仆马往寻叟。至旧处,迷村所在。周章逾时,夕暾渐坠;山谷甚杂,又不可以极望。乃与仆分上山头,以瞻里落;而山径崎岖,苦不可复骑,跋履而上,昧色笼烟矣。蹀躞四望,更无村落。方将下山,而归路已迷。心中燥火如烧。荒窜间,冥堕绝壁。幸数尺下有一线荒台,坠卧其上,阔仅容身。下视黑不见底。惧极不敢少动。又幸崖边皆生小树,约体如栏。移时,

The old man pointed to a mountain village in the distance, saying, "There is a fine young woman over there. If you will follow me there, I'll put in a word for you."

The student refused, saying that his sick mother was waiting for fish and he had no time to spare just now. The old man saluted him and assured him that if he ever did go to that village, he need only ask for Old Wang. With that he said goodbye and walked off.

The student returned home, cooked the fish and served it to his mother. With this nourishment in her system she bounced back to health in a few days.

That settled, he called for his servant and horse and started out in search of the old man. He came to the place they had met, but now he could not find a trace of the village. Time passed as they combed the area, until the evening sun began to drop over the horizon. The valley was so thickly grown it was impossible to see the length of it, so he and his servant separated to climb different peaks and see whether they could spot any settlements. The mountain path was too rugged to negotiate on horseback, so the student climbed to the top on foot. By this time the valley was veiled in the mists of twilight. Pacing back and forth, he looked in all directions: there was no village to be seen. He was ready to go down the mountain, but the road back was lost in gloom. Agitation burned like a fire within him. He began thrashing about, and blindly fell over the edge of a sheer cliff. Luckily, the merest sliver of a ledge covered with thick weeds broke his fall a few feet below. The ledge was only wide enough to hold his body: below was bottomless blackness. The student was so frightened of another fall that he dared not stir. By luck there were saplings growing up from the face of the cliff that held him like a railing. After a time he discovered, to his heartfelt joy, the mouth of a small cave next to his feet. Keeping his back pressed against the rock, he shifted position and wormed his way in. As his mood grew calm, he began to hope that the

见足傍有小洞口;心窃喜,以背着石,螬行而入。意稍稳,冀天明可以呼救。少顷,深处有光如星点。渐近之,约三四里许,忽睹廊舍,并无釭烛,而光明若昼。一丽人自房中出,视之,则青娥也。见生,惊曰:“郎何能来?”生不暇陈,抱袪呜恻。女劝止之。问母及儿,生悉述苦况,女亦惨然。生曰:“卿死年余,此得无冥间耶?”女曰:“非也,此乃仙府。曩时非死,所瘗,一竹杖耳。郎今来,仙缘有分也。”因导令朝父,则一修髯丈夫,坐堂上;生趋拜。女白:“霍郎来。”翁惊起,握手略道平素。曰:“婿来大好,分当留此。”生辞以母望,不能久留。翁曰:“我亦知之。但迟三数日,即亦何伤。”乃饵以肴酒,即令婢设榻于西堂,施锦裀焉。生既退,约女同榻寝。女却之曰:“此何

sound of his calls would bring help in the morning. Peering into the cave, he soon made out sparks of light in its depths. He proceeded three or four li inward, gradually approaching them. Suddenly he saw covered walkways and buildings before him. There were no lamps or candles, yet the place was bright as day. A beautiful woman came out of one of the houses: one look told him it was Qing-E.

She was shocked to see him: "How did you get here?"

The student wasted no time on explanations. He took hold of her sleeve and sobbed miserably. The girl consoled him till he was calm, and then asked of his mother and their son. The student told her how they had suffered, and the girl herself grew sad.

"You died over a year ago," he said. "This is the underworld, isn't it?"

"No, it isn't. This is the grotto of the immortals. I did not die then. What you buried was only a transformed bamboo pole. Your coming means we are fated to be immortal together." Then she led him away to pay a visit to her father—a long-bearded old man who sat at the head of a hall. The student hurried forward and kowtowed to him.

"Master Huo has come," the girl informed her father.

The old man rose in surprise, took the student's hand and spoke briefly of his past. "It's wonderful that you've come, son, you deserve to stay here."

The student declined, saying that he could not stay long because his mother was waiting. "I thought as much," said the old man. "But there won't be any harm in your lingering here a couple of days."

He treated the student to wine and dishes of food, then ordered a maid to get a bed ready in the west hall and cover it with a satin quilt. When they withdrew, the student asked the girl to sleep with him.

She refused, saying: "What makes you think you can behave lecherously in a place like this?" The student grabbed her arm and would

处,可容狎亵?”生捉臂不舍。窗外婢子笑声嗤然,女益惭。方争拒间,翁入,叱曰:“俗骨污吾洞府!宜即去!”生素负气,愧不能忍,作色曰:“儿女之情,人所不免,长者何当伺我?无难即去,但令女须便将随。”翁无辞,招女随之,启后户送之;赚生离门,父子阖扉去。回首峭壁巉岩,无少隙缝,只影茕茕,罔所归适。视天上斜月高揭,星斗已稀。怅怅良久,悲已而恨,面壁叫号,迄无应者。愤极,腰中出镵,凿石攻进,且攻且骂。瞬息洞入三四尺许。隐隐闻人语曰:“孽障哉!”生奋力凿益急。忽洞底豁开二扉,推娥出曰:“可去,可去!”壁即复合。女怨曰:“既爱我为妇,岂有待丈人如此者?是何处老道士,授汝凶器,将人缠混欲死!”生得女,意愿已慰,不复置辨;但忧路险

not let her go. The snorting giggles of a maid outside the window perturbed the girl even more. She was struggling to free herself when the old man walked in and spat out: "Your vulgar carcass is soiling my grotto! Get out now!"

The hot-tempered student could not bear to be shamed. A scowl came over his face, and he retorted: "Love between husband and wife is only natural. Why should an elder like you make it your business to peep at us? I'm going all right, but you must let your daughter go with me." The father had nothing to say against it: he instructed his daughter to go along, then opened the back door to see them out. When he had fooled the student into walking out first, father and daughter slammed the door behind them.

The student turned to see jagged rocks and a sheer cliff-face without the tiniest crack. There was nothing before him but his own forlorn shadow; he had nowhere to go. The crescent moon had climbed high in the sky, and the stars were few and far between. For a long while he was plunged in despair, until his brooding changed to anger. He turned to the wall and howled, but there was no response. In a fit of rage, he grabbed the spade that hung at his waist and laid into the rock, cursing with every stroke. In a flash he had made an opening three or four feet deep. He could hear a muffled voice saying "Damn him!" This roused him to dig even more frantically. Suddenly the inside of the tunnel sprung open like a two-leaved door, and Qing-E was pshed out with the words: "Go ahead!" The cliff-face closed back together.

"If you love me as a wife, how could you treat your father-in-law this way?" said the girl accusingly. "I'd like to know where the old Taoist came from who gave you this burglar's tool so you could pester me to death!"

Now that he had found her, the student was content and offered no argument. He was wondering how they would find their way home

难归。女折两枝,各跨其一,即化为马,行且驶,俄顷至家。时失生已七日矣。初,生之与仆相失也,觅之不得,归而告母。母遣人穷搜山谷,并无踪绪。正忧惶所,闻子自归,欢喜承迎。举首见妇,几骇绝。生略述之,母益忻慰。女以形迹诡异,虑骇物听,求即播迁。母从之。异郡有别业,刻期徙往,人莫之知。偕居十八年,生一女,适同邑李氏。后母寿终。女谓生曰:"吾家茅田中,有雉抱八卵,其地可葬。汝父子扶榇归窆。儿已成立,宜即留守庐墓,无庸复来。"生从其言,葬后自返。月余,孟仙往省之,而父母俱杳。问之老奴,则云:"赴葬未还。"心知其异,浩叹而已。孟仙

over the rugged terrain. The girl broke a stick into two halves, and each of them straddled one. The sticks transformed into horses that skimmed over the ground. In a flash they were home.

By that time the student had been missing for seven days. At first the servant had gotten separated from him and, after an unsuccessful search, returned to tell his mother. She sent men to comb the entire valley, but they failed to find a trace of him. Just when she was beginning to fear the worst, she heard her son arriving and went joyfully out to greet him. When she took her eyes off him and looked up, the sight of her daughter-in-law gave her a rude shock, but this turned to delight and relief once the student had given a brief explanation.

Concerned that her strange actions might give rise to fearful rumors, the girl asked to move out of the area. This the mother granted. Before long they set out on their journey unknown to anyone, bound for an estate the family kept in another prefecture. There they lived together for eighteen years and gave birth to a daughter, who married into the Li family of that district.

After this the mother died of old age. Then Qing-E said to the student. "In the pasture on our land there is a pheasant's nest with eight eggs that marks a good burial site. You and Mengxian take the casket to the grave. Since he is already grown up now, it is all right for him to stay to mourn in the hut by the grave. There is no need for him to come back with you." The student followed her instructions by returning alone after the burial.

A little over a month later, Mengxian went to visit his parents, but they had disappeared. He asked an old servant and was told: "They never came back from the burial." Mengxian knew that something unnatural had happened, but all he could do was heave a long sigh.

Mengxian made quite a name for himself as a writer, but the examination cell was a barrier he could not break through. By age forty, he still was not successful. Finally he was admitted as a senior licenti-

文名甚噪，而困于场屋，四旬不售。后以拔贡入北闱，遇同号生，年可十七八，神采俊逸，爱之。视其卷，注顺天廪生霍仲仙。瞪目大骇，因自道姓名。仲仙亦异之，便问乡贯，孟悉告之。仲仙喜曰："弟赴都时，父嘱文场中如逢山右霍姓者，吾族也，宜与款接，今果然矣。顾何以名字相同如此？"孟仙因诘高、曾，并严、慈姓讳，已而惊曰："是我父母也！"仲仙疑年齿之不类。孟仙曰："我父母皆仙人，何可以貌信其年岁乎？"因述往迹，仲仙始信。场后不暇休息，命驾同归。才到门，家人迎告，是夜失太翁及夫人所在。两人大惊。仲仙入而询诸妇。妇言："昨夕尚共杯酒，母谓：'汝夫妇少不更事。明日大哥来，吾无虑矣。'早旦入室，则阒无人矣。"兄弟闻之，顿足悲哀。

ate to the provincial examinations held in Peking prefecture. There he met and was attracted to seventeen-or-eighteen-year old scholar assigned to the same block as himself who was clever and carefree in manner. He looked at the young man's examination paper and found that it was marked Fellow Huo Zhongxian of Shuntian prefecture (Peking). His eyes grew wide in astonishment as he told the other his own name. Zhongxian too, thought this was strange and wanted to know his native place. Mengxian told him everything.

Zhongxian exclaimed delightedly: "When I left for the capital my father told me that if I were to meet someone named Huo from Shanxi he would be of my own clan and I should receive him accordingly. Now things have turned out just as he said! But how do you explain our names being so similar?"

Mengxian, after questioning the other on the family and given names of his great-grandparents, grandparents, and parents, exclaimed, "Those are my parents!" The disparity of age made Zhongxian dubious, but Mengxian said, "Our father and mother are both immortals. Their age cannot be taken at face value." Only when he had related all that had gone before was Zhongxian convinced. After the examination Zhongxian called for a carriage and they set out together for his home without a moment's delay. The servants met them at the gate with the news that the master and mistress had been missing since the night before. The two of them were dumbfounded. Zhongxian went in to get an explanation from his wife.

"I had a cup of wine with them just last night," said the wife. "Mother said 'You and my son are still not dry behind the ears, but I won't worry now that his older brother is coming here tomorrow.' I went to their room early this morning, but it was deserted." They brothers stamped their feet in disappointment when they heard this. Zhongxian was all in favor of going off in search of them, but was dissuaded by Mengxian, for it would do no good.

仲仙犹欲追觅;孟仙以为无益,乃止。是科仲领乡荐。以晋中祖墓所在,从兄而归。犹冀父母尚在人间,随在探访,而终无踪迹矣。

异史氏曰:"钻穴眠榻,其意则痴;凿壁骂翁,其行则狂;仙人之撮合之者,惟欲以长生报其孝耳。然既混迹人间,狎生子女,则居而终焉,亦何不可?乃三十年而屡弃其子,抑独何哉?异已!"

The outcome of the examination was a provincial re-commendation to the palace examination for Zhongxian. Since his ancestor's tombs were in Shanxi, he returned there with his brother. Still hoping that his parents re-mained in the human world, he made inquiries wherever he went, all without turning up a sign of them.

The Chronicler of the Tales comments: Tunnelling into a bedroom was a bit of lover's foolishness. Drilling through a wall to curse a loved one's father was the act of a manica. An immortal brought the two together nevertheless, so that a son's devotion to his mother could be rewarded with everlasting life. But seeing that Qing-E mingled her tracks with humans and lustfully gave birth to children, why not just stay on and come to a natural end? And how could she get away with abandoning her children repeatedly over a period of thirty years? Strange!"

宦　娘

温如春，秦之世家也。少癖嗜琴，虽逆旅未尝暂舍。客晋，经由古寺，系马门外，暂憩止。入则有布衲道人，趺坐廊间，筇杖倚壁，花布囊琴。温触所好，因问："亦善此也？"道人云："顾不能工，愿就善者学之耳。"遂脱囊授温，视之，纹理佳妙，略一勾拨，清越异常。喜为抚一短曲。道人微笑，似未许可。温乃竭尽所长。道人哂曰："亦佳，亦佳！但未足

GHOST-MAIDEN HUANNIANG

WEN As-Spring belonged to a noble Shaanxi family. When young he was inordinately fond of the lute, which he never put aside for a moment, even when staying at roadside inns. While traveling in Shaanxi he passed by an ancient temple and hitched his horse outside the gate to have a short rest. Inside, a Taoist priest dressed in homespun cloth sat cross-legged on the veranda, with a bamboo staff leaning against the wall next to him and a lute wrapped in gaily-patterned cloth.

Stumbling upon his favorite thing prompted Wen to ask: "Do you go in for this too?"

"I'm not accomplished," said the priest. "But I would like to study under a virtuoso." With that he removed the covering and handed it to Wen, who found the grain and texture of its surfaces exquisite. Moving his fingers lightly over the strings produced an extraordinarily clear, lilting sound. Wen gladly strummed a short piece to show what he could do. The priest smiled with something less than complete approval, which spurred Wen to play with his utmost skill.

The priest chuckled and said, "That's fine as far as it goes, but not good enough to teach me anything."

为贫道师也。”温以其言夸，转请之。道人接置膝上，裁拨动，觉和风自来；又顷之，百鸟群集，庭树为满。温惊极，拜请受业。道人三复之。温侧耳倾心，稍稍会其节奏。道人试使弹，点正疏节，曰：“此尘间已无对矣。”温由是精心刻画，遂称绝技。后归程，离家数十里，日已暮，暴雨莫可投止。路傍有小村，趋之。不遑审择，见一门，匆匆遽入。登其堂，阒无人。俄一女郎出，年十七八，貌类神仙。举首见客，惊而走入。温时未耦，系情殊深。俄一老妪出问客。温道姓名，兼求寄宿。妪言：“宿当不妨，但少床榻；不嫌屈体，便可藉藁。”少旋，以烛来，展草铺地，意良殷。问其姓氏，答云：“赵姓。”又问：“女郎何人？”曰：“此宦

Wen, thinking that he spoke presumptuously, invited him to play. The priest took the lute and put it on his knees. He had no more than run his fingers across the strings than a gentle breeze seemed to stir in the air around them. He had not played long before birds of all sorts gathered in flocks, till the courtyard trees were covered with them. Unable to contain his amazement, Wen bowed before him and asked to be his pupil. And so the priest repeated the tune times for him.

Wen cocked his head and poured his heart into listening until he had gained a certian feel for his teacher's rhythms. The priest had Wen try the piece while he tapped out the beat and made comments. "Already there is no match for you in this world," he said.

After that Wen absorbed himself in honing his skills until he could lay claim to unrivalled mastery. Then he set out on the return trip to Shaanxi. While still scores of li from home, the sun went down and he was caught in a sudden storm with nowhere to stay the night. There was a small village off to the side of the road, and he hurried toward it. He was in too much of a hurry to be particular, so he dashed through the first gate he saw and climbed a flight of steps into a gloomy, deserted house. Suddenly a young woman of seventeen or eighteen with the face of a goddess appeared. She raised her head, saw the stranger and ran to an inner room in alarm. Wen, who was still single, was drawn to her by feelings of unusual depth. Soon an old woman came out to greet him. Wen gave his name and asked to be put up for the night.

"There is no harm in staying the night," said the old woman. "But we are short on beds, so you will have to make do with a mattress of straw." Soon she brought a candle and graciously spread the straw on the floor for him. He asked her family name and learned that it was Zhao. He then asked who the young woman was.

"That was my niece Huanniang."

娘,老身之犹子也。"温曰:"不揣寒陋,欲求援系,如何?"妪颦蹙曰:"此即不敢应命。"温诘其故,但云难言,怅然遂罢。妪既去,温视藉草腐湿,不堪卧处,因危坐鼓琴,以消永夜。雨既歇,冒雨遂归。邑有林下部郎葛公,喜文士。温偶诣之,受命弹琴。帘内隐约有眷客窥听,忽风动帘开,见一及笄人,丽绝一世。盖公有一女,小字良工,善词赋,有艳名。温心动,归与母言,媒通之;而葛以温势式微,不许。然女自闻琴以后,心窃倾慕,每冀再聆雅奏;而温以姻事不谐,志乖意沮,绝迹于葛氏之门矣。一日,女于园中,拾得旧笺一折,上书惜余春词云:"因恨成痴,转思作想,日日为

Wen said, "In spite of my poverty and ignorance, what would you think if I asked to marry her?"

"I don't think I could go along with your wishes in that respect," said the woman, knitting her brows. Wen wanted to know why, but she would only say that it was an embarrassing subject, so Wen reluctantly dropped it. When the old woman left, Wen, seeing that the bed straw was too damp and mouldy to lie on, sat erect playing his lute to pass the long night. When the rain let up he risked a wetting by starting out for home.

In his district lived the retired Ministerial Secretary Master Ge, a man who relished the company of scholars. Once Wen visited him and played the lute at his request. A female member of the family could be dimly discerned listening from behind the screen. A quick gust of wind blew the screen open, revealing a girl with newly pinned back hair whose beauty was unmatched by any woman alive. Wen had heard that the master had a daughter whose childhood name was Lianggong, who excelled at poetry, and was known for her beauty, and now his heart leapt at the sight of her. He returned and spoke of this to his mother, after which a go-between was sent to broach the subject. Ge refused because of the declining state of the Wen family fortune. But the girl, after hearing Wen's lute, was secretly attracted to him and was continually hoped to hear his exquisite playing once again. But Wen, whose hopes had been dashed by the refusal, was no longer seen at the gate of her house.

One day when the girl was in the garden, she found a piece of letter paper. On it was a lyric to the tune of "Cherish the Lingering Spring" which went as follows:

Regret is now a foolish daze
And longing to dreaming has given way,
As passion sets my days awry.

情颠倒。海棠带醉，杨柳伤春，同是一般怀抱。甚得新愁旧愁，铲尽还生，便如青草。自别离，只在奈何天里，度将昏晓。今日个蹙损春山，望穿秋水，道弃已拚弃了！芳衾妒梦，玉漏惊魂，要睡何能睡好？漫说长宵似年；侬视一年，比更犹少：过三更已是三年，更有何人不老！”女吟咏数四，心悦好之。怀归，出锦笺，庄书一通，置案间；逾时索之不可得，窃意为风飘去。适葛经闺门过，拾之；谓良工作，恶其词荡，火之而未忍言，欲急醮之。临邑刘

The crab trees totter drunkenly
And willow trees droop listlessly—
What we cherish is the same.
Worries old and new oppress me:
I mow them down but they grow back
Just like fresh green shoots of grass.
Since we had to part
I bide the passing nights and days
Beneath a resignation-colored sky.
My smooth, soft brow is worn with frowning
My limpid pools are strained with gazing.
Goodbye to hope, goodbye forever!
These cozy covers keep me from my dreams;
The dripping timepiece startles me awake.
I try to sleep, but sleep eludes me.
Some liken dreary nights to years;
To me it seems that one whole year
Flies faster than this midnight watch.
Three nights, no, three long years have gone.
Can anyone tie time's wings down?

The girl recited the lyric repeatedly and, finding it to her liking, went home with it inside her blouse. She took out some fancy stationery and carefully made a complete copy, which she left on her desk. A while later she was unable to find it, so she concluded that it had been blown away by the wind. Actually Master Ge had passed by the door of her room and picked it up, thinking she had written it, and had then thrown it in the fire, disgusted with the wantonness of the words but unwilling to face her with them. He decided to arrange a betrothal right away. It was then that the son of Provincial Governor Liu from Lin Yi district, sent a go-between to ask for her hand. Ge was

方伯之公子,适来问名,心善之,而犹欲一睹其人。公子盛服而至,仪容秀美。葛大悦,款延优渥。既而告别,坐下遗女舄一钩。心顿恶其儇薄,因呼媒而告以故。公子亟辨其诬;葛弗听,卒绝之。先是,葛有绿菊种,吝不传,良工以植闺中。温庭菊忽有一二株化为绿,同人闻之,辄造庐观赏;温亦宝之。凌晨趋视,于畦畔得笺写惜余春词,反覆披读,不知其所自至。以"春"为己名,益惑之,即案头细加丹黄,评语亵嫚。适葛闻温菊变绿,讶之,躬诣其斋,见词便取展读。温以其评亵,夺而挼莎之。葛仅读一两句,盖即闺门所拾者也。大疑,并绿菊之种,亦猜良工所赠。归告夫人,使逼诘良工。良工涕欲死;而事无验见,

pleased to have an offer from such a person, but he wanted to meet him face to face. The governor's son came in formal clothes, a model of manly grace. Overjoyed at what he saw, Ge treated him to a sumptuous dinner. After dinner, when Liu had taken his leave, a girl's upturned slipper was found under his seat. Disgusted by his cavalier approach to women, Ge called for the go-between and told her what had happened. The governor's son hotly protested that he was being maligned, but Ge did not listen and finally cut off relations with him.

Prior to this, Ge had gotten hold of a green variety of chrysanthemums which he niggardly kept to himself, and Lianggong planted some in her chamber. Later a couple of chrysanthemums growing in Wen's courtyard suddenly turned green. Word of them reached his colleagues, and they visited him for the pleasure of gazing on them. This made Wen treasure them all the more. He rushed out to see them by the first light of dawn and found next to the flower bed a sheet of letter paper bearing a lyric to the tune of "Cherish the Lingering Spring." He unfolded it and read it repeatedly, not knowing where it was from. He was especially puzzled by the lyric's apparent reference to the word "Spring" in his name. He took it to his desk, where he painstakingly made emphasis marks with bright-colored inks and wrote indecorous comments. Just then Ge, shocked by the news that Wen's chrysanthemums had turned green, paid a personal call to Wen's studio, where he saw the lyric and commenced reading it. Wen, who did not care to let him see the suggestive comments, snatched it away and crumpled it, but not before Ge was convinced by the first line or two that this was the same lyric he had found up at the door of his daughter's bedroom. The green chrysantemums, which he guessed were a gift from Liang-gong, added to his suspicions. He returned home, told his wife and had her force the girl. Lianggong sobbed herself into insensibility, but there was no proof of her involvement and no way of arriving at the truth.

莫有取实。夫人恐其迹益彰，计不如以女归温。葛然之，遥致温。温喜极。是日招客为绿菊之宴，焚香弹琴，良夜方罢。既归寝，斋童闻琴自作声，初以为僚仆之戏也；既知其非人，始白温。温自诣之，果不妄。其声梗涩，似将效己而未能者。爇火暴入，杳无所见。温携琴去，则终夜寂然。因意为狐，固知其愿拜门墙也者，遂每夕为奏一曲，而设弦任操若师，夜夜潜伏听之。至六七夜，居然成曲，雅足听闻。温既亲迎，各述曩词，始知缔好之由，而终不知所由来。良工闻琴鸣之异，往听之，曰："此非狐也，调凄楚，有鬼声。"温未深信。良工因言其家有古镜，可鉴魑魅。翊日，遣人取至，伺琴声既作，握镜遽入；火之，果有女子在，仓皇室隅，莫能复隐。细审之，赵氏

Mrs. Ge figured that giving their daughter to Wen would be better than letting the matter be noised abroad, so they sent to tell him their plan. Wen was so overjoyed he invited friends to a dinner beside the green chrysanthemums. He lit incense and played the lute until well into the night. After he retired, his studio boy heard sounds coming from the lute. At first he thought that the other servants were playing a prank, but when he found no one there he reported it to Wen. Wen went there himself: the servant was not fooling him. The notes were a halting imitation of his own playing. Wen lit a torch and ran into the studio, but saw nobody there so he took the lute in his arm and left. The rest of the night was quiet. He guessed that it was a werefox and, since it had wanted to study under him, he played a piece every evening and left the lute out so the fox could imitate him. Every night he hid nearby to listen. In six or seven nights the disjointed notes surprisingly began to come together into a piece worth the attention of a cultivated ear.

Once their nuptial ceremonies had been performed, Wen and Lianggong exchanged recollections of lyric and began to realize that it was what had brought them together, but they still did not understand where it had come from. When Lianggong heard the strange story of the nightly lute music, she listened and said, "This music is not being played by a werefox. The tone is mournful. There is a ghostly ring to it."

Since Wen was not convinced, Lianggong told him of an antique mirror belonging to her family that could show the true colors of a spectre or ghoul. The next day she sent someone for it. The moment the lute music started she rushed in with the mirror in her hand, and in the glare of the lamp they brought in a young woman could plainly be seen cowering in a corner of the room, unable to hide. Wen questioned her closely and found to his great amazement that she was Huanniang of the Zhao family. She broke down under the questioning

之宦娘也。大骇,穷诘之。泫然曰:"代作蹇修,不为无德,何相逼之甚也?"温请去镜,约勿避;诺之。乃囊镜。女遥坐曰:"妾太守之女,死百年矣。少喜琴筝;筝已颇能谙之,独此技未有嫡传,重泉犹以为憾。惠顾时,得聆雅奏,倾心向往;又恨以异物不能奉裳衣,阴为君脯合佳偶,以报眷顾之情,刘公子之女舄,惜余春之俚词,皆妾为之也。酬师者不可谓不劳矣。"夫妻咸拜谢之。宦娘曰:"君之业,妾思过半矣;但未尽其神理。请为妾再鼓之。"温如其请,又曲陈其法。宦娘大悦曰:"妾已尽得之矣!"乃起辞欲去。良工故善筝,闻其所长,愿一披聆。宦娘不辞,其调其谱,并非尘世所能。良工击节,转请受业。女命笔为绘谱十八章,又起告别。夫妻挽之良苦。

and sobbed: "My services to you as go-between surely count for something. Why must you drive me into a corner?"

Wen offered to get rid of the mirror if she agreed not to run away. She gave her word. The mirror was put in a bag. She sat down at a distance and said: "I am the daughter of a prefect: I've been dead for a hundred years. As a girl I was able to learn something about the zither, but I never found anyone to pass the skill of lute playing down to me. I carried my regret over this with me into the underworld. When you so kindly visited us, I had a chance listen to your excellent playing. My heart went out to you, but, unfortunately, I could not serve you intimately because I am not of your kind. I worked behind the scenes to bring you together with the right person, as a way of repaying the regard you showed for me. The girl's slipper that young master Liu supposedly left and the banal lyric" Cherish the Remaining Spring "were my work. You cannot say that I did not put a lot of effort into repaying my teacher." Husband and wife bowed to her in appreciation.

"I have thought through most of what you taught, but the spirit that moves your music still escapes me," she said. "Would you please play for me again?" Wen did as she said, giving an elaborate demonstration of his fingering.

"Now I have it!" Huanniang exclaimed delightedly.

With this she excused herself and rose to leave. But Lianggong, herself an accomplished zither player, was fascinated to learn of the other's forte and wished to give ear to a sample piece. Huanniang did not refuse. *The music and her* rendering of it were unlike anything achievable in this world. Lianggong tapped along raptly as she listened, then asked if to learn something of her skill. Huanniang called for a brush and wrote down a score in eighteen sections, then rose and said goodbye. The couple held her back imploringly.

"You are like a matching lute and zither set," said Huanniang

宦娘凄然曰："君琴瑟之好，自相知音；薄命人乌有此福。如有缘，再世可相聚耳。"因以一卷授温曰："此妾小像。如不忘媒妁，当悬之卧室，快意时，焚香一柱，对鼓一曲，则儿身受之矣。"出门遂没。

gloomily. "You can appreciate each other's music. Fate has been too unkind to allow me such blessings. If we are linked by the ties of destiny, we will meet again in the next life." With this she handed Wen a scroll, saying: "This is a little portrait of me. If you don't want to neglect your matchmaker, you can hang it in your bed-room. When you are in the mood, burn a stick of incense and play a piece in front of it. It will be just as if I am here to enjoy it." Then she went through the gate and vanished.

局　诈

嘉祥李生，善琴。偶适东郊，见工人掘土得古琴，遂以贱直得之。拭之有异光；安弦而操，清烈非常。喜极，若获拱璧，贮以锦囊，藏之密室，虽至戚不以示也。邑丞程氏，新莅任，投刺谒李。李故寡交游，以其先施故，报之。过数日，又招饮，固请乃往。程为人风雅绝伦，议论潇洒，李悦焉。越日，折柬酬之，欢笑益洽。从此月夕花晨，未尝不相共也。年余，偶于丞廨中，见绣囊裹琴置几上。李便展

FRAUD(NUMBER THREE)

SCHOLAR Li of Jiaxiang was an accomplished lutanist. One day he happened to be in the eastern suburbs when some laborers uncovered an ancient lute while making an excavation. It was his for a negligible sum. Rubbed clean, it gave off an unearthly gleam. He strung it and played: the sound was piercingly pure. His joy could not have been greater than if he had found a piece of jade too big to hold in one hand. He kept it in a brocade bag hidden in a secret room, never showing it even to his closest relatives.

The newly arrived district commissioner Cheng announced himself with a calling card and paid Li a visit. Though Li seldom socialized, he returned the visit because the other had taken the initiative. Several days later he was invited for a drink, and, since the host was insistent, he went. Cheng was a charming, unconventional character, and Li enjoyed the animated ease of his conversation. After some days passed, Li sent a return invitation. This time the two found even more pleasure in each other's company. From then on there was not a moonlit evening or flower bedecked morning that they did not share.

More than a year had gone by when Li happened to notice a lute in an embroidered bag on the desk in Cheng's office. Li took it out and

玩。程问:"亦谙此否?"李曰:"生平最好。"程讶曰:"知交非一日,绝技胡不一闻?"拨炉爇沉香,请为小奏。李敬如教。程曰:"大高手!愿献薄技,勿笑小巫也。"遂鼓《御风曲》,其声泠泠,有绝世出尘之意。李更倾倒,愿师事之。自此二人以琴交,情分益笃。年余,尽传其技。然程每诣李,李以常琴供之,未肯泄所藏也。一夕,薄醉。丞曰:"某新肄一曲,无亦愿闻之乎?"为奏《湘妃》,幽怨若泣。李亟赞之。丞曰:"所恨无良琴;若得良琴,音调益胜。"李欣然曰:"仆蓄一琴,颇异凡品。今遇锺期,何敢终密?"乃启椟负囊而出。程以袍

turned in his hands.

"So you're conversant with this too, are you?" asked Cheng

"It's my life's passion," said Li.

Cheng exclaimed in surprise: "Our friendship doesn't date from yesterday. Why haven't I heard anything of your consummate skill?" He opened the censer, lit some gharuwood incense and asked Li to play a short piece. Li respectfully did his biding.

"You are quite an accomplished player! Now I would like to offer my paltry skill. Don't laugh at me for being like the little witch who went to see the sorceress."

He played "Riding the Wind" with a cool liquidity that carried one's thoughts away from the world and beyond its dust. Li conceived even more admiration for him and wanted to serve him as a teacher. From then on it was lute playing that brought the two together and deepened the bond between them. For more than a year Cheng passed on what he knew, but every time he called on Li, the latter was still reluctant to bring out what he had hidden, and so provided an ordinary lute.

One evening when they were slightly drunk the commissioner said, "I have just learned a new piece. Would you care to hear it?" He played the plaintive "Goddesses of the Xiang River" for his friend. Li praised it profusely.

"My only regret is that I do not have a fine lute," said the commissioner; "if I had one, the tone would be that much better."

Li piped up gladly: "I've been keeping a lute that is a cut above the ordinary article. Now that I've met a connoisseur, it would be a shame to keep it secret indefinitely."

He then opened a cabinet and lifted out a bag. Cheng brushed the dust off the lute with his sleeves, leaned toward the desk and played the piece again. It was a perfect interweaving of boldness and softness, played with virtuosity that was more than human. Li could

袂拂尘，凭几再鼓，刚柔应节，工妙入神。李击节不置。丞曰："区区拙技，负此良琴。若得荆人一奏，当有一两声可听者。"李惊曰："公闺中亦精之耶?"丞笑曰："适此操乃传自细君者。"李曰："恨在闺阁，小生不得闻耳。"丞曰："我辈通家，原不以形迹相限。明日，请携琴去，当使隔帘为君奏之。"李悦。次日，抱琴而往。程即治具欢饮。少间，将琴入，旋出即坐。俄见帘内隐隐有丽妆，顷之，香流户外。又少时，弦声细作；听之不知何曲，但觉荡心媚骨，令人魂魄飞越。曲终便来窥帘，竟二十余绝代之姝也。丞以巨白劝釂，内复改弦为《闲情之赋》，李形神益惑。倾饮过醉，离席兴辞，索琴。丞曰："醉后防有蹉跌。明日

not help but tap to the rhythm in appreciation.

"My limited and awkward skills have failed this fine instrument," said the commissioner. If my wife were allowed to play it, there would be a note or two worth hearing.

"You mean the lady of your house has mastered the lute too?" asked Li in shock.

"The exercise I just played was taught me by my wife," the commissioner chuckled.

"What a pity she is hidden away in your private cham-bers. I'll never be able to hear her," Li complained.

"We are such good friends that my family is your family," said the commissioner. "We should not let appearances restrict us. I wish you would take your lute to my house tomorrow. I'll have her play for you from behind the screen."

Li was delighted. The next day he went there, lute in arms. Cheng made preparations for a bout of convivial drinking. In a little while he took the lute inside, came right back and sat down. Then the faint shape of a beautifully dressed and coiffured woman appeared behind the screen, followed by a fragrance that wafted into the room. Before long the strings came delicately alive. Li did not know what piece it was, but sound of it swept his thoughts away and thrilled him to the marrow, so that his soul took leave of his body. At the end of her piece he went to peek around the screen: there was a woman in her early twenties who was surely one of the beauties of the age.

The commissioner urged huge cups of wine on Li, while the woman within the screen switched to a "Rhapsody of Leisure," which drove Li's body and mind to greater distraction. Having poured more than his measure of wine down his throat, he rose from the seat, started to say his goodbyes and asked for his lute.

"In your condition we must guard against your taking a flop with it," said the commissioner. "Visit us again tomorrow; I'll have my wife

复临，当令闺人尽其所长。”李归。次日诣之，则解舍寂然，惟一老隶应门。问之，云：“五更携眷去，不知何作，言往复可三日耳。”如期往伺之，日暮，并无音耗。吏皂皆疑，白令破扃而窥其室，室尽空，惟几榻犹存耳。达之上台，并不测其何故。李丧琴，寝食俱废，不远数千里访诸其家。——程故楚产，三年前，捐资授嘉祥。——执其姓名，询其居里，楚中并无其人。或云：“有程道士者，善鼓琴；又传其有点金术。三年前，忽去不复见。”疑即其人。又细审其年甲、容貌，吻合不谬。乃知道士之

perform all her best pieces."

Li went home. The next day he went back and found the office suite deserted except for an old servant who answered the door. When questioned the old man said, "He left with his family during the fifth watch this morning. I don't know what he plans to do, but he said it'll only take him three days to make the trip."

On the third day Li went to wait for them. He waited until sundown, but still there was no sign of them. The clerks and servants were mystified. They reported to the magistrate, who had the lock broken and the house searched. The house was completely empty: only desks and beds remained. The matter was communicated to higher authorities, but they too were unable to determine what had happened.

Li could not sleep or eat for grief over losing his lute. Disregariding the great distance, he set out on a few thousand-li search for the culprit's home—Cheng was a native of Chu who had paid for the post in Jiaxiang three years before. With a card bearing Cheng's name in his hand, Li made inquiries in the man's old neighborhood and learned that there was no such person in Chu. Someone told him: "There was a Taoist named Cheng who was good at the lute. Some say he possessed the golden touch. Three years ago he left and hasn't been here since."

Li suspected that this was the person. He asked detailed questions about the man's age and appearance: all the answers tallied perfectly with what he knew. He realized that the Taoist had procured an official title expressly for the sake of the lute. For the first year or more of their friendship, he had not said a word about music. Then slowly, but with well-timed certainty, he had left his lute out and then demonstrated his own skill and finally used the beautiful woman to distract Li. Three years of easing himself under Li's guard—then he had gotten the lute and left. The Taoist's obsession for the instrument

纳官，皆为琴也。知交年余，并不言及音律；渐而出琴，渐而献技，又渐而惑以佳丽；浸渍三年，得琴而去。道士之癖，更甚于李生也。天下之骗机多端，若道士，犹骗中之风雅者也。

was even greater than Li's. There are many angles from which to practice deception in this world. In the Taoist's case, there was a certain refinement in his trickery.

于 去 恶

北平陶圣俞，名下士。顺治间，赴乡试，寓居郊郭。偶出户，见一人负笈侄，似卜居未就者。略诘之，遂释负于道，相与倾语，言论有名士风。陶大说之，请与同居。客喜，携囊入，遂同栖止。客自言："顺天人，姓于，字去恶。"以陶差长，兄之。于性不喜游瞩，常独坐一室，而案头无书卷。陶不与谈，则默卧而已。陶疑之，搜其囊箧，则笔研之外，更无长物。怪而问之。笑曰："吾辈读书，岂临渴始

GHOST-SCHOLAR YU QU-E

TAO Shengyu of Beiping was a renowned scholar. During the Shunzhi reign of the first Qing emperor (1644-1661) he went up for the provincial examination and took lodgings on the outskirts of the capital. One day he went out and met a man with a wicker pack of books on his back scurrying about and apparently looking for a place to live. Tao asked him a few questions. The man set his pack down on the road and entered into a conversation. His manner of speech marked him a singular man of learning. Tao took a strong liking to him and invited him to room together. The delighted stranger carried his pack inside, and so they lived under the same roof. The stranger volunteered the fact that he came from Shuntian prefecture, his surname was Yu and he went by the name Qu-E. He addressed Tao, who was slightly older, as an older brother.

Yu was not fond of sightseeing. He often sat alone in a room, his desk empty of books. When Tao was not talking with him, he did little but lie in silence. Wondering about him, Tao looked through his pack and chest: there were inkbrushes and an inkstone but no other articles. He asked for an explanation of the mystery.

Yu answered with a laugh: "Do you think that for someone like me

掘井耶?"一日,就陶借书去,闭户抄甚疾,终日五十余纸,亦不见其折叠成卷。窃窥之,则每一稿脱,辄烧灰吞之。愈益怪焉。诘其故。曰:"我以此代读耳。"便诵所抄书,顷刻数篇,一字无讹。陶悦,欲传其术;于以为不可。陶疑其吝,词涉诮让。于曰:"兄诚不谅我之深矣。欲不言,则此心无以自剖;骤言之,又恐惊为异怪。奈何?"陶固谓:"不妨。"于曰:"我非人,是鬼耳。今冥中以科目授官,七月十四日奉诏考帘官,十五日士子入闱,月尽榜放矣。"陶问:"考帘官为何?"曰:"此上帝慎重之意,无论乌吏鳖官,皆考之。能文者以内帘用,不通者不得与焉。盖阴之有诸神,犹阳之有守、令也。得志诸公,目不睹坟、典,不过少

reading is a matter of 'waiting until thirsty to dig a well'?"

One day he borrowed one of Tao's books, shut himself in his room and copied from it furiously. By the end of the day he had over fifty pages, but there was no indication of his waiting to fold and bind them into a booklet. Furtive observation showed that he set fire to each page when he finished and swallowed the ashes. Tao's earlier puzzlement was nothing to what he felt now. He demanded to know the reason.

"I do this instead of reading," was the answer. In a few minutes Yu recited serveral chapters from the book he had been copying. Not a single word was amiss. Tao was excited by this demonstration and wanted Yu to let him in on the method. Yu thought it would not be a good idea. Tao suspected him of holding back and said so with a note of accusation in his words.

"Believe me, brother, you have not grasped my true intention. If I don't tell you the truth, there is no way to open my heart for you to see. If I come out and tell you, you'll likely be frightened of me for being a freak. What can I do?"

But Tao assured him: "It won't do any harm."

"Well, I'm not a man, I'm a ghost," said Yu. "They are awarding positions by examination now in the nether world. An examination to select examiners has been decreed on the fourteenth day of the seventh month. Candidates will enter their cells on the fifteenth and notice boards will be posted before the month is out."

"Why are there examinations to select examiner" asked Tao.

"It is the Lord on High's considered wish. Even the most minor officials will be subject to examination. Those who know how to write will be appointed examiners. Illiterates will not be given a chance. You see, the spirits down in the shades are like the governors and magistrates you have in this sunlit world. The ones that have realized their ambitions don't so much as glance at the classics. When young

年持敲门砖，猎取功名，门既开，则弃去；再司簿书十数年，即文学士，胸中尚有字耶！阳世所以陋劣幸进，而英雄失志者，惟少此一考耳。”陶深然之，由是益加敬畏。一日，自外来，有忧色，叹曰：“仆生而贫贱，自谓死后可免；不谓迍邅先生相从地下！”陶请其故。曰：“文昌奉命都罗国封王，帘官之考遂罢。数十年游神耗鬼，杂入衡文，吾辈宁有望耶！”陶问：“此辈皆谁何人？”曰：“即言之，君亦不识。略举一二人，大概可知：乐正师旷、司库和峤是也。仆自念命不可凭，文不可恃，不如休耳。”言已怏怏，遂将治任。陶挽而慰之，乃止。至中元之夕，谓陶曰：“我将入闱。烦于昧爽时，持香炷于东野，三呼去恶，我便至。”乃出门去。陶沽酒烹鲜以待之。东方既白，敬如所嘱。无何，于偕一少年来。问其姓字。

they only used them to batter through the gate to honor and fame. Once the gate was open they threw them aside. What is more, after a dozen years or so of handling documents, not even a learned man would have a word worth writing left in him, would he? In your world ignoramuses advance by sheer luck while men of mettle get nowhere, precisely bacause you lack this sort of examination." Tao was in complete agreement: now he was even more impressed with his guest.

Ond day Yu came in from outside with a despondent look on his face and sighed: "In life I was poor and under-priviledged. I told myself I would be spared that after death. How was I to know that Master Hardknocks would follow me underground?"

Tao asked what happened, and Yu replied, "The God of Literature was enfeoffed as Prince of Tula, and consequently the examination for examiners has been cancelled. For many decades idle spirits and parasitic ghosts have insinuated themselves into essay-evaluating positions. What hope is there for people like me?"

"Who are these people?" asked Tao.

"You wouldn't know even if I told you," said Yu. The blind music master Shi Kuang and treasurer He Chiao are two of them: that should be enough to give you an idea. I'm starting to think that since I can't rely on fate and my writing won't get me anywhere, I might as well give up. That said, he lapsed into brooding and made ready to pack his bags. Only when Tao dragged at his arm and comforted him did he stop.

On the eve of All Souls Day (the fifteenth day of the seventh lunar month) he said to Tao: "I'm about to go into the examination cell. Please take some incense to the fields east of the city and burn it there at dawn; call my name three times and I'll be there." Then he went out the door and left. Tao bought wine and prepared fresh meat to receive him. When the eastern sky whitened, he dutifully carried out Yu's instructions. Before long Yu cmae, together with a young man.

于曰："此方子晋，是我良友。适于场中相邂逅。闻兄盛名，深欲拜识。"同至寓，秉烛为礼。少年亭亭似玉，意度谦婉，陶甚爱之。便问："子晋佳作，当大快意？"于曰："言之可笑！闱中七则，作过半矣；细审主司姓名，裹具径出。奇人也！"陶扇炉进酒，因问："闱中何题？去恶魁解否？"于曰："书艺、经论各一，夫人而能之。策问：'自古邪僻固多，而世风至今日，奸情丑态，愈不可名，不惟十八狱所不得尽，抑非十八狱所能容。是果何术而可？或谓宜量加一二狱，然殊失上帝好生之心。其宜增与、否与，或别有道以清其源，尔多士其悉言勿隐。'弟策虽不佳，颇为痛快。表：'拟天魔殄灭，赐群臣龙马天衣有差。'次则《瑶台应制诗》、《西池桃花赋》。此三种，自谓场中无两

Tao asked his name.

"This is Fang Zijin, my good friend. We just met by chance at the examination. He has heard a great deal about you and wants very much to make your acquaintance." The three went to Tao's lodgings, where Tao and Fang exchanged bows by the light of a hand-held candle. Tao, much taken with the young man's fine, jadelike features and mild, humble manner, ventured, "I suppose Zijin was pleased with the quality of his writing."

"Just talking about it makes me laugh," said Yu. "He was over halfway through the seven assigned topics, but the minute he learned the presiding examiner's name, he wrapped up his stationery and walked straight out. A remarkable man, he is!"

Tao fanned the brazier to warm some wine and asked, "What were the assigned topics? Did you come out on top, Qu-E?"

"There was one section each on the Four Books and the Five Classics that a woman could have handled. The Policy question went like this: 'Multifarious evils have existed from ancient times, but in this day and age the treacherous and degenerate ways of men are beyond telling. The eighteen hells are not enough to punish all types of evil, nor are they large enough to hold all those found guilty. What then can be done? The proper course might be to add one or two to the number of hells, but this is at great variance with the Lord on High's love of living creatures. Should the hells be increased or not, or is there a different course open by which evil might be purged at the source? All candidates are urged to speak out exhaustively and without reservation.' My policy statement may not have been perfect, but I couldn't have been happier with it. The topic for the Memorial was: 'A Proposal for the Eradication of Demons in the Upper Abode and for Bestowal of Dragon Steeds and Heavenly Vestment on the Various Ministers by Rank.' After that there were a 'Poem on the Imperially Decreed Theme of Porphyry Pavilion,' and a 'Rhapsody on Peach Blossoms at

矣!”言已鼓掌。方笑曰:“此时快心,放兄独步矣;数辰后,不痛哭始为男子也。”天明,方欲辞去。陶留与同寓,方不可,但期暮至。三日,竟不复来。陶使于往寻之。于曰:“无须。子晋拳拳,非无意者。”日既西,方果来。出一卷授陶,曰:“三日失约,敬录旧艺百余作,求一品题。”陶捧读大喜,一句一赞,略尽一二首,遂藏诸笥。谈至更深,方遂留,与于共榻寝。自此为常;方无夕不至,陶亦无方不欢也。一夕,仓皇而入,向陶曰:“地榜已揭,于五兄落第矣!”于方卧,闻言惊起,泫然流涕。二人极意慰藉,涕始止。然相对默默,殊不可堪。方曰:“适闻大巡环张桓侯将至,恐失志

West Pond,' both of which dealt with the Queen Mother of the West. I'm convinced that nobody in the hall could equal my performance on these three sections." When finished speaking he clapped his hands.

"You're pleased with yourself now," said Fang laughing-ly. "We'll let you walk around with your head in the clouds for a while, in a few days you'll have to show what a man you are by not bawling out loud."

At daybreak Fang wanted to leave. Tao asked him to stay on as a roommate. He refused but promised to return in the evening. Three days passed without his coming back. Tao wanted Yu to go looking for him, but Yu said, "There is no need. Zijin has a good heart. Don't think he has no wish to make friends."

As the sun was westering Fang showed up after all. He pulled out a small volume and handed it to Tao, saying: "I broke my promise by three days, so I took the liberty of copying out a hundred or so of my old compositions that I'd like you to comment on."

Tao opened the book and read it with great delight, finding something to praise in every sentence. After reading briefly through one or two selections he put the book in a case. They talked deep into the night. Fang stayed and shared a bed with Yu.

From then on it was a regular thing. Fang visited every night without fail, and Tao would not have been happy without Fang. One evening Fang rushed in and said to Tao: "The notice boards have already been posted in the underworld. Fifth-Brother Yu was not selected!" Hearing these words, Yu started up from the bed and loosed a torrent of tears. The two of them had to do everything in their power to console him before he would leave off sniveling, Even then he looked at them in sullen silence, which they found unendurable.

"I just heard that Grand Circuit Inspector Zhang Fei, Marquis of Huan, will come soon," said Fang. "It could be no more than a rumor started by disappointed candidates. If it is true, the literary arena may get a good shaking up."

者之造言也；不然，文场尚有翻覆。”于闻之，色喜。陶询其故。曰：“桓侯翼德，三十年一巡阴曹，三十五年一巡阳世，两间之不平，待此老而一消也。”乃起，拉方俱去。两夜始返，方喜谓陶曰：“君不贺五兄耶？桓侯前夕至，裂碎地榜，榜上名字，止存三之一。遍阅遗卷，得五兄甚喜，荐作交南巡海使，旦晚舆马可到。”陶大喜，置酒称贺。酒数行，于问陶曰：“君家有闲舍否？”问：“将何为？”曰：“子晋孤无乡土，又不忍恝然于兄。弟意欲假馆相依。”陶喜曰：“如此，为幸多矣。即无多屋宇，同榻何碍。但有严君，须先关白。”于曰：“审知尊大人慈厚可依。兄场闱有日，子晋如不能待，先归何如？”陶留伴逆旅，以待同归。次日，方暮，有车马至门，接于莅任。于起握手

Yu's face lit up when he heard this. Tao asked the reason and Yu replied, "The Marquis of Huan inspects underworld functionaries once every thirty years and tours the sunlit world once every thirty-five years. The injustices of these two realms are done away with when that old gentleman appears." Then he stood up and led Fang away.

They did not return until two nights later, when Fang joyfully reported to Tao: "Aren't you going to congratulate Fifth-Brother? The Marquis of Huan arrived the night before last and tore the underworld ranking notice board to pieces. Only one third of the names on the list were allowed to remain. He read all the papers by unselected candidates and was tremendously pleased to find Fifth-Brother's. He recommended him as the Maritime Inspector of South China Sea. A coach and team should be sent for him any day."

Tao served wine and congratulated him with great joy. The wine had gone several rounds when Yu asked Tao: "Is there a room free in your house?"

"What would it be for?" asked Tao.

"Zijin is on his own and has no home to return to, but he can't bear to impose upon you. I was hoping that you might give him accommodations here."

"That would be wonderful," Tao exclaimed happily. "Since we don't have many rooms, he is free to share my bed. But I'll have to inform my father first."

Yu said, "I'm sure that we can depend on your father's kindness and generosity. You'll be going into the examination hall in a few days. If Zijin cannot wait for you, how about letting him go to your place first?"

Tao kept company with them in the inn, expecting that he and Fang would make the return trip together. The next day at sunset a coach and team pulled up at the gate, ready to take Yu to his post. Yu rose and shook Tao's hand, saying: "Well, this is goodbye. There is

曰："从此别矣。一言欲告，又恐阻锐进之志。"问："何言？"曰："君命淹蹇，生非其时。此科之分十之一；后科桓侯临世，公道初彰，十之三；三科始可望也。"陶闻，欲中止。于曰："不然，此皆天数，即明知不可，而注定之艰苦，亦要历尽耳。"又顾方曰："勿淹滞，今朝年、月、日、时皆良，即以舆盖送君归。仆驰马自去。"方忻然拜别。陶中心迷乱，不知所嘱，但挥涕送之。见舆马分途，顷刻都散。始悔子晋北旋，未致一字，而已无及矣。三场毕，不甚满志，奔波而归。入门问子晋，家中并无知者。因为父述之。父喜曰："若然，则客至久矣。"先是陶翁昼卧，梦舆盖止于其门，一美少年自车中出，登堂展拜。讶问所来。答云："大哥许假一舍，以入闱不得偕来。我先至

something I would like to tell you, but then again I don't want to dampen your fighting spirit."

"What is it?"

"It is your fate to see your aims frustrated. You were born in the wrong age. Your chances in this examination are one in ten. In the one after, the Marquis of Huan will appear in the world and justice will begin to prevail, so your chances will be three in ten. On the third try you can expect success." This made Tao wonder if it might not be better to give up the present attempt.

"You're wrong," said Yu. "All this is predestined. Even though you know they will be to no avail, you must weather through every one of your appointed sufferings." Then Yu turned to Fang and said, "Don't waste your time here. The year, month, day and hour new home in my carriage. I'll make my own way on horseback." Fang bowed an appreciative farewell.

Tao's mind was in such confusion that he was unable to think of any parting instructions. He simply waved a tearful farewell. He watched the horse and the carriage until they disappeared down different roads. Regret at not sending a single word homeward to the north with Zijin came over him, but it was too late. After he had sat through all three sessions, with results that were hardly encouraging, he made the tedious trek home. He asked about Zijin the minute he entered the door, but nobody in the house knew a thing. Then he told his father of the arrangements he and Fang had made.

His father was delighted: "If that is so, your guest was here some time ago." It turned out that the old man Tao had dreamed while napping of a carriage standing at the gate. A fine young man got out, walked into the hall and bowed in greeting. The old man asked in amazement why he had come, and he answered, "Older brother promised to give me the use of an apartment, but since he had to take an examination he couldn't come with me, so I came ahead without

矣。”言已，请入拜母。翁方谦却，适家媪入曰：“夫人产公子矣。”恍然而醒，大奇之。是日陶言，适与梦符，乃知儿即子晋后身也。父子各喜，名之小晋。儿初生，善夜啼，母苦之。陶曰：“倘是子晋，我见之，啼当止。”俗忌客忤，故不令陶见。母患啼不可耐；乃呼陶入。陶呜之曰：“子晋勿尔！我来矣！”儿啼正急，闻声辍止，停睇不瞬，如审顾状。陶摩顶而去。自是竟不复啼。数月后，陶不敢见之；一见，则折腰索抱，走去，则啼不可止。陶亦狎爱之。四岁离母，辄就兄眠；兄他出，则假寐以俟其归。兄于枕上教毛诗，诵声呢喃，夜尽四十余行。以子晋遗文授之，欣然乐读，过口成诵；试之他文，不能也。八九岁，眉目郎徹，宛然一子晋矣。陶两入闱，皆不第。丁酉，文

him." Then he begged leave to go inside and meet his friend's mother. The old man was trying to keep him out with all due politeness when an old woman servant entered to say: "Madame had given birth to a young master. The old man found himself awake, greatly puzzled by his dream."

Now the younger Tao was telling of events that tallied perfectly with the old man's dream. He realized at last that his baby son was a reincarnation of Zijin. In the gladness of the moment father and son decided that he should be called Little Jin.

At frist the baby was in the habit of crying at night, to its mother's dismay. Tao said, "If he is really Zijin reincarnated, his crying should stop when I go to see him." But unfamiliar faces were held by custom to be an unhealthy influence, so Tao was not allowed near the baby. But finally, when the mother's nerves could bear its howling no longer, she called for Tao.

Tao cooed to him: "Don't behave this way, Zijin. I'm here now." The baby abruptly stopped his mad squalling at the sound of Tao's voice and turned unblinking eyes on him as if to scrutinize him. Tao patted him on the head and left. From then on there was no more howling. After a few months Tao hesitated to visit the boy, for as soon as he did the boy fawned on him and begged to be held. If Tao walked away the boy would bawl uncontrollably. Tao, for his part, grew fond of the child. At the age of four the boy left his mother's side to sleep with his older brother. When his brother went out, the boy pretended to sleep and waited for his return. His brother taught him Mao's version of the *Book of Odes* in bed. The boy got through over fourty lines a night, twittering out the words like a swallow. When given essays that Zijin had left behind, he read with gay relish and learned them by heart after one reading. He was confounded when this was tried with other people's writings. By the age of seven or eight his bright, penetrating eyes showed him to be the very image of Zijin.

场事发，帘官多遭诛遣，贡举之途一肃，乃张巡环力也。陶下科中副车，寻贡。遂灰志前途，隐居教弟。常语人曰："吾有此乐，翰苑不易也。"

异史氏曰："余每至张夫子庙堂，瞻其须眉，凛凛有生气。又其生平喑哑如霹雳声，矛马所至，无不大快，出人意表。世以将军好武，遂置与绛、灌伍；宁知文昌事繁，须侯固多哉！呜呼！三十五年，来何暮也！"

Tao went for examinations twice and failed both times. In the year of 1657 abuses in the examination hall were exposed, many examiners were executed or banished, and the road to preferment by examination was thoroughly swept clean, all due to the efforts of Inspector Zhang. In the next examination Tao took an associate master of letters degree, and was soon chosen to be a senior licentiate. Despairing of further advancement, he went into retirement to teach his younger brother. He often told people: "I would not trade happiness like this for a place in Hanlin Academy."

The Chronicler of the Tales comments: "I often stop by the shrine to Mater Zhang and rest my eyes on his bewhiskered, beetle-browed visage, that is somehow charged with his awesome living force. I remember also that he was known in life for the ragged thunder of his wrathful voice. Wherever his lance and horse appeared, things were sure to be set aright with a briskness that no one expected. Because the general was fond of military exploits, people put him in a class with the Marquises of Zhou Bo and Guan Ying. How could they know the God of Literature has such a profusion of duties that the Marquis'help has always been sorely needed! Once every thirty-five years—what a long while to wait!"

凤 仙

刘赤水，平乐人，少颖秀。十五入郡庠。父母早亡，遂以游荡自废。家不中资，而性好修饰，衾榻皆精美。一夕，被人招饮，忘灭烛而去。酒数行，始忆之，急返。闻室中小语，伏窥之，见少年拥丽者眠榻上。宅临贵家废第，恒多怪异，心知其狐，亦不恐。入而叱曰："卧榻岂容鼾睡！"二人惶遽，抱衣赤身遁去。遗紫纨袴一，带上系针囊。大悦，恐其窃去，藏衾中而抱之。俄一蓬头婢自门罅入，向刘索取。刘笑要偿。婢请遗以酒，不应；赠以

PHOENIX SPRITE

LIU Chishui of Pingle district showed remarkable bril-liance at an early age and was admitted to the regional academy at fifteen. His father and mother died early, after which he wasted himself in idle pursuits. Though his family was of lower than average means, he had a fondness for ornamentation, and his bed and covers were of the finest quality. One evening he was invited to a party and, leaving his house, he forgot to blow out his candles. After several rounds of wine he remembered and hurried home, where he heard low voices in his room. Crouching, he peered into the room and saw a young man lying on his bed with a beautiful woman in his arms. Strange occur-rences were nothing new in his house, family. He realized that these were were-foxes, but was not afraid. He walked into the room, shouting"Do you think I want you sleeping and snoring on my bed?"

The two of them were so flustered that they ran off naked, clothes in arms. To his great joy, they left behind a pair of purple silk bloomers with a sewing pouch hanging from the belt. He held them in his arms under the cover, fearful that they might be taken away. Soon a mop-haired maid came in through a crack in the door and demanded the bloomers. With a laugh, Liu insisted on a reward. The maid asked

金,又不应。婢笑而去。旋返曰:"大姑言:如赐还,当以佳耦为报。"刘问:"伊谁?"曰:"吾家皮姓,大姑小字八仙,共卧者胡郎也;二姑水仙,适富川丁官人;三姑凤仙,较两姑尤美,自无不当意者。"刘恐失信,请坐待好音。婢去复返曰:"大姑寄语官人:好事岂能猝合?适与之言,反遭诟厉;但缓时日以待之,吾家非轻诺寡信者。"刘付之。过数日,渺无信息。薄暮,自外归。闭门甫坐,忽双扉自启,两人以被承女郎,手捉四角而入,曰:"送新人至矣!"笑置榻上而去。近视之,酣睡未醒,酒气犹芳,赪颜醉态,倾绝人寰。喜极,为之捉足解袜,抱体缓裳。而女已微醒,开目见刘,四

if wine would do, but he did not answer. She tried to give him gold: again he would not respond. The mai laughed and left, then returned in a little while to say: "Eldest Mistress says that if you will be kind enough to return them, she will repay you with a lovely mate."

"Who will it be?" asked Liu.

"We are the Pi family. Eldest Mistress is called Eighth-Sprite, and the one lying with her was Master Hu; Second Mistress is Water Sprite—she married Mater Ding of Fuchuan; and Third Mistress is Phoenix Sprite. She's even prettier than the others: surely you won't find anything to object to in her."

Afraid that she would go back on her word, Liu announced his intention to sit waiting for favorable news. The maid went out, then returned to say: "Eldest Mistress sends this message: Blessed events cannot be hurried. Just now we spoke to her about it, but got cursed for our pains. All you have to do is give her some time. Our family does not give its word lightly." Liu gave her the bloomers.

Several days passed without word. One day near sunset he came home, closed the door behind him and had just sat down when his double-leafed door opened without warning. Two persons came in holding the four corners of a blanket on which they carried a young woman and said, "Now we have delivered the bride!" They laughed as they placed her on the bed, then left. He took a closer look: the movement had not roused her from her slumbers, and her breath was pungent with wine. Her flushed face and inebriated sprawl would have overwhelmed any man alive. His happiness was compete. He grabbed her feet, pulled off her stockings, held her close and loosened her clothes. Now she was stirring. She opened her eyes and there was Liu: her four limbs were not hers to command. All she could do was complain: "Eight Sprite sold me down the river, that cheap chambermaid!"

Liu embraced her passionately: she started back at the iciness of his skin, then giggled, "'On this night of all nights, such a n-n-ice

肢不能自主，但恨曰："八仙淫婢卖我矣！"刘狎抱之。女嫌肤冰，微笑曰："今夕何夕，见此凉人！"刘曰："子兮子兮，如此凉人何！"遂相欢爱。既而曰："婢子无耻，玷人床寝，而以妾换袴耶！必小报之！"从此无夕不至，绸缪甚殷。袖中出金钏一枚，曰："此八仙物也。"又数日，怀绣履一双来，珠嵌金绣，工巧殊绝，且嘱刘暴扬之。刘出夸示亲宾。求观者皆以贽酒为贽，由此奇货居之。女夜来，作别语。怪问之，答云："姊以履故恨妾，欲携家远去，隔绝我好。"刘惧，愿还之。女云："不必，彼方以此挟妾，如还之，中其机矣。"刘问："何不独留？"曰："父母远去，一家十余口，俱托胡郎经

man is here with me! '"

Liu followed with:"'You angel, you! What will you do now that your n-n-ice man is here? '" And then they took their pleasure in one another.

When it was over she said, "That shameless little hussy, defiling people's beds and then trading me off for a pair of bloomers! I'll show her!"

From then on she came, never missing a night. Their tender love flourished. One day she pulled a gold bracelet from her sleeve and said, "This belongs to Eighth Sprite."

A few days later she came with a pair of embroidered slippers set with pearls and embroidered in gold bracelet from her sleeve and said, "This belongs to Eighth Sprite."

A few days later she came with a pair of embroidered slippers set with pearls and embroidered in gold thread of exquisite workmanship. These she gave to Liu with instructions to show them to everyone he met. When Liu went out he made much of showing them to his relatives and their guests. People who asked to look paid for the privilege with wine, and so he held on to them as if they were rare commodities.

But then the girl came out one night and hinted they would have to part. Mystified, he asked the reason.

"My eldest sister is angry with me because of the slippers. She wants our family to move far away to separate me from my love."

Liu was so frightened that he wanted to give the things back, but the girl said, "That isn't necessary. She is doing this to coerce me. If you return them, you'll be playing along with her scheme."

"Why not stay here by yourself?" asked Liu.

"My parents would be far away," she said. "The whole family, with over ten mouths to feed, relies on Master Hu to manage expenses. If I don't go along, that loose-tongued sister of mine will probably

纪，若不从去，恐长舌妇造黑白也。”从此不复至。逾二年，思念綦切。偶在途中，遇女郎骑款段马，老仆鞚之，摩肩过；反启障纱相窥，丰姿艳绝。顷，一少年后至，曰：“女子何人？似颇佳丽。”刘亟赞之。少年拱手笑曰：“太过奖矣！此即山荆也。”刘惶愧谢过。少年曰：“何妨。但南阳三葛，君得其龙，区区者又何足道！”刘疑其言。少年曰：“君不认窃眠卧榻者耶？”刘始悟为胡。叙僚婿之谊，嘲谑甚欢。少年曰：“岳新归，将以省觐，可同行否？”刘喜，从入萦山。——山上故有邑人避难之宅——女下马入。少间，数人出望，曰：“刘官人亦来矣。”入门谒见翁媪。又一少年先在，靴袍炫美。翁曰：“此富川丁婿。”并揖就坐。少

paint us in a bad light."

She did not come again after that. Two years went by, but that was not enough to ease his pangs of lovesickness. Then one day he met a young woman on the road riding an ambling horse led by an old servant. Their shoulders brushed in passing. She turned and raised her gauze veil to look at him. Her looks and bearing were exceedingly fair. In a moment a young man some distance behind her came by.

"Who is that woman? She seems to be quite a beauty." Liu praised her enthusiastically.

The young man joined his hands in deferential acknowledgement and laughed: "You flatter her too much. That is my wife."

Liu awkwardly begged his pardon.

"No harm done. After all, of the three Zhuges of Nanyang, you got the dragon. Three is not much worth saying about mine." Liu could make nothing of this.

"Don't you recognize the person who slept on your bed without permisson?" asked the young man. Liu finally realized that he was Master Hu. The two brothers-in-law got to know one another and had great fun exchanging jibes.

"Our father-in-law has just returned," said the young man. "We were on our way to visit him. Can you come along?"

Liu was glad to go. He followed them in their zigzagging path through the mountains. Atop one mountain was a dweling that a man of Liu's district used to go to in times of trouble. The girl dismounted and went in. In a little while several people came out to see them, saying: "Master Liu is here too!"

They went in to visit their parents-in-law and found another young man already there, resplendent in a hand-some robe and pair of boots. "This is my son-in-law Master Ding of Fuchuan," said the old man. He motioned them to take their seats. Soon the board was groaning under wine and roasted meats. The talk and laughter

时,酒炙纷纶,谈笑颇洽。翁曰:“今日三婿并临,可称佳集。又无他人,可唤儿辈来,作一团圞之会。”俄,姊妹俱出。翁命设坐,各傍其婿。八仙见刘,惟掩口而笑;凤仙辄与嘲弄;水仙貌少亚,而沉重温克,满座倾谈,惟把酒含笑而已。于是履舄交错,兰麝熏人,饮酒乐甚。刘视床头乐具毕备,遂取玉笛,请为翁寿。翁喜,命善者各执一艺,因而合座争取;惟丁与凤仙不取。八仙曰:“丁郎不谙可也;汝宁指屈不伸者?”因以拍板掷凤仙怀中,便串繁响。翁悦曰:“家人之乐极矣!儿辈俱能歌舞,何不各尽所长?”八仙起,捉水仙曰:“凤仙从来金玉其音,不敢相劳;我二人可歌《洛妃》一曲。”二人歌舞方已,适婢以金盘进果,都不知其何名。翁曰:“此自真腊携来,所谓

sparkled with conviviality.

"Today my three sons-in-law are all here at once. This is truly a wonderful occasion. Also, no stranger is here: we can call my daughters out and have a family get-together."

Shortly the sisters came out. Their father had chairs set for each next to her husband. Eighth Sprite did nothing but cover her mouth and laugh at the sight of Liu. Phoenix Sprite poked fun at him. Water Sprite did not quite come up to others in appearance, but she had a calmly graceful and reserved manner. While the conversation poured forth from all around the table, she did nothing but hold her cup, a smile lingering on her lips. By this time shoes and slippers were crossing beneath the table, and the air was heavy with orchid musk. They were euphoric from wine. Liu noticed a complete set of musical instruments at the head of the couch, so he got a jade-inlaid flute and offered to play to the old man's long life. The old man was delighted and ordered the musical ones each to take part. Everyone at the table raced to get an instrument, except for Ding and Phoenix Sprite.

Eighth Sprite said, "We'll allow that Master Ding knows nothing of music, but why should you keep your fingers curled up and not show what you can do?" She threw a clapper into Phoenix Sprite's lap. Then they struck up a melody in several parts.

The old man loved it. "There is nothing better than music made by a man's own family! My young ones are all good at singing and dancing—why not let each of them show us their best?"

Eighth Sprite got up and pulled Water Sprite with her, saying: "Phoenix Sprite always acts as if her voice is too good for people: I don't dare trouble her. The two of us can sing a piece called 'Nymph on the River Luo.'"

When they had finished singing and dancing, a maid brought a golden tray holding a kind of fruit whose name nobody knew. "These were brought from Cambodia," said the old man. "They call them

‘田婆罗’也。”因掬数枚送丁前。凤仙不悦曰：“婿岂以贫富为爱憎耶？”翁微哂不言。八仙曰：“阿爹以丁郎异县，故是客耳。若论长幼，岂独凤妹妹有拳大酸婿耶？”凤仙终不快，解华妆，以鼓拍授婢，唱《破窑》一折，声泪俱下；既阕，拂袖径去，一座为之不欢。八仙曰：“婢子乔性犹昔。”乃追之，不知所往。刘无颜，亦辞而归。至半途，见凤仙坐路旁，呼与并坐。曰：“君一丈夫，不能为床头人吐气耶？黄金屋自在书中，愿好为之！”举足云：“出门匆遽，棘刺破复履矣。所赠物，在身边否？”刘出之。女取而易之。刘乞其敝者。辴然曰：“君亦大无赖矣！几见自己衾枕之物，亦要怀藏者？如相见爱，一物可以相赠。”旋出一镜付之曰：“欲见妾，当于书卷中觅之；不然，相

Temphala." He reached for a few of them and put them in front of Ding.

Phoenix Sprite was not pleased: "It isn't right to discriminate among your sons-in-law because of differences in wealth." The old man chuckled but did not speak.

Eighth Sprite said, "Daddy did that because Master Ding is from a different district. That makes him the guest. If you're going to talk about precedence, Sister Phoenix is not the only one with a tight-fisted husband."

Phoenix Sprite remained unhappy. She took off her flowery adornments, gave the clapper to the maid and sang an air called "The Dilapidated Cave." Her voice quavered and the tears ran down. When the aria was over she walked straight out with an angry sweep of her sleeves, dampening the mood of all at the table.

"The little hussy is just as wayward as always," said Eighth Sprite. They chased after her, but did not know where she had gone. Unable to face them, Liu too took his leave and headed home. He was halfway there when he saw Phoenix Sprite sitting beside the road, calling him to sit beside her.

"You're a man," she said. "Can't you do something to bring credit on your own bedpartner? 'Inside of books a golden mansion is to be found.' Please try harder!" Then she lifted her leg and said, "I was in a hurry when I left: thorns tore clear through the lining of my shoes. Do you have the ones I gave you?"

Liu pulled them out. She took them and put them on instead of her own. Liu asked for the ruined pair. Agrin brightened her face as she said, "You really are nothing but a bum. Whoever saw a man hiding things from his own wife's wardrobe under his clothes? If you do care about me, there's one thing I can give you." With that, she pulled out a mirror and handed it on him, saying, "If you want to see me, search for me in your books. Otherwise, there can never be a

见无期矣。"言已,不见。怊怅而归。视镜,则凤仙背立其中,如望去人于百步之外者。因念所嘱,谢客下帷。一日,见镜中人忽现正面,盈盈欲笑,益重爱之。无人时,辄以共对。月余,锐志渐衰,游恒忘返。归见镜影,惨然若涕;隔日再视,则背立如初矣:始悟为己之废学也。乃闭户研读,昼夜不辍;月余,则影复向外。自此验之:每有事荒废,则其容戚,数日攻苦,则其容笑。于是朝夕悬之,如对师保。如此二年,一举而捷。喜曰:"今可以对我凤仙矣!"揽镜视之,见画黛弯长,瓠犀微露,喜容可掬,宛在目前。爱极,停睇不已。忽镜中人笑曰:"'影里情郎,画中爱宠',今之

time for us to meet again." The moment she finished speaking, she was gone.

Liu went home mired in dejection. He looked in the mirror: Phoenic Sprite was standing turned away from him, as if looking toward someone a hundred paces away. That made him think of her parting injunctions, so he refused to meet visitors and holed up in his room. One day he saw the woman in the mirror, her face toward him now, full of gaiety ready to spill over into laughter. His love for her redoubled. When no one was near, they would look at each other through the mirror. But after a month or so of this, his keen determination gradually weakened. When he went out to relax, the thought of going back often slipped his mind. Once he came back and looked at the image in the mirror. It seemed to be sniffling miserably. In a few days he looked again: now she had her back to him as before. It dawned on him that this was owing to the slackness of his efforts, whereupon he closed his door and pored over his books, not stopping night or day. In a little over a month the image was facing outward again. This was the proof of it: every time some distraction made him slacken, Phoenix Sprite's expression became forlorn, but a few days of hard study brought a smile to her face. And so he hung the mirror where he could see it night and day, as if he were in the presence of a mentor. After two years of this, victory came on his first attempt of the examina-tion. "Now I can face my Phoenix Sprite," he said happily.

He held the mirror up and looked: there were her eyebrows so finely shaped in black, and her melon-seed teeth slightly showing. The sweetness in her face was palpable, and it was right before his eyes. His love exceeded all bounds. He riveted his gaze upon her. Suddenly the figure in the mirror laughed and said, "So this is what they mean by 'a lover in the looking glass and a sweet heart on a scroll.'"

He looked about in joyful surprise, and there was Phoenix Sprite

谓矣。"惊喜四顾，则凤仙已在座右。握手问翁媪起居。曰："妾别后，不曾归家，伏处岩穴，聊与君分苦耳。"刘赴宴郡中，女请与俱；共乘而往，人对面不相窥。既而将归，阴与刘谋，伪为娶于郡也者。女既归，始出见客，经理家政。人皆惊其美，而不知其狐也。刘属富川令门人，往谒之。遇丁，殷殷邀至其家，款礼优渥。言："岳父母近又他徙。内人归宁，将复。当寄信往，并诣申贺。"刘初疑丁亦狐，及细审邦族，始知富川大贾子也。初，丁自别业暮归，遇水仙独步。见其美，微睨之。女请附骥以行。丁喜，载至斋，与同寝处。棂隙可入，始知为狐。女言："郎无见疑。妾以君诚笃，故愿托之。"丁嬖之，竟不复娶。刘归，假贵家广宅，备客燕寝，洒扫光洁。而苦

sitting beside him. He clasped her hands and asked if her parents were well. "I haven't returned home since we parted," she replied. "I secluded myself in a cave on the face of a cliff, as a way of sharing in your struggle."

Liu had been invited to a dinner in the prefectural seat, and Phoenix Sprite asked to go along. They went there, riding together, but people looked straight at her without seeing her. Afterward, as they set out for home, she and Liu made confidential plans to pass her off as his new bride from the prefectural seat. On their return she finally came out to meet guests and manage the household. Everyone was amazed at her beauty and had no idea she was a werefox.

Liu went to visit the magistrate at Fuchuan, under whom he had studied. There he met Ding, who graciously invited him home and treated him with lavish hospitality. "Our parents-in-law moved again recently. My wife went to pay her respects on them, and is just about to come back. I'll send a letter to her: then we can visit you together to extend our congratulations."

At first Liu suspected that Ding was also a fox, but once he made detailed inquiries into his clan affiliations, he learned that he was the son of a prominent Fuchuan merchant.

Earlier, Ding had come upon Water Sprite walking by herself as he returned from his retreat in the evening. Seeing her beauty, he gave her a sidelong glance. The girl asked if she might ride next to him on his horse. Ding was gald to oblige. He gave her a ride to his studio, where they slept together. She could enter through a crack in the window-frame, so he knew she was a werefox. She said to him, "Don't mistrust me. I wanted to put muself in your hands because of your honesty and earnestness." Ding made her his favorite and never got around to marrying anyone else.

Liu went home and borrowed a spacious house belonging to a genteel family. He prepared pleasant accommodations for his guests. He

无供帐；隔夜视之，则陈设焕然矣。过数日，果有三十余人，赍旗采酒礼而至，舆马缤纷，填溢阶巷。刘揖翁及丁、胡入客舍；凤仙逆妪及两姨入内寝。八仙曰：“婢子今贵，不怨冰人矣。——钏履犹存否？”女搜付之，曰：“履则犹是也，而被千人看破矣。”八仙以履击背，曰：“挞汝寄于刘郎。”乃投诸火，祝曰：“新时如花开，旧时如花谢；珍重不曾着，姮娥来相借。”水仙亦代祝曰：“曾经笼玉笋，着出万人称；若使姮娥见，应怜太瘦生。”凤仙拨火曰：“夜夜上青天，一朝去所欢，留得纤纤影，遍与

scrubbed and swept the place until it shone. The one thing that bothered him was the lack of ornaments and draperies. A night passed and a set of gleaming furnishings was there before his eyes. Within a few days, sure enough, over thirty people came bearing particolored banners and gifts of wine, in a flurry of coaches and horses that filled street and lane. Liu invited his father-in-law, Ding, and Hu to the guest house with a how, while Phoenix Sprite greeted her mother and sisters and took them to the inner bedrooms.

Eighth Sprite said, "Now that you're a person of conse-quence, you don't have to hold that old grudge against your match-maker any more, you little hussy. Do you still have my bracelet and slippers?"

The girl hunted them up and gave them to her, saying: "These are still your slippers, but they are worn out from being stared at by hundreds of people."

Eighth Sprite hit her on the back with a slipper, saying: "Take that for letting Young Liu keep them." With that she threw them in the fire and pronounced an invocation:

When new they were just like flowers
But passing time has made them wither.
Such precious things must not be worn:
Let Moon-Mistress fetch them thither.

Water Sprite also said an invocation for her:

Once these enveloped bamboo shoots of jade,
And multitudes raved when they were worn.
Should Moon-Mistress ever set eyes thereon,
She'd pity these slippers, so old and torn.

Phoenix Sprite stirred the ashes, chanting:

Night after night she soared into the sky,
But then one day she left her love behind.

世人看。”遂以灰捻柈中，堆作十余分，望见刘来，托以赠之，但见绣履满柈，悉如故款。八仙急出，推柈堕地；地上犹有一二只存者，又伏吹之，其迹始灭。次日，丁以道远，夫妇先归。八仙贪与妹戏，翁及胡屡督促之，亭午始出，与众俱去。初来，仪从过盛，观者如市。有两寇窥见丽人，魂魄丧失，因谋劫诸途。侦其离村，尾之而去。相隔不盈一矢，马极奔，不能及。至一处，两崖夹道，舆行稍缓；追及之，持刀吼咤，人众都奔。下马启帘，则老妪坐焉。方疑误掠其母；才他顾，而兵伤右臂，顷已被缚。凝视之，崖并非崖，乃平乐城门也；舆中则李进士母，自乡中归耳。一寇后至，亦被断马足而絷之。门丁执送太守，一讯

Now all that's left are these two slender shapes
That have been shown to all of humankind.

Then she scraped the ashes into a dustpan and formed them into ten piles. At Liu's approach, she held the dustpan out to him as a gift. It was full of embroidered slippers, all of exactly the same cut as the old pair. Eighth Sprite dashed over and knocked the dustpan to the ground. A couple of them remained until she leaned over to blow on them, causing them to vanish without a trace.

The next day Ding set out first on the long journey home with his wife. Eighth Sprite could not get enough of joking with her sister. Hu and the old man urged her repeatedly, but not until high noon did Hu and his wife go out and leave with their group.

Earlier, when they had just arrived, a marketlike crowd of onlookers had turned out for the impressive entourage. Two bandits who caught a glimpse of the beautiful lady were captivated by her, so they laid plans to abduct her on the road. Seeing her leave the village, they trailed along behind. They had closed in to less than an arrow's flight away, when her horses broke into a headlong gallop. They were left behind until the road went into a defile between two cliffs and the carriage slowed down. One of them overtook it, brandishing his sword and roaring. All her followers ran away. He dismounted and lifted the curtain: there sat an old woman. He wondered if he had accidently caputured the lady's mother, and just as he started to turn away from her, a sword bit into his right arm. Within moments he was bound hand and foot. A closer look showed that the cliffs were not cliffs: they were the gatetower on Pingle's city walls. In the carriage was the mother of Doctor of Letters Li, who had been returning from the country. The other bandit rode up from behind. One of his horse's legs was lopped off, and he too was bound fast. The gatekeeper turned them over to the prefect, to whom they admitted their guilt at the first

而伏。时有大盗未获，诘之，即其人也。明春，刘及第。凤仙以招祸，故悉辞内戚之贺。刘亦更不他娶。及为郎官，纳妾，生二子。

异史氏曰："嗟乎！冷暖之态，仙凡固无殊哉！'少不努力，老大徒伤'。惜无好胜佳人，作镜影悲笑耳。吾愿恒河沙数仙人，并遣娇女昏嫁人间，则贫穷海中，少苦众生矣。"

interrogation. Questioning revealed that one of them was a notorious bandit who had been at large.

In spring of the next year, Liu passed the third-degree examination. Phoenix Sprite turned down invitations to all her relatives' receptions so as not to court trouble. Liu did not marry anyone else. Once he got the position of a ministry secretary, he obtained a concubine and fathered two sons.

The Chronicler of the Tales comments: "Alas! Immortals can be just as cold, or just as warm, as mortals! 'If you don't make an honest effort when you're young, you're asking for misery in old age.' It is a pity to be without an ambitious, beautiful woman to cast images of gloom or laughter in your mirror. My wish is that immortals to the number of the grains of sand along the Ganges River would all send lovely girls down to be married into the human world. Then living beings would suffer less than they do in this sea of poverty and bitterness."

长亭

石太璞，泰山人，好厌禳之术。有道士遇之，赏其慧，纳为弟子。启牙签，出二卷，上卷驱狐，下卷驱鬼，乃以下卷授之，曰："虔奉此书，衣食佳丽皆有之。"问其姓名，曰："吾汴城北村玄帝观王赤城也。"留数日，尽传其诀。石由此精于符箓，委贽者踵接于门。一日，有叟来，自称翁姓，炫陈币帛，谓其女鬼病已殆，必求亲诣。石闻病危，辞不受贽，姑与俱往。十余里入山村，至其家，廊舍华好。入室，见

FOX-GIRL CHANGTING

SHI Taipu of Mount Tai took an interest in the art of exorcism. A Taoist priest met him and appreciated his intellect enough to accept him as a disciple. He took out a boxed set of books with an ivory label: the first volume dealt with exorcism of werefoxes, and the second with exorcism of ghosts. He handed the second volume to Shi, saying: "Study this carefully: food, clothing, and a beautiful woman will all be yours."

Shi asked the Taoist's name, and he replied, "I am Wang Chicheng of Dark Emperor's Shrine in the village north of Bian city."

For several days he kept Shi with him to pass on all his skills. Shi became so well versed in charms and books of incantations that people lined up at his gate to offer him acquaintance gifts. One day an old man came, introduced himself as Weng, and laid out a glittering array of cash and silken goods, saying that his daughter was gravely ill due to possession by a ghost. He begged earnestly that Shi make a personal call. When Shi heard the illness was critical, he turned down the gifts and went along to see what he could do.

After going a dozen li they entered a mountain village and came to the old man's house, which was a cluster of splendid buildings and gal-

少女卧縠幛中，婢以钩挂幛。望之年十四五许，支缀于床，形容已槁。近临之，忽开目云："良医至矣。"举家皆喜，谓其不语已数日矣。石乃出，因诘病状。叟言："日昼见少年来，与共寝处，捉之已杳，少间复至，意其为鬼。"石曰："其鬼也，驱之匪难；恐其是狐，则非余所敢知矣。"叟云："必非必非。"石授以符，是夕宿于其家。夜分，有少年入，衣冠整肃。石疑是主人眷属，起而问之。曰："我鬼也。翁家尽狐。偶悦其女红亭，姑止焉。鬼为狐祟，阴骘无伤，君何必离人之缘而护之也？女之姊长亭，光艳尤绝。敬留全璧，以待高贤。彼如许字，方可为之施治；尔时我当自去。"石诺之。是夜，少年不复至，女顿醒。天明，叟喜，以告石，请石入视。石焚旧符，乃坐诊之。见

leries. As he entered the room, a maid hitched aside the crepe curtian of the bed with a hook, revealing a girl lying inside. She appeared to be fourteen or fifteen years old. Her limbs rested limply on the bed, and her face was drawn with anguish. At his approach she suddenly opened her eyes and said, "Here is a doctor who knows what he is doing."

The whole family rejoiced at this and told him that she had not spoken for days. Shi then left the room to inquire into the symptoms. The old man Weng said, "A young man came in broad daylight and slipped into bed with her. When we went in to catch him, he was gone. In a little while he was back again, which leads us to think he is a ghost."

"If he's a ghost, driving him away won't be any trouble," said Shi. "But it might be a werefox, in which case I can't say what the outcome will be."

"No, it couldn't be that," said Weng. Shi gave them a written charm and stayed in their house that evening. During the night a well-dressed young man came into the room. Gussing he was a member of his host's family, Shi got up and asked him his name.

"I am a ghost. Everyone in the Weng family is a werefox. I took a fancy to his daughter Hong-Ting and attached myself to her for a lark. Ghosts do no damage to their innervirtues when they haunt werefoxes. Why should you interfere with someone else's attachments just to protect these werefoxes? Hong-ting's elder sister Changting is a dazzling beauty of the rarest kind. I have left that piece of jade intact for someone more deserving than myself. Wait to perform your cure until Changting agrees to marry you: when that time comes, I'll leave on my own." Shi assented.

The young man did not come back that night. In the morning the old man elatedly told Shi that the girl had suddenly revived, and asked him to go in for a look. Shi burned the charm he had written out earli-

绣幕有女郎,丽若天人,心知其长亭也。诊已,索水洒幛。女郎急以碗水付之,蹀躞之间,意动神流。石生此际,心殊不在鬼矣。出辞叟,托制药去,数日不返。鬼益肆,除长亭外,子妇婢女,俱被淫惑。又以仆马招石,石托疾不赴。明日,叟自至。石故作病股状,扶杖而出。叟拜已,问故。曰:"此鳏之难也!曩夜婢子登榻,倾跌,堕汤夫人泡两足耳。"叟问:"何久不续?"石曰:"恨不得清门如翁者。"叟默而出。石走送曰:"病瘥当自至,无烦玉趾也。"又数日,叟复来;石跛而见之。叟慰问三数语,便曰:"顷与荆人言,君如驱鬼去,使举家安枕,小女长亭,年十七矣,愿遣奉事君子。"石喜,顿首于地。乃谓叟:"雅意若此,病躯何敢复爱。"立刻出门,并骑而去。入视祟

er, and then sat down to diagnose her. Beside the embroidered curtain he saw a young woman, so beautiful she might have been from heaven, whom he called for water to sprinkle on the curtain. The young woman hurridely brought him a bowlful. As she tripped back and forth with sprightly steps, her manner expressed an inward excitement. At this point the ghost was the furthest thing from Shi's mind.

On the pretext of going to compound a prescription, Shi took leave of Weng and did not return for many days. The ghost went wild. With the exception of Changting, all the daughters-in-law, maids and other women molested. A servant and horse were sent to summon Shi, but he excused himself on grounds of illness. On the next day Weng came himself. Shi went to the door leaning on a staff, pretending his thighs were injured. With a bow, Weng asked what had happened.

"It was the sort of accident that can only happen to a widower. A few nights ago my maid stumbled as she stepped onto my bed. She dropped the warming pan and both my legs were scalded."

"Why haven't you remarried after all this time?" asked Weng.

"I can't be content with anything less than a good family like yours," said Shi. Weng went silently to the door. Shi walked him out, saying "I'll go to your place on my own when I recover. Don't wear out your delicate feet."

Several days later Weng came again. Shi hobbled out to meet him. After asking a few polite questions about Shi's condition, Weng said, "My wife and I had a talk. If you drive the ghost away and let my family sleep in peace, we are willing to send our little seventeen-year-old daughter Changting to do your bidding."

Shi happily bumped his forehead against the ground and told the old man: "Since you treat me so magnanimously, I would be ashamed to go on coddling my ailing body." They went out the gate immediately, riding shoulder to shoulder. After examining the victims of the disturbances Shi asked to discuss arrangements with Weng's wife, for

者既毕,石恐背约,请与媪盟。媪遽出曰:"先生何见疑也?"即以长亭所插金簪,授石为信。石朝拜之。已,乃遍集家人,悉为祓除。惟长亭深匿无迹;遂写一佩符,使人持赠之。是夜寂然,鬼影尽灭,惟红亭呻吟未已,投以法水,所患若失。石欲辞去,叟挽止殷恳。至晚,肴核罗列,劝酬殊切。漏二下,主人乃辞客去。石方就枕,闻叩扉甚急;起视,则长亭掩入,辞气仓皇,言:"吾家欲以白刃相仇,可急遁!"言已,径返身去。石战惧无色,越垣急窜。遥见火光,疾奔而往,则里人夜猎者也。喜。待猎毕,乃与俱归。心怀怨愤,无之可伸,思欲之汴寻赤城,而家有老父,病废已久,日夜筹思,莫决进止。忽一日,双舆至门,则翁媪送长亭至,谓石曰:"曩夜之归,胡再不谋?"石见长

fear that Weng would go back on his word.

The old woman rushed into the room, saying: "How could you doubt us, sir? She gave him a golden hairpin used by Changting as a token of faith. Shi bowed before her. Then he gathered all the members of the family for purification and casting-out. Changting alone was hidden from sight, so he wrote a charm for her to wear on her sash and had it sent to her. That night all was still: all signs of ghosts were gone. Only Hongting moaned without cease, but the moment Shi treated her with magic water, she seemed as if she had never been afflicted. Shi asked leave to go, but Weng courteously held him back. When evening came his host urged him even more insistently to enjoy the spread of meat dishes and fruit."

The water clock had gone down two notches when the host bid his guest good night and retired. As Shi's head touched the pillow an urgent knocking sounded at the door. He got up to look: Changting slipped in, closing the door behind her, and blurted out in confused agitation: "My family is going to take revenge on you with sharp knives. Run away quickly!" Having said this, she turned straight around and walked out the door.

Shi shuddered and turned pale. He scrambled frantically over the wall. In the distance he saw the glow of a fire. Hurrying up to it, he found men from his neighborhood who were out on a night hunting trip. He waited till they finished hunting, then went home with them.

Shi's heart seethed with outrage, but there was nowhere he could go to demand justice. He thought of going to Bian and hunting up the Taoist Wang Chicheng, but his old, debilitated father was with him at home. Day and night he considered the alternatives, but he could not decide whether to go or stay.

Suddenly one day two carriages drew up at his gate. Inside were the old man Weng and his wife, bringing Changting along. They said, "Why didn't you discuss things further with us after you went home

亭,怨恨都消,故亦隐而不发。媪促两人庭拜讫。石将设筵,辞曰:“我非闲人,不能坐享甘旨。我家老子昏髦,倘有不悉,郎肯为长亭一念老身,为幸多矣。”登车遂去。盖杀婿之谋,媪不之闻;及追之不得而返,媪始知之。颇不能平,与叟日相诟谇;长亭亦饮泣不食。媪强送女来,非翁意也。长亭入门,诘之,始知其故。过两三月,翁家取女归宁。石料其不返,禁止之。女自此时一涕零。年余,生一子,名慧儿,买乳媪哺之。然儿善啼,夜必归母。一日,翁家又以舆来,言媪思女甚。长亭益悲,石不忍复留之。欲抱子去,石不可,长亭乃自归。别时,以一月为期,既而半载无耗。遣人往探之,则向所僦宅久空。又二年余,望想都

that night?"

At the sight of Changting, Shi's resentment subsided and he kept his feelings about the past hidden. At the old lady's prompting, the two bowed in confirmation of their marriage. Shi wanted to arrange a banquet, but the old lady refused: "I have things to do. I can't sit around regaling myself with fine flavors and vintages. The old man of our house is in the final stages of senility. If there have been some oversights, I would feel fortunate if you would consider me for Changting's sake."

She climbed in her cart and they rode away. Actually, the old lady had not heard of the plan to kill their prospective son-in-law. She was not aware of it until the men returned from their unsuccessful chase. She was offended at the injustice done to Shi, and she railed at Weng day after day. Changting refused to swallow anything but her own tears. The mother insisted on taking the girl to Shi against her father's wishes. But Shi only learned of this after Changting came to live with him and he had time to question her.

Two or three months later, the girl's family wanted to take her home for a visit. Shi would not allow her to go, for fear that she would not return. From that time on, she often broke into crying fits. In a little over a year she gave birth to a son named Brilliant-Child. She hired a wet nurse to feed him; but the boy was choleric and insisted on sleeping with his mother at night.

One day her family sent a carriage with the message that the old woman dearly missed her daughter. Changting was more heartbroken than ever: Shi tried to take the child in her arms as she left, but Shi would not let her, so she returned alone. At her departure she agreed to see him again in a month, but half a year passed with no word from her. He sent someone to bring news of her, but the house her family once rented had long been vacant. The passing of two more years brought an end to Shi's wishing and hoping, but the child's nightlong

绝;而儿啼终夜,寸心如割。既而石父病卒,倍益哀伤;因而病惫,苫次弥留,不能受宾朋之吊。方昏愦间,忽闻妇人哭入。视之,则缞绖者长亭也。石大悲,一恸遂绝。婢惊呼,女始辍泣,抚之良久,始渐苏。自疑已死,谓相聚于冥中。女曰:"非也。妾不孝,不能得严父心,尼归三载,诚所负心。适家人由海东经此,得翁凶问。妾遵严命而绝儿女之情,不敢循乱命而失翁媳之礼。妾来时,母知而父不知也。"言间,儿投怀中。言已,始抚之,泣曰:"我有父,儿无母矣!"儿亦嗷啕,一室掩泣。女起,经理家政,柩前牲盛洁备,石乃大慰。而病久,急切不能起。女乃请石外兄款洽吊客。丧既闭,石始杖而能起,相与营谋斋葬。葬已,女欲辞归,以受背父之谴。夫挽儿号,

wailing pierced his helpless heart. Then his father weakened and died, which multiplied his misery. He was incapatitated by nervous exhaustion during the mourning period, and unable to receive the condolences of guests and friends.

Shi was wallowing in a demoralized muddle when he suddenly heard a woman come into his room crying. He looked up and saw Changting in hempen mourning clothes. Agreat surge of griet came over him and threw him into a faint. The maid's cries of alarm brought Changting out of her sobbing fit. She cradled him in her arms and stroked him a good while before he gradually revived. Thinking that he was dead, he told her that they were now united in the underworld.

"You are wrong," she said. "I am too disobedient to win my father's favor. He hindered me from coming back for three years. That is the reason I betrayed my trust. Recently a member of my family passed by here on his way from the East Coast, and so I learned the news of your father's death. I broke off my love for you in obedience to a parental command, but now I dare not neglect the observances for my father-in-law to submit to an irrational command. My mother knows I am here, but my father doesn't."

As she spoke, her child threw himself into her arms. When she had finished speaking, she stroked him and sobbed, "I have a father, but my son has had no mother. The child also wailed and howled. Everyone in the room brushed back their tears. Changting rose and set to work putting the house in order. Shi was greatly relieved to see ample offerings put neatly in place before the coffin. However, he had been ill for some time and could not get up at once, so Changting asked his cousin to receive and entertain callers. When the funeral was over Shi could at last get up with a cane to help arrange the burial.

After the burial, Changting excused herself to return home and receive the reprimand she had coming for deceiving her father. Shi tugged at her arm and her son wailed, which moved her to stay. Not

隐忍而止。未几,有人来告母病。乃谓石曰:"妾为君父来,君不为妾母放令去耶?"石许之。女使乳媪抱儿他适,涕洟出门而去。去后,数年不返,石父子渐亦忘之。一日,昧爽启扉,则长亭飘入。石方骇问,女戚然坐榻上,叹曰:"生长闺阁,视一里为遥;今一日夜而奔千里,殆矣!"细诘之,女欲言复止。请之不已,哭曰:"今为君言,恐妾之所悲,而君之所快也。迩年徙居晋界,僦居赵搢绅之第。主客交最善,以红亭妻其公子。公子数逋荡,家庭颇不相安。妹归告父;父留之,半年不令还。公子忿恨,不知何处聘一恶人来,遣神绾锁,缚老父去,一门大骇,顷刻四散矣。"石闻之,笑不自禁。女怒曰:"彼虽不仁,妾之父也。妾与君琴瑟数年,止有相好而无相尤。今日人亡家败,百口流离, 即不为父伤,宁不

long afterwards a servant came to say that her mother was ill, whereupon she said to Shi: "I came on account of your father. Won't you let me go for my mother's sake?"

Shi gave his approval. Changting had the nurse carry the boy away to another part of the house, then went sniveling out the gate. Once gone, she did not return for years. Shi and his son slowly forgot about her. Then one day he threw open the door at the break of dawn, and Changting glided in. As Shi questioned her in amazement, she sat dejectedly on the bed and sighed, Back in the days when I was growing up in secluded chambers, one li seemed far to me: Now I run a thousand li in one night. You can imagine how tired I am."

He questioned her closely. She opened her mouth to speak and then thought better of it. Under the weight of his ceaseless entreaties she said between sobs: "By telling you now, I'll probably make myself miserable and you delighted. A few years back we moved to Shanxi and rented living quarters in the mansion of Squire Zhao. Landlord and guests got along wonderfully, so we gave Hongting to be the young master's wife. But the young master strayed from home frequently, and their married life was by no means peaceful. When my sister went home and told our father how she was treated, he kept her at home for half a year and wouldn't hear of her going back. The young master was furious. He hired a wicked man from goodness knows where, who sent magic fetters to bind my father and take him away. Everyone in the house was horrified: within minutes they scattered to the four quarters."

Shi could not help but laugh when he heard this. The girl raged: "He may be cruel, but he's my father. You and I have been like lute and zither for years. There has been only love between us, never blame. Now my father is gone and my family is ruined. A hundred mouths are wandering with nowhere to turn. Even if you aren't sorry for my father, I thought you would at least sympathize with me. But

为妾吊乎！闻之忭舞，更无片语相慰藉，何不义也！”拂袖而出。石追谢之，亦已渺矣。怅然自悔，拚已决绝。过二三日，媪与女俱来，石喜慰问。母子俱伏。惊而询之，母子俱哭。女曰：“妾负气而去，今不能自坚，又欲求人，复何颜矣！”石曰：“岳固非人；母之惠，卿之情，所不忘也。然闻祸而乐，亦犹人情，卿何不能暂忍？”女曰：“顷于途中遇母，始知絷吾父者，盖君师也。”石曰：“果尔，亦大易。然翁不归，则卿之父子离散；恐翁归，则卿之夫泣儿悲也。”媪矢以自明，女亦誓以相报。石乃即刻治任如汴，询至玄帝观，则赤城归未久。入而参之。便问：“何来？”石视厨下一老狐，孔前股而系之。笑曰：“弟子之来，为此老

when you heard, you hopped about with a grin on your face and didn't say a word to comfort me. It just isn't right!" She went out with a sweep of her sleeve. Shi ran after her to blamed himself for letting her abandon him this way.

A few days later his wife turned up, together with her mother. Shi, in his joy to see them, questioned them solicitously. He was shocked when mother and daughter both went down on their knees before him, and demanded to know the reason. Both of them burst into sobs. It was the girl who answered: "I left you in anger. But I cannot harden myself now—I must ask for your help once again. I have no honor left to stand on."

"Even though my father-in-law is inhuman, I will never forget your mother's generosity and your love. You know it is human nature to delight in the misfortune of an unkind person. Couldn't you have overlooked that for a while?"

"Not long ago I ran into my mother on the road," said the girl. "It was then that I learned that your master is the man who bound my father."

"If he is, it's a simple matter," said Shi. "But as long as my father-in-law is detained, he and his children have to remain apart. I'm afraid that once he returns, your hus-band will weep and your son will mourn." His mother-in-law vowed to make her wishes plain, and Changting promised to repay his kindness, so Shi packed his bag right away and went to Bian. He asked the way to the Dark-Emperor's Shrine and found that Wang Chicheng had returned just a little while ago. Shi went in and opened the visit with a bow.

"What brings you here?" asked his master.

Shi, noticing an old fox tied in the kitchen by a cord passed through a puncture in its front leg, laughted and said, "This old ghoul is the reason for my visit." Chicheng asked what he meant.

"This is my father-in-law." He told his master the whole story.

魅。"赤城诘之,曰:"是吾岳也。"因以实告。道士谓其狡诈,不肯轻释。固请,乃许之。石因备述其诈,狐闻之,塞身入灶,似有惭状。道士笑曰:"彼羞恶之心,未尽亡也。"石起,牵之而出,以刀断索抽之。狐痛极,齿龈龈然。石不遽抽,而顿挫之,笑问曰:"翁痛之,勿抽可耶?"狐睛映闪,似有愠色。既释,摇尾出观而去。石辞归。三日前,已有人报叟信,媪先去,留女待石。石至,女逆而伏。石挽之曰:"卿如不忘琴瑟之情,不在感激也。"女曰:"今复迁还故居矣,村舍邻迩,音问可以不梗。妾欲归省,三日可旋,君信之否?"曰:"儿生而无母,未便殇折。我日日鳏居,习已成惯。今不似赵公子,而反德报之,所以为卿者尽矣。如其不还,在卿为负义,道里虽近,当亦不复过问,何不信之与有?"女次日去,二日即返。

The Taoist would not lightly let the fox go, claiming that it was cunning and devious, but he finally gave in to Shi's insistent pleas. Shi gave a complete account of the fox's deceitfulness, which made the fox slink under the stove as if in humiliation.

The Taoist said with a laugh: "At least he hasn't lost all sense of shame."

Shi rose and led the fox outside, where he cut the cord with a knife and began to pull it out. The fox, in the extremity of its pain, snapped its teeth at him. Instead of pulling the cord out all at once, Shi did it by fits and starts and laughingly asked, "Since this is so painful, old man, would you rather I didn't pull it out?" The fox's glowering eyes flashed fire, and a livid look came over its face. When he let it go, it took leave of the Taoist and started back. Three days before his arrival, word of Weng's release had reached the old woman, who went ahead to meet him, leaving her daughter to wait for Shi. When he arrived, Changting came out to greet him and went down on her knees. Shi helped her to her feet, saying, "As long as you don't forget our love, I don't care about gratitude."

"We have moved back to our old place not far from your village," said Changting. There will be nothing to hinder the exchange of messages and news. When I want to go home for a visit, I can make it there and back in three days. Do you believe me?"

My son came into this world with no mother to care for him: yet his life was not cut short. Now I've grown used to the life of a widower. Instead of behaving like Young Master Zhao, I repaid spite with kindness. I've done everything I could for you. You will do me wrong if you don't come back. The road may be short, but if you ignore me again, it will be better for me if I mistrust you." Changting left the next day, then returned two days later.

"Why so soon?" he asked.

"My father still won't forgive you for toying with his pride in

问:"何速?"曰:"父以君在汴曾相戏弄,未能忘怀,言之絮絮;妾不欲复闻,故早来也。"自此闺中之往来无间,而翁婿间尚不通吊庆云。

异史氏曰:"狐情反复,谲诈已甚。悔婚之事,两女而一辙,诡可知矣。然要而婚之,是启其悔者已在初也。且婿既爱女而救其父,止宜置昔怨而仁化之;乃复狎弄于危急之中,何怪其没齿不忘也!天下有冰玉之不相能者,类如此。"

Bian. He raved on and on about it. I didn't want to hear any more, so I left early."

From then on the women of the two houses visited back and forth constantly though father- and son-in-law made sure to stay out of touch, or so the story goes.

The Chronicler of the Tales comments: "The werefox's emotions were treacherous and unpredictable: that in itself indicated great deceitfulness. He fell into the rut of disavowing his two daughters' marriages, and from this his dishonesty can be seen. However, by maneuvering him into allowing the marriage, Shi invited his disavowal at the very beginning. Also, since the son-in-law saved the father for love of the daughter, he should have disregarded past injury and transformed the man with benevolence. Instead, he toyed with him at a crucial moment. Small wonder the werefox would not forget his anger till the end of his life. In this world there are many feuds like this between fathers-in-law and sons-in-law."

胭　脂

东昌卞氏，业牛医者，有女小字胭脂，才姿惠丽。父宝爱之，欲占凤于清门，而世族鄙其寒贱，不屑缔盟，以故及笄未字。对户龚姓之妻王氏，佻脱善谑，女闺中谈友也。一日，送至门，见一少年过，白服裙帽，丰采甚都。女意似动，秋波萦转之。少年俯其首，趋而去。去既远，女犹凝眺。王窥其意，戏之曰："以娘子才貌，得配若人，庶可无恨。"女晕红上颊，脉脉不作一语。王问："识得此郎否？"答云："不识。"王曰："此南巷鄂秀才秋隼，故

ROUGE

OLD Bian of Dongchang, a veterinarian by profession, had an intelligent, beautiful daughter whose childhood name was Rouge. Her father intended to find a mate from an esteemed family for his beloved, precious girl, but noblemen were too proud to connect themselves with him, for they despised his low rank and lack of means. Thus the girl reached hairpin age without being spoken for.

The wife of the Gong family across the street, n é e Wang, was a capricious, madcap sort who often spent time conversing in the girl's caught sight of a passing young man, commandingly handsome in his white gown and hat. She must have found him distracting, judging from the way the rippling glances of her eyes lingered after him. The young man lowered his head and hastened away. The girl's gaze remained fixed on him as he dwindled in the distance. Wang saw what was on her mind and poked fun at her: "With ability and looks like yours, young lady, I am sure there would be no regrets if you could be matched with such a man." Atinge of red spread over the girl's cheeks. She said nothing, but her pulse quickened.

"Do you know that genteman?" asked Wang.

"No, I don't" she answered.

孝廉之子。妾向与同里，故识之。世间男子，无其温婉。今衣素，以妻服未阕也。娘子如有意，当寄语使委冰焉。”女无言，王笑而去。数日无耗，心疑王氏未暇即往，又疑宦裔不肯俯拾。邑邑徘徊，萦念颇苦；渐废饮食，寝疾惙顿。王氏适来省视，研诘病因。答言：“自亦不知。但尔日别后，即觉忽忽不快，延命假息，朝暮人也。”王小语曰：“我家男子，负贩未归，尚无人致声鄂郎。芳体违和，非为此否？”女赪颜良久。王戏之曰：“果为此者，病已至是，尚何顾忌？先令夜来一聚，彼岂不肯可？”女叹息曰：“事至此，已不能羞。但渠不嫌寒贱，即遣媒来，疾当愈；若私约，则断断不可！”王颔之，遂去。王幼时与邻生宿介通，即嫁，

"That's Bachelor of Letters E Autumn – Falcon from South Lane, son of the late Exemplar. I used to live in his neighborhood, so I know him. No man in this world is as kind and gentle as he is. He's in plain dress now because the mourning period for his wife is not yet over. If you are willing I will carry a message telling him to send a matchmaker."

The girl did not speak. Wang went away laughing. Several days passed with no news. She surmised that Wang had not yet found time to pay a visit, and she also doubted if the son of an official would care to stoop and pick up what was left in his way. She whiled away her time despondently, suffering from thoughts that would not go away, till melancholy deprived her of appetite and rest. It was then that Wang came to see her and demanded to know the reason for her illness.

"I don't know myself," was her answer. "But since the last day you saw me, I've been restless and depressed. I'm living from breath to breath. It will be all over any day now."

Wang lowered her voice: "My husband hasn't gotten back from his selling trip yet: there is nobody to get the word to young E. Is that what is making you ill?"

The girl's face was crimson for a good while. Wang joked: "So that's what it's about. Now that you are in this condition, why bother about scruples? Have him come spend a night with you first. You don't think he'll turn you down, do you?"

"Things have gotten to the point that I can't play coy," said the girl. "If only he could see far enough past my poverty and low rank to send a matchmaker over, my illness would be cured. But if it takes having a rendezvous with him, I simply won't do it!

Wang nodded and left. In her younger days she had been involved with a young man named Su Jie who lived next door. Now that she was married, Su continued relations with her, watching for times when

宿侦夫他出，辄寻旧好。是夜宿适来，因述女言为笑，戏嘱致意鄂生。宿久知女美，闻之窃喜，幸其机之可乘也。将与妇谋，又恐其妒，乃假无心之词，问女家闺闼甚悉。次夜，逾垣入，直达女所，以指叩窗。内问："谁何？"答以"鄂生。"女曰："妾所以念君者，为百年，不为一夕。郎果爱妾，但宜速倩冰人；若言私合，不敢从命。"宿姑诺之，苦求一握纤腕为信。女不忍过拒，力疾启扉。宿遽入，即抱求欢。女无力撑拒，仆地上，气息不续。宿急曳之。女曰："何来恶少，必非鄂郎；果是鄂郎，其人温驯，知妾病由，当相怜恤，何遂狂暴如此！若复尔尔，便当鸣呼，品行亏损，两无所益！"宿恐假迹败露，不敢复强，但请后会。女以亲

her husband was elsewhere. Su happened to come this same night, so Wang amused him by repeating what the girl had said, and jokingly instructed him to relay the message to young E. Su, who had known of the girl's beauty long before, was glad to hear this, because of the opportunity it left open to him. He thought of discussing his plans with Wang but then reconsidered, fearing her jealousy. And so he plied her with seemingly disinterested questions to learn exactly where the girl's chamber was in the house.

The next night he climbed in over the wall, went right to the girl's room and tapped on a window with his finger.

"Who is it?" came a voice from inside.

"It's E" he replied.

"I want you for a lifetime, not for a single night. If you really love me, the only right thing to do is send a matchmaker soon. If you're talking about a secret affair I am afraid I can't satisfy your wishes."

Su pretended to agree and beseeched her to let him hold her delicate wrist as a pledge of trust. The girl felt too sorry for him to overdo her refusal, and so used all her strength to push the door open. Su darted in, embraced her and begged for joy. Lacking the strength to resist him, she fell to the ground, her breath coming in unconnected gasps. Su pulled her arm impatiently.

"What corner did you crawl out of, you scum? You couldn't be Master E. If you were E and knew the cause of my illness, you would be kind and considerate like him and feel pity for me, instead of acting like a brute. If you keep behaving this way I'll be forced to scream. It won't do either of us any good to have our good names ruined!"

Fearing that his deception would be uncovered, Su dared not force himself on her any further, so he only asked to meet her again. The girl set the bride-welcoming as the time for their next meeting. Su thought that was too long to wait and asked again. The girl, fed up

迎为期。宿以为远，又请之。女厌纠缠，约待病愈。宿求信物，女不许。宿捉足解绣履而去。女呼之返，曰："身已许君，复何吝惜？但恐'画虎成狗'，致贻污谤。今亵物已入君手，料不可反。君如负心，但有一死！"宿既出，又投宿王所。既卧，心不忘履，阴揣衣袂，竟已乌有。急起篝灯，振衣冥索。诘之，不应。疑妇藏匿，妇故笑以疑之。宿不能隐，实以情告。言已，遍烛门外，竟不可得。懊恨归寝。窃幸深夜无人，遗落当犹在途也。早起寻之，亦复杳然。先是，巷中有毛大者，游手无籍。尝挑王氏不得，知宿与洽，思掩执以胁之。是

with his clinging, asked him to wait for her recovery. Su begged her to give him a token of remembrance, but she would not, and so he grabbed her by the leg, pulled off her embroidered slipper and left.

The girl called him back saying: "I've already promised myself to you: why should I grudge you anything? My only fear is that 'the tiger might be painted to look like a dog.' We could become the objects of vile slander because of this. Now you are holding part of my intimate wardrobe in your hand. I see no hope of getting it back. If you betray me, death is my only way out."

After Su left he went to stay the night at Wang's place. He laid down in bed, but he could not stop thinking of the slipper. He furtively fumbled in his robe and was shocked to find that it was not there. He jumped up, turned the lampshade, then shook his clothes and felt around on the floor. He turned to ask Wang, who wouldn't answer his questions, so he began to wonder if she had hidden it. She laughed deliberately to heighten his suspicions. Su could not keep it to himself any longer: he told her the truth. When his story was finished he went over every inch of ground outside the gate, candle in hand, but still it did not turn up. He went back to bed greatly annoyed, cheering himself with the thought that nobody was out this late at night and that if he had dropped the slipper it would still be in the street. He got up early in the morning and searched for it, but it was still nowhere to be found.

Now there lived on the same street a shiftless vagrant named Mao the Elder, who had once made futile advances to Wang. Knowing that Su was having an affair with her, he had the notion to catch them in a compromising situation so that he could make demands. Walking by her gate this same night, he found it unlocked and slipped inside. Just outside the window he stepped on something soft and cottony. He picked it up to look: it was a woman's slipper wrapped in a handkerchief. Eavesdropping at the window, he heard Su give a complete ac-

夜，过其门，推之未扃，潜入。方至窗外，踏一物，软若絮帛，拾视，则巾裹女舄。伏听之，闻宿自述甚悉，喜极，抽身而出。逾数夕，越墙入女家，门户不悉，误诣翁舍。翁窥窗，见男子，察其音迹，知为女来者。心忿怒，操刀直出。毛大骇，反走。方欲攀垣，而卞追已近，急无所逃，反身夺刃；媪起大呼，毛不得脱，因而杀之。女稍痊，闻喧始起。共烛之，翁脑裂不复能言，俄顷已绝。于墙下得绣履，媪视之，胭脂物也。逼女，女哭而实告之；但不忍贻累王氏，言鄂生之自至而已。天明，讼于邑。邑宰拘鄂。鄂为人谨讷，年十九岁，见客羞涩如童子。被执，骇绝。上堂不知置词，惟有战栗。宰益信其情真，横加梏械。书生不堪痛楚，以是诬服。既解郡，敲扑如邑。生冤

count of his evening. Mao congratulated himself on his good luck as he crept away.

Several evenings later he climbed the wall and entered the girl's house. Being unfamiliar with the layout, he blundered into the old man's quarters. The old man looked out the window and saw a man who, judging from the sounds and movements he made, had evidently come for his daughter. Rage swelled in the old man's heart as he rushed out knife in hand. Mao turned in great fright and ran. He was about to climb the wall, but old Bian was close behind him. In desperation at having nowhere to run, he turned around and wrenched the blade away. Behind them the old woman let out a loud scream. Unable to free himself from the old man's grip, Mao put an end to him. The girl, who by this time had recovered somewhat from her illness, was roused up by the noise. Everyone went to the scene with candles: the old man's skull was split and he had lost the power of speech. In a short while he was no longer of this world. An embroidered slipper was found beneath the wall, and the old woman could see that it belonged to Rouge. When force was applied the girl sobbed out the truth. Not being hardhearted enough to implicate Wang, she claimed that young E had come on his own.

At daybreak charges were brought before the district court. The magistrate had E taken into custody. E was a quiet, reserved person, nineteen years of strangers. Being arrested frightened him out of his wits. He lacked the presence of mind to defend himself in the courtroom. All he did was tremble, which gave the magistrate all the more reason to accept the truth of the accusations. He put the finger-vise and cane to brutal use: the pain was more than a bookishly inclined person could stand, and in this way a confession was wrung out of E. Afterwards he was transported to the prefectural court, where he received as many floggings as he had in the district.

Young E was consumed with outrage. Over and over he wished

气填塞，每欲与女面相质；及相遭，女辄诟詈，遂结舌不能自伸，由是论死。往来复讯，经数官无异词。后委济南府复案。时吴公南岱守济南，一见鄂生，疑不类杀人者，阴使人从容私问之，俾得尽其词。公以是益知鄂生冤。筹思数日，始鞫之。先问胭脂："订约后，有知者否？"答："无之。""遇鄂生时，别有人否？"亦答："无之。"乃唤生上，温语慰之。生自言："曾过其门，但见旧邻妇王氏与一少女出，某即趋避，过此并无一言。"吴公叱女曰："适言侧无他人，何以有邻妇也？"欲刑之。女惧曰："虽有王氏，与彼实无关涉。"公罢质，命拘王氏。数日已至，又禁不与女通，立刻出审，便

for the chance to confront Rouge and demand the truth, but when they did meet she vilified him with such fury he was tongue-tied and could not state his own case, with the result that he was sentenced to death. None of the numerous officials he was sent back and forth to for further hearings opposed the sentence.

Finally the case was referred to Jian prefecture for a confirmatory decision. At that time Master Wu Nandai was the prefect of Jinan. One look at young E was enough to make him doubt that this man was a murderer. Wu secretly sent a person to question him informally and considerately, so that he could say his piece. The result convinced Wu that E had been unjustly accused. He spent a few days before the hearing devising a strategy.

First he asked Rouge: "Was anyone aware that you had agreed to a meeting?"

"No one," was the answer.

"Was anyone else present when you first saw young E?"

"No one."

Wu then called E to the stand and reassured him in kind tones. The scholar testified without being asked: "Once, when I was walking past her gate, I noticed my former neighbor Wang coming out of the doorway with this young woman. I quickened my steps right away to get past them. Since then I have not spoken so much as a word to her."

Master Wu roared at the girl: "You just said that nobody was with you. What was the neighbor woman doing there?" He ordered his men to prepare the instruments of interrogation.

"Wang was there," said the girl in fright: "But she really had nothing to do with him."

Master Wu adjourned the hearing and gave an order to arrest Wang. She was brought in a few days later and forbidden any communication with the girl. Wu resumed the hearing immediately.

问王："杀人者谁？"王对："不知。"公诈之曰："胭脂供言，杀卞某汝悉知之，胡得隐匿？"妇呼曰："冤哉！淫婢自思男子，我虽有媒合之言，特戏之耳。彼自引奸夫入院，我何知焉！"公细诘之，始述其前后相戏之词。公呼女上，怒曰："汝言彼不知情，今何以自供撮合哉？"女流涕曰："自己不肖，致父惨死，讼结不知何年，又累他人，诚不忍耳。"公问王氏："既戏后，曾语何人？"王供："无之。"公怒曰："夫妻在床，应无不言者，何得云无？"王供："丈夫久客未归。"公曰："虽然，凡戏人者，皆笑人之愚，以炫己之慧，更不向一人言，将谁欺？"命梏十指。妇不得已，实供："曾与宿言。"公于是释鄂拘宿。宿至，自供："不知。"公曰："宿

"Who is the killer?" he asked Wang.

"I don't know."

Then Master Wu laid a trap for her, saying: "Rouge has testified that you were familiar with the man who killed old Bian. Are you trying to conceal that fact?"

"It's a lie," wailed the woman. "The cheap chambermaid got all worked up over this man. I may have said something about acting as matchmaker, but I was only joking with her. How was I to know that she would lure a lover onto her property?"

Master Wu had to question her in detail before she would repeat what she had said jokingly on that and later occasions. He called Rouge to the stand and thundered: "You claimed she did not know a thing. Now she testifies that she was going to have you two introduced. Why is that?"

"My foolishness caused my father's cruel death," the girl wailed tearfully. "Who knows how many years it will take before this case is concluded? On top of that, I have involved other people. I just can't bear it."

Master Wuasked Wang: "After you had made those jokes, did you tell anyone about them?"

"I did not," *Wang testified.*

"There is nothing that a husband and wife don't talk about in bed," thundered Master Wu. "How can you say that you didn't?"

"My husband was away on a long trip," Wang testified.

"That may well be, but playing a joke on someone is invariably a matter of mocking another's dullness in order to show off one's own intelligence. Who do you think can fool by claiming that you didn't tell anyone?" He ordered the use of finger – vises on all ten fingers.

The woman had no choice. "I told Su about it," she admitted.

Then Master Wu released E and had Su arrested. When Su was brought into court he testified; "I don't know."

妓者必无良士!”严械之。宿自供:“赚女是真。自失履后,未敢复往,杀人实不知情。”公怒曰:“逾墙者何所不至!”又械之。宿不任凌籍,遂以自承。招成报上,无不称吴公之神。铁案如山,宿遂延颈以待秋决矣。然宿虽放纵无行,故东国名士。闻学使施公愚山贤能称最,又有怜才恤士之德,因以一词控其冤枉,语言怆恻。公讨其招供,反复凝思之。拍案曰:“此生冤也!”遂请于院、司,移案再鞫。问宿生:“鞋遗何所?”供言:“忘之。但叩妇门时,犹在袖中。”转诘王氏:“宿介之外,奸夫有几?”供言:“无有。”公曰:“淫乱之人,岂得专私一个?”供言:“身与宿介,稚齿交合,故未能

"Anyone who Sues for the favor of a whore is not a proper gentleman!"

A severe beating was all it took to make Su admit: "It's true that I tricked the girl, but after I lost the slipper I didn't dare go back. I swear that I know nothing of the murder."

"A man who would climb over a wall is capable of anything!" Again Master Wu had Su beaten. Unable to stand up to the torture, Su finally accepted the blame.

The confession was written up and reported to Wu's superiors. There was not one who did not praise Master Wu's perspicuity. It was an irrevocable case—as settled as a mountain—so there was nothing left for Su but to crane his neck and watch as the day of execution drew near. Still, even though Su was reckless and ill-behaved, he was a widely known intellectual in the eastern region. He had heard of the civil examiner Master Shi Yushan's superior ability as well as his fondness and solicitude for scholars of talent, so he complained of the wrong done to him in a touching and sorrowful petition. Master Shi reviewed his confession, poring over it again and again, and struck his desk, saying: "This young man has been wronged!"

Then Master Shi applied to the administrative and judicial authorities of the province for permission to hold another hearing.

He asked Su: "Where did you lose the shoe?"

"I don't remember," answered Su. "But it was still in my sleeve when I knocked on Wang's gate."

Shi then proceeded to question Wang: "How many lovers do you have besides Su Jie?"

"I have none."

"Why should a promiscuous woman restrict herself to one man?" asked Master Shi.

"I was involved with Su Jie since childhood," she testified. "That is why I could not break it off. It wasn't that no one made advances to

谢绝;后非无见挑者,身实未敢相从。”因使指其人以实之。供云:“同里毛大,屡挑而屡拒之矣。”公曰:“何忽贞白如此?”命搒之。妇顿首出血,力辨无有,乃释之。又诘:“汝夫远出,宁无有托故而来者?”曰:“有之,某甲、某乙,皆以借贷馈赠,曾一二次入小人家。”盖甲、乙皆巷中游荡子,有心于妇而未发者也。公悉籍其名,并拘之。既集,公赴城隍庙,使尽伏案前。便谓:“曩梦神人相告,杀人者不出汝等四五人中。今对神明,不得有妄言。如肯自首,尚可原宥;虚者,廉得无赦!”同声言无杀人之事。公以三木置地,将并加之;括发裸身,齐鸣冤苦。公命释之。谓曰:“既不自招,当使鬼神指之。”使人以毡褥悉幛殿窗,

me after that, but I really didn't care to accept them."

Shi told her to name such a man in order to substantiate her claim.

"Mao the Elder of my neighborhood made repeated advances; I refused him every time," she testified.

"How is it that you've become so chaste and pure all of a sudden?" asked Master Shi. He ordered his men to beat her. The woman bumped her innoncence, so he let her go. Then he resumed his questioning: "When your husband was far away, weren't there men who came claiming to have business with him?"

"There were. I let So-and-so A and So-and-so B into my house a few times to borrow money or leave gifts."

Actually A and B were idlers living in the same alley who had designs on Wang without being able to realize them. Master Shi had their names entered in the record and ordered them into court. When they were rounded up, Master Shi had them taken to the temple of the city god, where they were made to kneel before the altar. Then he told them: "A short while ago a spirit came to me in a dream and told me that one of you is the murderer. There can be no lying now that you are before the all-knowing god. If you give yourself up, there is still the possibility of forgiveness. If you speak falsely, there will be no pardon once the truth is out."

All of them claimed with one voice that they had not committed murder. The judge had wooden cangues, manacles and fetters laid out on the ground and was about to have them put on the suspects. Their hair was to be knotted atop their heads and they were to be stripped naked. All howled at the injustice of this harsh treatment. The judge ordered them untied and said, "Since you won't confess, I will have ghosts and spirits point out the murderer."

He had his men screen off all the windows in the main hall with blankets of felt, making sure that there was not the slightest crack of

令无少隙；袒诸囚背，驱入暗中，始授盆水，一一命盥讫；系诸壁下，戒令"面壁勿动。杀人者，当有神书其背。"少间，唤出验视，指毛曰："此真杀人贼也！"盖公先使人以灰涂壁，又以烟煤濯其手：杀人者恐神来书，故匿背于壁而有灰色；临出，以手护背，而有烟色也。公固疑是毛，至此益信。施以毒刑，尽吐其实。判曰："宿介：蹈盆成括杀身之道，成登徒子好色之名。祗缘两小无猜，遂野骛如家鸡之恋；为因一言有漏，致得陇兴望蜀之心。将仲子而逾园墙，便如鸟坠；冒刘郎而至洞口，竟赚门开。感帨惊尨，鼠有皮胡若此？攀花折树，士无行其谓何！幸而听病燕之娇啼，犹为玉惜；怜弱柳之憔悴，未似莺狂。而释幺凤于罗中，

light. Then he had the suspects' shirts pulled down to expose their backs, and drove them into the dark, where they were given a basin of water to wash their hands. That done, he had them tied near the wall and warned them: "Keep your face toward the wall and do not move. The god will write a sign on the back of whichever one of you is the murderer."

Before long he called them out for inspection, then pointed at Mao, saying: "This is the murderer!"

Actually the judge had told his men to smear ashes on the wall beforehand and put soot into the water in which they washed their hands. The murderer, afraid that the god would come to write on him, got ashes on his back by pressing it against the wall. On the way out he tried to protect his back with his hands, thus smearing it with soot. Master Shi's previous suspicions of Mao the Elder were confirmed. With the application of ruthless torture, Mao spat out the whole truth. Master Shi's verdict was as follows: Regarding Su Jie: This man flirted with death like Pen-cheng Kuo, and he nearly rivals Deng Tuzi for lechery. On the strength of a childish infatuation, he made a wild duck out of a household fowl. When the uttering of a few ill-placed words moved the conqueror of Long to hanker after Shu, he climbed unwanted over a garden wall and swooped down like a falcon. Fancying himself an irresistible magnet to fairy maidens, he proceeded to the mouth of Rouge's grotto and finally wheedled her door open. By disturbing a lady's girdle sash, he aroused a shaggy dog. Even a rat has skin on its face, but this man had no idea of shame. He clambered after flowers, snapping off branches on the way. A man of such low conduct does not deserve the name of scholar. It was a saving grace that he heeded the feeble sparrow's It was a saving grace that he heeded the feeble sparrow's cries; he had the heart to spare this piece of unblemished jade. Out of pity for her willowy frailness, he did not go wild like a March-mad oriole, but released the fledgling phoenix

尚有文人之意；乃劫香盟于袜底，宁非无赖之尤！蝴蝶过墙，隔窗有耳；莲花卸瓣，堕地无踪。假中之假以生，冤外之冤谁信？天降祸起，酷械至于垂亡；自作孽盈，断头几于不续。彼逾墙钻隙，固有玷夫儒冠；而僵李代桃，诚难消其冤气。是宜稍宽笞扑，折其已受之惨；姑降青衣，开其自新之路。若毛大者：刁猾无籍，市井凶徒。被邻女之投梭，淫心不死；伺狂童之入巷，贼智忽生。开户迎风，喜得履张生之迹；求浆值酒，妄思偷韩掾之香。何意魄夺自天，魂摄于鬼。浪乘槎木，直入广寒之宫；径泛渔舟，错认桃源之路。遂使情火息焰，欲海生波。刀横直前，投鼠无他顾之意；

from his grasp, as any man of learning should. Regrettably he wrested a fragrant token from beneath her petticoat, proving how truly worthless he was! That same night a different butterfly flitted over his lover's wall. A pair of ears lurked outside the bedroom window. The petal torn from the lotus was dropped on the ground and lost, and so it was that falsehood sprang up within falsehood. Who could imagine that a second injustice would lay beyond the first. Heaven sent calamity down upon our Su Jie – a vicious beating to the edge of death. His own wrongdoing caught up to him, and his head and body nearly ended up in different places. Climbing walls and trnneling through cracks is a stain on a scholar's cap, but when a peach – boring insect tries to infect a plumtree, the fumes of injustice are not easily blown clean. Thus it is proper to show some leniency: we will spare Su Jie the rod, to make up for the cruel pain he has already suffered, and open for him the road to self – renewal by demoting him to black robes.

Now as for Mao the Elder, that idle, weaselly ruffian of the marketplace: Though he met with a refusal from his neighbor girl as curt as a shuttle thrown in his face, his lustful intentions would still not die. He bided his time until a flippant young man slipped into the alley, and then a bright idea occurred to his devious mind. Later, outside an open sliding door, another wind blew his way, and he imagined himself going to meet his beloved. He was looking for homebrew, and caught the scent of fine wine. His delusions were like the heady fumes of an aphrodesiac perfume. How was he to know that his strength would be sapped by heaven, and his spirit would be carried off by ghosts? He got on his log·raft and rode the silvery waters straight toward the Moon Palace. He floated along in his fisherman's boat, thinking he knew the way to Peachblossom Spring. In the end his passionate flames were doused by a tidal wave in the sea of desire. With an unlooked – for knife coming straight at him, he

寇穷安往，急兔起反噬之心。越壁入人家，止期张有冠而李借；夺兵遗绣履，遂教鱼脱网而鸿离。风流道乃生此恶魔，温柔乡何有此鬼蜮哉！即断首领，以快人心。胭脂：身犹未字，岁已及笄。以月殿之仙人，自应有郎似玉；原霓裳之旧队，何愁贮屋无金？而乃感关雎而念好逑，竟绕春婆之梦；怨摽梅而思吉士，遂离倩女之魂。为因一线缠萦，致使群魔交至。争妇女之颜色，恐失'胭脂'；惹鸷鸟之纷飞，并托'秋隼'。莲钩摘去，难保一瓣之香；铁限敲来，几破连城之玉。嵌红豆于骰子，相思骨竟作厉阶；丧乔木于斧斤，可憎才真成祸水！葳蕤自守，幸白璧之无瑕；缧绁苦

lashed out, as robbers often do when backed against a wall. Even a cornered rabbit will use its teeth in desperation. He landed in this fix because he thought jumping the wall into someone else's courtyard would be as easy as 'Mr. Li wearing Mr. Zhang's hat'. Because he dropped the slipper while wrenching away the weapon, the fish swam through the net while a goose was caught. It hardly seems possible that an event so demonic should arise on the path of romance. How could a banshee like this exist in the land of warmth and softness? Mao the Elder's head shall be severed from his neck for the gratification of all.

Now as for Rouge: This girl has not yet been spoken for, though she is already of hairpin age. A fairy maiden straight from the moon palace should naturally have a bridegroom like jade. A member of the Rainbow Skirt Dancers can rest assured that a golden house awaits her. Now the mating cry of the osprey arouses her longing for a perfect mate; the time has come for Mistress Spring to wrap her up in dreams. Thinking of a likely gentleman, she resents the falling plum blossoms, and her soul goes out of her body in search of love. However beautiful other women may be, they cannot be compared to Rouge. No matter how fierce the other taloned birds may be, they all take wing at the sight of Autumn-Falcon.

A single entangling thread caused a horde of demons to converge upon this lovely girl. Once the lotus sliper was plucked away, the petal's fragrance was hard to keep. Intruders at the iron threshold nearly smashed a precious gem.

Just as the red dots inlaid in dice are etched by tears of disappointment, a love that is felt to the bone can be a gateway to disaster: An upright tree succumbed to the axe, and a sweet young thing became a 'swamp of perdition'. But she guardend her dignity, and luckity her white jade remains unflawed. She writhed in his grasp, glad for the brocade quilt that covered her. She is admirable for

争，喜锦衾之可覆。嘉其入门之拒，犹洁白之情人；遂其掷果之心，亦风流之雅事。仰彼邑令，作尔冰人。"案既结，遐迩传诵焉。自吴公鞫后，女始知鄂生冤。堂下相遇，腼然含涕，似有痛惜之词，而未可言也。生感其眷恋之情，爱慕殊切；而又念其出身微，且日登公堂，为千人所窥指，恐娶之为人姗笑，日夜萦回，无以自主。判牒既下，意始安帖。邑宰为之委禽，送鼓吹焉。

异史氏曰："甚哉！听讼之不可以不慎也！纵能知李代为冤，谁复思桃僵亦屈，然事虽暗昧，必有其间，要非审思研察，不能得也。呜呼！人皆服哲人之折狱明，而不知良工之用心苦矣。世之居民上者，棋局消日，绸被放

refusing an intruder who was already in her room. By remaining pure and clean, she has proven herself to be a person of character. Fulfilling her wish to throw her bouquet would be an elegant closing chapter to this romance. I trust the district magistrate will play the part of matchmaker.

After the case was settled, this verdict was spread and recited far and wide.

The girl did not know that she had wrongfully blamed Young E until after Master Wu's hearing. When they met outside the hall, she sniffled guiltily, as if she had words of remorse in mind but could not yet speak out. The young man, touched by her regard, began to feel strongly toward her. But the thought of her humble origins, along with her daily appearances in court where a thousand people had pointed and leered at her, made him fear he would be ridiculed for marrying her. He brooded night and day, but could not make up his mind. The words of the verdict when it was finally delivered put him at his ease. The district magistrate had the betrothal gifts sent to the girl's house on his behalf and furnished music for the wedding procession.

The Chronicler of the Tales comments: "How great the need for caution is in hearing legal cases! Even if one could know that the plumtree was damaged wrongfully, who would think that the peach as well was decimated by mistake? Still, even the most obscure matter must have openings that let light through. Without careful thought and shrewed observation these cannot be traced. What a regret it is that people admire the wise man's brilliant resolution of a court case, while they fail to recognize the painstaking efforts of a master mind. In this world people who hold positions of authority fritter away whole days playing chess and cancel their morning audiences so as to stay beneath silken covers, never bothering their heads about the sentiments or hardships of the people. When the drums sound the opening of

衙，下情民艰，更不肯一劳方寸。至鼓动衙开，巍然高坐，彼哓哓者直以桎梏静之，何怪覆盆之下多沉冤哉！”

magisterial sessions, they sit high and mighty on the bench, silencing those who cry out for justice by slapping them into irons. Small wonder that so many injustices are hidden from the light of day!"

瑞　　云

瑞云，杭之名妓，色艺无双。年十四岁，其母蔡媪，将使出应客。瑞云告曰："此奴终身发轫之始，不可草草。价由母定，客则听奴自择之。"媪曰："诺。"乃定价十五金，逐日见客。客求见者必以贽：贽厚者，接一弈，酬一画；薄者，留一茶而已。瑞云名噪已久，自此富商贵介，日接于门。余杭贺生，才名夙著，而家仅中资。素仰瑞云，固未敢拟同鸳梦，亦

COURTESAN RUI YUN

RUI Yun, a famous courtesan of Hangzhou, was unrivalled in beauty and accomplisments. When she was fourteen her madame, Matron Cai, was ready to bring her out to receive guests. Rui Yun told her: "I am just putting my foot onto the first rung of the ladder, and I mustn't do it haphazardly. You fix the price, Mother, and I will choose the guest myself."

"All right," said the matron. So Rui Yun's price was fixed at fifteen taels of gold, and she began to see guests daily. Guests who wished to meet her had to bring acquaintance gifts. The ones gave generously were invited to stay for a game of chess and rewarded with a painting. Givers of trifles were only asked to tea. Rui Yun's name had been well known for some time; now rich merchants and men of noble houses rubbed shoulders at her gate.

In Yuhang district there lived Scholar He, famed from an early age for his talent but raised in a family of only moderate wealth. He had admired Rui Yun all along, but the thought of sharing a lovebird dream with her had never entered his mind. He exhausted his funds to buy a meager gift in hopes that he too could be admitted to gaze on her beauty with her own eyes. He worried to himself that a girl on familiar

竭微贽，冀得一睹芳泽。窃恐其阅人既多，不以寒畯在意；及至相见一谈，而款接殊殷。坐语良久，眉目含情。作诗赠生曰："何事求浆者，蓝桥叩晓关？有心寻玉杵，端只在人间。"生得之狂喜。更欲有言，忽小鬟来白"客至"，生仓猝遂别。既归，吟玩诗词，梦魂萦扰。过一二日，情不自已，修贽复往。瑞云接见良欢。移坐近生，悄然谓："能图一宵之聚否？"生曰："穷踧之士，惟有痴情可献知己。一丝之贽，已竭绵薄。得近芳容，意愿已足；若肌肤之亲，何敢作此梦想。"瑞云闻之，戚然不乐，相对遂无一语。生久坐不出，媪频唤瑞云以促之，生乃归。心甚邑邑，思欲罄家以博一欢，而更尽而别，此情复何可耐？筹思及此，热念都消，由是音息遂绝。瑞云择婿数月，更不得一当，媪颇恚，将强夺之而未发也。一

terms with so many people would not be kindly disposed to one in his straitened circumstances, but when they met and talked she entertained him most graciously. They sat and conversed a good while and there was tenderness in her eyes. She gave him a poem that read:

What brings the seeker of rare elixirs
To knock on the Indigo Bridge at dawn?
If he hopes to find the pestle of jade
He should stard with the ground he stands upon.

Getting this poem sent the scholar into a paroxysm of joy. He wanted to have further words with her, but he left hastily when a maid came in and announced, "A guest is here."

Back home he chanted and savored the words of the poem until his soul was lost in dreams. A few days later, unable to suppress his feelings, he readied a gift and went again. Rui Yun was very happy to see him. She moved her seat close to him and murmured, "Can you arrange to have us spend a night together?"

"Devotion is the only thing a destitute scholar like me can offer to the one who understands him." This wisp of a gift stretched my meager resources to the limit. Being near to your beauty is a wish come true already. I cannot delude myself with hopes of intimacy."

Rui Yun listened in gloomy disappointment, her face turned wordlessly toward him. He sat there for a long time until the matron hurried him on his way by calling repeatedly for the girl to hurry him on his way. When he was back home, he moodily contemplated selling everything in his house to pay for a night of ecstasy, but that would mean parting with her at dawn, and what would happen to his love for her then? Thinking of this dampened his passionate impulses. Henceforth communication between the two was broken off.

Rui Yun had been months choosing a 'husband', but still she could

日，有秀才投贽，坐语少时，便起，以一指按女额曰："可惜，可惜！"遂去。瑞云送客返，共视额上有指印，黑如墨，濯之益真。过数日，墨痕渐阔；年余，连颧彻准矣。见者辄笑，而车马之迹以绝。媪斥去妆饰，使与婢辈伍。瑞云又荏弱，不任驱使，日益憔悴。贺闻而过之，见蓬首厨下，丑状类鬼。起首见生，面壁自隐。贺怜之，便与媪言，愿赎作妇。媪许之。贺货田倾装，买之而归。入门，牵衣揽涕，且不敢以伉俪自居，愿备妾媵，以俟来者。贺曰："人生所重者知己：卿盛时犹能知我，我岂以衰故忘卿哉！"遂不复娶。闻者共姗笑之，而生情益笃。居年余，偶至苏，有和生与同主人，忽问："杭有名妓瑞云，近如何矣？"贺

not find the right one. The matron, who was more than a little vexed, was determined to force the issue, though she had not yet taken action. One day a bachelor of letters called with a gift, sat talking for a short time and then got up. He pressed his finger against the girl's forehead, saying:" This should be cherished, "and then left. When Rui Yun came back from seeing him out, everyone noticed a fingerprint as black as ink on her forehead. Washing only made it show more plainly. In a few days the inky mark started getting larger, and, in little more than a year it had spread onto her cheek and all the way across her nose. People who saw her laughed. By this time the daily bustle at her gate had ceased. The matron stripped off her finery and jewels and put her to work with the maids. Delicate to drudgery as she was, Rui Yun grew daily more haggard.

Scholar He heard of this and went for a visit. She was in the kitchen when he saw her, hair hanging loose and her face as frightful as a ghost's. She looked up from her work and saw him there, then turned to the wall to hide her face. He felt sorry for her. He told the matron he would buy her freedom and make her his wife. The matron assented. By selling some land and emptying his strongbox, he was able to take her home. Once inside the gate she wiped the tears from her eyes on her robe. She did not consider herself his marital partner and wanted to serve as a maid or concubine to leave a place for his future wife.

He said, "The most valuable thing in life is an under - standing friend. You understood me for what I was when you were in your prime of beauty. I am not going to forget you just because that has faded."

He did not marry anyone else. Everyone who heard of this ridiculed him, but his affection only grew stronger. Nothing changed for over a year, until he happened to go to Suzhou. He stayed there in the same house with a certain Scholar Harmony, who suddenly asked

以“适人”对。又问:“何人?”曰:“其人率与仆等。”和曰:“若能如君,可谓得人矣。不知价几何许?”贺曰:“缘有奇疾,姑从贱售耳。不然,如仆者,何能于勾栏中买佳丽哉!”又问:“其人果能如君否?”贺以其问之异,因反诘之。和笑曰:“实不相欺:昔曾一觐其芳仪,甚惜其以绝世之姿,而流落不偶,故以小术晦其光而保其璞,留待怜才者之真鉴耳。”贺急问曰:“君能点之,亦能涤之否?”和笑曰:“乌得不能,但须其人一诚求耳。”贺起拜曰:“瑞云之婿,即某是也。”和喜曰:“天下惟真才人为能多情,不以妍媸易念也。请从君归,便赠一佳人。”遂与同返。既至,贺将命酒,和止之曰:“先行吾法,当先令治具者有欢心也。”即

him: "There was a famous singing girl in Hangzhou named Rui Yun. How are things with her these days?"

"She married somebody," answered Scholar He.

"Who was that?"

"A person very much like me."

"If he is like you, she found herself a good husband. I wonder how he paid for her."

"She was sold cheaply because of a strange affliction she had. Otherwise, how could someone like me have found a beautiful mate inside the balustrades of the gay quarters?"

"Could that person really be like you?" The strangeness of the question made Scholar He ask the meaning of it. Scholar Harmony laughed: "I won't mislead you. When I was admitted to her flowerlike presence, I felt sorry that such a sublime beauty should sink to the depths unmated, so I used a minor trick to dim her radiance and preserve her true nature, and to leave her for the discernment of a lover of beauty."

Scholar He hurriedly asked, "You were able to mark her with a touch. Are you able to wash it clean as well?"

"Why shouldn't I be able to?" laughed Harmony. "But the party concerned must ask from the heart."

He got up and sank on his knees, saying: "I'm the one who married Rui Yun."

"In this world only people of true ability can feel deeply for others, because their affections are not swayed by physical appearance," said Scholar Harmony approvingly. "I'll return with you, if I may, and deliver a beautiful woman into your hands."

So they went back together. Scholar He was going to call for wine on their arrival, but Harmony stopped him: "Let me practice my art first. I'd like to give the server something to be glad of before we start enjoying ourselves."

令以盥器贮水，戟指而书之，曰：“濯之当愈。然须亲出一谢医人也。”贺笑捧而去，立俟瑞云自靧之，随手光洁，艳丽一如当年。夫妇共德之，同出展谢，而客已渺，遍觅之不可得，意者其仙欤？

Harmony asked for a basin filled with water, then traced words over its surface and said, "Washing will cure her, but the patient must come out to thank the doctor personally." Scholar He laughed as he carried the basin in with both hands. He stood waiting while Rui Yun laved her face. As hands swept over her face, it grew radiant and clean. She was just as ravishingly beautiful as before. Both husband and wife appreciated the great kindness Scholar Harmony had done them. They came out to express their thanks, but he was gone. They looked everywhere without success. Could Scholar Harmony have been an immortal?

葛巾

常大用，洛人。癖好牡丹。闻曹州牡丹甲齐、鲁，心向往之。适以他事如曹，因假搢绅之园居焉。而时方二月，牡丹未华，惟徘徊园中，目注句萌，以望其拆。作怀牡丹诗百绝。未几，花渐含苞，而资斧将匮；寻典春衣，流连忘返。一日，凌晨趋花所，则一女郎及老妪在焉。疑是贵家宅眷，亦遂遄返。暮而往，又见之，从容避去。微窥之，宫妆艳绝。眩迷之中，忽转一想：此必仙人，世上岂有此女子

LINEN SCARF, THE PEONY SPIRIT

CHANG Dayong, a man of Luoyang, was inordinately fond of peonies. He longed to procure peonies from Caozhou prefecture, having heard that they outclassed all others in Shandong. It happened that other business took him to Caozhou, so he put up in an official's garden. This was still in the second month, before the peonies bloomed. All he could do was pace up and down the garden, fixing his eyes on the tender burgeons breaking through the soil and waiting for them to blossom. He wrote a hundred quatrains on"Yearning for Peonies." Befroe long the flowers began to form in their buds. When his funds were nearly depleted, he did not hesitate to pawn his spring clothes. He dallied there, forgetting to return. One day he hurried by light of dawn to where the flowers were. There he saw a young woman and an old matron. He scurried away, supposing them to be members of some wealthy household. That evening he went, saw them again and retreated out of sight, more calmly this time. He peered at the young woman from hiding: she was stunning in her palace robe. A thought came to him in his bedazzlement: she must be a fairy. Such a girl could not be of this world.

乎！急返身而搜之，骤过假山，适与妪遇。女郎方坐石上，相顾失惊。妪以身幛女，叱曰："狂生何为！"生长跪曰："娘子必是神仙！"妪咄之曰："如此妄言，自当絷送令尹！"生大惧。女郎微笑曰："去之！"过山而去。生返，不能徒步，意女郎归告父兄，必有诟辱之来。偃卧空斋，自悔孟浪。窃幸女郎无怒容，或当不复置念。悔惧交集，终夜而病。日已向辰，喜无问罪之师，心渐宁帖。而回忆声容，转惧为想。如是三日，憔悴欲死。秉烛夜分，仆已熟眠。妪入，持瓯而进曰："吾家葛巾娘子，手合鸩汤，其速饮！"生闻而骇，既而曰："仆与娘子，夙无怨嫌，何至赐死？既为娘子手调，与其相思而病，不如仰药而死！"遂引而尽之。

Hurriedly, he retraced his steps and went looking for them. He scuttled round a rockery, only to run right into the matron. The young woman, who was seated on a nearby rock, looked at him in surprise. The old matron shielded the girl with her body and snapped at him, "What are you up to, you maniac?"

The scholar knelt down and said, "The mistress must be an immortal."

The old matron scoffed, "You ought to be tied up and turned over to the sheriff for talking such nonsense." The scholar was thoroughly intimidated.

The young woman gave a little laugh: "Let's get away from him." They disappeared behind the rockery, and the scholar headed back, walking unsteadily. He feared that curses and humiliation would be in store for him once the girl went home and told her father and brothers. He threw himself down in the vacant studio, cursing himself for his thoughtlessness. He felt glad that her face had showed no sign of anger: perhaps she would not give it another thought. Mingled regret and apprehension weighed miserably on him all night through, but when the sun climbed above the horizon without bringing a punitive army his peace of mind gradually returned.

But her features and voice remained in his thoughts, and fear give way to longing. After three days of this he had nearly wasted to nothing. He was sitting beside a candle in the night, his servant deep in slumber, when the old lady came in holding a jar. She held it out to him, saying: "My mistress Linen Scarf made up this hemlock potion herself. Quick, drink it."

Her words struck terror in the scholar's heart, but he recovered enough to answer, "There has never been bad blood between your mistress and me—nothing that would make her hand me my death warrant. But since your mistress mixed it herself, better for me to die of poison than waste away pining for her."

妪笑，接瓯而去。生觉药气香冷，似非毒者。俄觉肺鬲宽舒，头颅清爽，酣然睡去。既醒，红日满窗。试起，病若失。心益信其为仙。无可夤缘，但于无人时，仿佛其立处、坐处，虔拜而默祷之。一日，行去，忽于深树内，觌面遇女郎，幸无他人，大喜，投地。女郎近曳之，忽闻异香竟体，即以手握玉腕而起，指肤软腻，使人骨节欲酥。正欲有言，老妪忽至。女令隐身石后，南指曰："夜以花梯度墙，四面红窗者，即妾居也。"匆匆遂去。生怅然，魂魄飞散，莫能知其所往。至夜，移梯登南垣，则垣下已有梯在，喜而下，果见红窗。室中闻敲棋声，伫立不敢复前，姑逾垣归。少间，再过之，子声犹繁；渐近窥之，则女郎与一素衣美人相对着，老妪亦在坐，一婢侍焉。又返。凡三往

Thereupon he raised the crock with a flourish and drained it. The old matron laughed, took the crock and left. The scholar found the potion fragrant and cooling; it did not at all seem to be poison. Soon he felt an expansiveness in his chest and a bracing clarity in his skull. A mellow feeling came over him, and he fell asleep. When he awoke, red sunlight filled his window. He got up to try his strength, and felt as if he had never been sick. Now more than ever he was convinced that she was immortal. Lacking a way to form a bond with her, he could only call up visions of her standing or sitting and bow reverently to them in silent prayer when no one else was around.

One day he went walking. Deep in a grove he suddenly met her face to face. Fortunately no one else was there. In great happiness he threw himself to the ground before her. As she came close to help body. He grasped her jade - liked wrist and pulled himself to his feet. The skin of her fingers had a soft sleekness that made his joints go limp.. She was just about to speak when suddenly the old matron came in view. The girl made him hide behind a rock and pointed to the south, saying: "Climb the ladder over the wall tonight. I live in the house with red windows on all four sides." With that she bustled quickly away.

The scholar was shaken. His spirits had flown from him, and he did not know where he was going. At nightfall he moved a ladder to the south wall and climbed it. Another ladder was already in position on the other side of the wall. He went down gleefully and saw the red window that he knew would be there. The clicking of go pieces could be heard inside. He stood stock still, not daring to advance farther, then climbed back over the wall and went home for the time being. After a short interval he crossed over again: the go pieces were still clicking away. He edged up to the window and peered in. Linen Scarf sat facing a beauty dressed in white. The old matron was sitting with them, and a maid was in attendance. He turned back again. When he

复，三漏已催。生伏梯上，闻妪出云："梯也，谁置此？"呼婢共移去之。生登垣，欲下无阶，恨悒而返。次夕，复往，梯先设矣。幸寂无人，入，则女郎兀坐，若有思者。见生惊起，斜立含羞。生揖曰："自谓福薄，恐于天人无分，亦有今夕耶！"遂狎抱之。纤腰盈掬，吹气如兰，撑拒曰："何遽尔！"生曰："好事多磨，迟为鬼妒。"言未及已，遥闻人语。女急曰："玉版妹子来矣！君可姑伏床下。"生从之。无何，一女子入，笑曰："败军之将，尚可复言战否？业已烹茗，敢邀为长夜之欢。"女郎辞以困惰。玉版固请之，女郎坚坐不行。玉版曰："如此恋恋，岂藏有男子在室耶？"强拉之，出门而去。生膝行而出。恨绝，遂搜枕簟，冀一得其遗物。而室内并无香奁，只床头有水精如意，

made his third trip, the second watch was nearly over. Crouched on the outside ladder, he heard the old lady come out and say, "There's a ladder. Who put it there?" She called the maid to help her move it away.

The scholar climbed back onto the wall but, having no way to climb down, turned back discouraged. He went again the next night and found the ladder ready for him. As luck would have it the place was still and empty. He went in. The young woman was sitting motionless, evidently absorbed in thought. Seeing him, she jumped up in surprise, leaning bashfully away. He clasped his hands and said, "I thought my blessings were too limited to ever call such a heavenly being my own. Is this night real?" He passionately took her in his arms. Her slender waist barely filled his grasp. She exhaled breath like orchid scent.

She straightened her arms and pushed him away, ex – claiming: "What's your hurry?"

"You can have good things without pushing and pulling. We'll make the demons jealous if we take too long," he said.

The discussion was still underway when they heard faraway voices. The girl blurted out, "My sister Jade Clapper is coming. Hide under the bed for now."

He did as he was told. In no time a young girl came in and said with a laugh: "Is the defeated general still ready for battle? I have some fine tea steeping now. May I ask you over for a night game?"

Linen Scarf declined, pleading drowsiness. Jade Clapper renewed her offer, but would not budge from her seat, which prompted Jade Clapper to say, "Such reluctance! Don't tell me you have a man hidden in here." She pulled her sister out the door by force.

The scholar walked out from under the bed on his knees, vexed to the limit. He rifled through the pillows and mats hoping to find something she had left behind, but there was no jewelry box in the room,

上结紫巾，芳洁可爱。怀之，越垣归。自理衿袖，体香犹凝，倾慕益切。然因伏床之恐，遂有怀刑之惧，筹思不敢复往，但珍藏如意，以冀其寻。隔夕，女郎果至，笑曰："妾向以君为君子也，而不知寇盗也。"生曰："良有之！所以偶不君子者，第望其如意耳。"乃揽体入怀，代解裙结。玉肌乍露，热香四流，偎抱之间，觉鼻息汗熏，无气不馥。因曰："仆固意卿为仙人，今益知不妄。幸蒙垂盼，缘在三生。但恐杜兰香之下嫁，终成离恨耳。"女笑曰："君虑亦过。妾不过离魂之倩女，偶为情动耳。此事要宜慎秘，恐是非之口，捏造黑白，君不能生翼，妾不能乘风，则祸离更惨于好别矣。"

only a crystal as - you - will scepter by the side of the bed. It was sparkling and lovely, and had a purple handkerchief tied to one end. He put it in his robe, went over the wall and returned home. He smoothed his sleeves and lapels, on which her bodily fragrance was still clinging, and this added to his longing. But the nervous shock of hiding under the bed had planted the dread of punishment in his mind. Considering the circumstances he dared not go again. The only thing to do was to stow away the scepter in hopes that she would come looking for it.

Linen Scarf did turn up the following night. "I thought you were a gentleman," she laughed. "I didn't expect you would turn out to be a burglar."

"There was good reason for it. I only relaxed my gentlemanliness this once out of my hope for an as - I - will. Then he pulled her body against his and undid the clasp of her dress. Her jade flesh was instantly revealed, and warm scent exuded from her. As they touched and embraced, he sensed no exhalation, whether breath from her nostrils or the pungency of her perspiration, that was not sweet."

So he said, "I thought you were a fairy maiden: now I'm sure that was no mistake. I'm happy that you are kind enough to care for me. The tie between us runs through the past, present, and future lives. But I fear that your descent into marriage will end in a sorrowful separation, like in the story of Du Orchid - Scent."

"Your qualms are overone," the girl said with a smile. "I am only a lovesick girl, and my soul has gone out to someone who happens to attract me. The main thing is for our affair to remain a carefully guarded secret, or judge - mental tongues will color things to suit themselves. Since you cannot grow wings and I cannot ride the wind, a disastrous·parting would be a good deal more miserable than an agreeable farewell."

Though the scholar agreed with her, he continued to suspect that

生然之，而终疑为仙，固诘姓氏。女曰：“既以妾为仙，仙人何必以姓名传。”问：“妪何人？”曰：“此桑姥。妾少时受其露覆，故不与婢辈同。”遂起，欲去，曰：“妾处耳目多，不可久羁，蹈隙当复来。”临别，索如意，曰：“此非妾物，乃玉版所遗。”问：“玉版为谁？”曰：“妾叔妹也。”付钩乃去。去后，衾枕皆染异香。由此三两夜辄一至。生惑之，不复思归。而囊橐既空，欲货马。女知之，曰：“君以妾故，泻囊质衣，情所不忍。又去代步，千余里将何以归？妾有私蓄，聊可助装。”生辞曰：“感卿情好，抚臆誓肌，不足论报；而又贪鄙，以耗卿财，何以为人矣！”女固强之，曰：“姑假君。”遂捉生臂，至一桑树下，指一石，曰：“转之！”生从之。又拔头上簪，刺土数十下，又曰：“爬

she was an immortal and insisted on knowing her lineage.

"Since you take me for an immortal, why must you remember me by name?"

"Who is the old woman?"

"She is Matron Mulberry. She protected me from the elements when I was young, so I don't consider her just another servant." With that she rose to go and said, "There are many eyes and ears at my place: I musn't stay away too long. I'll slip out again when the time is right." As she was about to leave, she motioned him to give her the as-you-will, saying "It isn't mine. Jade Clapper left it with me."

"Who is Jade Clapper?"

"She is my cousin." When he pulled the scepter from his robe and handed it to her, she left. Though she was gone, his pillows and covers were suffused with a rare fragrance.

After that she came once every two or three nights. The scholar was too obsessed with her to think any more of going home. By now his pouch was empty and he was on the point of selling his horse. When Linen Scarf learned of this she said, "It hurts me to think that you emptied your purse and pawned your clothes because of me. Now on top of that you are getting rid of your mount. How will you ever travel a thousand li home? I have some private savings that will help you get outfitted."

"I am so thankful for your love," he replied, "Even if I put my hand on my heart and pledged every fiber of my body to you, it would not be enough to repay you. How could ever face you if I spent your fortune greedily?"

But the girl pressed it on him, saying: "Let me lend it to you for now." She dragged him by the arm to the foot of a mulberrry tree, pointed to a stone and said, "Turn that over."

He did so. Then she pulled the hairpin from her head, poked it into the dirt several dozen times and said, "Dig here." Again he did as

之。"生又从之。则瓮口已见。女探入，出白镪近五十两许；生把臂止之，不听，又出十余铤，生强反其半而后掩之。一夕，谓生曰："近日微有浮言，势不可长，此不可不预谋也。"生惊曰："且为奈何！小生素迂谨，今为卿故，如寡妇之失守，不复能自主矣。一惟卿命，刀锯斧钺，亦所不遑顾耳！"女谋偕亡，命生先归，约会于洛。生治任旋里，拟先归而后逆之；比至，则女郎车适已至门。登堂朝家人，四邻惊贺，而并不知其窃而逃也。生窃自危；女殊坦然，谓生曰："无论千里外非逻察所及，即或知之，妾世家女，卓王孙当无如长卿何也。"生弟大器，年十七，女顾之曰："是有惠根，前程尤胜于君。"完婚有期，妻忽夭殒。女曰："妾妹玉版，君固尝窥见之，貌颇不恶，年亦相若，作夫妇可称嘉耦。"生闻之而笑，戏请作伐。女

she said, and the mouth of an urn came into view. She reached in and pulled out a string of silver pieces weighing somewhere around fifty taels. He held her arm and tried to stop her, but she would not listen. Again she pulled out over ten ingots. He insistently replaced half of them, then covered the urn.

One evening she said to him: "There has been a bit of gossip the last few days. Things cannot go on as they are. We simply have to take precautions."

"But what can we do?" he blurted in surprise. "I've always been a shy, overcautious person. But now, because of you, I'm like a widow who let her guard down—I can't decide things for myself any more. I'll do whatever you say without worrying over the consequences, even if there are swords, axes and saws waiting for me."

Linen Scarf made plans to elope together, telling him to return first and arranging to join him later in Luoyang. He packed his bags and headed home, intending to get there first and then go to meet her. When he arrived, her cart had just reached his gate. They went into the hall and payed their respects to the household. His surprised neighbors congratulated them, little knowing they had eloped. It all seemed precarious to him, but she was remarkably unruffled.

"A thousand *li* it beyond the range of pursuit, and even if we are found out, I come from a good family, so my relatives won't do a thing to the man who won their daughter's heart."

She took one look at the scholar's younger brother Daqi, a seventeen-year-old boy, and said, "This one has a prom-ising intellect; his career will overshadow yours."

The date for Daqi's wedding had been settled, but his wife died at an early age. Linen Scarf said, "You've had a peek at my sister Jade Clapper already. She is by no means bad looking, and her age is about right. If they were married they'd make a charming couple." The scholar laughed at this and jokingly asked her to be the go-between.

曰:“必欲致之,即亦非难。”喜问:“何术?”曰:“妹与妾最相善。两马驾轻车,费一妪之往返耳。”生惧前情俱发,不敢从其谋;女固言:“不害。”即命车,遣桑媪去。数日,至曹。将近里门,媪下车,使御者止而候于途,乘夜入里。良久,偕女子来,登车遂发。昏暮即宿车中,五更复行。女郎计其时日,使大器盛服而逆之。五十里许,乃相遇,御轮而归;鼓吹花烛,起拜成礼。由此兄弟皆得美妇,而家又日以富。一日,有大寇数十骑,突入第。生知有变,举家登楼。寇入,围楼。生俯问:“有仇否?”答言:“无仇。但有两事相求:一则闻两夫人世间所无,请赐一见;一则五十八人,各乞金五百。”聚薪楼下,为纵火计以胁之。生

"If you really want her to come, it won't be hard," said Linen Scarf.

"How can you get her here?" he asked happily.

"Sister and I are very close. Send a buggy with two horses. All it will take is a serving woman to go there and back."

The scholar, fearing that past events would be brought to light, dared not agree to her plan, but she insisted there would be no harm, so he called for the buggy and sent Matron Mulberry to Caozhou. In a few days she reached there. When she came close to the borough gate the matron stepped out of the buggy, told the driver to stay put and wait in the road, then entered the borough under cover of night. A good while later she appeared with a young girl. They climbed into the buggy and started back. At nightfall the next day they stayed in the buggy, then resumed their trip at the striking of the fifth watch. Linen Scarf, who had calculated their itinerary, had Daqi go out to meet them, dressed in a formal robe. He met with them over fifty *li* from his home.

They came home with Daqi at the reins. Amid drumming and blaring, and garlands and candles, they kowtowed to each other and performed the wedding ceremony. Now both brothers had beautiful wives, and the household grew daily more prosperous.

One day several dozen mounted bandits stormed into the yard. The scholar, realizing there would be trouble, led the family into an upstairs loft. The bandits rode about the yard and surrounded the house. The scholar looked down from a window and asked, "Do you have a score to settle with us?"

"No," they answered. "But we have two demands to make. First, we hear that the two ladies are like nothing on this earth. Give us a look at them. Second, there are fifty-eight of us, and we want five hundred pieces of gold each."

They piled firewood against the base of the house and threatened

允其索金之请;寇不满志,欲焚楼,家人大恐。女欲与玉版下楼,止之不听。炫妆而下,阶未尽者三级,谓寇曰:“我姊妹皆仙媛,暂时一履尘世,何畏寇盗!欲赐汝万金,恐汝不敢受也。”寇众一齐仰拜,喏声“不敢”。姊妹欲退,一寇曰:“此诈也!”女闻之,反身伫立,曰:“意欲何作,便早图之,尚未晚也。”诸寇相顾,默无一言,姊妹从容上楼而去。寇仰望无迹,哄然始散。后二年,姊妹各举一子,始渐自言:“魏姓,母封曹国夫人。”生疑曹无魏姓世家,又且大姓失女,何得一置不问?未敢穷诘,而心窃怪之。遂托故复诣曹,入境咨访,世族并无魏姓。于是仍假馆旧主人。忽见壁上有赠曹国夫人诗,颇涉骇异,因诘主人。主人笑,

to set fire to it. The scholar acquiesced to their demand for gold, but they were not satisfied and were on the point of burning the building down. Everyone in the family was terrified.

Linen Scarf wanted to go downstairs with Jade Clapper and would listen to no objections. They went down in their finest dresses. They stopped three steps from the bottom and said to the bandits: "We sisters are fairy maidens setting foot for a time in the world of dust. Bandits and brigands do not frighten us! We give you ten thousand pieces of gold, but we doubt if you'll accept it."

The crowd of bandits fell on their knees and chorused: "We wouln't take your money."

The sisters were about to withdraw, but one bandit piped up: "This is a trick."

At the sound of his voice, Linen Scarf turned, drew herself up to her full height and said, "If you're of a mind to do something, you'd best try it soon, while there's still time." The bandits looked wordlessly at each other as the sisters went calmly up the stairs. The bandits watched with upturned faces until the two were out of sight and then dispersed in noisy disorder.

Two years later both sisters gave birth to sons. It was not until then that they gradually started telling about themselves: "Our family name is Wei, and our mother was awarded the title Lady of Cao."

The scholar thought this suspicious, since there was no noble house by the name of Wei in Caozhou. Besides, how could a great clan ignore the loss of its daughters and not make some sort of inquiry. He did not dare to pry, but kept the doubt in his heart. And so he found a pretext for going back to Caozhou. When he crossed the district line he made inquiries and found that indeed, there were no Weis among the noble clans there. Then he borrowed lodgings from his former host. Right away he noticed a poem dedicated to the "Lady of Cao" on the wall—an unsettling development to be sure. He asked his host about

即请往观曹夫人，至则牡丹一本，高与檐等。问所由名，则以此花为曹第一，故同人戏封之。问其“何种”？曰：“葛巾紫也。”心益骇，遂疑女为花妖。既归，不敢质言，但述赠夫人诗以觇之。女蹙然变色，遽出，呼玉版抱儿至，谓生曰：“三年前，感君见思，遂呈身相报；今见猜疑，何可复聚！”因与玉版皆举儿遥掷之，儿堕地并没。生方惊顾，则二女俱渺矣。悔恨不已。后数日，堕儿处生牡丹二株，一夜径尺，当年而花，一紫一白，朵大如盘，较寻常之葛巾、玉版，瓣尤繁碎。数年，茂荫成丛；移

it. His host laughed and offered to take him to look at the lady of Cao. When they got there, it turned out to be an eave – high peony shrub. The scholar asked how it came by the name and learned that one of the host's colleagues had given it that title as a joke because it was unsurpassed in all of Caozhou.

"What variety is it?" he asked.

"It is a purple Linen Scarf."

His mind recoiled in amazement, and he began to suspect that the girl was a flower spirit.

Once home he could not bring himself to face her with the evidence; he merely told her of the poem to the Lady of Cao to see how she would react. She hurried out with a scowl on her face, called for Jade Clapper to bring their children and said to him: "Three years ago I was moved by your affection, so I offered myself to you in repayment. Now that you distrust me, I don't see how we can stay together." She and Jade Clapper lifted their children and threw them a great distance. Both of them disappeared the moment they fell to the ground. As the scholar looked on in astonishment, the two women also vanished. He cursed himself without end.

A few days later two peony shrubs sprang up where the children had fallen and grew to a foot in diameter overnight. They bloomed that year, one purple and one white, with flowers the size of saucers and petals even more numerous and finely delineated than those of ordinary Linen Scarves and Jade Clappers. In a few years they became lush, shaded thickets. When the roots were separated and transplanted, they changed into unique varieties that no one could name. From this time on the Luo River valley was unmatched for the splender of its peonies.

The Chronicler of the Tales comments: "Singleminded emotion makes itself felt by ghosts and spirits, while one who sways back and forth is not necessarily lacking in feelings. In one of his poems the

分他所，更变异种，莫能识其名。自此牡丹之盛，洛下无双焉。

异史氏曰："怀之专一，鬼神可通，偏反者亦不可谓无情也。少府寂寞；以花当夫人，况真能解语，何必力穷其原哉？惜常生之未达也！"

Magistrate Bai Juyi was so lonely he made a flower his wife. How much nicer it would be to find one that truly understands speech! What need would there be to delve into her origins? I feel sorry for Scholar Chang, who lacked a broad view of things."

黄　英

马子才，顺天人。世好菊，至才尤甚。闻有佳种，必购之，千里不惮。一日，有金陵客寓其家，自言其中表亲有一二种，为北方所无。马欣动，即刻治装，从客至金陵。客多方为之营求，得两芽，裹藏如宝。归至中途，遇一少年，跨蹇从油碧车，丰姿洒落。渐近与语。少年自言："陶姓。"谈言骚雅。因问马所自来，实告之。少年曰："种无不佳，培溉在人。"因与论艺菊之法。马大悦，问："将何往？"答云："姊厌金陵，欲卜居于河朔耳。"

YELLOW - BLOOM

MA Zicai was a man of Shuntian prefecture whose family had been fond of chrysanthemums for generations. But Zicai was even more fond of them than his forerunners. When he learned of a rare variety he never failed to buy it: a thousand - *li* trip did not deter him. One day a guest from Nanjing staying at Ma's house mentioned that his cousin had a variety or two not found in the north. Ma was so excited he packed his luggage that very day and set out with his guest for Nanjing. The guest kindly got busy hunting through various channels until he came up with two cuttings, which Ma wrapped and kept like jewels.

On his way home Ma met with a fine - looking, dashing young man mounted on a nag behind a curtained coach. He moved closer to make conversation with him. The young man gave his surname as Tao. His speech was easy and elegant. He asked where Ma was coming from, so Ma told him the whole story of his trip to Nanjing.

"Both of these varieties are prime, but how they are mulched and watered depends on the gardener," said the young man. This led to a discussion on the techniques of chrysanthemum growing.

In a burst of elation Ma asked, "Where are you headed?"

马欣然曰:"仆虽固贫,茅庐可以寄榻。不嫌荒陋,无烦他适。"陶趋车前,向姊咨禀。车中人推帘语,乃二十许绝世美人也。顾弟言:"屋不厌卑,而院宜得广。"马代诺之,遂与俱归。第南有荒圃,仅小室三四椽,陶喜,居之。日过北院,为马治菊。菊已枯,拔根再植之,无不活。然家清贫,陶日与马共食饮,而察其家似不举火。马妻吕,亦爱陶姊,不时以升斗馈恤之。陶姊小字黄英,雅善谈,辄过吕所,与共纫绩。陶一日谓马曰:"君家固不丰,仆日以口腹累知交,胡可为常。为今计,卖菊亦足谋生。"马素介,闻陶言,甚鄙之,曰:"仆以君风流高士,当能安贫;今作是论,则以东篱为市井,有辱黄花矣。"陶笑曰:"自食其力不为

"My elder sister is tired of Nanjing: we'd like to find a place to live in the north."

"I know I am poor, but you can put up in my cottage anyway," Ma offered with pleasure. "If you don't mind roughing it, you needn't bother to go elsewhere."

Tao rode up to the coach to consult with his sister. The one who pushed aside the curtain to speak with him was a world - class beauty in her twenties. She looked at her brother and siad, "I have no objection to a poor dwelling, but the yard should be spacious." Ma offered his assurances, and so they went home with him.

South of the house was a neglected garden plot with nothing but a shanty four or five beams long. Tao liked it and moved in. Every day he visited the north yard and tended Ma's chrysanthemums, which had withered. He pulled them up by the roots and replanted them: not one of them failed to survive. Tao and his sister lived in austere poverty. He took his meals daily with Ma, who noticed that they never seemed to have a fire burning in their house. Ma's wife, n é e Lü, was also fond of Tao's sister and gave her a quart here and a peck there by way of assistance. Tao's sister went by her childhood name Yellow - Bloom. Being an agreeable conversationalist, she began dropping in at Lü's rooms to sew and spin thread with her.

One day Tao said to Ma: "You are not well off either. I can't go on making demands on a friend every day to fill my belly. For now I think selling chrysanthemums will do for a living."

Ma, who tended to be scrupulous in such matters, listened contemptuously and said, "I took you for a spirited, high - minded man who could be content in poverty. What you are saying amounts to turning the East Hedge into a marketplace. That would be an insult to these yellow flowers!"

"Earning one's own keep is not greediness," said Tao with a smile, "nor is it banal to sell flowers for a living. True, people should

贪，贩花为业不为俗。人固不可苟求富，然亦不必务求贫也。”马不语，陶起而出。自是，马所弃残枝劣种，陶悉掇拾而去。由此不复就马寝食，招之始一至。未几，菊将开，闻其门嚣喧如市。怪之，过而窥焉，见市人买花者，车载肩负，道相属也。其花皆异种，目所未睹。心厌其贪，欲与绝；而又恨其私秘佳本，遂款其扉，将就诮让。陶出，握手曳入。见荒庭半亩皆菊畦，数椽之外无旷土。劚去者，则折别枝插补之；其蓓蕾在畦者，罔不佳妙：而细认之，皆向所拔弃也。陶入屋，出酒馔，设席畦侧，曰：“仆贫不能守清戒，连朝幸得微资，颇足供醉。”少间，房中呼“三郎”，陶诺而去。俄献佳肴，烹饪良精。因问：“贵姊胡以不字？”答云：“时未至。”问：“何时？”曰：“四十

not amass wealth dishonestly, but, then again, they need not purposely make themselves poor."

Ma had nothing to say. Tao got up and walked out. Afterwards Tao gathered up and carried away all the broken stems and stunted plants Ma threw away. He no longer slept and ate at Ma's, except when invited. Before long, when the time came for chrysanthemums to bloom, there was a clamor that made Tao's gate sound like a marketplace. Wondering what this was about, Ma went over to observe. He saw market vendors coming to buy flowers, their carts and shoulder poles brushing past one another on the road. The flowers were all exotic varieties Ma had never seen before. He was disgusted by such aquisitiveness and wanted to break off their friendship. What was more, he was irked that Tao had kept the best varieties for himself. He knocked on Tao's gate, intending to give him a piece of his mind. Tao came to the gate, grasped his hand, and pulled him inside. The once barren courtyard had become half a *mu* of chrysanthemum beds. There was not an empty piece of ground for several rafter lengths around the house. Of all the buds swelling into bloom in the flowerbeds, none were less than exquisite. Tao had stuck cuttings in the ground to replace dug-up plants. Close inspection proved that all the cuttings were the ones Ma had pulled up and discarded earlier. Tao went into his room, brought out wine and food, and set places next to the flowerbeds.

"I am not one to abide by austere discipline when times are hard," he said. "Fortunately I have made a slight amount of money these last few days—more than enough to drink my fill."

Soon a voice called from inside: "Third-Brother!" Tao shouted in answer as he went in. Before long he brought out a number of delicacies, stewed and braised to perfection, which prompted Ma to ask, "Why isn't your sister engaged?"

"The time has not come yet."

三月。"又诘:"何说?"但笑不言。尽欢始散。过宿,又诣之,新插者已盈尺矣。大奇之,苦求其术。陶曰:"此固非可言传;且君不以谋生,焉用此?"又数日,门庭略寂,陶乃以蒲席包菊,捆载数车而去。逾岁,春将半,始载南中异卉而归,于都中设花肆,十日尽售,复归艺菊。问之去年买花者,留其根,次年尽变而劣,乃复购于陶。陶由此日富:一年增舍,二年起夏屋。兴作从心,更不谋诸主人。渐而旧日花畦,尽为廊舍。更于墙外买田一区,筑墉四周,悉种菊。至秋,载花去,春尽不归。而马妻病卒。意属黄英,微使人风示之。黄英微笑,意似允许,惟专候陶归而已。年余,陶竟不至。黄英课仆种菊,一如陶。得金益

"What time?" asked Ma.

"The forty - third month."

"What's that supposed to mean?" Ma asked again. Tao only laughed in reply.

They did not call it quits until they enjoyed themselves thoroughly. Ma went to visit the next day, and saw that the cuttings which had recently been stuck in the ground were already a full foot tall. Greatly amazed, he begged to know Tao's technique.

"Actually, this cannot be imparted with words. Besides, you would not make your living with it, so what use would it be to you?"

After a few more days, when the bustle in his gate and yard had quieted down somewhat, Tao wrapped his chrys - anthemums in rush mats, loaded bundles of them onto a number of carts and left. He came back the following year, when spring was nearly halfway over, with a load of rare botanicals from the south, which he used to set up a florist's shop in town. Ten days later everything was sold out, and he went back to tending chrysanthemums. Ma learned from his customers of the previous year that they were buying from Tao again, since the bulbs they kept had all reverted to plants of low quality.

From then on Tao got richer every day. He added rooms one year and raised a new manor the next. He started new buildings when the spirit moved him, without so much as discussing it with his host. The old flower beds gave way little by little to galleries and buildings. Then Tao bought a piece of land on the other side of the wall, surrounded it with a tall wall and planted it full of chrysanthemums. With the coming of fall he carried off a load of flowers. Spring passed, but he did not return.

Then Ma's wife died. He thought of marrying Yellow - Bloom and sent someone to broach the subject. Yellow - Bloom smiled in seeming approval. All she had to do was wait for her brother's return.

More than a year went by, and still Tao did not come back. Yel-

合商贾，村外治膏田二十顷，甲第益壮。忽有客自东粤来，寄陶生函信，发之，则嘱姊归马。考其寄书之日，即妻死之日；回忆园中之饮，适四十三月也，大奇之。以书示英，请问"致聘何所"。英辞不受采。又以故居陋，欲使就南第居，若赘焉。马不可，择日行亲迎礼。黄英既适马，于间壁开扉通南第，日过课其仆。马耻以妻富，恒嘱黄英作南北籍，以防淆乱。而家所须，黄英辄取诸南第。不半岁，家中触类皆陶家物。马立遣人一一赍还之，戒勿复取。未浃旬，又杂之。凡数更，马不胜烦。黄英笑曰："陈仲子毋乃劳乎？"马惭，不复稽，一切听诸黄英。鸠工庀料，土木大作，马不能

low – Bloom instructed the servant to plant chrys – anthemums just as he had done. The money she earned was added to her business investments. She had twenty *qing* of fertile land under cultivation outside the village, and built a main residence more imposing than the last one.

Then a stranger came unexpectedly from Guangdong province with a letter from Tao, instructing his sister to marry Ma. The letter had been sent on the very day Ma's wife had died. Ma recalled with amazement that the party in Tao's garden had been exactly forty – three months before. After showing the letter to Yellow – Bloom, he asked, "Where should I send the betrothal gift?"

Yellow – Bloom would not accept his gift. Due to the rundown condition of his dwelling, she wanted him to live in the south house, as if he were marrying into her family. He refused and chose a suitable day to perform the bride – welcoming ceremony.

After Yellow – Bloom married Ma, she added a walkway leading through the dividing wall to the south house. Every day she walked over to her own house to supervise her servants. Ashamed of his wife's wealth, Ma constantly reminded Yellow – Bloom to keep separate ledgers for the north and south households so as to prevent confusion. But Yellow – Bloom brought whatever she needed for the north house from the south residence. Within half a year, Tao's possessions were everywhere in the house. On the spur of the moment Ma ordered the help to move each and every object to its original spot. He forbade her to bring them back, but before ten days passed, their possessions were mingled again. They went back and forth so many times that Ma could not keep up with them.

"Aren't you over – exerting yourself, Mr. Purity?" laughed Yellow – Bloom. This embarrassed Ma: he discontinued his inspections and left everything to her. She assembled laborers and gathered materials for a major construction project. There was nothing he could do

禁。经数月,楼舍连亘,两第竟合为一,不分疆界矣。然遵马教,闭门不复业菊,而享用过于世家。马不自安,曰:“仆三十年清德,为卿所累。今视息人间,徒依裙带而食,真无一毫丈夫气矣。人皆祝富,我但祝穷耳!”黄英曰:“妾非贪鄙;但不少致丰盈,遂令千载下人,谓渊明贫贱骨,百世不能发迹,故聊为我家彭泽解嘲耳。然贫者愿富,为难;富者求贫,固亦甚易。床头金任君挥去之,妾不靳也。”马曰:“捐他人之金,抑亦良丑。”黄英曰:“君不愿富,妾亦不能贫也。无已,析君居:清者自清,浊者自浊,何害。”乃于园中筑茅茨,择美婢往侍马。马安之。然过数日,苦念黄英。招之,不肯至;不得已,反就之。隔宿辄至,以为常。黄英笑曰:“东食西宿,廉者当不如是。”马亦

to stop her. After several months the north and south residences were joined by continuous frame buildings and living quarters. There was nothing to mark the boundary between the two.

Yellow-Bloom did, in deference to Ma's instructions, close the gate and stop dealing in chrysanthemums. Still, they lived more luxuriously than a noble family. This made Ma uncomfortable.

"I had thirty years of purity before you imposed on me," complained Ma, "Now I'm in this world just to stare and breathe. I get my food by hanging on to a petticoat. There isn't a wisp of manliness left in me. Everybody else prays for wealth, but I pray for poverty."

"It's not that I'm greedy," said Yellow-Bloom. "But if I do not make sure that we have a fair amount of wealth, people will be saying for thousand years that my poet-ancestor Tao Qian was a born pauper whose bloodline could not thrive even after a hundred generations. Therefore I resort to this so that people will no longer ridicule our dear Magistrate of Pengze District. Anyway, a poor person who wants wealth has a hard time ahead of him, but a rich person who looks for poverty can be satisfied very easily. You can squander the gold under the beds as you wish-I'm not tight."

"There is something very unseemly about throwing away another person's money," answered Ma.

"You don't want to be rich, and I refuse to be poor," said Yellow-Bloom. "Since there is no otherway, I'll live separately from you. The pure will be left to his purity; the polluted will be left to her pollution. What could be wrong with that?"

And so she had a thatched hut built in the garden and chose a nice-looking maid to wait on him there. Ma was content. But after several days he missed Yellow-Bloom painfully. He sent for her, but she would not come. The only thing he could do was to go to her. He made a habit of showing up every other night.

"Eating at your own house and sleeping with your neighbor-

自笑，无以对，遂复合居如初。会马以事客金陵，适逢菊秋。早过花肆，见肆中盆列甚烦，款朵佳胜，心动，疑类陶制。少间，主人出，果陶也。喜极，具道契阔，遂止宿焉。要之归。陶曰："金陵，吾故土，将婚于是。积有薄资，烦寄吾姊。我岁杪当暂去。"马不听，请之益苦。且曰："家幸充盈，但可坐享，无须复贾。"坐肆中，使仆代论价，廉其直，数日尽售。逼促囊装，赁舟遂北。入门，则姊已除舍，床榻裀褥皆设，若预知弟也归者。陶自归，解装课役，大修亭园，惟日与马共棋酒，更不复结一客。为之择婚，辞不愿。姊遣两婢侍其寝处，

that's not the way a man of purity would act," Yellow - Bloom said with a smile. Ma himself had to laugh: "there was nothing he could say to that. So it was that he went back to living with her as in the beginning."

It happened that Ma travelled to Nanjing to see to a certain matter just when the chrysanthemums were in full bloom. He went by a florist's shop one morning and saw a profuse array of magnificent potted flowers. This gave him quite a start, since he noticed a resemblance to Tao's handiwork. Sure enough, the shopkeeper who came out a moment later was none other than Tao.

Ma was overjoyed. After exchanging greetings Ma stayed the night. He invited Tao to go back, but Tao said, "Nanjing is my home territory, and I'm going to marry here. I've built up some meager funds that I'd like you to take back to my sister. I'll probably make a short trip there at the end of the year." Paying no heed to this, Ma redoubled his pleas and said, "Your family is this, Ma redoubled his pleas and said, "Your family is blessed with ample means. You should do nothing but sit back and enjoy it. You don't need to stay in business any more."

As they sat in the shop, Tao had servants price his goods for him. By keeping prices low, he sold everything in a few days. Then he made short work of packing his baggage, hired a boat and headed north.

Entering the gate, they found that his sister had already cleared a suite for him, with bed and bedding already in place, as if she had known her brother was coming.

Now that Tao was back, he unpacked his possessions and directed laborers in laying out extensive gardens and pavilions. He spent his days playing chess and drinking with Ma, without even befriending a house guest. He refused offers to help him find a wife. His sister assigned two maids to serve him at bedtime. After three or four years

居三四年，生一女。陶饮素豪，从不见其沉醉。有友人曾生，量亦无对。适过马，马使与陶相较饮。二人纵饮甚欢，相得恨晚。自辰以讫四漏，计各尽百壶。曾烂醉如泥，沉睡座间。陶起归寝，出门践菊畦，玉山倾倒，委衣于侧，即地化为菊，高如人；花十余朵，皆大于拳。马骇绝，告黄英。英急往，拔置地上，曰："胡醉至此！"覆以衣，要马俱去，戒勿视。既明而往，则陶卧畦边。马乃悟姊弟菊精也，益爱敬之。而陶自露迹，饮益放，恒自折柬招曾，因与莫逆。值花朝，曾来造访，以两仆舁药浸白酒一坛，约与共尽。坛将竭，二人犹未甚醉。马潜以一瓻续入之，二人又尽之。曾醉已惫，诸仆负之以去。陶卧地，又化为菊。马见惯不惊，如法拔之，守其旁以观其变。久之，叶益憔悴。大惧，始告黄英。英闻骇曰：

one of them bore him a daughter.

Tao was a heavy drinker, but no one ever saw him in a stupor. When a friend named Zeng, whose capacity for wine was also unrivalled, came to visit Ma, Ma instigated rregretting that they had not met each other sooner. From midmorning until the fourth watch of night they each finished a hundred pots in all. Zheng was so plastered he sprawled in his chair and passed out. Tao stood up to go to bed, but he walked out the door and into a chrysanthemum bed instead. Like a jade mountain he tottered and fell. As he hit the ground he turned into a chrysanthemum plant with a heap of clothes lying around it. It was tall as a man and had at least ten blossoms, each bigger than a fist.

Greatly shaken, Ma told Yellow-Bloom. She rushed to the spot, pulled up the plant and laid it on the ground, saying: "Look how drunk you are!" She covered it with the clothes and asked Ma to come away with her, warning him not to look. The next morning he went there and found Tao lying by the flowerbed. At last Ma realized that brother and sister were both chrysanthemum spirits, which was all the more reason for him to love and respect them.

Tao, now that he had revealed his true identity, drank with greater abandon. He constantly sent invitations to Zeng, and their friendship grew till nothing could come between them. Then it was Flower-Morning. Zeng came to visit with two servants carrying an urn of white wine infused with herbs, which he invited Tao to share to the bottom. The two of them nearly emptied the urn without getting especially drunk. Ma stealthily added another crockful, and was not startled. He pulled up the plant in the usual way and waited beside it to watch the transformation. After a time the leaves started looking wilted. Greatly frightened, he went to tell Yellow-Bloom. She was aghast at the news.

"You've killed my brother!" she said. She ran to look: the root and stalk were already shriveled. She was crushed. She nipped off the

"杀吾弟矣!"奔视之,根株已枯。痛绝,掐其梗,埋盆中,携入闺中,日灌溉之。马悔恨欲绝,甚怨曾。越数日,闻曾已醉死矣。盆中花渐萌,九月既开,短干粉朵,嗅之有酒香,名之"醉陶",浇以酒则茂。后女长成,嫁于世家。黄英终老,亦无他异。

异史氏曰:"青山白云人,遂以醉死,世尽惜之,而未必不自以为快也。植此种于庭中,如见良友,如对丽人,——不可不物色之也。"

stem, put soil around it in a pot and carried it to her room. She watered it every day. Ma tormented himself with regret and felt great resentment toward Zeng. After several days news came that Zeng had drunk himself to death.

The plant in the pot slowly sent forth a sprout. In the ninth month it bloomed. It had a short stem, a powder - white bloom and gave off a winelike fragrance. They named it "Drunken Tao." It grew best when watered with wine. Afterwards Tao's daughter grew up and married into a noble family. Yellow - Bloom lived to old age without any other strange occurrences.

The Chronicler of the Tales comments: "Like Fu Yi, whose epitaph was 'a man of green mountains and white clouds,' Tao ended up dying of drink. Everyone pities him, but who is to say it was not an exciting life for him? Plant this variety in your courtyard. It's as good as seeing a close friend or being with a beautiful woman. You simply have to go looking for it."

书 痴

彭城郎玉柱，其先世官至太守，居官廉，得俸不治生产，积书盈屋。至玉柱，尤痴：家苦贫，无物不鬻，惟父藏书，一卷不忍置。父在时，曾书《劝学篇》粘其座右，郎日讽诵；又幛以素纱，惟恐磨灭。非为干禄，实信书中真有金粟。昼夜研读，无间寒暑。年二十余，不求婚配，冀卷中丽人自至。见宾亲，不知温凉，三数语后，则诵声大作，客逡巡自去。每

A FOOL FOR BOOKS

LANG Yuzhu of Pengcheng was the heir of a former prefect. He had been a scrupulous office-holder, and had put what income he had into collecting a houseful of books instead of investing it productively. Now it was Yuzhu's turn to be an even greater fool for books. He lived in poverty and sold every possession, but he could not bear to part with a single book from his father's collection. While alive his father had copied out the "Exhortation to Learning" by the Song emperor Zhen Zong(r. 998-1022), and pasted it on his desk. Yuzhu read it aloud daily. He covered it with a gauze overlay for fear that it would become frayed.

He was not out to command a salary: he truly believed that wealth and sustenance were to be found within books. He ground away at his studies night and day, and no extreme of weather could interrupt him. He was in his twenties but did not seek a mate, expecting that some beautiful woman would come to him unbidden from inside a book. He didn't know how to make small talk around guests and relatives. He would make a few remarks, but then as the sound of his reciting started to ring out, his guest would back hesitantly out the door. Each time the civil examiner came to give a qualifying exam, he was placed at the

文宗临试，辄首拔之，而苦不得售。一日，方读，忽大风飘卷去。急逐之，踏地陷足；探之，穴有腐草；掘之，乃古人窖粟，朽败已成粪土。虽不可食，而益信“千锺”之说不妄，读益力。一日，梯登高架，于乱卷中得金辇径尺，大喜，以为“金屋”之验。出以示人，则镀金而非真金。心窃怨古人之诳己也。居无何，有父同年，观察是道，性好佛。或劝郎献辇为佛龛。观察大悦，赠金三百、马二匹。郎喜，以为金屋、车马皆有验，因益刻苦。然行年已三十矣。或劝其娶，曰：“‘书中自有颜如玉’，我何忧无美妻乎？又读二三年，迄无效；人咸揶揄之。时民间讹言：天上织女私逃。或戏郎：“天孙窃奔，盖为君也。”郎知其戏，置不辨。

head of the list of candidates, but he was miserably unsuccessful in higher examinations.

One day, while he was reading, a gust of wind blew his book from his hand. As he was rushing after it, a spot of ground he stepped on gave way under his feet. He probed with his hand and found a cavity containing mouldy straw. Dug up, it proved to be an ancient cellar full of millet, which had already rotted into dirt. Though it was inedible, it strengthened his belief that the "thousand bushels" mentioned in the "Exhortation to Learning" was no lie. He studied with renewed vigor. On another day while climbing a stepladder to reach a high shelf, he found a foot-long golden model of a cart in a disorderly pile of books. He was beside himself with joy, since he took this as a confirmation of the words "golden room" in the "Exhortation." When a person he showed it to pronounced it gilt instead of gold, he was miffed at the ancients for hood-winking him.

Not long afterward, a man who passed the examinations in the same year as his father and who was devoted to the Buddha stopped there on a tour of inspection. Someone urged Lang to present the miniature cart to him for his Buddha niche. The inspector was so pleased he gave Lang three hundred taels of gold and two horses. Happy in his belief that the promise of a golden room, carriage and horses in the "Exhortation" had come true, Lang redoubled his diligence. Still, he was already thirty years of age. When someone advised him to marry, he quoted the "Exhortation" : "'In books you will find a countenance like jade,'" and said, "I am not worried that there will be no beautiful wife for me."

Over the next few years of fruitless study, he became a butt of common ridicule. There was a rumor going round that the Weaving Maid had run away from heaven, and people poked fun at Lang, saying: "The heavenly princess must have run away for your sake."

Lang let it pass, realizing it was only in fun. One evening he was

一夕,读汉书至八卷,卷将半,见纱翦美人夹藏其中。骇曰:“书中颜如玉,其以此应之耶?”心怅然自失。而细视美人,眉目如生;背隐隐有细字云:“织女。”大异之。日置卷上,反复瞻玩,至忘食寝。一日,方注目间,美人忽折腰起,坐卷上微笑。郎惊绝,伏拜案下。既起,已盈尺矣。益骇,又叩之。下几亭亭,宛然绝代之姝。拜问:“何神?”美人笑曰:“妾颜氏,字如玉,君固相知已久。日垂青盼,脱不一至,恐千载下无复有笃信古人者。”郎喜,遂与寝处。然枕席间亲爱倍至,而不知为人。每读,必使女坐其侧。女戒勿读,不听。女曰:“君所以不能腾达者,徒以读耳。试观春秋榜上,读如君者几人?若不听,妾行去矣。”

reading the eighth fasicle of the *History of the Han Dynasty* and had gotten almost to the middle when he found a gauze cutout of a beautiful woman pressed between the leaves.

"Is this supposed to answer to the prediction of a countenance like jade within a book?" he asked himself, stunned. He was crestfallen and disheartened. However, a closer look at the cutout showed lifelike features. On the back the words "Weaving Maid" were written faintly in hairline characters. He thought the portrait quite marvelous and each day he placed it on a pile of books to gaze at admiringly again and again, to the point that he forgot food and sleep. One day as his eyes were fixed on it the beautiful woman bent forward at the waist, got up and sat smiling on his books. Startled to the utmost, Lang prostrated himself before the desk. On rising he was amazed to see that she was a full foot long. Again he touched his head to the ground, and this time she stepped down from the desk wish statuesque poise, looking every bit as beautiful as any woman alive.

"Which goddess are you?" Lang asked with a bow.

"My surname is Countenance, and I am called Like-Jade," she said with a smile. "You've known about me for a long while, and every day you've been kind enough to look my way. If I had neglected to show myself, I'm afraid nobody for the next thousand years would trust fully in the ancients again." Lang felt wonderful.

So it was that he found himself in bed with a beautiful woman, but even though nestling among the mats and cushions was conducive to intimacy, he did not know how to play a man's part.

Whenever he read, he had her sit beside him. She told him not to read, but he ignored her.

"Your reading is precisely what keeps you from soaring to success. Look at the spring and fall bulletins of master's and doctor's degree holders: how many of those men study as much as you do? If you don't listen to me, I'm leaving."

郎暂从之。少顷，忘其教，吟诵复起。逾刻，索女，不知所在。神志丧失，嘱而祷之，殊无影迹。忽忆女所隐处，取汉书细检之，直至旧所，果得之。呼之不动，伏以哀祝。女乃下曰："君再不听，当相永绝！"因使治棋枰、樗蒲之具，日与遨戏。而郎意殊不属。觑女不在，则窃卷流览。恐为女觉，阴取汉书第八卷，杂溷他所以迷之。一日，读酣，女至，竟不之觉；忽睹之，急掩卷，而女已亡矣。大惧，冥搜诸卷，渺不可得；既，仍于汉书八卷中得之，叶数不爽。因再拜祝，矢不复读。女乃下，与之弈，曰："三日不工，当复去。"至三日，忽一局赢女二子。女乃喜，授以弦索，限五日工一曲。郎手营目注，无暇他及；久之，随指应节，

Lang went along with her for a while, but soon he forgot her instructions and commenced his reciting again. After a while he tried to find her, but she was gone. Without her he was bereft of spirit and senses. He invoked her with a prayer, but she showed no sign of appearing. Suddenly remembering where she had once hidden, he took down the *History of Han Dynasty* and leafed through every page of it, until he came to the old place, and there she was. He called to her, but she did not move. Then he crouched before her in woeful supplication.

At last she stepped out of the picture, saying: "If you ignore me again, I will part with you forever." She made him set up a *weiqi* board and a dicepot. Day after day they amused themselves, but Lang's heart was simply not in it. He watched for her to go away, then sneakily grabbed a book and started skimming through it. He was afraid that she would find out, so he secretly took the eighth fascicle of the *History of the Han Dynasty* and put it among a jumbled pile of other books to mislead her. One day he was so carried away with his reading that he did not notice her return. The instant he saw her he closed his book hurriedly, but she had already disappeared. Greatly frightened, he searched haphazardly through a number of books without success. Later he found her once again in the eighth fascicle of the *History of the Han Dynasty* on the very same page. Then he prostrated himself before her and begged her to reappear, promising that he would study no more. At last she came down from the desk. She started a game of *weiqi*, saying: "If you don't master this in three days, I'll leave again."

On the third day he surprised them both by coming out two pieces ahead at the end of a game. Pleased with his progress, she began teaching him stringed instruments and allowed him five days to master a piece. Lang's hands were busy and his eyes were occupied; there was no leisure for getting sidetracked. With time the rhythm sprang to life

不觉鼓舞。女乃日与饮博,郎遂乐而忘读。女又纵之出门,使结客,由此倜傥之名暴著。女曰:"子可以出而试矣。"郎一夜谓女曰:"凡人男女同居则生子;今与卿居久,何不然也?"女笑曰:"君日读书,妾固谓无益。今即夫妇一章,尚未了悟,枕席二字有工夫。"郎惊问:"何工夫?"女笑不言。少间,潜迎就之。郎乐极,曰:"我不意夫妇之乐,有不可言传者。"于是逢人辄道,无有不掩口者。女知而责之。郎曰:"钻穴逾隙者,始不可以告人;天伦之乐,人所皆有,何讳焉。"过八九月,女果举一男,买媪抚字之。一日,谓郎曰:"妾从君二年,业生子,可以别矣。久恐为君祸,悔之已晚。"郎闻言,泣下,伏不起,曰:"卿不念呱呱者耶?"女亦凄然。良久曰:"必欲妾留,当举

at his fingertips: his whole body moved spontaneously to the beat. From then on she drank and played with him every day, and he had too much fun to remember his studies. What was more, she freed him to get out of the house and into society. Soon he became known as a zestful and convivial man.

"Now you're ready to go and take the examinations," she said.

One night Lang said to her: "As a rule men and women who live together give birth to children. We have lived together for quite a while. Why are we the exception?"

"I always said it did you no good to study every day," she laughed. "Even now the chapter on husbands and wives has you baffled. There is an art to 'pillowing' together."

"What art?" Lang asked in surprise. She laughed and said nothing, but in a little while she snuggled up against him under the covers.

Lang's delight knew no bounds. "I didn't suspect that the happiness of married couples had something incommunicable in it," he said.

He told everyone he met of his discovery, and there were none who were not forced to hold back their laughter. She learned of this and scolded him, but he protested, "Tunneling through walls and squirming through crannies is the sort of thing you can't tell people, but the joy of a natural relationship is shared by everyone. Why should I scruple to mention it?"

Sure enough after eight or nine months Like - Jade gave birth to a son. They hired a nurse to raise him. One day Like - Jade said to Lang: "I've been with you for two years and I've given you s son: now I can leave you. I'm afraid if I stay too long I'll bring trouble for you: when that happens our regrets will not do us any good."

Tears ran down his face when he heard these words. He threw himself down and would not rise. "Won't you miss our little baby?" he asked.

She was heartbroken also. After a long pause she said, "If you in-

架上书尽散之。”郎曰:“此卿故乡,乃仆性命,何出此言!”女不之强,曰:“妾亦知其有数,不得不预告耳。”先是,亲族或窥见女,无不骇绝,而又未闻其缔姻何家,共诘之。郎不能作伪语,但默不言。人益疑,邮传几遍,闻于邑宰史公。史,闽人,少年进士。闻声倾动,窃欲一睹丽容,因而拘郎及女。女闻知,遁匿无迹。宰怒,收郎,斥革衣衿,梏械备加,务得女所自往。郎垂死,无一言。械其婢,略能道其仿佛。宰以为妖,命驾亲临其家。见书卷盈屋,多不胜搜,乃焚之;庭中烟结不散,瞑若阴霾。郎既释,远求父门人书,得从辨复。是年秋捷,次年举进士。而衔恨切于骨髓。为颜

sist on my staying, you should do away with every last book on your shelves."

"Those books are your birthplace, and they are my life. How can you say such a thing?!" protested Lang.

She did not force the issue: "Anyway I know this is predestined. I had to let you know beforehand, that's all."

Prior to this, some of Lang's kin had caught glimpses of the girl, and every one of them had been thoroughly amazed. What was more, they had not heard which family he was connected with by marriage, so they went to him in a group and demanded an answer. Unable to tell an untruth, Lang simply held his tongue. People grew more suspicious. News spread as if by mail until it reached Master Shi, the district magistrate. Shi, a native of Fujian, had taken his doctorate at an early age. What he heard stirred in him an impulse to set eyes on Like-Jade's beautiful face, and so he gave an order to take Lang and the girl into custody. The girl got word of this and fled without a trace. In order to learn where she had gone, the angry magistrate arrested Lang, stripped him of his scholar's robe, and had him flogged and his hands clamped in pressure manacles, until he was within an inch of his life, but still he said nothing. Then the magistrate had the maids beaten, and they gave an account bearing some semblance to the truth. The magistrate decided that the girl was an evil spirit. He called for his coach and went to Lang's house to make a personal inspection. He found a roomful of books, The smoke hung over the courtyard in clouds that would not disperse, gloomy as stormclouds.

On his release Lang travelled to see a former student of his father's, who gave him a letter that brought about his reinstatement as an academicain in good standing. That year he won success at the fall examinations and the next year he took the doctorate. But still he harbored rage against Shi in the very marrow of his bones. He made an altar to Countenance Like-Jade and prayed to it morning and night: "If

如玉之位,朝夕而祝曰:“卿如有灵,当佑我官于闽。”后果以直指巡闽。居三月,访史恶款,籍其家。时有中表为司理,逼纳爱妾,托言买婢寄署中。案既结,郎即日自劾,取妾而归。

异史氏曰:“天下之物,积则招妒,好则生魔:女之妖,书之魔也。事近怪诞,治之未为不可;而祖龙之虐,不已惨乎!其存心之私,更宜得怨毒之报也。呜呼!何怪哉!”

your spirit lives, help me get an assignment in Fujian."

Later he did indeed make an inspection tour in Fujian as a court-appointed censor. After a three-month stay there he uncovered evidence of shi's wrongdoings and had his property confiscated.

At that time, a cousin of his who was serving as a prosecutor had taken a concubine by force and left her in Lang's compound, claiming that she was an indentured maid. On the very same day that the confiscation case was settled, Lang declared himself unfit for office, married the concubine and returned home.

The Chronicler of the Tales comments: "All possessions in this world invite envy when accumulated and when loved give rise to deviltry. The deviltry of books was at the root of the girl's seductive magic. Lang's actions were so preposterous that it was not necessarily wrong to straighten them out, but to burn the books like the first Qin emperor was too ruthless. The magistrate's selfish motives deserved vengeful retribution. My, what an odd tale!"

晚　霞

五月五日，吴越间有斗龙舟之戏：刳木为龙，绘鳞甲，饰以金碧；上为雕甍朱槛；帆旌皆以锦绣；舟末为龙尾，高丈余；以布索引木板下垂，有童坐板上，颠倒滚跌，作诸巧剧。下临江水，险危欲堕。故其购是童也，先以金啖其父母，预调驯之，堕水而死，勿悔也。吴门则载美妓，较不同耳。镇江有蒋氏童阿端，方七岁，便捷奇巧，莫能过，声价益起，十六岁犹用之。至金山下，堕水死。蒋媪止此子，哀鸣

GHOST – GIRL WANXIA

ON the fifth of the fifth month dragon boat contests are held in the Wu – Yue area. Hewn logs are shaped into dragons, which are painted with scales and ornamented in gold and green. On top are sculptured tiles and vermilion railings, and the sails and banners are all embroidered satin. The stern of each boat projected upwards in the shape of a dragon tail over ten feet high. Wooden slats are suspended from these by cloth ropes, and boys support themselves on the slats as they somersault, spin and perform all sorts of stunts in constant danger of plunging into the water below. For this reason the boys are procured by cash pyments made to their parents, and then they are trained to perform, so that no one can complain if they fall into the water and die. The Suzhou boats are somewhat different in that they carrry pretty singing girls.

In Zhenjiang district there was a boy performer of the Jiang clan named A – Duan. At the age of seven he was unequalled for his agility and remarkable reflexes. His reputation kept growing, and at sixteen he was still at work. Then he died falling into the water at the foot of Mt Gold. His mother, who had only this one son, could only wail in misery. A – Duan himself was not aware that he had died. He only

而已。阿端不自知死，有两人导去，见水中别有天地；回视，则流波四绕，屹如壁立。俄入宫殿，见一人兜牟坐。两人曰："此龙窝君也。"便使拜伏。龙窝君颜色和霁，曰："阿端伎巧可入柳条部。"遂引至一所，广殿四合。趋上东廊，有诸年少，出与为礼，率十三四岁。即有老妪来，众呼解姥。坐令献技。已，乃教以钱塘飞霆之舞，洞庭和风之乐。但闻鼓钲喤聒，诸院皆响。既而诸院皆息。姥恐阿端不能即娴，独絮絮调拨之；而阿端一过，殊已了了。姥喜曰："得此儿，不让晚霞矣！"明日，龙窝君按部，诸部毕集。首按夜叉部，鬼面鱼服。鸣大钲，围四尺许；鼓可四人合抱之，声如巨霆，叫噪不复可闻。舞起，则巨涛汹涌，横流空际，时堕一点星光，及着地消灭。龙窝

knew that two men led him away under the water, to another heaven and earth. Looking behind him, he saw perpendicular walls of water flowing on all sides. Soon he wa[illegible]n inside a palace, where a man in a battle helmet sat. The two [illegible]aid, "This is the Lord of Dragon Lair." They directed A-Duan to b[illegible] to the ground. The Lord of Dragon Lair softened the expression on his face.

"A-Duan, your mastery has qualified you for admission to the Willow-Wand Troupe," he said.

A-Duan was then led to where the view on all sides was blocked by huge palaces. As he hurried down the east gallery, a number of young men, mostly thirteen or fourteen years old, came out and bowed in greeting. Then came an old woman whom everyone addressed as Granny Xie. She sat down and told A-Duan to show off his skills. When he was finished, she taught him dances called Thunder on the Qiantang River and Dongting Lake Breeze. The din of the drums and gongs could be heard reverbrating from every courtyard. After a while the court-yeards all quieted down. Granny was worried that A-Duan would not learn all the moves smoothly, so she took special care to give him long-winded instructions for each step, but he knew exactly what he was doing after one time through.

Granny exclaimed happily: "With a boy like this, our troupe will be in the same class as Wanxia's."

The next day, the Lord of Dragon Lair was to review the troupes, and every last troupe gathered. First he reviewed the Yaksa Troupe, with their ferocious faces and fishskin costumes. They struck a large gong some four feet in circumference, and their thunderous drum needed four men to hold it. They struck up a deafening chorus of yells and whoops. As they started dancing, giant waves surged across the sky above, dropping sparks of starlight that went out when they hit the ground. The Lord of Dragon Lair orderd them to stop abruptly and then called for the girls of the Nestling Oriole Troupe: all of them

君急止之，命进乳莺部，皆二八姝丽，笙乐细作，一时清风习习，波涛俱静，水渐凝如水晶世界，上下通明。按毕，俱退立西墀下。次按燕子部，皆垂髫人。内一女郎，年十四五以来，振袖倾鬟，作散花舞；翩翩翔起，衿袖袜履间，皆出五色花朵，随风飏下，飘泊满庭。舞毕，随其部亦下西墀。阿端旁睨，雅爱好之。问之同部，即晚霞也。无何，唤柳条部。龙窝君特试阿端。端作前舞，喜怒随腔，俯仰中节。龙窝君嘉其惠悟，赐五文袴褶，鱼须金束发，上嵌夜光珠。阿端拜赐下，亦趋西墀，各守其伍。端于众中遥注晚霞，晚霞亦遥注之。少间，端逡巡出部而北，晚霞亦渐出部而南；相去数武，而法严不敢乱部，相视神驰而已。既按蛱蝶部，童男女皆双舞，身长短、年大小、

were sweet sixteen and beautiful. The delicate notes of mouth organs rose into the air. In an instant a cool breeze breathed across the water and the crashing waves were silent. The water slowly grew still like the everywhere - transparent limits of a crystal world. At the end of the performance all the troupers withdrew to stand beneath the west steps.

The next to be reviewed was the Swallow Troupe, made up of girls young enough to wear their hair long. Among them was a young woman somewhere around fourteen or fifteen. In the Flower - Strewing Dance she waved her sleeves and dipped her head. Then she fluttered and took soaring leaps, while flowers of all colors fell form her sash and sleeves and stockings, floating down the wind and drifting over the whole courtyard. At the end of the dance she too followed her troupe to the bottom of the west steps.

A - Duan cast a sidelong glance in her direction and lost his heart to her. He asked a fellow trouper and learned that her name was Wanxia. Before long the call went out for the Willow - Wand Troupe. The Lord of Dragon Lair gave A - Duan a special audition. A - Duan performed the dances he had just learned. His dancing was a perfect embodiment of the feelings in the music, and his every movement was made in perfect rhythm. The Lord of Dragon Lair commended his intelligence and presented him with a pair of rainbow pantaloons and a fish - whisker hair clasp of gold set with a golw - in - the - dark pearl. A - Duan bowed in gratitude, then hurried to the west steps, where each troupe drew up in its own formation. A - Duan gazed at Wanxia from afar through the crowd and she gazed back at him. Soon A - Duan edged out of rank and moved northward; Wanxia also edged southward out of her troupe. They were only a few steps apart, but neither dared cross over the line between formations. All they could do was gaze soulfully at one another.

Then the Butterfly Troupe was reviewed. This was made up of

服色黄白，皆取诸同。诸部按已，鱼贯而出。柳条在燕子部后，端疾出部前，而晚霞已缓滞在后。回首见端，故遗珊瑚钗，端急纳袖中。既归，凝思成疾，眠餐顿废。解姥辄进甘旨，日三四省，抚摩殷切，病不少瘥。姥忧之，罔所为计，曰："吴江王寿期已促，且为奈何！"薄暮，一童子来，坐榻上与语，自言："隶蛱蝶部。"从容问曰："君病为晚霞否？"端惊问："何知？"笑曰："晚霞亦如君耳。"端凄然起坐，便求方计。童问："尚能步否？"答云："勉强尚能自力。"童挽出，南启一户；折而西，又辟双扉。见莲花数十亩，皆生平地上；叶大如席，花大如盖，落瓣堆梗下盈尺。童引入其中，曰："姑坐此。"遂去。少时，一美人拨莲花而入，则晚霞也。相见惊喜，各道相思，略述生平。遂以

little boys and girls who danced in pairs of matching height, age and wing color.

When all the troupes had been reviewed, the dancers walked out in single file. The Willow - Wand Troupe was to follow the Swallow Troupe. A - Duan hurried to take the first place in his troupe, while Wanxia dawdled in the rear of hers. She turned and saw A - Duan, then let her coral clasp fall. He immediately put it in his sleeve. On his return he made himself ill thinking of her to the exclusion of sleep and meals. Granny Xie served him rich and savory foods. She checked on him several times a day and tended him solicitously, but he did not improve in the slightest. She worried for him, but had no idea what to do.

"The birthday celebration for the King of Wu River is drawing near. What are we going to do?"

That night a young boy came, sat on the edge of the bed and talked with A - Duan.

"I belong to the Butterfly Troupe," he said. Then he asked with studied calmness: "Are you ill because of Wanxia?"

"How did you know?" A - Duan asked incredulously.

"She is in the same shape you are," laughed the boy. A - Duan sat up gloomily and asked what could be done.

"Can you still walk?" adked the boy.

"If I push myself I can make it," he said. The boy led him out by the arm, opened a door to the south, turned west, then went through another double door. There before them was a large expanse of lotus flowers, growing on dry land, with leaves as large as mats and flowers as large as canopies. Fallen petals were piled a full foot high around the stems.

The boy led him among them, saying, "Sit here for now," and walked away. After a short while a young beauty parted the lotuses and walked into the clearing: it was Wanxia. When they got over the

石压荷盖令侧，雅可幛蔽；又匀铺莲瓣而藉之，忻与狎寝。既订后约，日以夕阳为候，乃别。端归，病亦寻愈。由此两人日一会于莲亩。过数日，随龙窝君往寿吴江王。称寿已，诸部悉还，独留晚霞及乳莺部一人在宫中教舞，数月更无音耗，端怅惘若失。惟解姥日往来吴江府；端托晚霞为外妹，求携去，冀一见之。留吴江门下数日，宫禁森严，晚霞苦不得出，怏怏而返。积月余，痴想欲绝。一日，解姥入，戚然相吊曰："惜乎！晚霞投江矣！"端大骇，涕下不能自止。因毁冠裂服，藏金珠而出，意欲相从俱死。但见江水若壁，以首力触不得入。念欲复还，惧问冠服，罪将增重。意计穷蹙，汗流浃踵。忽睹壁下有大树一章，乃

happy surprise of seeing one another, they each told how much the other had been on their thoughts and gave brief accounts of their lives. Then they weighed down lily pads with stones to make them lean sideways, which did nicely for a screen, spread an even layer of petals to recline on, and gleefully lay down beside each other. Afterward, having set sundown as the time for their daily rendezvous, they parted.

Back with his troupe, A-Duan recovered from his illness soon afterward. From then on the two met every day in the locust patch. After several days they went with the Lord of Dragon Lair to the King of Wu River's birthday celebration. When they had commemorated the king's longevity, all the troupes returned, leaving only Wanxia and one other member of the Nestling Oriole Troupe at the palace as dancing teachers. For several months there was no news of them. A-Duan was miserable and spiritless. The only ray of hope was Granny Xie, who made daily trips to the Wu River palace. A-Duan asked to be taken along to see Wanxia, claiming that she was his cousin. He stayed within the Wu River gates for a few days, but the stringent palace discipline kept Wanxia from coming out of the women's section, so he went back discouraged. When little more than a month had passed, his lovesickness threatened to be the end of him.

One day Granny Xie came in mournfully to console him: "How sad! Wanxia has thrown herself into the river."

A-Duan was stunned: there was no controlling the tears that ran down his cheeks. He destroyed his hat and tore up his robe, then ran out with the gold and pearl clasp in his sleeve, intending to follow her in death. But the river water formed a wall that would not give way even then he batted his head against it. He considered going back but thought of the aggravated punishment he would receive when taken to task for the hat and robe. He was at wit's end: sweat poured off him till it trickled over his ankles. Just then he noticed a large tree beside the wall of water. He shinnied up to the top most branches and took a

猱攀而上，渐至端杪；猛力跃堕，幸不沾濡，而竟已浮水上。不意之间，恍睹人世，遂飘然泅去。移时，得岸，少坐江滨，顿思老母，遂趁舟而去。抵里，四顾居庐，忽如隔世。次且至家，忽闻窗中有女子曰："汝子来矣。"音声甚似晚霞。俄，与母俱出，果霞。斯时两人喜胜于悲；而媪则悲疑惊喜，万状俱作矣。初，晚霞在吴江，觉腹中震动，龙宫法禁严，恐旦夕身娩，横遭挞楚；又不得一见阿端，但欲求死，遂潜投江水。身泛起，沉浮波中，有客舟拯之，问其居里。晚霞故吴名妓，溺水不得其尸。自念衏院不可复投，遂曰："镇江蒋氏，吾婿也。"客因代贳扁舟，送诸其家。蒋媪疑其错误，女自言不误，因以其情详告媪。媪以其风格韵妙，颇爱悦之；第虑年太少，必非肯终

mighty leap. Unexpectedly he broke through without so much as wetting his clothes, and found himself floating on the surface. Before he realized what was happening, the world of the living was before his eyes. He swam with the current until he came to the bank. Sitting momentarily beside the river he began to think of his old mother. He hailed a passing boat that was going his way, and as he reached his ward, the cottages he saw on all sides were like a memory from a previous lifetime.

Then he came to his house, where a girl's voice rang out from the window: "Your son is here."

The voice was very much like Wanxia's. In a moment the speaker came out with his mother. It was Wanxia herself. In an instant the young couple's sadness gave way to joy, while the matron's emotions ran the gamut from puzzlement and sorrow to shock and elation.

Earlier, while staying at the Wu River Palace, Wanxia had felt rapid movements in her abdomen. Owing to the severe discipline in the palace, she feared that when the time came to give birth she would be brutally beaten. On top of that she could not see A-Duan. Wishing only to end her life, she stole out and threw herself into the river. Her body floated upward until it was bobbing on the waves. A traveler's boat came along and pulled her to safety. The passengers asked her which ward she lived in. Wanxia - originally a well-known courtesan from Wu whose corpse had not been recovered when she drowned - thought to herself that a brothel was no place to go back to, and so she answered, "My husband is of the Jiang family in Zhenjiang."

The passengers rented a boat for her and took her home. Matron Jiang thought that she had come to the wrong place, but Wanxia assured her that it was no mistake. She told her whole story to the matron. The matron was quite taken with her lively, attractive manner, but worried that such a young woman could not possibly endure widowhood. Still, the girl was obedient and attentive. Seeing the difficult

寡也者。而女孝谨,顾家中贫,便脱珍饰售数万。媪察其志无他,良喜。然无子,恐一旦临蓐,不见信于戚里,以谋女。女曰:“母但得真孙,何必求人知。”媪亦安之。会端至,女喜不自已。媪亦疑儿不死;阴发儿冢,骸骨具存。因以此诘端。端始爽然自悟;然恐晚霞恶其非人,嘱母勿复言。母然之。遂告同里,以为当日所得非儿尸。然终虑其不能生子。未几,竟举一男,捉之无异常儿,始悦。久之,女渐觉阿端非人,乃曰:“胡不早言!凡鬼衣龙宫衣,七七魂魄坚凝,生人不殊矣。若得宫中龙角胶,可以续骨节而生肌肤,惜不早购之也。”端货其珠,有贾胡出资百万,家由此巨富。值母寿,夫妻歌舞称觞,遂传闻五邸。王

circumstances the matron lived in, she took off her jewelry and sold it for hundreds of strings of cash. The matron was much gladdened to learn that she had no ulterior motive. But her son was not there and the fear remained that neighbors and relatives would distrust Wanxia as her pregnancy advanced. The matron broached this subject to her.

"As longas you get your own true grandson. Mother, why should other people have to know?" This put the matron's mind at ease.

Wanxia was beside herself with delight when A – Duan arrived. The matron shared her joy and even began to question the fact that her son had died at all. She secretly opened his grave and found his remains intact, which prompted her to question him. The truth finally dawned on A – Duan, but he warned his mother not to mention it again for fear that Wanxia would reject him for not being human. His mother agreed with him, so she told the neighbors that the corpse which had been recovered that day was not her son's. Still, she continued to worry that he might not be able to father a child. But before long Wanxia gave birth to a boy that felt no different to the touch than a normal child. At last the matron was happy.

In time Wanxia realized that A – Duan was not a living human.

"Why didn't you tell me sooner? For a period of forty – nine days after the wearing of ghostly garments or dragon palace garments, a person's soul remains undissipated, just as if he were alive. If we had managed to get dragon horn glue from the palace during that time I could have joined your bones at the joints, and your flesh would have grown back. What a shame we did not buy it earlier!"

A – Duan put his pearl up for sale. A foreign trader gave a million in cash for it, which made them into a wealthy family overnight. On his mother's birthday he and his wife sang and danced between toasts. When word of this reached the mansion of the local prince, he wanted to seize Wanxia for himself. A – Duan was frightened, and he went before the prince to confess: "My wife and I are both ghosts."

欲强夺晚霞。端惧,见王自陈:“夫妇皆鬼。”验之无影而信,遂不之夺。但遣宫人就别院,传其技。女以龟溺毁容,而后见之。教三月,终不能尽其技而去。

A test was performed proving that the two did not cast shadows, which convinced that this was true, so he gave up his plan of abduction. He did, however, assign women from his palace to study under Wanxia in a side courtyard. Wanxia would not see him until she had disfigured herself by applying tortoise urine to her face. She left after teaching for three months, when it became clear that mastery such as hers was more than her students could ever learn.

白 秋 练

直隶有慕生，小字蟾宫，商人慕小寰之子。聪惠喜读。年十六，翁以文业迂，使去而学贾，从父至楚。每舟中无事，辄便吟诵。抵武昌，父留居逆旅，守其居积。生乘父出，执卷哦诗，音节铿锵。辄见窗影憧憧，似有人窃听之，而亦未之异也。一夕，翁赴饮，久不归，生吟益苦。有人徘徊窗外，月映甚悉。怪之，遽出窥觇，则十五六倾城之姝。望见生，急避去。又二三日，载货北旋，暮泊湖滨。父适他

FISH DEMON BAI QIULIAN

SCHOLAR Mu of Zhili, known by his childhood name Changong, was a son of the merchant Mu Xiaohuan. He was intelligent and loved reading. When he was sixteen his father, considering a literary profession impractical, made his son learn business instead by taking him along on a trip to Chu. Whenever there was nothing to do aboard the boat, he passed his time chanting and reading aloud. They arrived in Wuchang, where the father left him at an inn to watch over their assets. Changong took advantage of his father's every absence by picking up a scroll and chanting poems in rhythic tones. At times like he could see a shadow wavering at the window, as if someone were secretly listening to him, but he thought nothing of it.

One night when his father stayed out late at a party, the scholar chanted with a fervor unusual even for him. The figure of a person walking back and forth outside the window was plainly visible in the moonlight. Curious, he rushed out to get a better look and saw a fifteen- or sixteen-year-old girl — the sort of beauty that can bring a city tumbling down. At the sight of the scholar she darted into hiding.

A few days later father and son headed north loaded with a load of merchandise. At sundown they were moored by the side of a lake and

出，有媪入曰："郎君杀吾女矣！"生惊问之。答云："妾白姓。有息女秋练，颇解文字。言在郡城，得听清吟，于今结想，至绝眠餐。意欲附为婚姻，不得复拒。"生心实爱好，第虑父嗔，因直以情告。媪不实信，务要盟约。生不肯。媪怒曰："人世姻好，有求委禽而不得者。今老身自媒，反不见纳，耻孰甚焉！请勿想北渡矣！"遂去，少间，父归，善其词以告之，隐冀垂纳。而父以涉远，又薄女子之怀春也，笑置之。泊舟处，水深没棹；夜忽沙碛拥起，舟滞不得动。湖中每岁客舟必有留住守洲者，至次年桃花水溢，他货未至，舟中物当百倍于原

the father happened to be elsewhere, when a matron came aboard and said, "You'll be the death of my daughter, young fellow!"

Taken aback, the scholar asked what that meant. "My name is Bai," she answered. "I have a daughter named Qiulian who knows a thing or two about the written word. She says she first heard your musical chanting in the prefectural seat. Now she's so desperate thinking of you that she won't eat or sleep. I would like to marry you to her. You won't get the chance to refuse a second time."

In his heart, the scholar really felt for the girl, but he worried that his father would disapprove, and he said so frankly. The matron did not believe him and insisted that he give his pledge of honor. He would not.

The matron exploded: "Plenty of people in this world try to arrange marriages through go-betweens and don't get what they want. Now I come in person to discuss this with you, yet you turn me down. I can't think of a greater humiliation! Don't be too sure you'll make it back north across the river after this!" With that she left.

In a short time his father came back. The scholar told him of what had happened, putting it in the best possible light in the hopes that he would approve of a marriage. But his father thought there was too great a distance involved and laughed it off as the amorous impulse of a young woman.

The water at their mooring that evening was too deep for their oars to touch tottom, but during the night sand and gravel suddenly bulged up under their boat and stranded it. The father was not very alarmed at this, because every year some of the traders pulled their boats onto sandbars in the lake and stayed there until the peach-blossom waters rose in the third month after New Year's. Then the merchandise in their boats would be worth many times its original price, since no other goods would arrive for some time. The old man simply figured that he still needed to scour up capital for next year's trip

直也,以故翁未甚忧怪。独计明岁南来,尚须揭赀,于是留子自归。生窃喜,悔不诘媪居里。日既暮,媪与一婢扶女郎至,展衣卧诸榻上。向生曰:“人病至此,莫高枕作无事者!”遂去。生初闻而惊,移灯视女,则病态含娇,秋波自流。略致讯诘,嫣然微笑。生强其一语。曰:“‘为郎憔悴却羞郎’,可为妾咏。”生狂喜,欲近就之,而怜其荏弱。探手于怀,接脑为戏。女不觉欢然展谑,乃曰:“君为妾三吟王建‘罗衣叶叶’之作,病当愈。”生从其言。甫两过,女揽衣起坐曰:“妾愈矣!”再读,则娇颤相和。生神志益飞,遂灭烛共寝。女未曙已起,曰:“老母将至矣。”未几,媪果至。见女凝妆欢坐,不觉欣慰。邀女去,女俯首不语。

simply figured that he still needed to scour up capital for next year's trip south, so he left his son with the boat and went home himself.

The scholar was pleased for his own reasons, but he was sorry he had not asked the matron's address. That evening the matron and a maid showed up supporting a young woman. They loosened her clothes, lay her on the bed and, as they left, turned to the scholar and said:

"When a person gets this sick, you shouldn't lay back and act like it doesn't concern you!"

When he had gotten over the shock of hearing this, the scholar moved the lamp closer to get a look at the girl. There was a touch of coquetry in her frailness and rippling glances stirred in the pools of her eyes. He asked a few brief questions, but she only smiled winsomely. He pressed her to say something.

"'I pine for him but feel shy before him, is the line that fits me,'" she said. This drove him wild with joy. He wanted to get close to her, but her frailness gave him pause. His hand explored her breast and he playfully touched his lips to hers. Before she knew it, she was teasing him exuberantly and saying: "If you recite Wang Jian's 'Dress of Shimmering Gauze' three times for me, my illness will be cured."

He did as she said. After only the second time through she pulled her robe over her shoulders, sat up and said, "I'm cured." As he read it the third time her coy looks were mixed with trembling. Now his soul was soaring. He blew out the candle and lay down with her.

The girl got up before daybreak, saying: "My mother will be here soon."

Before long the matron did arrive. She was naturally relieved to see her daughter sitting there in good spirits and dressed up quite presentably. The mother asked her daughter to leave, but she lowered her head and did not answer. With that the matron went out by herself, saying:

媪即自去，曰："汝乐与郎君戏，亦自任也。"于是生始研问居止。女曰："妾与君不过倾盖之友，婚嫁尚不可必，何须令知家门。"然两人互相爱悦，要誓良坚。女一夜早起挑灯，忽开卷凄然泪莹，生急起问之。女曰："阿翁行且至。我两人事，妾适以卷卜，展之得李益江南曲，词意非祥。"生慰解之，曰："首句'嫁得瞿塘贾'，即已大吉，何不祥之与有！"女乃稍欢。起身作别曰："暂请分手，天明则千人指视矣。"生把臂硬咽，问："好事如谐，何处可以相报？"曰："妾常使人侦探之，谐否无不闻也。"生将下舟送之，女力辞而去。无何，慕果至。生渐吐其情。父疑其招妓，怒加诟厉。细审

"You like having fun with this fine young man, so do as you wish."

At last the scholar got around to asking about her family background.

"Our friendship is no more than the meeting of two carts along the road," she said. "We can't be sure that marriage is in store for us. Why should I tell you about my family."

Yet the two found joy in one another and meant the vows they made with all sincerity. One night Qiulian got up at an odd hour and trimmed the lamp. She opened a book and in a moment her face turned glum and glistened with tears. The scholar jumped up and asked what was wrong.

"Your father is about to arrive," said the girl. "Just now I used a book to divine what will happen to us. It opened to 'Melody of Jiangnan' by Li Yi. The mean of this lyric is not promising."

"The first line is 'I married a trader from Qutang': that in itself is encouraging," he said to console her. "What is so unpromising about that?"

This made her feel a bit better. She got up and took leave of him, saying: "Let's part company for the time being. When day comes all sorts of people will start pointing and staring at us."

He took her arm and choked back a sob.

"Where can I let you know if the joyous event is settled?" he asked.

"I'll have someone shadowing you all the time. I'll hear about it, whether it works out or not." He wanted to go ashore to see her off, but she refused vigorously and left.

Before long Mu the elder came back. The scholar coughed up the truth little by little. His father berated him angrily, suspecting he had entertained a prostitute. A careful inventory of the valuables in the boat showed that nothing was missing, so he gave his son another

舟中财物，并无亏损，谯诃乃已。一夕，翁不在舟，女忽至，相见依依，莫知决策。女曰："低昂有数，且图目前。姑留君两月，再商行止。"临别以吟声作为相会之约。由此值翁他出，遂高吟，则女自至。四月行尽，物价失时，诸贾无策，敛资祷湖神之庙。端阳后，雨水大至，舟始通。生既归，凝思成疾。慕忧之，巫医并进。生私告母曰："病非药禳可痊，唯有秋练至耳。"翁初怒之；久之，支离益惫，始惧，赁车载子，复如楚，泊舟故处。访居人，并无知白媪者。会有媪操柁湖滨，即出自任。翁登其舟，窥见秋练，心窃喜；而审诘邦族，则浮家泛宅而已。因实告子病由，冀女登舟，姑以解其沉痼。媪以婚无成约，弗许。女露半面，

scolding and forgot about it.

One night when the old man left the boat the girl suddenly appeared. They gazed at each other longingly, but there was nothing to be done.

"Ups and downs are predestined—we should think about the present," she said. "For now I'll have you stay for two months; we'll discuss where to go from there later."

On her way out she prescribed the sound of reciting as the signal for a rendezvous. After this whenever his father went out he would start chanting, and the girl would come by herself. The fourth month ran its course, and the time of optimum prices was past. The desperate traders took up a collection for an offering at the lake god's temple. The big rains did not come until after Dragon-Boat Festival, and then at last the boats could get through.

Once the scholar got home he fell ill pining for the girl. His concerned father had both a shaman and a doctor come to treat him. The scholar told his mother in private:

"My sickness cannot be healed by herbs or exorcism. The only way is for Qiulian to come."

At first the old man was angry, but when time only made his son's debility worse, he grew afraid. He hired a coach to carry his son, went back to Chu and moored a boat at the old spot. He questioned the people living there, but none of them knew of Matron Bai. Then an old woman came poling her boat along the lakeshore, identifying herself as the person he was seeking. Climbing aboard her boat, the old man was delighted with the glimpse he caught of Qiulian. But then he inquired into their clan affiliations and found that they were nothing but a drifting houseboat family. He frankly told them the reason for his son's illness, hoping that the girl would board his boat and relieve his son's depression for the time being. The matron would not allow it because no agreement on the marriage had been made.

殷殷窥听，闻两人言，眦泪欲堕。媪视女面，因翁哀请，即亦许之。至夜，翁出，女果至，就榻呜泣曰：“昔年妾状，今到君耶！此中况味，要不可不使君知。然羸顿如此，急切何能便瘳？妾请为君一吟。”生亦喜。女亦吟王建前作。生曰：“此卿心事，医二人何得效？然闻卿声，神已爽矣。试为我吟‘杨柳千条尽向西’。”女从之。生赞曰：“快哉！卿昔诵诗余，有采莲子云：‘菡萏香连十顷陂。’心尚未忘，烦一曼声度之。”女又从之。甫阕，生跃起曰：“小生何尝病哉！”遂相狎抱，沉痾若失。既而问：“父见媪何词？事得谐否？”女已察知翁意，直对“不谐”。既而女去，父来，见生已起，喜甚，但慰勉之。因曰：“女子良佳。然自总角时，把柁棹歌，无论微贱，抑亦不贞。”生不

Part of the girl's face showed around a corner as she listened breathlessly; tears nearly dropped from the corners of her eyes at what she heard them say. At last the sight of the girl's face, along with the old man's pleading, made the matron give in.

Sure enough, when the old man went out that night, the girl appeared. She moved to the edge of the scholar's bed and sobbed, "So now it is your turn to be in the condition I was in last year! I had to let you know what it felt like, but you've wasted away so badly I can't cure you right away. Let me recite something for you."

The scholar's mood also brightened. Qiulian recited the same poem by Wang Jian. "That was a specific remedy in your case," said the scholar. "It may not work for a second person. I have to admit that hearing your voice is exhilarating in itself. Try reciting 'All the willow wands are trailing to the west' for me."

She did as he asked, and he paid her a compliment: "Wonderful! You used to chant a ditty set to 'The Lotus Gatherer' that started like this: 'Blossoms of water lily scent the spacious slope.' I've never forgotten it. Please go through it once, and linger over every word." Again she did his bidding.

Just as she brought the lyric to a close, he leapt up and said, "When was I ever sick?" Then they held each other tightly, as if he had never been ill.

Afterward he asked, "What did my father and your mother say to each other? Did they reach an agreement or not?"

Qiulian, who was aware of the old man's feelings, answered straightforwardly: "No agreement."

After she left, the father came. He was very glad to see his son up and about, but he would do no more than tell him to take heart and comfort him. Then he came to the point: "She's a fine girl, but she's been at the rudder singing oarsman's songs ever since her hair has been in a topknot. I won't mention her low birth, but you can be sure

语。翁既出,女复来,生述父意。女曰:"妾窥之审矣:天下事,愈急则愈远,愈迎则愈距。当使意自转,反相求。"生问计。女曰:"凡商贾志在利耳。妾有术知物价。适视舟中物,并无少息。为我告翁:居某物,利三之;某物,十之。归家,妾言验,则妾为佳妇矣。再来时,君十八,妾十七,相欢有日,何忧为!"生以所言物价告父。父颇不信,姑以余资半从其教。既归,所自置货,资本大亏;幸少从女言,得厚息,略相准。以是服秋练之神。生益夸张之,谓女自言,能使己富。翁于是益揭资而南。至湖,数日不见白媪;过数日,始见其泊舟柳下,因委禽焉。媪悉不受,但涓吉送女过

she's no virgin. The young man had nothing to say."

When the old man had gone out, Qiulian came back. The scholar related his father's opinion. "I saw well enough already," she said. "In this world the more impatient we are for something, the further it recedes from us. When we go more than halfway with someone, they push us away. What I'll do is cause a turnabout in his opinion of me, so he will ask me instead." The scholar wanted to know her plan. The girl said: "Merchants have one aim—to make a profit. I have a method for finding out the prices of commodities. I just looked at the goods in your boat: you don't stand to gain a thing by them. Tell your father for me that if he invests in such-and-such an item he'll get three times the profit and with such-and-such goods he'll get ten times his investment. Then, when you return hom and my words come true, I'll make a wonderful wife for you. By the time you come back you'll be eighteen and I'll be seventeen. There will be plenty of time to be happy together—don't worry!"

The scholar told his father the goods and prices she had mentioned. The father didn't give them much credit, but he agreed to go along with her instructions using half of his remaining funds. On their return the goods he had stocked himself lost a great deal of money. It was lucky for him he had partially heeded the girl's advice, since the fat earnings on the goods she recommended were just about enough to offset his losses. This made him acknowledge the girl's foresight. The scholar laid the praise on thicker, telling how the girl had said she could make a rich man of him. At this the old man raised additional funds and headed south.

They reached the lake and stayed there for several days without seeing Matron Bai. Several more days passed before they saw her boat moored by a willow, whereupon they presented the engagement gifts. The matron would not accept any, and simply chose a favorable day to send her daughter over to the old man's boat. The old man rented

舟。翁另赁一舟为子合卺。女乃使翁益南，所应居货，悉籍付之。媪乃邀婿去，家于其舟。翁三月而返。物至楚，价已倍蓰。将归，女求载湖水；既归，每食必加少许，如用醯酱焉。由是每南行，必为致数坛而归。后三四年，举一子。一日，涕泣思归。翁乃偕子及妇俱如楚。至湖，不知媪之所在。女扣舷呼母，神形丧失。促生沿湖问讯。会有钓鲟鳇者，得白骥。生近视之，巨物也，形全类人，乳阴毕具。奇之，归以告女。女大骇，谓夙有放生愿，嘱生赎放之。生往商钓者，钓者索直昂。女曰："妾在君家，谋金不下巨万，区区者何遂靳直也！如必不从，妾即投湖水死耳！"生惧，不敢告父，盗金赎放之。既返，不见女，搜之

another boat for his son's goblet – sharing ceremony.

After this the girl told her father – in – law to go farther south and gave him a ledger listing the goods he should invest in. The matron invited her son – in – law to make himself at home in her boat. Three months later the old man returned, bringing goods that increased two to five times in value when he brought them to Chu.

Before they set out for home, the girl asked to take along a load of lakewater. Back home she invariably added a smidgin of it to every meal, as if it were*sauce piquante*. Henceforth, every time the old man travelled south, he had to bring back several urns of it for her. A couple of years later she gave birth to a son.

One day they found her sniffing and sobbing from home – sickness, so the old man took his son and her with him to Chu. They arrived at the lake, but there was no telling where the matron was. The girl beat against the gunwale and shouted for her mother in despair. She urged the scholar to go along the shore asking for her whereabouts. It so happened that a man who fished for sturgeon had just caught a white carp. The scholar walked over for a closer look. It was a huge creature, quite similar to a human in form and complete with breasts and private parts. Impressed with such an oddity, he went back to tell Qiulian. She was greatly shaken. She told him that she had long ago vowed to set some living thing free and instructed him to pay for the fish's freedom. He went to bargain with the fisherman, who asked an exorbitant price.

"Since I've been in your family I've brought in a good ten thousand taels of gold," Qiulian said. "Why must you haggle over such a measly sum? If you insist on going against my wishes, I will throw myself into the lake and drown myself this minute!"

The scholar was frightened. Not daring to tell his father, he stole gold to buy the fish's freedom. On his return to the boat, he did not see Qiulian. He looked for her without success until the last watch,

不得，更尽始至。问："何往？"曰："适至母所。"问："母何在？"腼然曰："今不得不实告矣：适所赎，即妾母也。向在洞庭，龙君命司行旅。近宫中欲选嫔妃，妾被浮言者所称道，遂敕妾母，坐相索。妾母实奏之。龙君不听，放母于南滨，饿欲死，故罹前难。今难虽免，而罚未释。君如爱妾，代祷真君可免。如以异类见憎，请以儿掷还君。妾去，龙宫之奉，未必不百倍君家也。"生大惊，虑真君不可得见。女曰："明日未刻，真君当至。见有跛道士，急拜之，入水亦从之。真君喜文士，必合怜允。"乃出鱼腹绫一方，曰："如问所求，即出此，求书一'免'字。"生如言候之。果有道士蹩躠而至，生伏拜之。道士急走，生从其后。道士以杖投水，跃登其上。生竟从之而登，则

when she finally appeared.

"Where were you?" he asked.

"I went to my mother's place."

"Where is your mother?"

In a voice halting with embarrassment she said, "I have to tell you the truth now. The fish you paid for a while ago was my mother. The Dragon-Lord of Dongting Lake had ordered her to serve on his entourage. Recently when concubines were being chosen for the palace, certain gossipy people spoke highly of me, so an order was given to confine my mother pending my return. My mother wrote a truthful memorial to the throne, but the Dragon-Lord paid no attention. He banished my mother, almost dead from starvation, near the south shore: that is why she met with yesterday's disaster. Although she is now out of that predicament, the sentence against her has not been re-voked. If you love me, you can save her by praying to the True Lord. If I am repugnant to you because I am not of your kind, let me hand your son over to you and leave. There could well be a hundred times more riches for me in the dragon palace than in your house."

The scholar was overwhelmed, and he worried that he would not be able to meet with the True Lord.

Qiulian said, "Tomorrow afternoon between two and four o'clock the True Lord will appear. When you see a lame Taoist, bow down to him immediately. Stay with him, even if he goes into the water. The True Lord is fond of literary men: he is sure to be sympathetic." With this she took out a sheet of fine, fishbelly-white cloth and said, "If he asks what you want, show him this and reguest that he write the word 'pardon'."

The scholar waited as she had told him. Sure enough, a Taoist priest came hobbling along. The scholar prostrated himself before him. He hurried away with the scholar following behind. Then he

非杖也，舟也。又拜之。道士问："何求？"生出罗求书。道士展视曰："此白骥翼也，子何遇之？"蟾宫不敢隐，详陈颠末。道士笑曰："此物殊风雅，老龙何得荒淫！"遂出笔草书"免"字，如符形，返舟令下。则见道士踏杖浮行，顷刻已渺。归舟，女喜，但嘱勿泄于父母。归后二三年，翁南游，数月不归。湖水既罄，久待不至。女遂病，日夜喘急。嘱曰："如妾死，勿瘗，当于卯、午、酉三时，一吟杜甫梦李白诗，死当不朽。候水至，倾注盆内，闭门缓妾衣，抱入浸之，宜得活。"喘息数日，奄然遂毙。后半月，慕翁至，生急如其教，浸一时许，

threw his staff into the water and jumped onto it. The scholar, too, jumped after him and found it was not a staff but a boat. Again he bowed down to the Taoist.

"What are you after?" asked the Taoist.

The scholar pulled out the piece of fine silk and asked him to write the word. The Taoist unrolled it and looked at it, saying: "This is from the fin of a white carp. How did you come by it?"

The scholar dared not hold anything back; he revealed everything from start to finish.

"She is quite a delicate elegant creature," the Taoist laughed. "What makes the old dragon think he can get away with such dissipation?" He proceeded to take out his brush and write the word "pardon" in a cursive style used in charms. Then he turned the boat back and let the scholar go ashore. The scholar watched the Taoist skim away across the water, feet planted on the staff, until he swiftly dwindled away.

The scholar returned to his boat. Qiulian was happy, but cautious enough to warn him not to let a word of this slip out to his parents.

Two or three years after their return north, the old man made a trip south, from which he did not return for many months. The lake water was used up, and no more arrived after a long wait. Qiulain fell ill: day and night she gasped for breath.

"If I die," she instructed him, "don't bury me. Recite Tu Fu's 'Dream of Li Po' for me once each morning, noon, and evening. Then I will not decay even in death. Wait until the water comes and pour it into a tub. Remove my clothes behind closed doors, carry me to the water and soak me in it. That should bring me back to life."

She drew a few more days of wheezing breaths and then died a lingering death. Half a month later when old Mu arrived, the scholar hastened to carry out her instructions. A little more than two hours of soaking gradually revived her. After this she was preoccupied with

渐苏。自是每思南旋。后翁死，生从其意，迁于楚。

thoughts of returning south. Later the old man died and the scholar followed her with by moving to Chu.

竹　青

鱼客，湖南人，忘其郡邑。家贫，下第归，资斧断绝。羞于行乞，饿甚，暂憩吴王庙中，拜祷神座。出卧廊下，忽一人引去，见王，跪曰："黑衣队尚缺一卒，可使补缺。"王曰："可。"即授黑衣。既着身，化为乌，振翼而出。见乌友群集，相将俱去，分集帆樯。舟上客旅，争以肉向上抛掷。群于空中接食之。因亦尤效，须臾果腹。翔栖树杪，意亦甚得。逾

THE BIRD NYMPH ZHUQING

YU Ke was a native of Hunan, from which district and town I do not recall. His circumstances were straitened to begin with, and after he failed to make the roll in civil examination, he ran out of money on his way home. He was ashamed to beg, though desperately hungry, so he stopped to rest at a temple to the King of Wu and prostrated himself in prayer before the image of the deity. Then he went out and lay down on the veranda. Soon a man came and led him away to see the king. The man knelt and said, "There is still an opening for a soldier in the black-robe corps. We can have this gentleman fill it."

"Good," said the King of Wu.

The man handed Yu a suit of black clothes. The instant he put them on, Yu was transformed into a crow. Out he went with flapping wings to where he saw his fellow crows gathered in a flock. They took him along to some sailboats, where they perched on the spars. The passengers in the boats vied with one another in throwing bits of meat up for the crows to catch in midair. By imitating his fellows, Yu soon filled his belly. He glided to a perch on top of a tree feeling quite content.

After a few days the King of Wu, pitying him for not having a

二三日，吴王怜其无偶，配以雌，呼之“竹青”。雅相爱乐。鱼每取食，辄驯无机。竹青恒劝谏之，卒不能听。一日，有满兵过，弹之中胸。幸竹青衔去之，得不被擒。群乌怒，鼓翼扇波，波涌起，舟尽覆。竹青仍投饵哺鱼。鱼伤甚，终日而毙。忽如梦醒，则身卧庙中。先是，居人见鱼死，不知谁何，抚之未冷，故不时令人逻察之。至是，讯知其由，敛资送归。后三年，复过故所，参谒吴王。设食，唤乌下集群啖，祝曰：“竹青如在，当止。”食已，并飞去。后领荐归，复谒吴王庙，荐以少牢。已，乃大设以飨乌友，又祝之。是夜宿于湖村，秉烛方坐，忽几前如飞鸟飘落，视之，则二十许丽人，辗然曰：“别来无恙乎？”鱼惊问之。曰：“君不

mate, matched him with a female called Zhuqing. They were perfectly delighted with a female called Zhuqing. They were perfectly delighted with one another.

Yu's efforts at foraging were invariably meek and unre – sourceful. Zhuqing often urged him to be bold, but he was never able to follow her advice. One day a passing Manchu soldier shot him in the chest with a slingshot. Luckily for him Zhuqing carried him away in her beak, so he was not caught. The flock of sacred crows was outraged. They beat their wings until they stirred up waves that overturned the boats. Zhuqing busily fetched bits of food and fed them to Yu, but he was badly wounded and died before the day was out.

Suddenly, like waking from a dream, he found himself lying in the temple. Prior to this, the local inhabitants had seen an unidentified man lying there, apparently dead, but since he was still warm to the touch they had left him there and checked on him at intervals. Now, learning what had happened to him, they took up a collection to pay for his way home.

Passing by the same place three years later, Yu stopped to pay homage to the King of Wu. He set out some food, called the crows down in a flock to eat it, and prayed: "If Zhuqing is among you, I want her to stay behind." But when the crows finished eating, all of them flew away.

Later, on his way home after being recommended to the provincial chief examiner, he visited the King of Wu's temple once again. When he had finished making the lesser offering of pork and mutton, he set the meat out as a feast for his crow friends and prayed to them again. That evening he stopped in a lakeside village. He was sitting up by candlelight when a birdlike creature came fluttering to rest before his desk. Lifting his eyes, he saw a beautiful woman of about twenty flashing him a smile as she asked, "Have you been well since we parted?"

识竹青耶?"鱼喜,诘所来。曰:"妾今为汉江神女,返故乡时常少。前乌使两道君情,故来一相聚也。"鱼益欣感,宛如夫妻之久别,不胜欢恋。生将偕与俱南,女欲邀与俱西,两谋不决。寝初醒,则女已起。开目,见高堂中巨烛荧煌,竟非舟中。惊起,问:"此何所?"女笑曰:"此汉阳也。妾家即君家,何必南!"天渐晓,婢媪纷集,酒炙已进。就广床上设矮几,夫妇对酌。鱼问:"仆何在?"答:"在舟上。"生虑舟人不能久待。女言:"不妨,妾当助君报之。"于是日夜谈宴,乐而忘归。舟人梦醒,忽见汉阳,骇绝。仆访主人,杳无音信。舟人欲他适,而缆结不解,遂共守之。积两月余,生

Yu asked incredulously who she was.

"Don't you recognize you Zhuqing?"

Yu elatedly asked where she had come from.

"I'm a nymph of the Han River now: I hardly ever get a chance to come back to my own home. The crow messengers brought word twice of the state you were in, so I have come for a reunion with you."

Yu was overjoyed. Like husband and wife after a long separation, they could not contain the joy of their togetherness. He wanted to take her south with him, while she wished to invite him west, but they let the matter remain undecided when bedtime came.

On awakening Yu noticed that she had already risen. His eyes were greeted by a spacious hall lit by large, radiant candles: this was not the boat cabin he had slept in last night! He stood up in surprise and asked, "Where are we?"

"This is Hanyang," she said laughingly. "My house is your house. What need is there to go south?"

As the day brightened a flurry of maids gathered around them. Before he realized it, wine and viands had been served. Yu and his wife drank to one another across the short-legged table they set up on the roomy bed.

"Where is my servant?" asked Yu.

"On the boat," she answered. Yu was concerned that the boatmen could not wait long for him. "Don't worry," she said. "I'll help you make it worth their while." And so the two of them spent their days and nights in intimate conversation. In his bliss Yu gave no thought to going home.

The boatmen were shocked when they awoke from their dreams to find themselves in Hanyang. Yu's servant went looking for him, but he was nowhere to be seen. The boatmen wanted to leave, but the knots in the mooring cable would not come loose, so they were forced to stay there together to watch over the boat.

忽忆归，谓女曰："仆在此，亲戚断绝。且卿与仆，名为琴瑟，而不一认家门，奈何？"女曰："无论妾不能往；纵往，君家自有妇，将何以处妾乎？不如置妾于此，为君别院可耳。"生恨道远，不能时至。女出黑衣，曰："君向所着旧衣尚在。如念妾时，衣此可至；至时，为君解之。"乃大设肴珍，为生祖饯。即醉而寝，醒，则身在舟中。视之，洞庭旧泊处也。舟人及仆俱在，相视大骇，诘其所往。生故怅然自惊，枕边一袱，检视，则女赠新衣袜履，黑衣亦折置其中。又有绣橐维絷腰际，探之，则金资充牣焉。于是南发，达岸，厚酬舟人而去。归家数月，苦忆汉水，因潜出黑衣着之。两胁生翼，翕然凌空，经两时许，已达汉水。回翔下视，见孤屿中有楼舍一簇，遂飞堕。有婢子已

More than two months went by before the Yu recollect – ed his intention of returning home and said to Zhuqing: "As long as I stay here, I'm cut off from my relatives. Besides, you could say that the two of us are husband and wife, yet you have not yet been to my house. Shouldn't we do something about that?" "In the first place my going is out of the question. But even if I could go, you have your own wife back home. What would I be to you then?" "It would be better to leave me here to make a home away from home for you."

The scholar complained that the distance was long and that he would not be able to come often, but Zhuqing brought out a suit of black clothes, saying "I still have the clothes you used to wear. If you miss me, put these on and you can come. When you come, I'll take them off for you."

That night a feast of delicacies was set out to send Yu off. He went to bed feeling the effects of the wine and found himself, on awakening, back in the cabin of his boat. One look outside told him that this was his old mooring place on Dongting Lake. His servant and the boatmen, who were all there, looked at him in amazement and demanded to know where he had been. He was lost in bewilderment.

Beside his pillow lay a bundle. Inspecting it, he found that it was a gift of new clothes, stockings, and shoes from Zhuqing, with the black robe folded among them. Fastened at the waist of the robe was an embroidered pouch which, when opened, proved to be filled to the mouth with gold coins. At this he set out for the south. When the boat touched shore, he paid the boatmen generously and went on his way.

A few months after his return home, his thoughts turned longingly to the Han River, so he secretly took out the black robe and put it on. Wings grew from under his arms and bore him aloft with measured strokes. In little more than four hours he reached the Han River. Looking downward as he turned a gliding circle, he noticed a cluster of buildings situated on a long islet, so he swooped down. A maid who

望见之,呼曰:“官人至矣!”无何,竹青出,命众手为缓结,觉羽毛划然尽脱。握手入舍曰:“郎来恰好,妾旦夕临蓐矣。”生戏问曰:“胎生乎?卵生乎?”女曰:“妾今为神,则皮骨已硬,应与曩异。”越数日,果产,胎衣厚裹,如巨卵然,破之,男也。生喜,名之“汉产”。三日后,汉水神女皆登堂,以服食珍物相贺。并皆佳妙,无三十以上人。俱入室就榻,以拇指按儿鼻,名曰:“增寿”。既去,生问:“适来者皆谁何?”女曰:“此皆妾辈。其末后着藕白者,所谓‘汉皋解珮’,即其人也。”居数月,女以舟送之,不用帆楫,飘然自行。抵陆,已有人絷马道左,遂归。由此往来不绝。积数年,汉产益秀美,生珍爱之。妻和氏,苦不育,每思一见汉产。生以情告女。女乃治任。送儿从父归,约以三月。既归,和爱之过于己出,过十

had seen him coming called, "The gentleman has come!"

In no time Zhuqing came out and ordered all hands to help undo his clothes. He could feel his coat of feathers split down the middle and peel off him. Zhuqing led him inside by the hand, saying: "You came just in time: I'm ready to go into confinement any day."

"Will it be an oviparous or viviparous birth?" Yu joked.

"Now that I am a goddess, my flesh and bones are more substantial. This one should be different than the ones I had before."

After several days she did indeed deliver something in a placenta so thick it resembled a huge egg. This was broken open to reveal a baby boy. The delighted scholar named the boy Han-Born. Three days later the nymphs of the Han River, all in the fresh bloom of youth, filed into the hall with congratulatory gifts of clothes, food and precious stones. Each of nymphs entered the bedroom, stood by the bed, and pressed a thumb on the baby's nose, a custom which they called "life-lengthening."

When they were gone Yu asked, "who were those ladies that just came?"

"They are my sister nymphs. The two at the very end, who were dressed in lotus-stem white, were the nymphs in the story 'A Gift of Jade Pendants on Mt Hangao.'"

After a few months'stay, Zhuqing sent him off in a boat which glided forward on its own, without the use of sail or pole. On disembarking he found a man beside the road holding a horse, so he returned on horseback. From then on he was continually going back and forth. Han-Born grew with the passing years into a fine young boy - Yu's treasure. Yu's first wife, née He, who was pained by her failure to conceive a child, constantly longed to meet Han-Born. The scholar told Zhuqing of this, so she bundled up the boy's things and sent him off with his father, on the understanding that they would be back in three months.

余月,不忍令返。一日,暴病而殇,和氏悼痛欲死。生乃诣汉告女。入门,则汉产赤足卧床上,喜以问女。女曰:"君久负约。妾思儿,故招之也。"生因述和氏爱儿之故。女曰:"待妾再育,令汉产归。"又年余,女双生男女各一:男名"汉生",女名"玉珮"。生遂携汉产归。然岁恒三四往,不以为便,因移家汉阳。汉产十二岁入郡庠。女以人间无美质,招去,为之娶妇,始遣归。妇名"卮娘",亦神女产也。后和氏卒,汉生及妹皆来擗踊。葬毕,汉生遂留;生携玉珮去,自此不返。

After their arrival, his wife He developed greater affec - tion for the boy than if he had been her own. More than ten months passed, but still she could not bear to let him go back. One day the boy fell victim to a sudden illness and died. His wife came close to dying herself of grief. Yu travelled to the Han River to break the terrible news to Zhuqing, but on entering the door he found the boy lying on the bed, ready for nap. Yu joyfully asked her how it could have happened.

"You stayed past the agreed time," she said. "I missed my son, so I called him back."

Then Yu told her how much his wife loved the boy, at which Zhuqing said, "Wait until I am with child again, so I can let you take Han - Born back with you."

A little over a year later she gave birth to twins, a boy and a girl. The boy they named Han - Grown and the girl, Jade - Pendant. Then Yu took Han - Born home with him. Making three or four annual trips seemed troublesome, so he moved his family to Hanyang. Later Han - Born was admitted to the district academy at the age of twelve. Zhuqing, feeling that the most beautiful feminine qualities were lacking in the human world, called the boy to her and found him a wife before she let him return. The wife's name was Goblet - Mistress, who was also the child of a goddess. After a time Yu's first wife He died. Han - Grown and his sister both went to mourn her. When the burial was over, Han - Grown stayed there, but Yu took Jade - Pendant away with him, never to return again.

石清虚

邢云飞，顺天人。好石，见佳石，不惜重直。偶渔于河，有物挂网，沉而取之，则石径尺，四面玲珑，峰峦叠秀。喜极，如获异珍。既归，雕紫檀为座，供诸案头。每值天欲雨，则孔孔生云，遥望如塞新絮。有势豪某，踵门求观。既见，举付健仆，策马径去。邢无奈，顿足悲愤而已。仆负石至河滨，息肩桥上，忽失手，堕诸河。豪怒，鞭仆。即出金，雇善泅

STONE PURE - VOID

XING Yunfei, from Shuntian prefecture, had a fondness for rocks. If he found a fine-looking rock, he did not mind paying a substantial price for it. Once as he was fishing in the river something became tangled in his net. He dove down to free it and brought up a stone a foot in diameter, with finely detailed peaks and ridges on every side. He felt the boundless delight of one who has acquired a rare treasure. Upon returning home, he carved a stand of red sandalwood for it and gave it the place of honor on his desk. Whenever rain was imminent, all of the little openings on the surface emitted little clouds. From a distance they appeared to be stuffed with floss.

Then a certain local despot came to his door asking for a look at the stone. When he saw it, he seized it and handed it to his brawny servant, then spurred his horse away without a word. Xing could do nothing but stamp his feet in grief and vexation.

The despot's servant carried the stone on his back as far as the riverside, Suddenly he lost his grip, and the stone fell into the river. The boss flew into a rage and whipped his servant. Later he paid skilled divers who tried everything imaginable to locate it on the bottom but were nevertheless unsuccessful. The boss drew up an open

者,百计冥搜,竟不可见。乃悬金署约而去。由是寻石者日盈于河,迄无获者。后邢至落石处,临流于邑,但见河水清澈,则石固在水中。邢大喜,解衣入水,抱之而出。携归,不敢设诸厅所,洁治内室供之。一日,有老叟款门而请。邢托言石失已久。叟笑曰:“客舍非耶?”邢便请入舍,以实其无。及入,则石果陈几上。愕不能言。叟抚石曰:“此吾家故物,失去已久,今固在此耶。既见之,请即赐还。”邢窘甚,遂与争作石主。叟笑曰:“既汝家物,有何验证?”邢不能答。叟曰:“仆则故识之。前后九十二窍,巨孔中五字云:‘清虚天石

contract offering a reward to the finder of the stone and then went on his way. After that the banks of the river were crowded with stone seekers, none of whom had any success.

Xiang later went to the spot where the stone had fallen in and stared dejectedly down into the current. To his eyes the river water was clear right to the bottom: the stone was plainly lying there, under the water. Jumping for joy he took off his clothes and dove in. He walked ashore with the stone in his arms, its sandalwood stand still intact. Once home he readied an inner room, making it austerely clean, and set the stone in a place of honor there, not daring to place it in his living room.

One day an elderly man knocked on his gate asking to see the stone. Xing claimed that it had been lost long ago. The old man laughed and said, "Isn't it in your guest room?"

Xing invited him into the guest room to prove it wasn't there, but when they entered the stone was in plain view on the table. Xing was dumbfounded. The old man patted the stone as he said, "This is a family heirloom of mine that has been missing for a long time. Now it has turned up here, hasn't it? Now that I've seen it, I hope you will return it to me."

Xing's wounded pride prompted him to dispute the old man's right to the stone. The old man said laughingly: "Well, since it's your possession, can you name any identifying marks?" Xing could not answer.

"I know them fully well. There are ninety-two openings around the stone, and within the largest of them are the words 'Rock Decoration from Pure-Void Heaven.'"

Xing inspected the stone and, sure enough, found words as tiny as millet grains within one of the openings. It took all his powers of eyesight to make them out. He counted the same number of openings that the old man had said there were. He had no answer to give to the old man, but still he would not give up the stone.

供。'"邢审视，孔中果有小字，细如粟米，竭目力裁可辨认；又数其窍，果如所言。邢无以对，但执不与。叟笑曰："谁家物，而凭君作主耶！"拱手而出。邢送至门外；既还，已失石所在。邢急追叟，则叟缓步未远。奔牵其袂而哀之。叟曰："奇哉！径尺之石，岂可以手握袂藏者耶？"邢知其神，强曳之归，长跽请之。叟乃曰："石果君家者耶、仆家者耶？"答曰："诚属君家，但求割爱耳。"叟曰："既然，石固在是。"入室，则石已在故处。叟曰："天下之宝，当与爱惜之人。此石能自择主，仆亦喜之。然彼急于自见，其出也早，则魔劫未除。实将携去，待三年后，始以奉赠。既欲留之，当减三年寿数，乃可与君相终始。君愿之乎？"曰："愿。"叟乃以两指捏一窍，窍软如泥，随手而闭。闭三窍，已，曰："石上窍数，即君寿也。"作别欲去。邢苦留之，辞甚坚；问其姓

"You had better make sure whose family this belongs to before you try to lay claim to it," the old man laughed. He raised his clasped hands politely and went out. Xing saw him out the gate. Then, when he got back inside, the stone was not there. He rushed after the old man, who was still ambling along not far away. Xing ran to him, grabbed his sleeve, and pleaded with him.

"Now that's strange!" said the old man. "How could a stone one foot in diameter fit in my hand or up my sleeve?"

Realizing that the man had supernatural powers, Xing dragged him back into the house and knelt before him to beg for the stone.

"Does the stone belong to your family or to mine after all?" asked the old man.

"It truly does belong to yours, but I beg you to part with it."

"If that is the case, the stone has been here all along," said the old man. They went to the inner room, and there it was in its old place. "The truly precious things in this world should go to those who appreciate them. This stone has the ability to choose its owner, and I too was pleased with its choice. Still, it was anxious to show itself, which made it come out prematurely before its period of calamity was lifted. I intended to take it with me and wait for three years before presenting it to you. Since you want it left here, yo must give up three years of your allotted lifetime. That way you and the stone can be together until the end. Is that your wish?"

"It is."

The old man pinched the mouth of one of the openings with his fingers; the stone there turned soft as clay at his touch and the opening was moulded shut. When he had shut three of the openings, he said, "Three are as many openings in this stone as there will be years in your life." With that he took his leave and turned to go. Xing beseeched him to stay, but his refusals were quite firm. He left without even answering Xing's questions as to his name.

字,亦不言,遂去。积年余,邢以故他出,夜有贼入室,诸无所失,惟窃石而去。邢归,悼丧欲死。访察购求,全无踪迹。积有数年,偶入报国寺,见卖石者,则故物也,将便认取。卖者不服,因负石至官。官问:“何所质验?”卖石者能言窍数。邢问其他,则茫然矣。邢乃言窍中五字及三指痕,理遂得伸。官欲杖责卖石者,卖石者自言以二十金买诸市,遂释之。邢得石归,裹以锦,藏椟中,时出一赏,先焚异香而后出之。有尚书某,购以百金。邢曰:“虽万金不易也。”尚书怒,阴以他事中伤之。邢被收,典质田产。尚书托他人风示其子。子告邢,邢愿以死殉石。妻窃与子谋,献

A little more than a year later, when Xing was out on business, a burglar broke into his house at night and stole the stone, leaving all else untouched. On his return Xing was sick to death at his loss. He asked everywhere and offered to pay for information, but no sign of it turned up.

A few years later he happened to visit the Temple of Patriotic Obligation. There he saw a man selling decorative stones, and his own was among them. Xing claimed right on the spot that the stone on his back and went to the magisterial court. The magistrate asked, "How can you prove ownership?"

The stone - seller was able to tell the number of openings on the stone, but he was at a loss when Xing demanded further proof. Xing told of the words inside the large opening and the marks left by the old man's fingers. In this way the case was judged in his favor. The magistrate was about to punish the stone - seller with a beating, but the seller protested that he had bought the stone in a market for twenty pieces of gold, and so he was released.

Returning home with his stone, Xian wrapped it in brocade and stored it in a chest. On the occasions when he took it out to contemplate it, he always lit rare incense first.

A certain board minister offered to buy the stone for one hundred pieces of gold, but Xing said, "I wouldn't give it up, even for ten thousand pieces." This made the minister angry. Working behind the scenes, he implicated Xing in an unrelated offense. Xing was put under arrest, and his property was confiscated. Then the minister sent someone to drop a hint to Xing's son. When his son told him of this, Xing vowed to die for his stone. His wife and son, however, discussed the matter and decided without Xing's knowledge to offer the stone to the minister's family. Xing did not learn of this until he was released from hung himself several times if the servants had not caught him in time.

石尚书家。邢出狱始知，骂妻殴子，屡欲自经，家人觉救，得不死。夜梦一丈夫来，自言："石清虚。"戒邢勿戚："特与君年余别耳。明年八月二十日，昧爽时，可诣海岱门，以两贯相赎。"邢得梦，喜，谨志其日。其石在尚书家，更无出云之异，久亦不甚贵重之。明年，尚书以罪削职，寻死。邢如期至海岱门，则其家人窃石出售，因以两贯市归。后邢至八十九岁，自治葬具；又嘱子，必以石殉。及卒，子遵遗教，瘗石墓中。半年许，贼发墓，劫石去。子知之，莫可追诘。越二三日，同仆在道，忽见两人，奔蹶汗流，望空投拜，曰："邢先生，勿相逼！我二人将石去，不过卖四两银耳。"遂

One night a man calling himself Stone Pure – Void came to him in a dream. He admonished Xing not to grieve at his loss: "I'll only be parting with you for a little more than a year. Next year on the twentieth day of the eighth month come to Haidaimen at dawn. You'll be able to buy my freedom for two strings of coppers." Xing, who found this a heartening dream, took the precaution of writing down the date.

Once it was taken into the minister's house, the stone no longer emitted its remarkable clouds. As time went by no one there valued it highly. A year after, the minister died shortly after being removed from office for his crimes. Xing went to Haidaimen on the assigned day: there he found the minister's servant, who had stolen the stone and was offering it for sale. And so Xing bought it for two strings of coppers.

Years later, upon reaching the age of eighty – nine, Xing made preparations for his own burial and instructed his son to bury the stone with him. When he died his son carried out his last wish and entombed the stone with him. Half a year later robbers broke into the grave and took the stone away. Young Xing learned of this but was unable to trace them. Two or three days afterward he was out with a servant when he saw two men coming toward him on the road, dashing and stumbling and sweating profusely. Their eyes were fixed on the air above their heads as they threw themselves down on the ground, crying, "Mr. Xing, don't torment us this way. All we did was take the stone and sell it for four pieces of silver."

Young Xing had them bound and taken to court, where they confessed at the first interrogation that they had sold the stone to a man named Gong. The stone was brought into the courtroom. It was much to the liking of the magistrate, who ordered it deposited in the strongroom, hoping to lay hands on it later. As a clerk was lifting the stone it fell to the floor, and broke into dozens of pieces. Everyone went pale. Then the magistrate gave the two robbers a heavy beating and

絷送到官，一讯即伏。问石，则鬻宫氏。取石至，官爱玩，欲得之，命寄诸库。吏举石，石忽堕地，碎为数十余片。皆失色。官乃重械两盗论死。邢子拾碎石出，仍瘗墓中。

异史氏曰："物之尤者祸之府。至欲以身殉石，亦痴甚矣！而卒之石与人相终始，谁谓石无情哉？古语云：'士为知己者死。'非过也！石犹如此，何况于人！"

sentenced them to death. Young Xing picked up the stone fragments and buried them again in his father's grave.

The Chronicler of the Tales comments: "Exceptional things of any kind are a storehouse of calamity. As for the stone, his wish to die for it was fondness carried the extreme! But in the long run stone and man were together until the end: who can say that stones have no feelings? The old saying, 'A man of quality dies for the one who recognizes his ability,' is no exaggeration. If a stone can do this, how much more fitting it is that men should also!"